Introduction

Scattered all across Great Britain and Ireland are the ...f ancient monuments. For many hundreds of years people have ... past, but in recent times, scientific interest has increased dram... ...eologists, prehistorians, scientists and scholars have been investigating the burial ... ...g barrows and cairns, enormous earthworks and rows of mysterious standing stones and stone circles that were built by our prehistoric ancestors. These monuments, tombs and temples are the most visible remains of several Neolithic and Bronze Age civilisations that began more than five thousand years ago. They flourished for hundreds of years, then declined and finally faded out around 1100 BC. After that time came a period of social degeneration and increasing unrest, culminating in a dramatic increase in intertribal warfare with the start of the production of iron weapons some time around 800 BC.

Despite centuries of intensive research, these age-old cultures have stubbornly refused to yield many of their secrets. The most obvious of these enduring mysteries is the purpose and function of the massive stone structures that they built and the nature of the societies that built them, from about 3,500 BC to 1500 BC. The conventional theories that have been put forward to explain these monuments are based largely on the scientific evidence provided by the skeletons and other physical remains of the people who have been excavated, together with the tools, weapons and pottery that they used. This information has been greatly helped by new environmental data and the physical attributes of the structures themselves. But despite *three centuries of intensive investigation* the major problem in the interpretation of prehistoric ruins has always been that they belong to a time before writing was invented and as a result of this lack of written records, they have remained a major puzzle for our archaeologists. Even with a vast amount of new, highly detailed scientific information about those far-off times, in many ways the nature of prehistoric Britain is as uncertain and mysterious as it was in the 1700's. Fundamental questions about our ancestor's way of life, their social organisation and their religious beliefs remain unanswered.

When I first became interested in our distant past, one of the many questions I asked myself is this:

Why has it been so difficult for our prehistorians, academics and archaeologists to understand what our forefathers were doing and why they did it, when every other science has made such enormous progress in the last three hundred years?

For more than a decade I have been doing my own research, exploring the places where our distant ancestors lived, worked and died and looking with my own eyes, rather than just relying on the information other people have supplied.

As a result of my own investigations, I have made a series of revolutionary discoveries and insights that will transform our knowledge and understanding of who we are and where we came from.

In my opinion, the reason why so little progress has been made with the big questions is that in the late 17th century the first investigators of our prehistoric past set off on the wrong path and we have been blindly following in their footsteps ever since. *Each successive generation has made exactly the same mistakes as the previous generation.*

The classic view of our distant past has been handicapped by a form of racism and prejudice towards people who were classed as primitive because they only developed simple tools and simple pottery. The oral history of our distant ancestors has disappeared over the millennia, probably as a result of a socially disruptive and brutal Iron Age, followed by six centuries of Roman influence and then later invasions of other peoples such as the Angles, Saxons, Vikings and then the Normans. In addition, the recorded history of earlier centuries was in the hands of the literate few, mainly Christian priests and nobles, who recorded contemporary events that interested them and unlike in Ireland, no one seems to have recorded the folklore of previous millennia. Our early antiquarians and amateur archaeologists had no historical basis for the interpretation of what they saw; they could only do this by comparison with the classical civilisations of Ancient Greece, Rome and Egypt.

They weren't impressed.

Yet instead of looking back at the early British settlers with disdain, what should have been recognised is just how much they managed to achieve, despite having only simple technology. And indeed, many prehistoric stone structures have already survived more than twice as long as the buildings of the much more recent Roman Empire.

The myth that our distant ancestors were just simple hunters and gatherers, then peasant farmers, barely able to scratch a living, is deeply engrained in our cultural beliefs and we look back to the distant past as though our forefathers achieved virtually nothing. Yet this is clearly a very prejudiced viewpoint for in fact we owe them a great deal, because they were the first to open up the forested landscape for farming and agriculture. These pioneers were the first to produce bread, beer, pork, beef, lamb, milk, butter, cheese, wool, cloth and pottery. Their descendants went on to develop new technology by using metals such as copper and tin to make bronze, and later on they produced iron.

The other reason that the old prejudiced viewpoint was so wrong is that primitive, ignorant, simple or stupid people could never have built the world's most famous prehistoric monument, the architectural marvel we know as Stonehenge. And although Stonehenge is unique, there are many other complex structures all over Britain and Ireland. Obviously there is a conflict here, between the popular viewpoint of ignorant *'barbarians'* and the sophisticated architectural, constructional and organisational techniques necessary to construct huge tombs, like Maeshowe in Orkney, Newgrange in Ireland, the West Kennet Long Barrow in Wiltshire, and earthworks such as the huge, man-made mound known as Silbury Hill or enormous outdoor temples such as the stone circles we know as Avebury, Stanton Drew or the Ring of Brodgar in Orkney.

The stones used to make Neolithic (New Stone Age) monuments and open-air temples can be enormous, some weigh as much as sixty tons and recent experiments have shown just how extremely difficult it is to move such giant blocks of stone with no machinery, but a great deal of skill and ingenuity. One example of this is the immense prehistoric site of Avebury, Wiltshire that originally boasted hundreds of colossal stones. There was a circle of about a hundred megaliths (large standing stones), two smaller circles, one of twenty-seven and the other had twenty-nine stones, an enormous pillar known as the Obelisk and a three-sided arrangement known as the Cove. All this was erected inside an enormous, roughly circular, ditch that was over a kilometre long, about twenty-one metres wide and eleven metres deep (69 x 36ft) and was surrounded by a high bank. There were also two long avenues, each of about a hundred pairs of megaliths. So it is obvious that such an extraordinary arrangement could only have been the result of intelligent people who had planned, organised and engineered their temple with a specific purpose in mind.

This was not the result of simple-minded, primitive, barbarians or peasant farmers but of a clever and hard-working people who were united in a common goal to build a very special place for celebration and worship. A temple that must have taken decades to build.

To return to the problem of interpretation of the unwritten past. As most people are aware, our very distant ancestors painted marvellous images of Ice Age animals, such as mammoths, bison, elk, deer, wild cattle, reindeer and horses in special caves in southwestern France and Northern Spain. Their earliest images date from about 32000 BC and this tradition of decorating caves continued for another *twenty thousand years*, right up until the end of the Ice Age, in other words, ten times as long as the current Christian era. According to conventional archaeology, some of the descendants of these cave painters and sculptors from what are now France and Spain and others from Germany,

Multiple images of faces on a 4 metre high Neolithic sculpture at the Ring of Brodgar, Orkney, Scotland
PICTURES FROM THE PAST - copyright MARTIN RINGER 2013

'PICTURES FROM THE PAST'

Martin Ringer

SOLVING THE MAJOR MYSTERIES OF THE MEGALITHIC TRADITION
IN GREAT BRITAIN AND IRELAND
DURING THE NEOLITHIC AND BRONZE AGE
(from about 3500 BC to 1000 BC)

	Introduction	5
1	Simple is not the same as stupid	8
2	Astronomy, symbolism and religious beliefs	26
3	Newgrange and new beginnings	60
4	Symbols of power, symbols of stone	80
5	A new look at Stonehenge	99
6	The art of Ancient Britain	133
7	Stonehenge art	159
8	Inside the Temple	181
9	The symbolism and meaning of Stonehenge	205
10	Calanais and Brodgar	227
11	Stanton Drew	260
12	Avebury	282
13	Conclusions	345

First published in Great Britain by Marrin Publishing
29 Carnarvon Road, Bristol BS6 7DU

Copyright © 2012 by Martin Ringer

www.martinringer.co.uk

The right of Martin Ringer to be identified as the Author
of the Work has been asserted by him in accordance
with the Copyright, Designs and Patents Act 1988.

All rights reserved. No part of this publication may be
reproduced, stored in a retrieval system, or transmitted in
any form or by any means without the prior written
permission of the publisher, nor be otherwise circulated
in any form of binding or cover than that in which it is
published.

A CIP catalogue record is available for this title from the British Library

Paperback ISBN: 978-0-9572843-0-2

Printed and bound in the UK by Biddles, part of the MPG Books Group,
Bodmin and Kings Lynn

ACKNOWLEDGEMENTS

First and foremost, I owe an enormous debt of gratitude to the American author Jean M. Auel. Her marvellous series of fiction books entitled *'Earth's Children'*, the story of her heroine, Ayla, mesmerised me from the very first time I read *'The Clan of the Cave Bear'* and all of the sequels that followed, including *'The Valley of Horses'*, *'The Mammoth Hunters'*, ending with the last book in the series: *'The Land of Painted Caves'*. Without these wonderful stories about people who lived during the last Ice Age, I would never have become interested in the lives of our distant ancestors and I would not have gone on to challenge the accepted viewpoint about our forefather's artistic abilities and consequently I would never have made all the fantastic discoveries that I have made. I owe it all to Jean.

I would also like to thank my sister Gillian, for her support with my long term project, which was undertaken entirely in my spare time. Although she was sceptical about what I was doing, she nevertheless helped me financially when my resources were very low and I couldn't get to the sites I desperately wanted to visit in northern Scotland and Ireland. Thank you, Gill.

A big thank you to my friend Michelle Rainey, whose interest, belief and encouragement has helped enormously over the last five years, especially when my enthusiasm was flagging, and another big thank you to Brian Perrett, for his ongoing interest and support for the project.

My thanks also to the Dutch astronomer Victor Reijs, who helped me to understand some of the complexities of the lunar cycles, my opinions and any subsequent errors I may have made, are entirely my own.

All of the photographs and diagrams in this book were done by the author, with the exception of the revised plan of the Avebury Henge by Peter Roberts. His wonderfully authoritative website on Avebury is at http://www.avebury-web.co.uk

Denmark, the Netherlands and Portugal came north with the warming climate, and the retreating ice, and they settled in Britain. Yet despite the hundreds of thousands of people who lived in Britain from 8000 BC onwards, right through to the arrival of iron working, around 800 BC, very few works of art have been discovered, even though far simpler societies, such as the Aborigines of Australia and the Bushmen of the Kalahari desert in Africa, had a rich artistic and cultural side to their societies for tens of thousands of years.

The conventional theory is that art, and the creation of art, died out with the warming of the planet and the melting of the glaciers and ice sheets around 12000 years ago. By the time of the first farming communities, more than six millennia later, art was just a distant memory, with only a few people creating simple art and craft objects. The nearest thing to a written language was the invention and production of signs, symbols and motifs on the large stones known as megaliths, at special places such as Newgrange and Loughcrew in Ireland, and in northwest Scotland and Northumberland. According to our experts, art would only be re-invented in the Iron Age, along with the production of exquisite metal working, fine jewellery and lethal weapons.

I have discovered that the experts are completely wrong.

As you will see from the following pages, I have discovered that our prehistoric ancestors developed extraordinary new styles and new forms of art and they created a vast amount of amazing and highly complex works of art, some of which I think are the best that have ever been created in stone.

The discoveries that I have made over the last ten years, and the insights I have gained as a result of these discoveries, have enabled me to solve many of the major mysteries surrounding the lives and religious beliefs of our Neolithic and Bronze Age ancestors. As a result of these completely new insights into their belief systems it has been possible for me to work out the meaning of the monuments that they built and why they built them.

These discoveries and insights, **revealed here for the very first time**, will revolutionise and transform our knowledge and understanding of our prehistoric ancestors. In years to come our attitudes towards them will change profoundly and we will give them the respect that they so richly deserve.

***And let's not forget that without them,
we wouldn't be here at all.***

1 SIMPLE IS NOT THE SAME AS STUPID

The early part of the human story is no longer part of the school curriculum, so it is perhaps a good idea to start with a bit of background information about our distant origins, and how those who came before us changed the natural world so that we could become the people we are today. It is so easy to forget that, without them, we would not be here at all. In other words, we owe our ancestors everything, even our very existence.

The study of our past is usually divided into two parts, prehistory and history, and prehistory is the term used to describe the time before written records were made. Although there are systems of signs and symbols that date from much, much earlier periods, one of the first forms of writing that we currently understand dates from about five thousand years ago. However, even this information system started out much earlier on. A simple, but highly effective, system was used across thousands of miles of the Middle East and it used small, geometrically shaped pieces of baked clay including cones, spheres, disks, cylinders, tetrahedrons and a variety of other shapes. Archaeologist Denise Shmandt-Besserat was the first to realise that these counters were tokens and that they represented a special system, one that was widely used for counting and trading commodities such as cattle, sheep and goats, measures of grain and oil and some were even used to represent a day's labour. The beauty of this apparently simple system was that it could be used by people who spoke very different languages, for although their names for the same things were different, everyone understood that a particular shape represented a particular item.
The token system eventually developed into a writing system that used wedge-shaped marks pressed into clay tablets, which were then baked in a very hot oven. This system is known as cuneiform writing and was invented in Sumeria, a part of ancient Mesopotamia between the Tigris and Euphrates rivers, in what is now Iran and Iraq. Cuneiform was initially used for registering the business accounts of temples but later on it developed into a more generalised method of recording information. One of the most famous mythical stories of the Sumerian civilisation that was recorded in cuneiform is a poem known as the 'Epic of Gilgamesh', the story of a warrior king and it featured a Great Flood caused by the god Ea. A few centuries later, Egypt developed the well-known form of picture writing we call hieroglyphs, which are famous for recording the religious beliefs of ancient Egypt and the lives of the Pharaohs. All the major civilisations of the ancient world invented some form of writing for recording important parts of their culture; particularly the exploits of their leaders and kings and information concerning their religious beliefs. They also invented methods for counting and for recording transactions for commercial purposes, including international trade, but most of all, for the dreaded taxation. Have things really changed that much over the last 5,000 years?

Unfortunately our own written records go back a mere two thousand years, to just before the time of the Roman Conquest in AD 43, but our unrecorded past accounts for a much, much longer period than our historical record suggests. Prehistory accounts for more than 95 per cent of the time since our species, Homo sapiens sapiens, evolved in Africa from our more archaic ancestors. Current estimates suggest this happened well over 150,000 years ago, although unfortunately some influential scholars still like to think that we only became truly intelligent human beings around 40,000 years ago. This more recent epoch corresponds to the time when people like us ('*anatomically modern humans*') first arrived in southern Germany, western France and northern Spain at a time when Europe was still in the grip of an Ice Age, at the start of the period that scientists call the Upper Palaeolithic era. These early ancestors of ours are known by palaeontologists as the Aurignacians, after the town of Aurignac, in southwest France, where their remains were first discovered. However, they are really identified after the new types of tools and hunting weapons that they invented. But it wasn't just the tools and weapons that were important, they needed to develop new skills and expertise in order to successfully hunt the big game animals that were typical of that part of the world during the last Ice Age. Their prey included woolly mammoth, woolly rhinoceros, bison, giant wild cattle called aurochs, reindeer and horses. This era, and those that followed, the Gravettian, Solutrian and Magdalenian periods, marked the appearance in the European archaeological record of profound social and cultural changes, reflected in the tools, weapons, and decorations that people made during the last Ice Age. This was also a time for the development of many new forms of art, including cave painting and the creation of small sculptures and carvings, items that could be carried by the hunters and their families as they moved back and forth across the Continent following the migrating herds of reindeer and bison. The Aurignacian period also appears to mark the spreading out of modern humans far to the east, travelling thousands of miles into Asia and going even as far as Borneo and Australia. The oldest human remains so far discovered are those from Liujiang in Southern China, dating from some 67,000 years ago. And some archaeologists believe that the first people arrived in the Americas more than 40,000 years ago, although many still think this occurred much more recently, towards the end of the last Ice Age. This is a matter of some controversy, but more and more people are beginning to accept the idea that America was visited and occupied long before the more conventional date of around 10000 BC.

The invention of written languages has enabled us to understand a great deal about our more recent ancestors, but the lack of written records has meant that very little is known about ancient societies whose knowledge, customs and history were transmitted from one generation to the next by just talking to each other. Their system for recording knowledge was in the form of songs, poems and stories. Unfortunately one of the downsides to the invention of writing is that it has also created an artificial boundary in time, a boundary that has divided the whole of humanity into two distinct parts - it is as if those without a written language were far less intelligent than those who had invented writing.

But where do we get such a stupid idea from? Well it comes from people who depend on the written word for their jobs, in other words, our academics, professors and teachers. And it is this simple idea that has given rise to the erroneous belief that people without a written language must have been far less capable and far less intelligent than those who invented writing. But you didn't need a written language to keep yourself alive, warm and well-fed during an Ice Age winter! It was their knowledge, skill, experience and intelligence that allowed the big game hunters of the last Ice Age the possibility of moving away from the warmer lands around the Mediterranean and move northwards to the incredibly rich sources of meat on the steppe of central Europe. For that to happen they needed to be able to make fire when they needed it most, and produce warm clothing and make superior weapons from flint and other special types of stone. Their intelligence guaranteed their survival, and they evolved, simply because stupid people didn't survive for very long...

The false idea that our ancestors were not very bright has also given rise to the impression that a written language was the only viable means of recording information for the benefit of future generations. But in my opinion the use of writing is very much an artificial boundary, because people are physically, mentally and emotionally the same the world over, regardless of whether or not they can read and write. And although we are all born with the same potential, in every group of people some are smarter than others and some are more inventive and more willing to try new ways of doing things. We can therefore assume that, although their attitudes, customs and traditions may have varied considerably, people in the past were in many ways similar to ourselves, with exactly the same emotions and needs, hopes and fears. Just like us, they were human beings, regardless of when or where they lived. Human nature doesn't change. We know from written records that people in Mesopotamia, Ancient Egypt and Ancient Rome, or even in Shakespearean England, may have lived very different lives but they behaved in very similar ways to each other, and to us, simply because they were ruled by the same mix of emotions that we all have, for both good things and bad.

Since Victorian times, and even earlier, we have been encouraged to mentally distance ourselves from prehistoric people, as though we could not possibly have anything in common with such 'primitive' people. At one point it was even fashionable to think of them as sub-human. But make no mistake about it. These people are our distant relatives. And we owe them a lot, for without them, few of us would be here today. Recent research in genetics by Professor Bryan Sykes has suggested that 95 per cent of Europeans are related to just seven Ice Age clan mothers. (See his 2001 book *'The*

Seven Daughters of Eve') According to his research, over 47% of us are distantly related to just one woman who lived 20,000 years ago along the Mediterranean coastline near Marseilles. Some of her descendants travelled a long way north, almost as far as the edge of the ice sheet that covered most of Wales, central England and nearly all of Scotland. It was in 1986 that an excavation, led by Chris Stringer of the Natural History Museum, discovered the jawbone of a young man whose body had been buried around 12,000 years ago in Gough's Cave in the Cheddar Gorge in Somerset. But the ancient hunter was by no means a complete stranger, because modern genetic science has shown that many of us are related to him. When Professor Sykes extracted some mitochondrial DNA from inside the fossil teeth of Cheddar Man he discovered samples that matched around 7% of the modern European population. And it is simply extraordinary to realise that many of us are related to this Ice Age hunter of mammoths, bison and reindeer and that he is a very distant member of our own families. According to the DNA found in the skeletons of those individuals who have been tested, around two thirds of European Mesolithic hunters were related to him. And around six per cent of Europeans are related to another famous ancient person, Ötzi, the five thousand year old Iceman, whose frozen body was discovered in 1991 high up in the Italian Alps near the Austrian border with Italy. Many more of us are related to ancient farming people who originated from further to the south, from Anatolia and the Near East. Within the last decade further ancient lineages have been discovered, bringing the total number of haplogroups of mitochondrial DNA in modern Europeans to twelve. After more than three centuries of research the true nature of life for people in prehistoric Britain remains almost a complete mystery. It is like a gigantic jigsaw puzzle, with nearly all of the pieces missing, a jigsaw that has proved very hard to put together from the evidence and the information that has survived and was then lucky enough to have been recovered in excavations. Prehistoric archaeology is now in possession of thousands upon thousands of miscellaneous facts and figures regarding our distant forefathers, but unlike people who lived in Ancient Egypt, Rome or Greece, we still do not know what they looked like, nor any of their names, the languages they spoke, the histories of their families, communities or leaders, and we have only a few details about their daily lives.

After more than three hundred years of study, we understand little about prehistoric social organisation, customs, laws, morals and attitudes and we know next to nothing of their myths and legends, religious beliefs or scientific knowledge.

Yet it is not all bad news. Modern scientific expertise has helped a great deal by providing more insights than ever before in the form of a mass of new data derived from such diverse sciences as ecology, geology, botany, zoology, forensic science and through new research techniques obtained from progress in physics, chemistry and genetics. Since the 1950's, Radiocarbon 14 dating has become vitally important for giving us the approximate age of organic material such as bones, charcoal, wood and even nuts and seeds, enabling a time-based table of events to be structured. Unfortunately in the early days radiocarbon dating was by no means an exact science, the earliest techniques used for dating proved inaccurate and samples could in fact be several hundred years older than was originally thought. More recently, archaeologists have had access to much more exact dating through dendrochronology, the study of tree rings, which can show the age of a tree and the growth patterns during its lifetime, which in turn reflect changes in the climate. Small samples of wood can then be matched by dendrochronology to a particular year, even to the season the tree was felled. In addition, pollen examination and soil samples can reveal changes in vegetation and show what sorts of crops were grown. Even the study of different species of tiny snails in the soil can reveal changes in what the countryside looked like and how it was used.
Geophysical and aerial surveys can show what lies buried underground, whilst microscopic examination of samples can show how pottery and stone tools were made and then used, even from where the samples of clay or stone originated. However, in spite of all these advances in science and technology, it is hard to understand a culture from these sorts of clues on their own. It's a bit like someone trying to understand the story of your life, just from the contents of your rubbish bin. Even with societies that had a written language, not all of them used an alphabet. Many ancient cultures used symbols, signs, or images to represent events, the sounds of spoken words or just ideas. Most of these

early sign systems have remained undeciphered and await explanation. One example that predates Egyptian hieroglyphs comes from the Vinca culture of Yugoslavia, and by about 5000 BC the system had developed to such an extent that over two hundred different symbols were being used to decorate pottery, figurines and spindle whorls (a perforated disc used as a weight on a spindle for spinning wool and thread). Other early civilisations used carvings, sculptures and paintings to represent their thoughts, daily lives, mythology, history and religious beliefs. The carvings and paintings were often used to decorate the walls of their homes, tombs and temples, and appeared as decoration on pottery, tools, weapons and other artefacts. But according to conventional theory, there were no records made of life in Ancient Britain, or at least, not until the arrival of Julius Caesar in 55 BC.

Traditionally the prehistorical past is artificially divided into distinct periods by the sort of innovations and technology that became available over time. The oldest and by far the longest period was the Stone Age, followed by the Bronze Age, then the Iron Age. Although these divisions are useful, they are not strictly accurate because the different periods overlap each other in time and place. However, the different ages do still have their uses in a general way for speaking of a particular moment in time. The era covered by the prehistoric sites in this book runs through the Neolithic (or New Stone Age), which dates from about 4500 to 2300 BC and then up to the middle of the Bronze Age, about 1500 BC. This is an enormous period of time when you consider all the changes that have taken place during the last hundred years. However, unlike the way we live today, the ancient world showed slower changes, people lived at a much more reasonable pace and their lives remained unchanged for many generations. When change came it was often dramatic and shows up in the archaeological record in the form of social and cultural upheaval, as radical changes in religious beliefs and burial practices, the appearance of new foods, new ways of doing things, new styles of pottery, weapons and tools etc. There would also have been changes in hairstyles, fashions, furnishings, clothing and language but these do not show up easily in the archaeological record.

A very, very long time ago, long before the Neolithic period that features so heavily in this book, our Ice Age ancestors produced superb carvings of animals in ivory, bone and wood, and they created marvellous paintings and engravings of bison, horses, mammoths cattle and deer in famous caves such as those at Lascaux in France and Altamira in Spain. The earliest cave art found so far dates from around 32,000 years ago and comes from Chauvet Cave in the Ardèche region of France. And this tradition of artistic creativity lasted for more than twenty thousand years, right through some of the harshest climate in European history. But according to traditional wisdom, the artistic temperament died out around ten thousand years ago because of changes in lifestyle brought on by a rapidly warming climate and the retreat of the glaciers. People spread out into new areas and lived in much smaller groups than before and because of this reduction in social interaction and trade, people no longer specialised in their traditional skills and crafts and so their artistic capabilities died out.

But I have discovered that this traditional theory is simply not true. Prehistoric art continued to evolve and to flourish and it is there for anyone to see, if you know how and where to look, which is one of the main reasons I have written this book.

It is vitally important to understand and to accept the idea that the great civilisations of ancient history did not suddenly spring up from nowhere or nothing, nor in some giant leap forwards from 'primitive' to 'civilised', nor was there any need for some outside source of knowledge or wisdom from another planet, or from some mythical lost civilisation such as Atlantis. Instead, civilisations have always evolved as a result of the development of new inventions, new knowledge and new techniques based upon a solid foundation of earlier wisdom derived from the innovations, inventions, techniques and discoveries of previous generations. Cereal growing for example was indispensable to the growth of Dynastic Egypt, yet it had already been around for a very long time before the first Pharaoh was in power. The idea of growing crops had started at least three thousand years earlier, far to the northeast, in the Fertile Crescent, an area of land running from Israel to Northern Syria and Northern and Eastern Iraq. Other prehistoric developments that were indispensable to the evolution of later civilisations included the manufacture of pottery, metals, mining, art, medicine, record keeping, religion and scientific thought. And the origin of some of these innovations can be traced back tens of thousands of years. (See Richard Rudgeley's book *'Lost Civilisations of the Stone Age'* for his excellent insights and a good overview of some of the basics). In much the same way, our modern world is based upon a solid core of Victorian knowledge and engineering that was in turn derived from many of the scientific discoveries that were made in the previous century. For example, the initial research into the nature of electricity that was carried out by William Gilbert, in around 1600, has culminated in the production of atomic power and the development of the sophisticated electronics that we use today in so much of our lives. The pace of change has increased dramatically over the last few decades and although manned flight is a recent innovation, we have already come a very long way in the century or so since the first powered flight by the Wright brothers, at Kitty Hawk, North Carolina in 1903.

In the past, prehistorians tended to concentrate on what they called 'industries' or 'lithic assemblages', a rather fancy way of speaking of a range of stone tools and weapons. But it was not just the hardware that people used that ensured the survival of our species, it was the software that they developed that was equally, if not more, important, and it was the training of hunting techniques and survival skills, and knowledge and experience that they gained as they were growing up that counted more than the tools and weapons that they made and used. Anyone could make a spear but if they didn't want to go hungry, they also needed excellent tracking and hunting skills, as well as patience, experience and endurance. Across the world, indigenous people are renowned for their knowledge of the local fauna and flora and much of this knowledge about the natural world goes back to the Dawn of Mankind, and the wisdom gained was passed down from father to son and from mother to daughter through countless generations. Although the ancient hunters and foragers depended on what nature could offer, they had an intimate knowledge of their environment and as they grew up they were taught how to hunt and to forage for wild foods and they learned to stockpile nature's bounty to last them through the winter months. By drying, smoking and salting meat, fish and game, as well as collecting and storing plant foods, such as seasonal fruit and berries, seeds, nuts, roots, tubers and mushrooms, they survived over countless millennia. If they had not been such experts at what they did, they simply would not have survived and many of us would not be here today.

The ancient nomadic lifestyle is usually seen as being inferior to a settled way of life, but the desire to travel, to see new places and to have new experiences is hard-wired into our genes. That is why Homo sapiens has colonised the entire planet and the reason global tourism is with us today. The distant descendants of those archaic nomads have even ventured into Space. Far from being simply aimless drifters, the ancients were adventurous and brave. They crossed deserts, mountains, rivers, seas and oceans, always wondering what was over the next hill. They were courageous people, who ventured into the unknown, proud of their abilities to survive difficult times and to face unknown perils. But sometimes people tired of travelling and they settled down in one place, usually along coastal areas or in river valleys because locally rich natural resources allowed good fishing, fowling, hunting, foraging and gathering. And throughout the ancient world these settlements grew and became large villages, and even towns. They predate the advent of livestock farming and agriculture by thousands of years. Like us, these people enjoyed their lives. They raised their children and they hunted, fished and harvested natural foods and medicines and they traded raw materials and finished products with other communities. The traditional skills and knowledge that they inherited meant that they could look after themselves and it wasn't always a constant struggle to survive. They were successful in what they did, although sometimes disease, natural disasters or even warfare took a heavy toll.

One of the most important things in our nature which separates us from other animals is our care and concern for others of our kind, particularly when they are ill, wounded or dying. Although maternal instincts are strong in the animal kingdom, it is only a few creatures, such as the African elephant, that seem to care for their own when they are sick or dying. Elephants that have died from natural causes are often covered in leaves and branches by others of their group and the animals seem to mourn the deceased, sometimes staying in the area for two or three days. They have even been known to cover up dead human hunters that have unsuccessfully tried to kill them. For humans the start of the idea of burial of the dead is lost in the mists of time and different strategies evolved over countless generations. Just as today, very few early societies thought that when you die, that was it, the end of everything. It is an almost universal hope and belief across the globe that although the body dies, the spirit carries onwards to another destiny. For many people our time here on Earth is just one part of a long journey from one form to another and from one place to another and that in the afterlife we will be reunited with our loved ones and those that have already passed onwards. There are a wide variety of such themes throughout prehistory and into historical times. Some of these sacred beliefs include a return to Mother Earth; rebirth; reincarnation; joining with the ancestral spirits; journeys to other worlds; going to a better world (heaven/paradise) and eternal life amongst the stars, etc.

Although parts of much earlier fossil human remains have been found, dating as far back as half a million years, the earliest human burial in Britain that has been discovered so far dates back thirty three thousand years, to around the middle of the last Ice Age. Wrongly identified as a woman, the skeletal remains were found at a cave site known as Paviland Cave (Goat's Hole Cave) on the Gower Peninsula in south Wales near Swansea. Like burials from even earlier periods on the Continent, the twenty-five year old man had been covered with a layer of powdered ochre, a red iron ore known as haematite. The red earth was probably used to symbolise the flow of blood associated with birth. And by rubbing a paste of ground up pigment into the skin of the deceased and by scattering more red earth over the corpse I think that the mourners were symbolising the process of being reborn, with the cave representing the womb of Mother Earth and the passageway into a cave representing the birth canal.

Contrary to popular belief, people of that time didn't usually live in caves, or at least not all year round, and the numbers of corpses buried inside caves was very low. (I think it likely that they were buried inside because the ground outside the cave was frozen too hard, winters during the Ice Age could get down to minus 40 degrees Celsius.) During most of the year it is likely that corpses were laid out on wooden platforms above the ground and left to decay naturally, and as a result of this practice their skeletal remains have simply not survived. But sometimes people were buried in a grave dug in the ground and in the fullness of time, their body returned to Mother Earth. To accompany the deceased on their journey to the next world it was often customary to bury the person with a tool or favourite hunting weapon that would help them get started in their new life. The single most important tool was a flint knife, for without this basic tool the newly reborn people would struggle to fend for themselves. No one knew what awaited them at the end of the journey, but a knife was essential to cut wood, start a fire, make other tools and weapons, hunt and butcher animals and make clothes. Sometimes there were other grave goods to accompany the deceased person. These included personal decorations in the form of bracelets or necklaces made from seashells or pierced stones, and another favourite were strings of ivory beads. Bear, fox or wolf teeth were often worn as decoration on clothes or as pendants by both males and females. Many ancient hunting cultures had fraternities and male societies with special rites, traditions and taboos, each with their own totem spirit that was said to guide them. Sometimes hunters were interred with animal skulls, deer antlers or animal teeth and claws and these were probably a symbol of their totem or indicative of belonging to a particular hunting fraternity, tribe or clan.

There are also representations of the Earth Mother or the Mother Goddess in many ancient cultures, including the celebrated 'Venus' figures made from stone, ivory or even in ceramics and dating from around 25,000 years ago. This particular Creation belief seems to have been based on the idea that since all life is born from the female of the species, so there must have been one female that gave birth to all the other forms of life, hence the Great Earth Mother. They would also have noticed that almost all animals and birds cared for their young, feeding them and caring for them until they were old enough to look after themselves. This is what we call instinctive behaviour but to the ancient peoples perhaps they saw it as an expression of the spirit of the Earth Mother, her way of looking after all of her children, so that they survived, grew and multiplied to produce the next generation.

In the developed countries we tend to forget that there are many people in the world who are still closer to our ancestor's way of life, than they are to our own artificial lifestyles. Yet the small bands of people who still live in the Stone Age are fundamentally different to our own Stone Age ancestors because they have continued to retain the ancestral way of life for tens of thousands of years.
Perhaps what made the precursors of the classical civilisations special was that they had a different way of thinking and a different way of acting, which eventually led to the evolution of farming, agriculture, metallurgy, science and technology, which in turn has radically changed the natural world. Even our ancestors of 15,000 years ago, the cave painters, sculptors and craftsmen of the Magdalenian period, appear to be more culturally and artistically advanced than many simple tribal societies of the modern era. But regardless of their way of life, our ancestors not only managed to survive, they were successful in what they did. By as early as 50,000 years ago, modern humans had settled in parts of Europe, Siberia, China, Japan, Australia and a few may also have ventured into the Americas. But much of central, and all of northern Britain, was covered in very thick ice and Britain and Ireland were joined to mainland Europe by low-lying land. So much of the planet's water was locked in the gigantic ice sheets that global sea levels were up to a hundred metres below current levels. The beginning of the end of the last Ice Age started around thirteen thousand years ago, and by about 8000 BC the glaciers had gone and the landscape of southern Britain was changing from open steppe grassland to becoming dense birch and pine forests. At that time there was no North Sea or English Channel, and it would have been possible to walk from 'Ireland', across 'England' and on towards 'Denmark', crossing streams and rivers en route.
In recent years it has been realised that the European Mesolithic hunter/gatherers were not very different from their Ice Age forefathers. They were essentially doing the same things as before, but in the new hunting grounds that had become available with the profound changes in climate that in turn greatly influenced changes in fauna and flora. During the post-glacial period, people such as the descendants of the Magdalenian reindeer hunters of Spain and France, the fishermen of the Danube and the mammoth hunters of Siberia had an entire continent to choose from, a vast area with few humans, but enormous quantities of wildlife. With so much choice they moved with the seasons to areas with outstanding natural resources, locations that were particularly rich in animal and plant life, and they stayed in places where migrating animals, birds or fish were so concentrated that they ensured easy hunting and provide a guaranteed supply of food in spring, summer or autumn.
When the local resources were used up, they simply moved to other areas where new food resources were reaching their peak. Apart from big game animals, seasonal resources included the eggs of nesting birds, migrating salmon and wintering wildfowl. They would also have foraged for a wide variety of plants, tubers, roots and herbs. One of the most nutritious plants that were widely available in freshwater habitats is the reed mace, (known as the cattail in America). The rhizomes can be baked in the fire or ground into flour, the bases of young leaves can be eaten raw or cooked and the pollen can be used as a flour-like thickener in soups and stews. In autumn people often stayed for a while in areas where there were large quantities of fruit, berries, seeds and nuts, particularly hazel nuts. Together with mushrooms and other edible fungi, these could be processed and stored, for use throughout the winter and into early spring when fresh food was harder to find. As the years went by, and the climate improved, life became easier, population levels grew and they were able to explore and to spread out a great deal more, travelling to places that had previously been buried under thick ice. As the centuries passed, the early hunting people of Continental Europe returned to the northern parts of their ancestral lands in ever increasing numbers. The reindeer hunters and herders followed the reindeer further and further north, moving into Scandinavia and eastwards into Russia. Other groups of people moved north to Brittany, Germany, Denmark, Ireland and Britain.

The local wildlife was changing with the vegetation and so the lifestyle of the hunters had to change with it. Their prey was different from those of their distant ancestors, who had pursued the enormous herds of steppe animals, such as the woolly mammoth, bison, horse and reindeer, and the woolly rhinoceros, giant deer and red deer. The largest animal species had either become extinct or had changed their regional locations and migration patterns because of the warming climate. However, it was still bitterly cold in winter, especially in the far north, so the hunters needed a way of knowing in advance when it would be time to move south to their winter camps, in short, they needed a simple calendar based around the sun and moon. Their ancestors had been noticing the movements of the moon and the sun for thousands of years already, so they were well aware that the sun and the phases of the moon could measure time. Many ancient societies used a calendar based around the moon, naming each month after special events at a particular time of year.

These included events such as the flowering of particular plants, pronounced changes in the weather, the falling of leaves in autumn or the appearance of certain migrating birds and animals. Over many centuries this knowledge expanded and much later on, during the Neolithic period around 3000 BC, it formed the basis of new religions, culminating in enormous sacred sites and vast constructions of earth, wood and stone. These people revered their ancestors and the tombs and burial mounds that they built were dedicated to those family members who had passed away or had gone on their final journey long before. This is usually called 'ancestor worship', but I think that it is more about the respect and love for those who had gone before and who were still remembered in a multitude of stories and songs, poems, myths and legends. (Like the Viking Sagas)
Around eight thousand years ago, forests of birch and pine trees covered much of Britain and even though the ice had already retreated much further north, it was still colder than it is today. Later on, as the weather changed and the climate improved, the forest changed to become predominantly pine, hazel, willow and juniper and then finally the mixed forest included deciduous varieties of trees, particularly oak, lime, and elm. This was the start of the Mesolithic era, the Middle Stone Age. Although we speak of an age of stone, it was really a time when only natural materials, such as wood, wicker, fur and fibres - both animal and vegetal, bone, antler, stone and clay were in use.

When the first settlers arrived in Britain, they lived by hunting and gathering natural foods along the coast, then moved upriver and ventured further inland along animal trails into the dense forests. In the wild woods were red and roe deer, elk, bears, wolves, lynx, wild pigs, beaver and aurochs (huge wild cattle). Contrary to what most people think, they enjoyed a healthy lifestyle, even if it could be a bit precarious at times. The bushcraft skills and knowledge gained from the tracking and hunting of animals was passed down to them from previous generations. This increased their ability to adapt to local conditions of scarcity of a particular food. However, the unpolluted rivers were full of fish, including eels, tench, bream, pike and seasonal salmon. The hunters and foragers knew when the salmon would run and when ducks, geese and swans from the Arctic would arrive for the winter and they knew all the other invaluable know-how and ingenuity that made a big difference to their survival. They knew for example that traps and snares have a big advantage over actively pursuing prey, because they work twenty-four hours a day, seven days a week and one hunter can set many traps, multiplying the chance of success and a good meal for him and his family. Even in those early days people travelled widely, with some living as far north as the Western Isles (Outer Hebrides), northwest of Scotland. They certainly did not swim to get there and although ancient middens (rubbish heaps) show evidence of deep-sea fishing, no remains of boats or canoes from this period have been found in Britain. However, along with their stone axes they also produced adzes. These are woodworking tools that were used for shaping timber and making planks and they would have been particularly useful for making dugouts. An adze looks like a sort of axe, but with the blade at right angles to the shaft. The best-preserved remains of Mesolithic canoes come from the bogs of Tybrind Vig, Denmark where two canoes, one measuring over thirty feet long (9.5 metres) and capable of carrying eight people, were found. Such boats were used not only for travel but also for deep-sea fishing and enabled them to hunt seals and porpoises. Sometimes they even had a fireplace on board in the stern, to keep them warm and for fishing at night. Seals were important not just for food but because the hide is waterproof and is very resistant to the cold. (Reindeer hide and sealskin makes better arctic clothing than most modern fibres.) Other contemporary finds of wood, antler or bone tools include many different kinds of arrows, spears, harpoons, wickerwork baskets, fish traps and fish hooks, as well as textiles, nets and even pottery. There was also a wide range of flint and stone tools, showing evidence of an ever-increasing range of skills and techniques to make new forms of hunting weapons and other useful tools. They also produced bone and ivory pendants and other decorations for clothing. Thick birch bark was widely used to make domestic utensils such as pouches, baskets and bowls and other storage containers. It was also tough and light enough to be cut into large sheets and rolled up, ready for use as the roofing for temporary hunting shelters. And they probably made sophisticated birch bark canoes, since they had the necessary boring tools to enable them to fasten the sewn pieces of bark to the framework, using withies or animal sinew. They would also have used birch bark tar to waterproof the seams.

Our very distant ancestors learned what was edible by trial and error and by observing other animals. What a bear could eat, so could a man. But hunting was only one activity. Children, their mothers and the sick and elderly were making a very important contribution as they collected a wide range of plant food and shellfish for their families. The botanical knowledge they inherited was a result of living off the land for hundreds of thousands of years. This knowledge was also used for medicinal purposes and some of that ancient knowledge is still with us today in the form of herbal teas, herbal remedies and medicines. And most of our fruits, vegetables and cereals are just domesticated varieties of wild plants. In all they had a reasonably balanced diet, but their biggest problem was to last through the long winters and that entailed stockpiling food in the form of dried, salted or smoked supplies. Contrary to popular belief, a hunting and gathering existence can result in a great deal of leisure time, especially when Mother Nature is particularly bountiful.

In mainland Britain, archaeologists have found little trace of these remote ancestors of ours. Apart from the sites of a few hunting camps, all that seems to remain are some of the stone tools they made, in particular very small flint blades known as microliths. These have traditionally defined the culture of the Mesolithic, or Middle Stone Age, hunters. The microliths were set into shafts to form complex weapons such as barbed arrows, harpoons and spears, fish spears with two or three barbed prongs, and tools such as knives, saws, borers and chisels, called burins, for carving ivory, antler, bone and wood. There are even sites that show that these little blades were made on an industrial basis, but very little trace of the people and their habitations have been discovered. (In recent years it has become more obvious that microliths are not just post-glacial tools, instead they were first manufactured during the Palaeolithic era, thousands of years before the glaciers melted and the Mesolithic era began.)

Very few Mesolithic skeletons have been found in Britain, but in January 1797 two young men hunting a rabbit first discovered the cave of Aveline's Hole, near Cheddar in Somerset. They opened up its burrow to find the entrance to a large cavern and were surprised to discover that it contained the skeletons of over fifty bodies, lying side by side, in a sort of recess near the entrance next to the wall. Some were coated with a natural covering of calcite (the material that forms stalactites) and were lying with their heads facing north. The cave had obviously been used as a cemetery, since at least another thirty skeletons were found in subsequent excavations. Grave goods included many necklaces of beads made from seashells and typical Mesolithic flint tools, as well as seven fossil ammonites with one burial and one small, very well made antler harpoon with three barbs on each side. According to F.A. Knight in his book 'The Heart of Mendip', earlier finds included 'flint knives and roughly fashioned bone dice (?)'. Although the bones were taken away, some to Oxford, it is believed that these, together with the grave goods, date from the middle of the Mesolithic period, about eight thousand years ago.

It seems likely that there were many different lifestyles and patterns of settlement. People often stayed in one place for the winter and lived at other sites in spring, summer and autumn. Whilst some members of the community stayed near the main sites, others went off on hunting trips or went looking for flint and other types of stone to make their essential tools. A few hunting camps have been found, such as the one at Starr Carr in Yorkshire, dating from about 7500 BC, but the generally accepted picture of life in Mesolithic Britain is one of very low population levels for hundreds of years. This lack of evidence may be partly due to more recent settlement and the fact that coastal fishing villages vanished when so much of our ancient coastline disappeared under the sea around 6000 BC. It was also during the Mesolithic Era that Britain became progressively cut off from the Continent as sea levels rose drastically and flooded low-lying land to form what are now called the Irish Sea, the Channel and the North Sea. This also had a profound effect on later colonisation by delaying the arrival of new immigrants from Portugal, Spain and Brittany and from Denmark, Germany and the Netherlands. The final flooding of the last land bridge that made mainland Britain into a large island may date to around 5600 BC. This is the same time as a great flood in the Mediterranean area drowned low-lying land, creating numerous islands in the Aegean and a catastrophic breakthrough of the Bosphorus into the Black Sea. Throughout the Mesolithic period low-lying coastal land all over the globe, together with many coastal settlements and towns, sank beneath the waves at different intervals. Tales of Great Floods are common in many legendary tales from around the world.

The distant memory of some widespread, disastrous event in the Mediterranean may well have given rise to the story of the Flood and Noah's Ark in the Bible.) By the time the next archaeologically distinct group of people settled permanently in Britain, thousands of years had passed. This period is known as the Neolithic or New Stone Age and has been traditionally associated with the development of livestock farming and agriculture, typified by the widespread use of new forms of pottery, polished stone axes and the use of stone querns for grinding cultivated grain. For many, this was the beginning of 'the daily grind'. The distinction between the end of the Mesolithic and the beginning of the Neolithic period is very fuzzy, people did not suddenly all stop hunting and foraging, and then start raising livestock and growing crops. Instead, the transition varied from place to place and community to community over hundreds of years. Pottery was known from earlier periods but was rarely made and used by nomadic people because of its fragility whilst travelling. Wooden bowls, birch bark and leather containers were much more effective, durable and easier to produce. People on the move had few possessions simply because everything had to be carried from place to place. However, not everyone was nomadic at this time, in Eastern Europe and the Near East there were small towns with industries based on the exploitation of local resources, such as salt and a volcanic black glass called obsidian, and other settled communities lived and traded the products of farming and agriculture. However in Britain, things seem to have moved on very slowly indeed. It wasn't until about 4300 BC that agriculture started on an identified basis. This is probably because growing crops can be very hard work, sometimes with little or no return and it would have taken a lot longer to become an accepted way of life.

In comparison, the raising of pigs, cattle, sheep and goats was relatively easy because guarding the herds and flocks was a lot less physically demanding; even children could do it whilst the adults were busy elsewhere. Early crops were emmer and einkorn wheat, barley, oats, flax, and vetch (a type of edible bean). At a time when there was no complex machinery the growing of plants for food demanded that everything was done by hand. It started with clearing away the ancient woodland, digging up rocks, stones, weeds and roots, tilling the soil, sowing the seed, then weeding and constantly guarding the plants from birds and animals, and when the crop was ripe, harvesting the grain. After that came threshing, winnowing, parching and storage and then finally grinding the grain to make flour. Initially it would certainly have made many people wonder if all that effort was justified.

To begin with perhaps the native hunters and foragers just traded with the cereal growers, exchanging game, dried fish and furs for bread, beer and flour. And cakes made with wild honey and flavoured with hazelnuts and berries would have been a rare treat. Eventually the benefit of having an almost guaranteed reserve of food gained from growing crops must have outweighed the incredibly hard work involved, and agriculture became more widespread. However, it would be inaccurate to think of it in terms of our modern farms with acres upon acres of land under the plough. Early crops were invariably grown in smallholdings, simply because of the significant effort required to prepare the soil and then to reap the harvest, then process, store and grind the grain. Initially the farming of livestock was by far the main method of food production and large areas of the forested landscape were cleared for pasture. In time many such areas became unproductive and covered with weeds and were allowed to return to secondary woodland, then cleared again decades later. In some places the cultivation of crops was so intensive over such a long time that it led to soil erosion and the creation of moorland, including Exmoor, Dartmoor and the North Yorkshire Moors.

When moving to a new area, the forest would have to be cleared away using stone tools to cut down the trees and then used fire to burn away the brush. Stone and flint axes are not very efficient, the stump looks as though it has been gnawed away by a beaver, but an expert can fell a medium-sized tree in an hour or so. Sometimes the stumps of trees such as hazel were pollarded, that is they were left to sprout for a couple of years, then cut back and the coppiced branches used for making baskets, walls and fencing. Initially small areas of forest would be cleared and burned to make small gardens and fields for growing crops, but when the soil was exhausted, they simply moved to a new area, using the slash and burn process still used today in many parts of the world, with the same devastating results.

Later on, using more efficient axes, made of metal, rather than stone or flint, Bronze Age farmers started to clear the densely forested primeval landscape in earnest, eventually transforming much of the countryside into an open pastoral and agricultural landscape. Their domesticated animals included new breeds of cattle, sheep, horses and pigs. Over time they invented food production techniques that would have provided regular supplies of beef, lamb and pork, milk, butter and cheese, flour, bread and beer. And in addition to clothes made from the fur and skins of wild animals they would have made themselves a wide range of clothing from sheepskin, suede and leather. Other garments were woven from plant fibres such as nettle and flax, and then coloured with vegetable dyes and decorated with beads and fur. The domestication of wild animals did not happen overnight, but must have its origins much further back in time. Young animals, particularly pigs, must have been brought back from a successful hunt to be eaten at a later date, when game was scarce and in time along came the idea of letting the less aggressive ones grow to adulthood and always selecting the tamer ones for breeding. The dogs they kept are particularly interesting as these were the distant descendants of wolves, showing that 'man's best friend' has been with us for a very long time indeed. Whether they were pets in the modern sense is debatable, but they would certainly have been very useful as guard dogs, as well as a hunting companion and in times of great hardship, they would probably have been on the menu!

A commonly held belief is that along with their nomadic lifestyle, our hunter/gatherer forefathers were all living a hand-to-mouth existence, with starvation just round the corner. Then finally, around 4500 BC, along came farming to save the day. The truth is that life expectancy **declined** with the widespread adoption of agriculture. The scientific analysis of teeth and bones shows that the hunter/gatherers had enjoyed a better and far more varied diet and were generally healthier and fitter than the farmers were. With only simple tools, agriculture was very hard work, the skeletons of many of the early farmers reveal the terrible toll that clearing the ground, tilling the soil, and planting, weeding and reaping crops had on their bodies. Farming was incredibly labour intensive and osteo-arthritis of the joints and spine was common, even amongst children and adolescents. Nevertheless, however unattractive the hard work was, the change from an unfettered way of life was made and eventually the farming way of life prevailed. Permanent agricultural villages meant that although many people worked much harder than their ancestors, bread, meat and dairy products were usually present, although they were sometimes unable to adapt to a poor harvest and crop failures caused famine. However, arable farming was usually sufficient to produce food surpluses and a high carbohydrate diet resulted in increased fertility in women and hence a big increase in population levels, although life expectancy for the young was low, especially for babies and children, and only a few people reached their forty-fifth birthday. In addition to their farm work, they also created massive monuments in the landscape that required them to work harder than ever.

Most of us still believe the propaganda we were taught as schoolchildren, Roman propaganda that has endured for two thousand years. Even now our own history starts with the invasion of our lands by the Roman Legions, and it gives the very false impression that nothing important happened until they appeared on the scene. Julius Caesar recorded his version of events in his conquest of Gaul, (France) and he wrote about the savages he encountered during his invasion of Britain in 55 BC and 54 BC. (The actual conquest of Britain began later on under the Emperor Claudius, in 43 AD.) The general consensus of opinion amongst Roman soldiers, writers and historians was that the Britons were barbarians, who only became 'civilised' under the influence of the Romans. This attitude has persisted to the present day, because only their version of the truth has survived. This perversion of the facts has meant that many people are still under the impression that our forefathers were running around in tattered animal skins and living like beasts in caves. However, the real truth is very different, for scattered across Britain and Ireland are the ruins and remains of early forms of civilisation that predate the coming of the Romans by well over two thousand years. These ancestors of ours may have lived and worked with simple technology, but they were far from being backward, instead they built enormous and very complex monuments of earth, wood and stone, some of which took well over a million man-hours to construct.

Everything they used was made by hand from natural materials - there were no metals and no glass, concrete, or paper and certainly no plastics. Everything had to come from plant, animal or mineral origins. Their tools and weapons were skilfully made from bone, antler, flint and stone. And they used many different woods, selected according to what the tool would be used for. Oak, ash, elm and hazel all have their own distinct properties. Ash for example is a shock-resistant wood and is often used for the handles of axes, spades and hammers. Oak is often used in construction because of its strength and both oak and beech are good for making furniture. The pottery they produced was quite simple, but it was reasonably effective for cooking food, particularly for making gruel (wheat or barley boiled in water or stock) and for cooking stews in the embers of an open fire. Some pottery would have been used for storing liquids and other pots were for the storage of salt, herbs, fats and preserved foods.

The ancient hunting and gathering lifestyle changed forever once farming became firmly established, people became rooted to the same spot for generation after generation. The population was initially quite small, so people had plenty of space to themselves, often living on small isolated farms with just a few neighbours. They had room to grow their crops and raise their animals, although in special places where the soil was particularly fertile, such as the Boyne Valley in Ireland or on the loess soils of Wiltshire, there were much higher concentrations of people.

One of the first groups of permanent Neolithic settlers in England are known as the Windmill Hill Culture, named after a site near Avebury, Wiltshire, and dated to about 3700 BC. They constructed causewayed camps, which were large earth circles consisting of one or more raised banks and ditches, with gaps in the bank and passageways across the ditch. The use of these enclosures varied from place to place and from time to time, initially they were used as seasonal meeting places, stock enclosures, fairs and markets and later on some of these sites seem to have become cemeteries where the dead were laid out to decay naturally. In historical times in New Guinea and India, as well as with certain Native American tribes, the dead were laid out on tall wooden platforms, so that their spirits or souls could rise up into the sky, and as a result these are sometimes called sky burials. In addition to human remains, the ditches of causewayed enclosures often contain broken pottery and animal bones, the rubbish of everyday living, the remains of feasts or when people shared one last meal with the dead. And of course this truly ancient tradition of a final banquet or wake, with all the friends and family of the deceased, is still with us today. In some places the dead were cremated, then buried, rather than allowed to decay naturally in the open air, the customs varied according to tradition and belief.

It was also about this time that some human skeletons, probably those of the new social elite, were buried in elongated mounds of earth called longbarrows. These communal graves are thought to have had their origins on the continent and the techniques and traditions of such burials varied greatly over time. Unlike the hunters, the farmers were used to digging and as time went by, the long mounds of earth became more substantial and more elaborate, with some examples containing wooden chambers and others having passageways and side chambers with stone roofs and walls. Drawings done by early Georgian researchers, such as John Aubrey and William Stukeley, show that some barrows had arrangements of standing stones around them. The tradition of building longbarrows lasted for well over a thousand years and in some cases many successive generations were interred inside, until eventually the tomb was sealed forever. The earliest burials in the famous West Kennet longbarrow near Avebury date to around 3500 BC, whilst the last burials date from the Beaker period of the early Bronze Age, around 2300 BC.

In many instances the skeletons of the dead were buried inside longbarrows without much in the way of grave goods, that is practical items, such as tools, pottery or weapons, or else decorative items, such as jewellery, which would show their status and help them in the afterlife. So it seems to me that some people in those days believed that the spirits of their dead ancestors had no need for grave goods since they would stay in the vicinity to look after their children and grandchildren. However, other people thought that the spirits would only return at special times of the year and that they would have a need for tools and weapons in the other world. Some five hundred years later, their descendants built a new style of large earthwork called henges, which consisted of circular, or slightly oval, ditches with an external bank and distinct entrances. On the chalk lands of Wiltshire and Dorset, the gleaming white ring of the chalky bank would have been visible from afar. In other parts of the country, the earth bank was sometimes considered to be too dark, so in places such Thornborough, Yorkshire, the earth bank was given a coating of white gypsum. At other sites the bank was even sprinkled with pieces of white quartz that would have sparkled in the sun and glistened by moonlight. Sometimes these earth circles contained circular arrangements of wooden posts or standing stones. The first stone circles are attributed to just before 3000 BC, but as with many constructions of earth and stone, the building styles and traditions continued for many centuries, overlapping in time and space with new and old versions intermixed as the local populations changed.

Although the megalithic tradition of building large stone tombs was long-lived and widespread across Europe, it is important to note that circular monuments of earth and/or standing stones were almost exclusively a tradition in Great Britain and Ireland, and not often built on the Continent. And as we shall see further on, the development and proliferation of earth circles, timber structures and circles of standing stones were very indicative of the spread of belief systems and philosophies linked to the cyclical nature of the sun and moon, the natural world and the farming year.

In the south of England, the Neolithic farmers gave way in turn to the Beaker people, named after their distinctive pottery and perhaps their fondness for beer made from barley and for mead made from honey and sometimes flavoured with herbs such as meadowsweet. The Beaker people buried their dead as either cremations or inhumations in round barrows. Sometimes excavators have found skeletons of men clutching a drinking pot, as though even in death they wouldn't let go of their favourite beaker. This was perhaps a way of showing the cause of death or maybe it was customary to go to parties in the afterlife with your own drinking vessel, something like the Viking Valhalla? They were the first people to manufacture copper and introduce bronze into Britain. They first appeared in southern England about 2500 BC, but were widespread in Europe long before then. The Beaker people brought with them many new ideas and techniques, to do with pottery and metalworking, architecture, agriculture and religion.
The subject of the Beaker people is still controversial. Currently they are thought by many experts not to have been a separate people at all, as previous generations of archaeologists had thought and many now see them simply in terms of an imported cultural influence. I am not happy about this interpretation for several reasons, firstly because the original inhabitants of these islands were famous for their long narrow skulls, whilst those who were buried in round barrows often had a much more rounded skull, hence the expression: Long skull, longbarrow; Round skull, round barrow. Secondly, there were more profound cultural changes in the five centuries after 2500 BC than in previous years. Our history has shown time and time again that profound changes in society are often the product of incoming groups of new people with new ideas and different ways of doing things. Gradually the local population adopts these ideas and inventions, blending the new and the old, until a 'marriage' occurs between the two groups of peoples, a marriage that is a product of the two ways of living and working. In time, 'old-fashioned' products no longer find a ready market and so local artisans have to adopt and adapt to the new methods of working and produce only the latest fashions.
I suspect that this interpretation of non-existent Beaker people is just another fad amongst academics that think that our prehistoric ancestors weren't very clever and that at such an early epoch there were few gifted boat builders, daring merchants or adventurous sailors. And so it is easier for them to imagine a new society developing from the effects of trade on native cultures, rather than as

the outcome of a fleet of immigrants that had travelled across the sea and taken away the power of local chiefs. (Doesn't it remind you of historical invaders such as the Romans, Angles, Saxons, Vikings and Normans?) Beaker burials of men show that they were quite a warlike people, their grave goods often featured battle-axes, triangular arrowheads, bronze axes and daggers and stone wrist guards, indicating powerful bows. Sometimes just one arrowhead has been found with the skeleton. In modern times we use arrow signs to show directions, but in earlier times an archer's arrow could be lethal. So perhaps an arrow was not just a traditional symbol for a warrior, but like the axe, it also represented an ancient symbol for death and the journey to the afterlife. Around 2300 BC there were many social, religious and cultural changes going on right across Northern Europe, brought on by the movement of people leaving their traditional homelands and moving north. In Britain the changes are obvious in the form of improved weapons and pottery styles, in some places Grooved Ware ceases to be made, Beaker pottery takes over, and ritual monuments alter because of new religious influences. At about this time longbarrows were no longer in active use, some were even sealed up with rubbish, small stone circles appear more widespread and the first burial mounds known as round barrows were constructed.

Some of the last groups of people covered by this book were named the Wessex Culture by Professor Stuart Piggott, and according to him, were characterised by comparatively rich grave goods of gold, copper, bronze, amber and jet, and who evolved from the local population around 2300 BC. They built the final version of Stonehenge, the ruins of which we can still see today. By the middle Bronze Age much of the area surrounding Stonehenge had changed radically over the centuries, from the ancient forest of the Mesolithic into one of open pastureland interspersed with small woods and areas of intensive crop production for growing bread wheat, barley and oats. At some time around 1500 BC, the religious centres of Avebury and Stonehenge were mysteriously deserted, no new major construction projects were organised, although there were still a few farmers living in the area. However, if this break up of society had not happened, history would have been very different, my analysis of the final temple at Stonehenge shows that they were starting to take a more scientific route to understanding the nature of the world around them.

The architectural techniques employed at Stonehenge show they were close to inventing new building techniques to move away from wood and make more permanent structures, such as bridges and houses of stone. The proliferation of industrial processes, of mining and smelting copper ore and the production of bronze would have encouraged a different way of thinking and a different way of life and it was the start of a new society based on more modern principles, similar perhaps to those that eventually created the classical civilisations of Ancient Greece and Rome. What actually seems to have happened is that the basic infrastructure of much of their society fell apart. Groups in southern Britain that had lived together in large communities became isolated and fragmented. Even the pottery changed from the highly decorated, thin-walled beakers to the rough, thick-walled pottery of the late Bronze Age and early Iron Age, as though important skills had been lost or forgotten.
The most likely explanation is that this was brought about by some sort of major change in society, perhaps caused by an external influence such as a change in climate, an outbreak of cattle disease or a virulent plague, thus causing a major shift in religious belief. A very wet spring would cause the seed to rot in the ground and if summer skies were overcast for long periods, the remaining grain would not ripen properly, resulting in a poor harvest and little seed grain for the next sowing season. If this scenario were repeated for several years in a row, just as it did in the late 11th Century AD, population levels would have plummeted and all the religious, cultural and scientific progress that had taken thousands of years to fully develop, must have changed dramatically for the worse. In many places the old religions based on the sun and moon were replaced by new ideas involving sacrifices and tributes paid to the gods of the Underworld, many ornaments and weapons, such as bronze swords, were cast into lakes, rivers and bogs.
By the time of the invasion by the Celtic Peoples from the Continent, around 750 BC, people no longer lived in harmony with each other. And with the advent of iron weapons, provided by the new technology of high temperature smelting of iron ore, matters only got worse. By the time recorded

history began, the country was filled with rival clans and warring tribes that lived, or sought refuge, on fortified hill tops, the Iron Age hill forts. And these sorts of profound changes in customs, ways of life and belief continued when the Romans arrived and the official version of British history began, some two thousand years ago. (But it should be remembered that conquerors tell their version of events and rewrite history accordingly.)

Traditionally, the invention of writing in the Middle East has been seen as the hallmark of the beginning of civilisation. Elsewhere, people were just as intelligent; it's just that they did not develop in the same direction as the Babylonians and Egyptians, or later on, the Minoans, Phoenicians, Greeks and Romans. Instead, their simple civilisations were more subtle and had a greater affinity with the seasonal changes to the natural world. Ancient Egypt had only one high point of the year, the annual flooding of the Nile, but in more northern latitudes, the movements of the sun had seasonal changes that influenced agriculture on a different basis. These seasonal variations and their effects on livestock and crops had a profound effect on the lives and attitudes of the early European farmers. In northwestern Europe, people had plenty of room to spread out and go their own way, resulting in a diffused population with only a few regions with large communities such as those around Carnac in Brittany, Stonehenge and Avebury in Wiltshire and the Boyne Valley in Ireland.

Around 3200 BC, the people of the Boyne Valley in Ireland constructed enormous burial mounds with chambered tombs such as those at Newgrange, Dowth and Knowth. Although they could just as easily have constructed such tombs with squared-off slabs of stone, they preferred to use more natural forms for the walls and roofs. It was not a question of the increased amount of work needed to produce regular-sided oblongs that makes these different to the architecture of the Middle East; they could have done so, if they had wanted to. The amount of time and effort needed for the construction of their monuments was almost irrelevant to them, what is important was the different way of thinking that this shows, which came directly from the influences of their ancestors, their own way of life and their religious beliefs.

This non-linear way of thinking, of using more natural forms for their buildings and monuments, is a key element to understanding the minds of our distant ancestors. Their lives were in relative harmony with nature and their monuments reflect this attitude since they are much less artificial and unnatural looking than those of later cultures. Their earthworks and stone circles seem to be an integral part of the landscape, rather than apart from it. As we shall see later on, their symbolism reflects this as well, for instead of having just one meaning, their use of complex symbolism reflects different levels of comprehension and purpose, much of which is hidden but with observation, insight and empathy it can be unravelled. In our modern world, symbols and symbolism usually have just one meaning, but in prehistoric societies this was not always the case. Simple designs are often deceptive in their apparent simplicity. The same symbolic image could have many different meanings that were not exclusive to each other but instead reflected a multi-layered way of thinking and an abstract rather than a logical way of looking at things. We are different. We have imposed artificial order and control on the natural world through science and technology, and we like to think that we have tamed the wild world - although from time to time Mother Nature reminds us just who is boss!

Although our ancestors were like us in many ways, in other ways they were vastly different, they had a different way of seeing and doing things and sometimes the things they did were very, very strange indeed. After studying their cultures for more than ten years, it seems to me that their 'scientific' knowledge was a curious mixture of strange rituals that blended together astronomy, spirituality and astrology, mixed with magic and superstition. Many of the tombs and temples they built reflect the persistent belief in an afterlife and the presence of ancestral spirits and ghosts. Their astronomers and priests accumulated knowledge of the movements of the sun, moon, stars, and the visible planets. Over time these developed into a wide range of religious beliefs and customs, some of which were linked to nature and the cycles of the farming year.

Even if they were poor by our standards of wealth, they were only poor in terms of material possessions. Our ancestors had simple civilisations that seem to have been relatively peaceful and flourished for thousands of years. Of the hundreds of thousands of people that lived here from the end of the last Ice Age, around eleven thousand years ago, until about 1500 BC very little seems to remain which shows who they were and what they were like. However, from the Neolithic period onwards they have left behind some very obvious proof in the form of ritual burial mounds, tombs and temples and some evidence of their daily lives in the form of the tools and pottery that they used, clues also come from the sort of crops they grew and the domesticated animals they raised.

What has not survived are the vast majority of the things they made and used, all the things that were composed of perishable materials of wood, bone, horn, leather, rope, plant and animal fibres, wicker or cloth. There appeared to be very little evidence of an artistic or creative side of their culture and as a result, they have often been seen as not having had much intelligence or capable of sophisticated thinking. From reading much of the literature on prehistoric Britain one is left with the impression of people who did very little to improve their way of life, a way of life that remained practically unchanged for millennia. They seem to have just repeated more or less the same things as their ancestors had done centuries beforehand. They raised crops, looked after livestock, raised their children and sometimes built ritual monuments of earth, wood and stone. They used simple but very effective tools made from flint, bone, antler and wood and gradually adopted the use of metals. For many people their lives were short and hard, a seemingly endless cycle of drudgery involving the daily chores of cutting firewood, fetching water and grinding grain interspersed with the seasonal activities such as tilling the soil, planting and harvesting their crops.

But is this a true picture of what life was really like? Were they really so insensitive to art and culture?

The landscape of Britain has changed dramatically since the Bronze Age. Over the centuries the earth banks of causewayed enclosures, henges and barrows have eroded way and been ploughed out, the ditches have filled up and the wooden buildings have rotted away, leaving just a memory of their existence as depressions or holes in the ground. All that is left are the big stones, the megaliths and even they have suffered terrible depredations, many have been broken up, others lie half buried in the ground and some have fallen and then been re-erected the wrong way round. The ancient Britons built their monuments to be used and to show others who they were and what they believed in and they demonstrated what could be accomplished with simple technology, even though like so many other civilisations across the world the people declined and vanished. They built many of their monuments out of stone because they knew that they would last forever but what they did not realise is that their descendants, four thousand years later, would not understand them. This has happened because the oral traditions of passing on the ancient wisdom and knowledge of countless generations has been lost and as a result, they have been robbed of their identities, leaving a great deal of confusion and misunderstanding behind. And in the past we have made the classic error of mistaking simplicity for ignorance and stupidity.

The idea that our ancestors of four or five thousand years ago were just primitive, pagan sun-worshippers is really propaganda that has been handed down to us through the Roman, Saxon, Medieval, Georgian and Victorian eras. Christian writers of history were quick to denounce their distant forefathers as barely human and hardly able to scratch a living because the old 'pagan' religions were seen as a threat. Because of this misinformation, to many people, the old religions and the ancient way of life was the realm of primitive wild men, and their lunar beliefs were the human equivalent of wolves baying at the full moon. Even higher civilisations, such as Ancient Egypt, Greece and Rome, were pagan according to the Christian faith, because each had revered and worshipped a variety of Gods and reserved special roles for the Sun and the Moon in their mythology and religious belief systems. The Ancient Britons also revered the sun and moon, but in a different way, as an integral part of the human life cycle and as vital elements in the natural world. In other words, **the sky above, affected the world below.**

Ancient mythology often contained important knowledge and cultural lessons disguised in an entertaining form that were easy to learn, remember and understand. And some myths have been proved later on to be true accounts of actual events. Only a few of the really ancient traditions, myths and legends survive in our own superstitions, folklore or fairy tales. Most of our ancient oral history is descended from the Celtic mythologies and religions of a much more recent date, sometime after 600 BC. Contrary to popular belief, the Iron Age priests, the Druids, did not build Stonehenge. The very long period during which Stonehenge was built and used belongs to a much earlier era, starting around 3000 BC, but, until radiocarbon dating came along, in the minds of many Victorian and Edwardian scholars the two completely different time periods and religions were one and the same. As a result of religious and intellectual racism, to many people, the early settlers in Britain were sub-human and were not very different to those that had lived a million years before.

Nothing could be further from the truth.

They had the same emotions and feelings that we all share, the characteristics, emotions and sentiments that make us human. Initially, they lived in relative harmony with the natural world, taking only what they could use and they tried to make sense of the world around them and the sky above. But it would be wrong to think of it as a Golden Age. People worked extremely hard and died young, (just as they did until very recent times in the West and still do in many parts of the world, particularly in Africa and Asia). However, they did live in quite close-knit communities and they continued the old traditions of their ancestors, living in comparative harmony with the natural world and were relatively peaceful and happy for generation after generation. This is not to say that they did not have thefts, rapes, murders, fights or disputes, since human nature has changed little over the millennia but there is not much evidence for the large-scale warfare associated with other civilisations. However life was not always peaceful, excavation has found evidence of defensive wooden palisades at several sites, such as the one at Mount Pleasant, Dorset, which featured a continuous circle of some 1600 large tree trunks enclosing a 4.5 hectare site, 270 metres across, with two narrow entrances inside a ditch on the top of a hill. It was further revealed that the fort had been destroyed by fire, and that some megaliths had been burned and smashed up. At the Neolithic site of Carn Brae in Cornwall, attackers had fired over 750 arrows into its hilltop enclosure, then all the wooden structures inside were burned to the ground. Elsewhere several skeletons have been found that show that people had been killed by arrows, one at Stonehenge had been shot with four arrows, the skeleton of a man in the West Kennet longbarrow showed he had been shot in the throat. And during the early Neolithic period around 2850 BC, archers attacked another settlement at Hambledon Hill, in Gloucestershire and at least one man had been shot in the back. Other ancient skeletons from both long and round barrows show evidence of murderous attacks or the brutal punishment of wrongdoers, the corpses had smashed or crushed skulls. Some had been beheaded and some people had their hands or feet cut off. Such scenes show that life wasn't always peaceful and that occasionally there would be outright battles fought between rival groups, but it appears that little occurred on the epic scale of what was to come during the following millennia. Let's not forget that over a hundred **million** men, women and children died in the 'civilised' wars of the 20th Century.

The construction of the major sites shows strong evidence of a complex society. Religious and social leaders governed the construction projects, organised the necessary labour force to extract and move huge stones, and erect them to a particular design, provided the necessary tools and equipment, directed the digging of thousands of cubic metres of soil and generally looked after everyone and kept them fed. Some of these ancient construction projects are thought to have taken twenty or thirty years to complete. Perhaps it was not an idyllic society in the way some would see it, but it was a time of great stability due to common ideals, beliefs and social behaviour, a way of life that lasted hundreds of years. And with a relatively low population there would be less to argue over and contact between neighbouring groups could be cemented in friendship by the giving and receiving of gifts, such as stone or flint axes, food, handicrafts and above all, help with large construction projects. The population came from many different ethnic backgrounds but some groups in the western part of the country had their cultural origins in Brittany. The distribution of stone circles shows that mainland Britain was divided into at least two main areas by religious beliefs, with open air stone temples scattered to the west and the north of a line drawn from Southampton to Sheffield and across to the east, towards Grimsby. However, even the stone circle tradition shows many different localised beliefs, varying greatly from one community to another and from one time period to another. Over the centuries, the amateur and professional excavation of many stone circles has revealed very little about their use and purpose. Often there are just a few clues available from pieces of charcoal, flint tools, animal and human bones, or broken pottery.

Looking at early British pottery and the absence of figurines and statuettes, gives an impression of people who cared very little for art, but this is not the case at all because I have discovered that the Neolithic artists were busy elsewhere, producing works of art in a more traditional, satisfying and permanent material, **stone**.

The most obvious remains of the ancient ritual centres are the megaliths, the big standing stones, yet surprisingly they have received the least attention and the least understanding. Most research has been concerned with their geology, astronomy and the folklore around the stones. Rarely have the experts looked closely at the individual stones, even though, like the pages in a book ***each stone has its own story to tell, if you know how to read it.***

Although they did not produce great stone palaces, our distant forefathers, the ancient Britons, were far more subtle and more sophisticated than we have been led to believe. Of the hundreds of thousands of people, who were born, lived and died, some were extremely gifted individuals and of everything they achieved, their most extraordinary success story is the world-famous prehistoric temple we call Stonehenge. But even this achievement was in doubt until a few decades ago. Until the 1970's many scholars, archaeologists and prehistorians believed that the architecture of Stonehenge was far too good to be work of the native population and therefore its sophisticated structural techniques had to be the result of outside influences, probably by architects from Mycenae, the precursor of Ancient Greece.

How wrong they were.

So to recap, for several centuries our scientists have been investigating the mysteries surrounding the people and monuments of the megalithic tradition. Yet amazingly they have ignored the most obvious signs and spent most of their time pursuing tiny clues revealed through excavation and the analysis of the things that have been recovered, instead of looking more closely at the very things that defined the culture itself, the big stones known as megaliths.

As a direct result of looking and thinking for myself, rather than just blindly accepting that earlier theories were correct, I have made a series of ground-breaking observations about the standing stones. As we shall see in the following chapters, these observations have resulted in new discoveries and in completely new insights into the lives of our ancestors and in turn these insights have solved many of the mysteries surrounding the enigmatic stone circles, standing stones and megalithic tombs that our Neolithic and Bronze Age ancestors created.

2 ASTRONOMY, SYMBOLISM AND RELIGIOUS BELIEFS

The traditional method of studying the world of our prehistoric ancestors has usually been undertaken through the examination, analysis and cataloguing of scientific evidence, derived principally from excavations. By comparing the results from different digs, archaeologists have tried to develop theories to account for what they have unearthed. These insights have formed part of a framework that has identified the characteristics of different cultures in different eras and it has been successful in identifying the series of technological changes to weapons, tools and pottery that took place over time. But although this method has worked quite well in terms of providing knowledge about physical objects, it is far from ideal about revealing what people were actually doing, and it often fails to provide any understanding of the reasons why such changes took place. After all, people have always been motivated to make changes to their way of life for a very wide variety of different reasons. For example, change may come about through variations in weather patterns that have caused environmental transformations or more simply, through the social and cultural development of older traditions. Change may also happen because of new influences from outside the local area. These may come about through trade or even the arrival of immigrants who have different or better ways of doing things. Change may also come about through the actions of one key individual, whose behaviour has been motivated by such basic human emotions as greed, anger, fear, jealousy, desire, lust or a need for revenge. Or change may come about because of more positive emotions, such as love or devotion in this key individual, but of all the different root causes for change, one of the most powerful of the forces that have driven humanity, either forward (or backward), is religious belief. But what exactly were the beliefs of our Neolithic and Bronze Age ancestors?

The answer is that after more than three centuries of investigation we still don't know...

Without any contemporary written records to go by, all we have had, until now, is the physical evidence of the few things that have survived buried in the ground and the ruined remains of the buildings, monuments, tombs and temples that were constructed such a long time ago. And at present all that our experts know for certain is that many of the religions of Neolithic and Bronze Age Britain had something to do with the sun and the moon. So perhaps one of the best starting points to a new understanding of the religious beliefs of our distant ancestors is to forget for a moment our own knowledge and understanding of how the natural world works and try to think in the same way as they did. Let's try and see things as they saw them, in effect to look at their world through their eyes, rather than through our own modern, scientifically based ones.

Five thousand years ago it was a very different world to the one we know. Dense mixed forests covered most of Britain and Ireland, with only scattered farmsteads and small villages, and with just a few tribal centres where the local population rose above a few hundred people. This is a far cry from the millions of people who are crammed into today's towns and cities. In those far-off times life was a lot simpler and a great deal quieter but it was much harder, infant mortality was high and life expectancy was low and few people lived to see their forty-fifth birthday. Many skeletons of ancient farming people show periods of malnutrition when the crops had failed and life had become very precarious. Yet in spite of all their difficulties, we can be certain that they had the same human emotions as ourselves and they would have had similar joys, hopes and fears, and just like us, they would have loved (and hated) each other and worried about their children and what the future had in store for them.

In northern latitudes people could not have failed to notice that each year the seasons always followed each other in the same rhythmic cycle of spring, summer, autumn and winter, just as they always have done and always will do. The people of Ancient Britain were well aware of the seasonal changes of the natural world and how the lives of animals and plants altered with the passing seasons. In spring, new life was born, grew through the summer months and reached maturity in the autumn, and although many would die during the winter, a new generation of plants and animals would always appear the following spring.

In other words, the natural world has a never-ending cycle of **Birth, Life and Death,** followed by **Rebirth.** The early farmers lived close to the land and as they worked they watched the seasons pass and their families, herds and crops grow. They lived and worked outdoors and looked for changes in the natural world of plants and animals to gauge the right moment to sow their seeds, and looked to the sky above for the right time to make hay and harvest their crops. All the way through the growing and ripening season life was a constant worry, until the harvest had been safely gathered, with enough food stored to last through the winter and into early spring. Over time, the farmers appreciated more and more just how much the ever-changing seasons affected the way they lived their lives. This was not just a practical issue for them but one that profoundly affected their way of thinking and how they saw themselves and their place in the greater scheme of things. Although their interpretation of cosmic events changed with time and place, the ancient sky watchers would have noticed that the movements of the sun, moon, stars and planets repeat themselves on a regular basis. And those people who were curious about such things knew that to fully understand these cycles they had to work out what the sequences were and how long each lasted.

Yet in addition to the annual cycle of the sun, the monthly phases of the moon and the repetitive sequence of the changing seasons, there is a much more frequent sequence of cyclical events. One that is so commonplace that we rarely think about it. Each and every day the sun goes through the same pattern of behaviour, despite the weather. As dawn approaches, the sky to the east grows lighter and the darkness of the night gives way to the coming day. On a clear day the sky brightens further until at last the sun rises over the eastern horizon. The sun rises further into the sky, travels round part of the horizon and then sinks down below the western side of the horizon, it disappears from view and the sky progressively darkens until night falls and the day ends. The following day the sequence repeats itself and the never-ending cycle continues. This process can also be seen in terms of an eternal cycle, as the daily cycle of the **Birth, Life, Death and Rebirth of the Sun.**

As the years passed it became more and more evident to the farmers that the sun, and the moon, brought about many of the transformations in the natural world, and that changes to their own lives were often a reflection of cosmic events. They could see that there was a clear and direct link between the sky above and the land below. During the annual cycle of the sun, the different amounts of sunlight received caused the seasons to change and in turn these events dramatically changed the lives of all living things. The sun determined the vegetation cycle and this in turn had a direct effect on the lives of people, because the energy from sunlight made their crops germinate, grow and then ripen. The sun made the grass grow and their cattle and sheep could eat, grow and multiply. The hay that the farmers cut and stored ensured the survival of their animals through the cold months of the year. In short, the energy from the sun was of vital importance since it was the starting point for the production of all their food. Their lives depended on it. Just as our lives do today.

Over countless millennia the sun, moon, stars and planets must have been the subjects for many campfire tales and they would have played a key role in many beliefs, myths and legends. During the long hot days of summer the sun was overwhelmingly bright, and painful to look at, more powerful than an enormous campfire, and because of this powerful energy it was often considered to be a masculine entity. In contrast, the moon mysteriously changed its shape during its monthly cycle. It changed from just a thin crescent to becoming round and full. Just like the swelling belly of a pregnant woman and pregnancy itself lasted about nine moons, so for reasons such as these the moon was often considered to be a feminine entity. During the long nights with little in the way of artificial illumination, the light of the full moon allowed people to hold ceremonies, parties and feasts and they could travel and even hunt by moonlight. In addition, the moon was important in coastal regions since it controlled the twice-daily tides that brought fish into their nets and allowed the collection of seafood from the shoreline when the tide was out. Each month the moon went through her endlessly repeated cycle of phases, mysteriously appearing out of the darkness, growing to fullness, and then fading away to completely disappear at the end of the cycle, only to be reborn again as a new moon. And this monthly sequence was yet another everlasting cycle of **Birth, Life** and **Death**, followed by **Rebirth** and the start of the next cycle.

The inescapable logic that accumulated from such simple and obvious observations was the driving force behind many of the religious practices that followed. The ancient farmers could see that life on earth closely followed the cycles of the heavens above. So to sum up this way of thinking, the Sun was masculine and the Moon was feminine, and powerful forces influenced and controlled Life on Earth, and the cycles that took place in the sky above governed events on the earth below.

As above, so below.

There is plenty of physical evidence to show that our prehistoric ancestors were well aware of the cycles of the sun and moon, but just how good their astronomical knowledge was is a matter of lively debate. However, despite all the differences of expert opinion, everyone acknowledges that one of the many skills that the ancient builders had was to build their monuments, tombs and temples in very specific ways tied to horizon events. The most common alignments were set up to highlight and permanently record the position of the rising or setting sun at special times of the year. However, despite claims to the contrary, in most cases these alignments were not highly accurate; I think that the intent was more religious symbolism than scientific accuracy. Many monuments contained features that had references to the northeast or southwest, but these were usually just a sort of directional indicator, rather than an ultra-precise alignment that was valid on just one particular day of the year. It was usually religious symbolism, not science and astronomy that was important to them. However later on, particularly in Northern Scotland during the Bronze Age, there were places where they erected standing stones with quite accurate alignments towards the sun or the moon. And we can perhaps see these observation points as the result of a change in attitude, a change towards a more scientific way of thinking and a desire for a greater understanding of cosmic events.

Rising with the sun, their lives were governed by the sun and the demands of the farming year, not by alarm clocks, timetables or deadlines. They lived at a hard but relatively slow pace and many activities were controlled by the way that the number of hours of daylight varied according to the time of year. In short they simply weren't as obsessed with time as us. Instead they often used simple religious calendars that were based on the high, middle and low points of the annual cycle of the sun, and many people believe that these events were often permanently marked by erecting standing stones that indicated the special seasonal rising and setting points of the sun and the extreme positions of the moon.

These must also have been tied in with some of their holy days and were part of a sacred calendar that varied from place to place, according to the beliefs of the people involved.
The timing of religious events and ceremonies was important to them and made even more impressive because they usually took place at sunrise or sunset, or as the moon rose or set and so there was often a beautiful natural light show to accompany the moment and make it truly spiritual. It is very likely that making music, singing songs and performing dances were an integral part of these celebrations. (We must stop thinking of our Neolithic ancestors as savage brutes, with no appreciation of natural beauty and no artistic temperament - the clues that they appreciated such things have been there for anyone with an open mind to realise!)

So let us try and decipher what some of their beliefs were and how they could have evolved from observation of the sky, and how my discoveries and new insights fit in with traditional theories and the currently available archaeological evidence. But first it is essential to know some basic astronomical principles and to be aware of how the movements of the heavens form cyclical patterns over time.

And by trying to look at the sky through our ancestors' eyes, we should then be able to understand (at long last!) the basic symbolism inherent in many of their monuments, temples and tombs.

The Cycles of the Sun and the Moon

From a purely observational viewpoint the Earth seems to be at the centre of the Universe. This is simply because the stars, planets, sun and moon all move around us in a clockwise direction above our heads. To us, the sun and moon appear to be about the same size as they travel around the Earth, always rising somewhere along the eastern horizon and then setting along the western horizon. However, the actual points of sunrise and sunset vary according to the time of year and the sun only rises within an arc between northeast and southeast. It travels round the sky during the day, then sets somewhere in another arc between the northwest and the southwest. Moonrise and moonset positions are different, although similar to the movements of the sun they vary according to the time of month. People living in equatorial regions see a very different picture, the sun always rises almost due east and sets due west. During the year it varies between the Tropic of Cancer and the Tropic of Capricorn and for many areas there are only two seasons, a dry season and a rainy season.

To an observer it looks as though the sun orbits the earth each year, however thanks to Copernicus, and then Galileo, we now know that in reality it is the Earth that orbits the sun in a year and that the moon orbits around the Earth in about a month. We tend to think of the moon being around only at night but of course this is wrong, since all the different phases of the moon appear at different times of the day and night. Cloudy skies in Britain often make the moon harder to see, particularly in summer when the moon is fairly low down. So it is more common for us to notice the moon in winter, simply because daylight hours are reduced, the moon rides higher in the sky and stays above the horizon for longer. It is also interesting to note that the sun can resemble the full moon when seen through thin cloud. Most of the time the sun looks white, its colour changes around dawn and dusk when it goes through the almost magical changes we are all familiar with.

One complete orbit of the Earth around the sun takes 365.24 days, which also explains why we have three consecutive years of 365 days in our calendar and then a leap year of 366 days every fourth year. This calendar is still based on the one invented by Julius Caesar in which there were alternate months of 30 and 31 days (366 days). However, other calendars across the globe were based on having twelve lunar months to the year, each of thirty days. In reality, problems always occur with these sorts of calendars because the moon has a monthly cycle lasting averaging 29.53 days. It means that unless extra days are added to the calendar, the months and the seasons can quickly get out of order. (29.53 x 12 = 354.36 i.e. about 11 days short, and after 16 years the date from a 'monthly' calendar like this would be nearly six months out of sequence with the seasons! A lunar calendar based on 30 days to the month is slightly better when compared with the solar cycle since 30 x 12 = 360, i.e. 5¼ days short).

The Islamic calendar solves some of the problems by being based on a 30-year cycle of 12 lunar months, although an extra day needs to be added every two or three years during the complete cycle to keep it regular. Each month of the Muslim calendar has its own name and officially starts with the first appearance of the crescent moon, which is one reason why the crescent is such a holy symbol throughout the Islamic world. An extra month also needs to be added every three years to the Jewish calendar since this too is based on a lunar year of twelve lunations, rather than on a solar year of just over 365 days. The Chinese lunar calendar was based on a 19-year cycle, and in addition they use a twelve-year cycle of zodiac animal characters to name each year. The sequence for this cycle is: rat, ox, tiger, hare, dragon, snake, horse, sheep, monkey, cock, dog and pig. Our year 2000 AD was the Year of the Dragon. Expert opinion is divided about the sorts of calendars that were used in prehistoric Britain and how accurate they were. All sorts of different combinations have been suggested, although probably the best idea is that the annual cycle of the sun was used to mark religious festivals, whilst the visible phases of the moon were more practical for keeping track of time on a short-term basis.
Every day the sun rises somewhere on the eastern horizon and then travels slowly around the sky in a clockwise direction, until it sets in the evening on the western horizon. Each day the sun rises

and sets in slightly different places from where it did the day before. It moves around the horizon in an arc that varies in length according to the season. The longer the arc, the more hours of daylight there are. In addition, the arcs vary in height. At midday in summer the sun is high overhead, whilst in winter it is quite low down in the sky to the south. As winter changes slowly to spring, sunrise occurs a couple of minute earlier each day and sunset takes place a couple of minutes later than the day before, so the days get longer simply because the sun stays above the horizon for longer. As the seasons advance, the position where the sun rises moves steadily northwards each day, until by the spring equinox, usually on the 20th or 21st of March, it rises due east and sets due west. From then on it carries rising earlier and earlier each day and by the midsummer solstice it reaches its maximum rising point, in the northeast. For several days, the time and the position of sunrise hardly seems to change and so on its annual journey, from southeast to northeast and back again, the sun seems to stop and stand still for a while. The standstill or solstice is usually centred on the 21st of June and it is also the longest day of the year. Thereafter the position of the rising sun moves back the way it came, rising later and setting earlier each day.

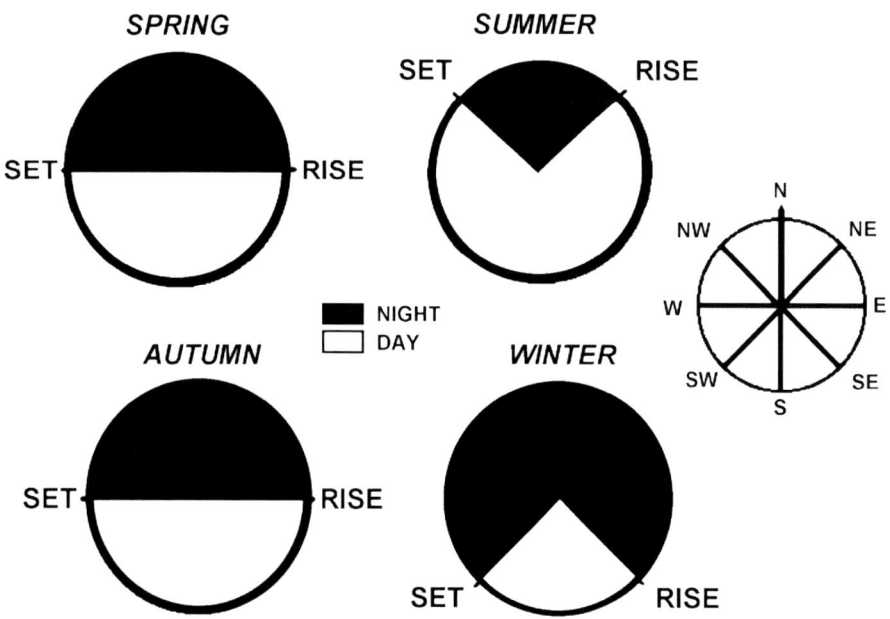

Three months later, at the autumn equinox, usually on September 23rd, it rises due east and sets due west. Then during the second half of the year, the sun slowly returns towards the southeast, until by midwinter the sun reaches its most southerly rising point in the southeast, and again its rising point seems to stand still for several days. This is usually centred on the 21st December and is the shortest day of the year and known as the midwinter solstice. Once the solstice has passed, the daily sunrise position starts moving north once more. It takes the sun six months to go from one solstice position to the other and a whole year to complete the full cycle. Of course in reality the sun hasn't risen or set at all, instead this apparent movement corresponds to the Earth spinning round and round on its axis each day as we move along the path of our annual orbit around the sun. Midsummer just refers to the middle point of the solar cycle, rather than the middle of the summer weather. This is because the sea, land and air take a while to heat up, so the hottest part of our summer usually occurs about a month or so after the summer solstice and our coldest weather is usually in late January or early February, rather than at the winter solstice, just before Christmas.

Five thousand years ago, the solstice sun rose slightly further north in summer and a bit further to the south in winter than it does now. This change is due to an effect known as precession, which is the result of a slow change in the angle of tilt of the earth's axis. Four thousand years ago for example, the midsummer solstice sun rose at Stonehenge almost a full degree further to the left of its current rising position. Precession also affects our orbit around the sun and hence, the date of astronomical events. For example, in 2000 BC, the spring equinox, which now happens on the 20th or 21st of March, took place on the 8th of April. This phenomenon is known as the *'precession of the equinoxes'* and over a long period the dates of the equinoxes and solstices shift backwards. And a complete cycle takes an astonishing 25,800 years to unfold.

Like the rising sun, the setting sun moves back and forth along the horizon according to the time of year. Its position moves from northwest in summer to southwest in winter. At the summer solstice the sun rises in the northeast and sets in the northwest. Six months later, at the winter solstice, the sun rises in the southeast and sets in the southwest. In other words, the seasonal movements of the sun are like a giant pendulum, swinging in huge arcs around the horizon. And it is this apparent motion of the sun moving north or south that seems to cause the seasons to change. However, as we now know, the Earth spins anti-clockwise on its axis and is tilted at a 23.44 degree angle to our path around the sun and this tilting affects the angle at which the incoming rays of sunlight strike the Earth. The heating effects are greater when the angle is higher and temperatures at the equator are so fierce because the sun is directly overhead. And so it is this tilt of the planet's axis and the angle of the incoming rays that makes all the difference, not how close or far away we are from the sun during our annual orbit around it. In fact we are at perigee, our closest position to the sun, in winter, and although the sun appears to be slightly larger, the Northern Hemisphere is tilted away from the sun, so the heating effect of sunlight is lessened and the weather is colder. Six months later it is the turn of the Southern Hemisphere to be tilted away from the sun and so it has the colder weather, during our summer. The angle of tilt of the earth's axis varies on a 41,000 year cycle, which is combined with another cycle taking 21,000 years in which the Earth behaves like a spinning top, with its axis tracing out a full circle in space. Thirdly, there is another very long cycle lasting about 100,000 years in which our orbit around the sun changes from an ellipse to a circle and back again. A combination of all these cycles affects the amount of energy the planet receives from the sun and in turn this has had a direct bearing on the creation and ending of Ice Ages. The sun also has a cycle of sunspot activity that lasts about 11 years and we receive an increase in radiation when sunspot activity is high, which can adversely affect our satellites and hence international communications.

The apparent movement of the sun gives us different day lengths according to the time of year. Rising and setting times, and the corresponding increase or decrease in the amount of daylight hours, vary according to where you live and the latitude of the site. For example, southern England gets approximately sixteen and a half hours of daylight in summer, twelve hours at the equinoxes but only eight hours in winter. But in the north of Scotland this changes to about eighteen hours of daylight in summer but unfortunately only about six and half hours in winter. Although the height of the sun varies from season to season, the one thing in common to all the different seasons is that the sun reaches its maximum height due south at about midday, then it starts to slowly descend until it sets. (N.B. British Summer Time, BST, is one hour ahead of GMT, Greenwich Mean Time.) It should be noted that for the sake of clarity this is a generalised explanation of events since rising and setting times have many small anomalies caused by gravitational effects of the moon, the shape and orbit of the earth, the effect of parallax and changes in our atmosphere can alter viewing conditions.

As the seasons change from winter to summer and back again, the daily path of the sun forms a series of arcs that seem to spiral across the sky. The spiral increases as the sun rises earlier and further north and moves higher in the sky, then it decreases again after the summer solstice, it is a bit like winding or unwinding thread around a bobbin. The rising and setting positions of the full moon are in opposition to those of the sun. So for example, as the winter sun sets in the southwest, the full moon rises opposite it in the northeast. When the summer sun is high in the sky, the full moon is low, and in winter, when the sun is low on the horizon, the moon is high. So as one of the spirals increases, the other decreases. The greatest diameter of the spirals climax with the midsummer sun and the midwinter moon, and the smallest diameters are for the midwinter sun and the summer full moon. Not very surprisingly, spirals were common designs on prehistoric pottery and as rock carvings, although as we shall see later on, their significance has usually been misunderstood.

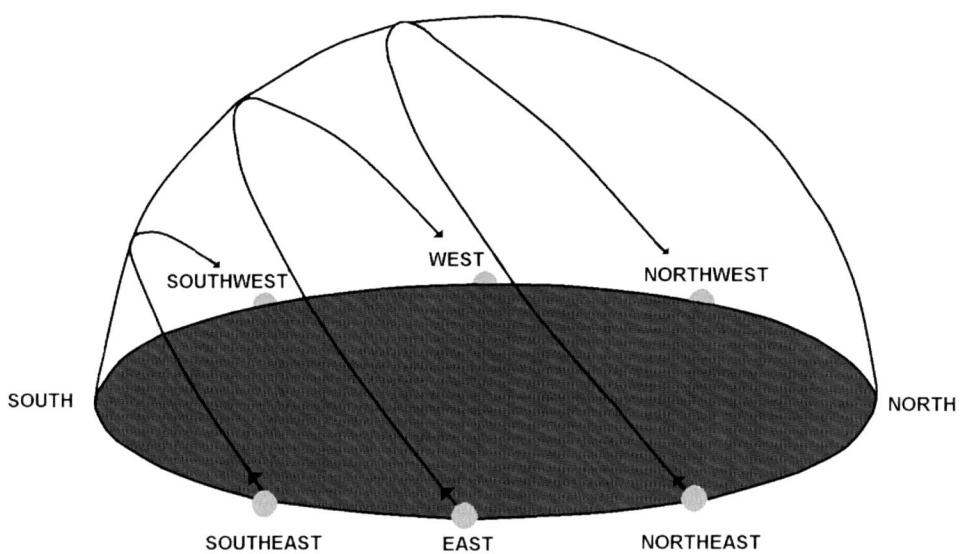

Seasonal rising and setting positions of the sun

At the winter solstice, the sun rises in the southeast and sets in the southwest.
At the spring and autumn solstices, the sun rises in the east and sets in the west.
At the summer soltice, the sun rises in the northeast and sets in the northwest.

Athough the movements and cycle of the sun are quite straightforward, those of the moon are much more complicated because the moon has a number of different cycles. The most obvious cycle, the one that we are most familiar with, is the Synodic month. In this cycle the moon goes through the complete sequence of its different phases in a lunation, which lasts on average 29.53 days. The times of moonrise and moonset vary according to the phase and the season, sometimes they occur before sunset whilst at other times the moon rises after the sun has set, which is why we sometimes notice the moon in the morning and other times in the afternoon or evening. Unfortunately because the Earth orbits the sun and the moon orbits the Earth, there is no direct correlation between the number of lunations and a solar year. However, the sun and moon do synchronise again every 19 years, which is also 235 lunations. (365.24 x 19 = 6,939 days; 235 x 29.53 = 6,939 days). This is now called the Metonic cycle, named after the Greek astronomer Meton, but I don't think that he was the first person to have noticed the cycle; he was simply the first person whose written records have survived. Yet another cycle is the Draconic month. In this cycle the moon orbits slowly around the Earth and takes 27.21 days to return to where it crossed over the ecliptic, the apparent path of the sun.

Let's start with the simplest cycle, the synodic month. During the period astronomers know as new moon, the moon rises close to the sun, both in time and position along the horizon, but because of the sun's glare it remains invisible for a day or two. The first time the new crescent moon is usually visible is in the early evening and it takes the form of a thin crescent facing to the left, like this) and it is sometimes known as a young moon. The distinctive crescent shape is formed because only the right side of the moon is lit by the sun's rays. As it orbits the Earth, the moon rises each day a bit later than when it rose the day before. As the days pass, the moon waxes, that is more of the surface is lit up by the sun, and it grows fatter, until about a week after new moon, it forms the classic semi-circular, half-moon shape, a bit like the letter D, usually called first quarter. The moon continues to rise later and later after sunrise and it waxes over the next week or so until at full moon, the entire round orb is visible as it reflects the maximum light from the sun.

Full moonrise often occurs close to sunset. A day or two later, the moon starts to wane, passing through the same sequence as before but with the shadow growing from the right, until about a week later it becomes another semi-circle, like a reversed letter D (third quarter). The moon continues to wane, becoming a thinner and thinner crescent each day, until it looks like this **(**. It is also a bit like our letter **C**. So the standard lunar cycle starts with a new moon, then goes on to first quarter, then full moon, third quarter and then new moon again. We usually call the time of no visible moon, the new moon, but it seems to me that this makes little sense and that it is very unlikely that the ancients would have used the same sort of terminology as us. And so I think it far more likely that the ancients would have interpreted the first crescent moon to be seen as the new moon and then about three weeks later, the last crescent to be seen was probably called the old moon. And finally at the end of the cycle, when there was a period of complete darkness and no moon was visible, they called this time something like '*the Dark Moon*' or '*the Dead Moon*'. So my revised version of the monthly cycle starts with the appearance of a new crescent moon. This waxes to form a half moon, reaches its optimum at full moon, and then wanes to form the other half moon and then continues to wane until it becomes an old moon, which dies and disappears, to be reborn anew a day or two later.

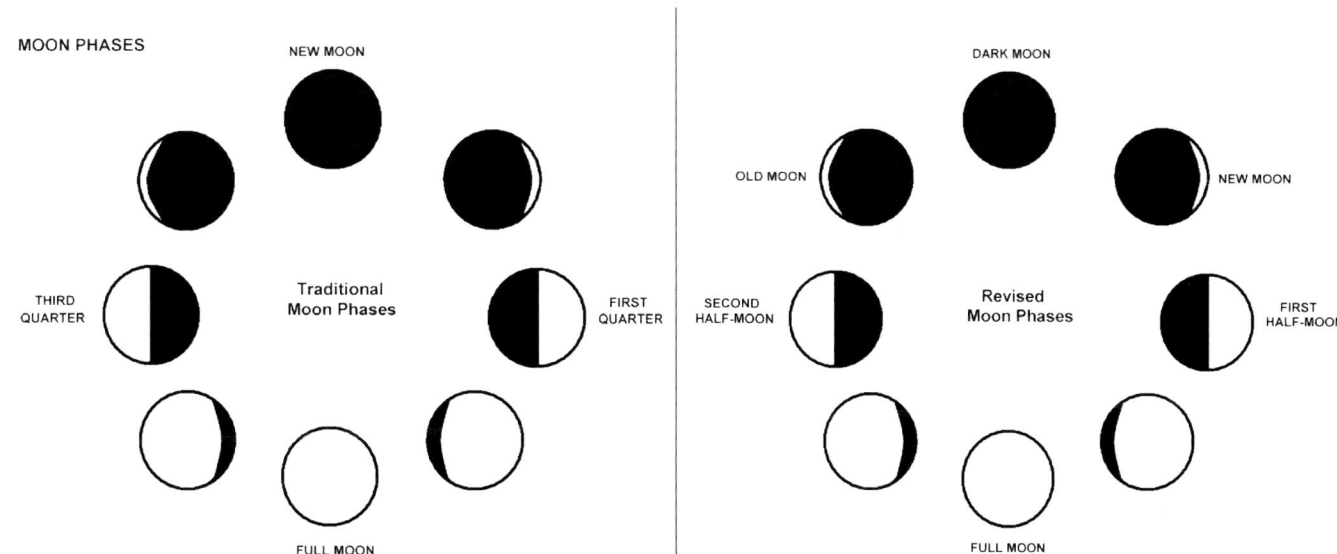

My revised monthly cycle of phases is: New moon, first half-moon, full moon, second half-moon, old moon, dark moon, and then new moon again. The cycle of lunar phases of new moon, full moon, old moon and dark moon also corresponds to the human life cycle of birth, maturity, old age and then finally death. So in this way, both the daily and the annual cycles of the sun and the monthly cycle of the moon are examples of the eternal cycle of **Birth, Life**, and **Death**, followed by **Rebirth** and a new cycle.

The movements and cycles of the moon are much more complicated than those of the sun but in some respects they are similar. The position along the horizon of each successive moonrise changes with the phase, and the sequence of different phases moves back and forth along roughly the same arc of horizon as the sun, however, instead of taking a whole year, the moon takes only a month to complete this journey. As far as the lunar phases are concerned, their position along the horizon varies according to the position of the Earth in its annual orbit around the sun and the position of the moon in its monthly orbit around the Earth. This combination affects how much sunlight is reflected by the moon and produces the different phases that we see. So for example, if a new moon rises in the northeast on the summer solstice, then each day this crescent moon will grow more and its point of rising will move further south. About a week later a first half-moon (first quarter) will rise due east and then a week after that the full moon will appear in the southeast. Then the moon retraces its journey and about a week later the second half-moon (third quarter) will rise in the east again. With each subsequent cycle the movement of phases shifts a bit further along the horizon, so that by the autumn equinox the new moon rises in the east and sets in the west. And by the time of the winter solstice the new moon rises in the southeast, close to the point where the sun rises. (Please note that the date of the new moon rising nearest a solstice varies greatly from year to year.)

Very generally, soon after the midsummer sun sets in the northwest, the full moon rises in the southeast. Later on, near dawn, the moon sets in the southwest and the sun rises in the northeast. Then three months later, at the equinoxes, the sun rises in the east and the full moon sets in the west. And when the sun sets in the west, the full moon rises again in the east. At midwinter, the full moon rises in the northeast as the sun sets in the southwest and the moon is visible during the night for about sixteen hours. So the movements of the sun and the full moon appear to be opposite each other and to complement each other: sun/moon; northeast/southwest; northwest/southeast; east/west. They are true opposites, not just in the amount of heat and light that is generated, but also where they appear along the horizon. There are also many other dualities that complement each other, pairs such as rise/set; day/night; midday/midnight; spring/autumn; summer/winter; hot/cold; male/female; man/woman and boy/girl.

At the winter solstice, the midday sun is low in the sky whilst at the summer solstice the midday sun is at its highest, almost overhead. However, the sun and full moon are opposite each other so although the summer full moon at midnight is low down on the southern horizon, in winter it is high up in the sky and provides useful illumination for much of the night. As a direct result, in the days before artificial lighting, many night time activities and of course, ceremonies, parties and feasts were linked to the time of the full moon.

THE SIMILARITIES BETWEEN THE SOLAR AND LUNAR CYCLES

N.B. The first half-moon is usually called first quarter and the second half-moon is usually known as third quarter

As we saw earlier, the phase of the moon that we can see is the result of its position in its monthly orbit around the Earth. Each moon phase depends on how much of it is lit up by the sun and as the month progresses, more and more of the disc is illuminated until it reaches full moon, then it starts to wane until it disappears a fortnight later at dark moon. The sun and the full moon rise and set opposite each other, so as the summer sun rises in the northeast the full moon sets in the southwest and when the setting sun of midsummer disappears in the northwest, the full moon rises in the southeast. The rising sun moves from northeast to southeast and back in an annual cycle but the moon covers the same range in just one monthly cycle.

The full moon does not rise on exactly the same date each year, this is because the cycle of phases in a synodic month does not fit exactly into a year of 365.25 days. (12 x 29.53 = 354.36) However, because of the Metonic cycle, every nineteen years the same phase of moon does appear on the same date (not every twenty-nine years). In other words, if the full moon rises on Midsummer's Eve it will be nineteen years before it happens again. (235 lunar months equals 19 solar years). Another very dramatic and complex type of lunar sequence is known as the lunar nodal cycle. This cycle has caused a lot of confusion amongst scholars, prehistorians, archaeologists, and even some astronomers. So I'll do my best to try and make it clear, once and for all.

The moon's orbit around the Earth is not circular, it is an ellipse, and the distance between us varies according to changing gravitational forces in our annual orbit around the sun. In practise this means that, unlike the sun, the moon does not rise in exactly the same position as the previous cycle, or indeed the previous year. So it must have been very disconcerting to early astronomers to find that the position of the full moonrise nearest the winter solstice moved backwards and forwards a few degrees each year. Over a period of about nine years this can form a very noticeable arc in the northeast of as much as twenty degrees. And when the midsummer full moon, that is the full moon nearest the summer solstice, rises in the southeast sector its rising point varies in the same way over successive years.

In addition, the full moon looks much larger at perigee, when its elliptical orbit brings it closer to the Earth in midwinter, whilst the moon looks smaller at midsummer because it is at apogee, the furthest its orbit takes it from the Earth. There is also an optical illusion that makes the moon look larger when it is nearer the horizon than when it is high in the sky. All these factors can sometimes make the moon seem very close to the Earth, (conveniently close for spirits to travel).

The actual lunar phase on a particular day depends on the moon's relationship to the sun as it orbits around the Earth. This orbit is not circular and it is affected by a combination of gravitational effects that make it appear over the horizon at different places each cycle. Every eighteen or nineteen years these gravitational effects are at their strongest and the moon rises at its most northerly point, followed two weeks later by its most southerly rising position. The extreme positions of the rising and setting moon are known as the major points, or sometimes, the major standstill limits.

The major northern moon rises in the north-northeast, travels round the sky and sets in the north-northwest. Two weeks later the moon rises at its major southern position in the south-southeast then sets a short time later at the major moonset position in the south-southwest. However, as the years go by the most extreme rising and setting positions of the moon move slightly each year, until after nine years the other extreme position is reached, this is known as the minor point. After that, the extreme rising and setting points return slowly north (or south) again until the cycle is complete and the moon is rising and setting at its major positions once again. The cycle from the major position to the corresponding minor position and back again is in a sequence that lasts about nineteen years and this is often known as the lunar nodal cycle. (The nodes are the two points where the moon crosses over the ecliptic, the apparent path of the sun.)

So the movement of the moon between its major rising and setting positions form a series of arcs that are similar, but greater than, the seasonal movements of the sun. The arc of the northern major moon is very great, all the way round the horizon from north-northeast to north-northwest and the moon rises very high into the sky. However, two weeks later the arc of the major southern moon, from its rising in the south-southeast to the setting position in the south-southwest, is much, much less. The major southern moon does not rise very high in the sky and the further north one travels, the lower this arc becomes. (In the Shetland Isles, the major southern moon does not even rise above the horizon.)

So to recap, starting at its major point in the north-northeast, the position of the most northerly moonrise (major) will move slightly further east each year for about nine years, attain its other extreme position (minor) and then move back to the start again, **completing the cycle in 18 or 19 years**. This is often misleadingly quoted as 18.61 years, but this figure is just an average. (The cycle is usually in a sequence of 18, 19, 19 years.) It is a common mistake to think that the major position is always a full moon, it isn't. At the time of a major moonrise the moon is usually a roughly semi-circular shape, close to either the first or last half-moon depending on the season. The major moonrise represents the moment that the moon is at its furthest point away from the Earth, and this will only occur when the sun is near an equinox position. And as I mentioned previously, the most northerly and southerly positions of the full moon are not quite as far north (or south) as the major rising and setting positions. It is always important to try and make this distinction between the major standstill positions of the moon, and the most northerly (or most southerly) rising or setting positions of the full moon. And it is important to remember that the full moon will rise at its most northerly position in winter and its most southerly in summer.

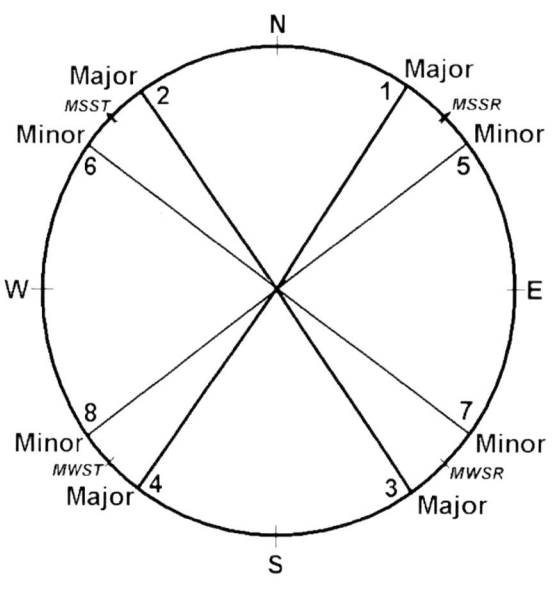

POSITIONS OF MOONRISE AND MOONSET
DURING THE 19-YEAR SWING CYCLE

MSSR midsummer sunrise   MWSR midwinter sunrise
MSST midsummer sunset   MWST midwinter sunset

In the first year the moon rises at its most northerly point, its major position, point 1, travels all the way round the horizon and sets at point 2.

Each day it rises a little bit further south, until after two weeks it rises at its most southerly position, point 3, and sets a short time later at 4.

Over the next eight or nine years the most northerly moonrise position changes each monthly cycle, moving further east each year, until by the ninth year the most northerly moonrise is at minor position 5, and moonset is at point 6.

Each day it rises a little bit further south, until after two weeks it rises at its minor position, point 7 and sets at 8.

Over the next nine years the moon swings slowly back to its extreme rising points again, to the major northern moonrise in the north-northeast at point 1 and to the major southern moonrise position at point 3.

At some sites it was the rising or setting position of the full moon that was recorded in stone and at other sites it was the major or minor moon that was monitored. Of course throughout this long cycle the moon goes through the complete set of phases each month as usual and these phases all appear at different places along the horizon and within the large arc between the major northern and the major southern positions. Halfway through the complete swing cycle the moon will only rise within a shorter arc, between the two minor positions in the north and south, and these are full moon positions. In addition, there is also the dramatic visual disparity between the major northern moonrise that travels round most of the horizon and rises very high into the sky, whilst sometimes the rising moon hardly makes it above the skyline, in its short arc along the horizon between its major southern positions.

The most famous lunar temple in the British Isles is at Calanais (or Callanish, as it is pronounced and often written) on the Isle of Lewis in the Western Isles (Outer Hebrides), which lie off the northwest coast of Scotland. It is deservedly famous since it is a truly awe-inspiring place and one that deserves a visit. The principal temple can be seen from miles around since it is on a promontory that runs roughly north/south. It is a bit like a backbone that rises out of the surrounding area of low-lying land and lochs. Calanais is situated on the northwestern side of the isle of Lewis, on the coast, due west of the principal port and town of Stornoway. Nearby are several other circles of standing stones but it is the main temple at Calanais that is the most interesting. The northeast avenue was built in such a way that from the far end of the avenue, the summer full moon appears very low over the southern horizon and then minutes later sets inside the circle. At this unique time it seems as though our worlds are very close to each other. This viewing of the full moon must have been a very special time in the sacred calendar, but what is particularly sad is that life expectancy in those days was so low and many people would not have lived to see this exceptional event more than once in their lives. Local folklore has a garbled account of this phenomenon. It speaks of *'The Shining One'*, who walked along the avenue at midsummer sunrise. (However, since the midsummer sun rises far to the east of the avenue this is much more likely to have been a reference to the appearance of the rising and dramatic setting of the moon at the southern end of the monument.) In recent years the most southerly rising and setting positions achieved by the midsummer full moon at Calanais were in 2006, on the 11th of June. However, the most extreme major lunar moonrise positions were attained by a waning second half-moon, near dawn on the 23rd of March and then in late afternoon on the 29th of September by a waxing first half-moon. The most northerly position was obtained a fortnight earlier, by the major moonrise on the 15th of September.

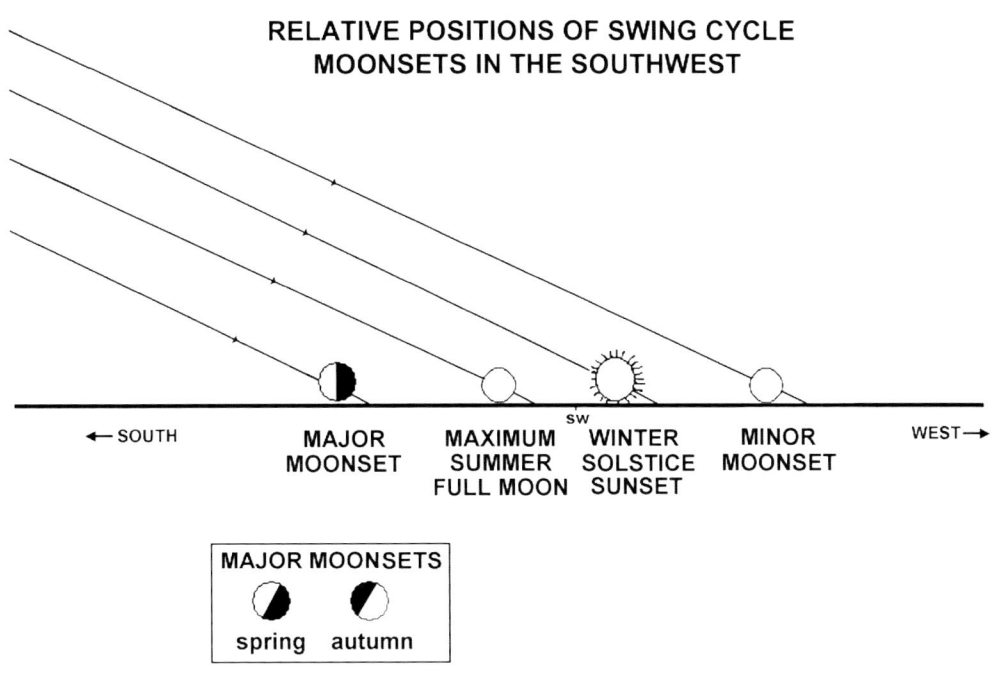

Other good examples of lunar temples that were built to celebrate the lunar swing cycle are the dozens of recumbent stone circles in the countryside around Aberdeen. Each of these stone circles was built with a horizontal altar stone laid between two flanking upright stones and there are far more circles where the recumbent stone was aligned with the major moonset rather than towards the minor position. And there were also many burial sites, such as the Clava cairns near Inverness, and many other types of barrows and graves across the British Isles that were built with alignments towards the extreme southern positions of the lunar swing cycle. The visual part of the ceremony would probably have included the passage of the full moon in the background, either rising or setting or just passing over the horizontal, recumbent, altar stone. However, one of the problems concerning such alignments is that the measurement of the azimuth is often taken from the centre of the ring and by just moving one pace forwards, backwards or sideways the data can be drastically altered. Many alignments with important lunar events were a bit rough and ready, simply because of the wideness of the target area needed to cope with a range of celestial events that took place over long periods. It is also important to remember that the majority of stone circles were local meeting places for everyday worship, rather than erected as highly accurate astronomical observatories and they needed to be able to be used for ceremonies throughout the seasons and not just for one special occasion once every nineteen years.

The apparent path of the sun around the Earth is called the ecliptic and the orbit of the moon intersects the ecliptic at two points, the ascending and the descending nodes. And it is only when the moon is at one of these nodes that the moon can hide the sun from view and an eclipse can take place. If the dark moon and the sun appear to be in the same place at the same time, we may be lucky enough to see a total solar eclipse, and such an awe-inspiring sight must have had a profound impact on people, just as it does today (even if we are far more cynical and blasé). Such an important phenomenon may have been explained in Neolithic mythology as the mating of the moon and the sun, when the sun finally catches its elusive partner. Or perhaps they saw it differently, as the dark moon creeping up to overshadow the sun but with the sun winning through and a triumph for light over darkness and of good over evil? A solar eclipse can only occur when the moon is directly in line between the sun and the Earth. And a lunar eclipse can only occur when the Earth is directly between the sun and the moon, and the moon passes into the shadow of the Earth. So a solar eclipse can only occur at dark moon and a lunar eclipse can only occur at full moon. Lunar eclipses are visible to far more people, often half the globe, and are much more frequent than total solar eclipses, which are much more localised. Total solar eclipses only last for a few minutes, whilst a full lunar eclipse lasts for well over an hour.

As I mentioned before, the Metonic cycle produces the extraordinary effect that every nineteen years the same moon phase appears on the same day of the year. The date of each full moon varies each year over the nineteen-year period because the monthly cycles of the moon do not fit exactly into a solar year. So the full moon nearest the summer solstice could be on any day either side of the solstice itself, but nineteen years after the full moon rose on the eve of the summer solstice, the phenomenon would repeat itself. The following dates are for the day when the full moon is nearest to the summer solstice, starting with 20th June 1997. 20, 10, 28, 16, 05 (July), 24, 14, 02 (July), 21, 11, 30, 18, 07, 26, 15, 03 (July), 23, 13, 02 (July), and the next full moon in this Metonic cycle is on the 20th June 2016. The next full moon in the cycle is on 20th June 2035, followed by 20th June in 2054. And in the same way, if it were the old moon just before the winter solstice it would be nineteen years before the observer would experience the same combination again, the dying moon and the dying sun. A day or two later at sunrise it would be a New Moon and a New Year, giving ample excuse for celebrations of new beginnings and hopefully, the start of a new era of health and prosperity.

If the weather had been good, a young visitor to the 2004 BC summer solstice festival could have witnessed the full moon rising on Midsummer's Eve, followed about eight hours later by the rising of the sun on the longest day of the year, on the 11th of July. And it is a sobering thought that they might not have lived long enough to see the same visually significant phenomenon repeat itself nineteen years later. The Metonic cycle can also have an impact on witnessing and predicting lunar eclipses. There was a lunar eclipse on the 21st January 2000 and the next one in the cycle is on the same date in 2019. During lunar eclipses the moon can sometimes appear red, because of the refraction of sunlight by the Earth's atmosphere. Such an awesome spectacle must have caused panic in the distant past, not only did the full moon darken but it started to turn the colour of blood.

But with knowledge of the Metonic cycle the ancient astronomer/priests could have predicted that it might happen again nineteen years later. (The cycle only lasts for one or two repeats of the initial lunar eclipse and please note that this is a very, very different proposition to being able to accurately predict the local arrival of a total solar eclipse.) The most recent lunar eclipse that I watched occurred on the night of the 3rd March 2007. The rounded shadow of the Earth slowly darkened the full moon, moving upwards across the surface until the last rays of sunlight just shone on the very top of the disc. Totality lasted for about an hour; with the moon reflecting only a faint amount of light from the Earth and it looked like a very large, but dirty, golf ball. Then the first glimmers of sunlight appeared on the left side of the lunar disc, with more and more of the surface gradually reflecting sunlight, until after about half an hour later a semi-circular shape could be seen, this slowly waxed until finally the whole disc of the moon reappeared. (Although it was still less bright than normal, since it remained in the penumbral shadow of the Earth for another hour or so.) What was odd about this is that the surface of the moon gets lit up and gets larger from the left, the complete opposite of the normal sequence of phases, since during the normal monthly sequence the left side of the waning moon becomes a thinner and thinner crescent as the days pass. And perhaps this unusual sequence of a waxing moon, which happened only after a total lunar eclipse, was seen in ancient times as one more manifestation of the rebirth of the moon, in yet another **Birth, Life, Death** and **Rebirth** cycle.

So to go over the main points of the annual cycle of the sun and the moon once again: The midsummer sun and the midwinter full moon rise in the northeast and set in the northwest. The midwinter sun and the midsummer full moon rise in the southeast and set in the southwest. In each case, the time and direction of rising or setting is symbolic of one aspect of the life, death or rebirth of the sun (and the moon). In the daily cycle of the sun, the day starts at sunrise and ends at sunset but in the annual cycle of the sun, the year starts with the midwinter sunrise and ends a year later, at midwinter sunset, then a new year starts on the following day, at sunrise. And therefore since winter sunset is the ultimate symbol of death, and winter sunrise symbolises birth and rebirth, so midsummer sunrise must symbolise the mid-point of the solar lifecycle (and the human one as well). In the monthly lunar cycle, the new moon is at the start and the dark moon is at the end of the cycle, with the full moon at the middle of the lunar lifecycle. And it is this combination of astronomical phenomena that supports my idea that some of the most important times for many religious purposes were midsummer sunrise and midwinter full moonrise, since each was a time of optimum vitality in one of the Birth, Life and Death cycles. But although midwinter sunrise and moonrise were both symbolically linked to Rebirth, it was the midwinter sunset and the midsummer full moonset that were synonymous with Death and marked the final stages in the different life cycles.

Our Neolithic ancestors must have tried to gain a better understanding of the complexities of the different cycles of the heavenly bodies and in particular the complex relationship between the Earth, the sun and the moon. They embodied some of this knowledge, and parts of their religious beliefs, in symbolic form in their mysterious open-air temples, the legendary stone circles. One problem with understanding the astronomy and symbolism of stone circles is that the stones were set up to mark the visible movements of the sun and the moon under local landscape conditions and at many locations the horizon is not level. This means that maps and magnetic compass bearings are not always helpful when trying to determine the exact positions of seasonal sunrise and sunset along a horizon that varies considerably in height. One way is to return to the circle at different times of the day and at different times of the year to see what actually happens and to make allowance for the passage of time, for example in the Neolithic, the midsummer sun used to set almost a whole degree further north, (to the right) than it does today.

According to some archaeoastronomers there is evidence to support the view that, at certain sites, precise layouts using simple trigonometry were constructed to gain a better understanding of very complex celestial mechanics. The problem with such theories is that they usually have to be proved by complex mathematical formulas, and there is no indication at present that our ancestors were capable of such calculations. However, we do know that the Egyptians used clever but very simple techniques of surveying to erect many of their monuments, including the pyramids, without the need for complex calculations. So what is most likely is that our ancestors used quite simple methods to lay out and construct many of their stone circles, and would have used several sighting poles, some semi-permanent marker posts and some lengths of rope to set out the initial arrangements, which would then become permanent by the erection of standing stones.

It is my belief that, at the majority of stone circles, the builders were concerned more with symbolic direction and ceremonial meaning, rather than a rigorously scientific exactness. The stones at small circles are much too close together to form highly accurate sightlines across the diameter of the circle towards the sun or moon. However, in some instances outlying stones were erected at least thirty metres away, to continue the sightline outwards from the circle towards specific astronomical events. Another common error is to suppose that they always used the centre of a circle as the base for sightings, but only very rarely is there anything in the middle of stone circles to indicate where the observer needed to stand. Without measurements it can be quite hard to work out exactly where the centre lies, so I think it was probably more common to stand behind, or in front of, one particular stone and look out across the ring towards another stone and then onwards towards the sun or moon.

A circle is not an ideal instrument for establishing alignments; it is far better to set up three stones in a line. At an Early Bronze Age site, near Temple Wood in the Kilmartin Valley, Argyle, in the north-west of Scotland there is a good example of such an astronomical structure. The early astronomers set up five stones in a long X-formation, with the tallest stone at the centre and one axis aligned with the major southern moonset.

There is great variation in stone circles, some have an axis on a north/south line, others align east/west and many are northeast/southwest. Others were built towards a particular rising or setting of the sun on a special date and many are aligned with the moon at special times, particularly the major southern moonset. So in my opinion, at the start of circle construction there was always at least one key solar or lunar alignment that dictated the subsequent arrangement and positioning of all the other stones. And it would have taken a minimum of nine years of observation to sort out all the extreme rising and setting points of the lunar swing cycle under local conditions. Not all stone circles are circles, some are ovals or ellipses, and they seem to me to be a representation of the elliptical orbit that the moon takes around our planet.

In addition to key alignments, a significant factor in rediscovering the intent of the builders can involve the original number of stones that were erected in the ring. Unfortunately many circles are in a ruined state but at the Merry Maidens, a Cornish stone circle near Penzance, the temple of nineteen stones is situated on rising ground below the crest of the hill to the northeast. This means that at the time of the summer solstice the sun had already risen well into the morning sky long before it appeared above the local horizon. Therefore it could not have been sited to celebrate the rising sun on the longest day of the year. Instead there is a wonderful panoramic view to the south and southwest and this seems to indicate that it was a lunar temple and that it was the setting of the summer full moon that was important. Confirmation of this is provided by the number of stones in the circle, nineteen, clearly referring to the 19 years of the lunar swing cycle and the 19-year Metonic cycle. I have already mentioned the special relationship with the moon at the principal circle of Calanais (Callanish) in the Western Isles of Scotland, which originally had an avenue to the north-northeast of two rows of upright stones; one that contained nine stones and the other side had ten stones. However, the most famous use of the number nineteen has to be at Stonehenge, where there was a U-shaped arrangement of nineteen pillars of the famous Bluestones inside the circle of massive sarsen stones.

As we have seen above, the relationships between the orbits and cycles of the moon, the Earth and the sun are far from simple. This would have posed problems to devising a calendar for religious purposes. The priests would have needed to be able to make plans for special ceremonies, celebrations and feasts long in advance and for that they needed to know the date of future events. Although a solar-based calendar is not too hard to establish, a priest or astronomer trying to devise a calendar based on the cycles of both the moon and the sun would find it much harder. The cycles of the moon and the sun are out of synchronisation most of the time, although 235 lunar months is close to 19 solar years. Some stone circles, such as the enormous Ring of Brodgar in the Orkney's, had sufficient stones to chronicle two complete lunations of the moon, (2 x 29½ = 59). Instead of counting on their fingers, the sixty or so standing stones at Brodgar could have been used as an impressive but easy and accurate calculator to predict the date of future moon phases linked to religious festivals and ceremonies, in other words, a moon phase calendar, set in stone.

The construction and the orientation of ancient monuments varied considerably from place to place, and according to local beliefs and traditions. So how does the astronomical and religious symbolism I have suggested above tie in with the observed archaeology?

Religious Beliefs

Many burial places had a deep spiritual meaning for their builders. One of the earliest and most impressive sites is the huge mound of earth and stone at Newgrange in Ireland that archaeologists call a passage grave tomb. It was constructed to face towards the southeast, the direction of midwinter sunrise and featured a long passageway that opened outwards towards the midwinter sunrise.
Other passage graves, such as at nearby Knowth and the one known as Cairn T at Loughcrew, in County Sligo, Ireland were directed towards the spring equinox sunrise. To the east of Newgrange is another large mound called Dowth and this huge mound has an entrance and passageway facing towards the southwest, towards the setting sun at midwinter. In Orkney, the magnificent, stone-built, chambered tomb at Maes Howe has a long passageway facing outwards to the southwest and along this passage the rays of the setting midwinter sun enter, symbolic of the dying sun on the last, and longest, night of the year.

The enormous chambered cairn at Maes Howe, Orkney

Passageways are often thought of as simply a means of entering a cairn or tomb but they could also have been intended as a spirit pathway. The stone-lined passageway inside the enormous mound at Maeshowe is so low that one has to walk crouched down, bent over like an old man. This was deliberate. It forces you to think about what you are doing. Perhaps the idea was to get people to adopt a penitent and respectful attitude. In other Orcadian cairns, such as at Isbister and Cuween Hill, you have to crawl down a long passageway to get inside. A secondary reason for the construction of these low passageways was perhaps intended as a pathway to show the direction for spirits to travel in order for them to be reborn in the next world in the *'Land of the Dead'*. (This is certainly the case for the two shafts leading upwards and outwards from the King's Chamber inside the Great Pyramid at Giza.) Or possibly, the passage was a two-way street and they thought that when time stood still between the end of one year and the beginning of the next, a doorway between the worlds opened, leaving the way clear for the ancestral spirits to visit the living. We are used to doorways that are taller than ourselves but the idea of having to bend down to enter a room is also known from the famous prehistoric village of Skara Brae in Orkney, dating from about 3100 BC. The houses of this extraordinary village were constructed from slabs of the local sandstone and they were linked together by low passageways roofed over by more slabs. Then these were covered by a thick layer of turf. This helped with waterproofing and kept out the bitter winter winds sweeping down from the Arctic Circle and from across the Atlantic. These building techniques were also used in other constructions in Orkney, particularly for the chambered cairns of Cuween Hill, Wideford Hill, Isbister (Tomb of the Eagles), Unstun, Blackhammer and Quoyness. The chambers inside these stone cairns have high ceilings, allowing you to stand up easily and they suggest that special ceremonies were held inside, perhaps with some sort of magical ritual involving herbal smoke, taking psychedelic mushrooms, such as the Psilocybe genus of 'magic mushrooms' or perhaps they used powerful hallucinogenic mushrooms such as the dangerous red and white spotted Fly Agaric, Amanita muscaria. Such rituals and strange experiences would have been designed to make people hallucinate and experience a different reality, and perhaps make them think that they were communicating with the spirits of their ancestors.

The design of a special chamber with a passage leading into it also seems to indicate a symbolic parallel with the vagina and the uterus, the birth passage and the womb. And the mound itself is reminiscent of the swollen belly of a pregnant woman lying on her back, but this time not of flesh and bone, but of earth and stone, the basic fabric and skeleton of the land. In addition to these ideas, the semi-circular profile of a burial mound resembles the rising sun and the rising moon. And of course when viewed in the opposite direction, the domed mound resembles the setting sun or moon as it sinks below the horizon. Although this symbolism is incredibly obvious, until now no one seems to have understood that the shape of circular burial mounds was a clever way of linking a special place for the dead with the dying sun at sunset. And seen from the other direction, the dome of the rising sun is symbolic of a new day and a new life.

History and prehistory are littered with new and improved versions of ancient ideas and customs. The long, stone-lined passageway of Maeshowe also resembles a natural tunnel into a cave, with the central burial chamber acting as a cavern inside. People in those far-off days would have experienced similar sensations to modern people who have survived near-death experiences. People who have almost died because of a serious accident or severe illness have related how as they were dying they seemed to travel down a passageway towards a bright light. And there are similarities here with passage graves that are lit by the sun at key times of the year, particularly the spring and autumn equinoxes and the winter solstice. At Stonehenge, some 700 years after Maeshowe was built, the idea of a stone passageway was replaced with 'the Avenue', parallel lines of banks of earth, dug from long ditches leading into the temple from the northeast and these earth banks were marked by short rows of standing stones, although these have long since disappeared.

Other chambered cairns are aligned with the rising sun at midwinter, and as I explained earlier, the rising sun at this time of year is symbolic of rebirth, so clearly there was a local difference of opinion and religious belief and corpses were treated accordingly. Stonehenge, the nearby Coneybury henge and Woodhenge were all aligned northeast/southwest. On the eastern side of Britain, at Arminghall in Norfolk, funeral customs were different, around 3150 BC the locals constructed a henge, a high, circular bank of earth with a deep ditch, and then erected a U-shaped arrangement of eight large posts inside, with the entrance/exit to the southwest, towards the dying sun of midwinter. Other monuments, such as the Stonehenge Cursus and some longbarrows were aligned eastwards towards the rising sun (or moon) at the spring and autumn equinoxes.
These events seems to indicate the reaching of a half-way point, not just between day and night but also between winter and summer, summer and winter; life and death and death and rebirth. In the natural world, the spring equinox marks the end of winter and the first hesitant beginnings of spring

and the rebirth of nature, but as far as the solar cycle is concerned, the sun was reborn months earlier and the spring equinox is simply half way between the winter and summer solstice, the equivalent of adolescence in the Birth, Life, Death, Rebirth cycle. But the autumn equinox is at the midpoint between summer and winter, between life and death so the symbolism here indicates a staging point, after which the spirit could move on to its final resting place, either staying locally in a purpose-built 'House of the Dead', or else in the next world, in the heavens above. Traditionally, autumn was also a time for getting ready for the long, cold, winter months ahead and this meant gathering nature's bounty of tubers, roots, fruits, berries and nuts and collecting the last of the winter fodder. Late autumn was the time when the cooler temperatures meant culling excess animals, then smoking, salting and storing the meat and fat and collecting a hell of a lot of firewood!

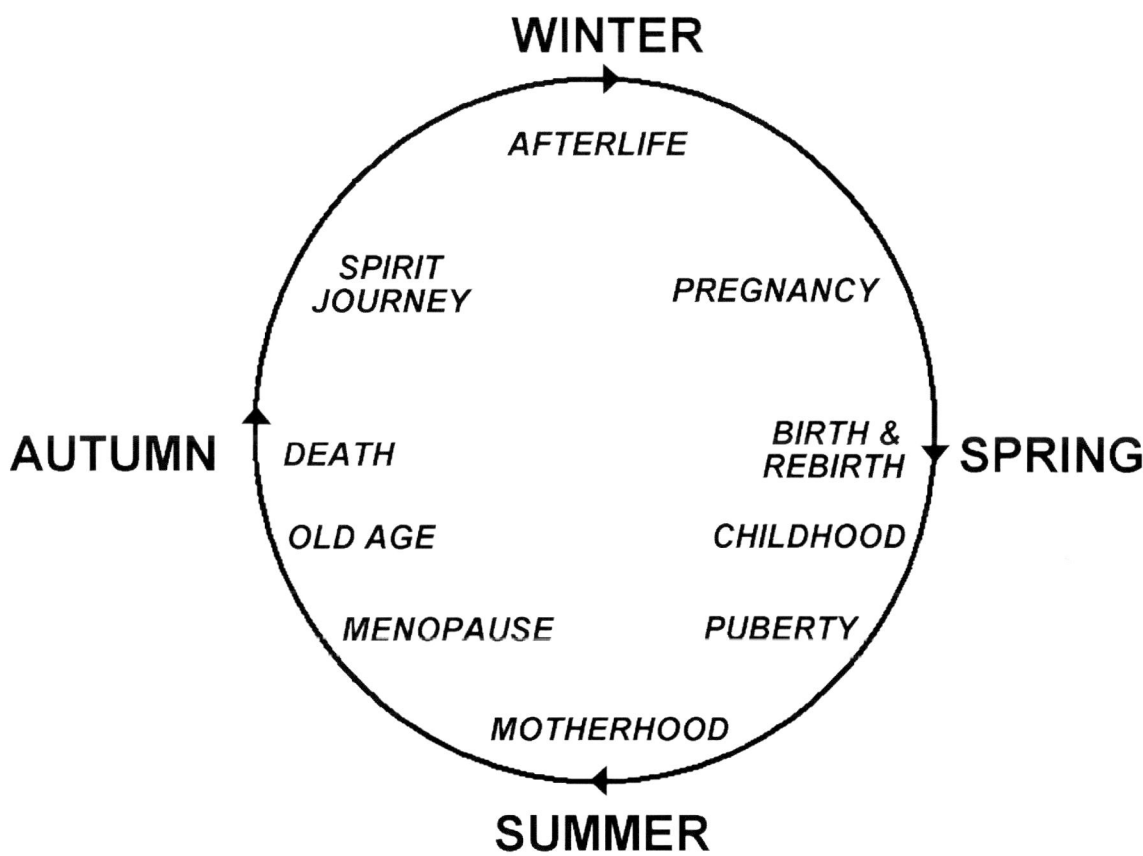

THE CYCLE OF THE SEASONS AND THE CYCLE OF LIFE

For a long time I was puzzled about some of the reasons why the ancients had such a profound reverence for the moon. Although its cycles, phases and movements have explicit symbolism in their own right, these alone did not seem sufficient reason to justify such intense emotions and often such extraordinary amounts of constructional labour over many, many years, but finally I realised that I had been thinking along modern lines, with the 'benefit' of modern knowledge. We know that the planets rotate around the sun at different rates, also that the earth spins on its axis in a day and orbits around the sun in a year and that the moon is a satellite that orbits the earth in slightly less than a month, but did all the ancient peoples know and understand this? The ancients had been watching the moon for thousands of years and it is likely that many different myths, legends and theories were developed to try and make sense of its different phases and its appearance and disappearance each month.
I am not sure if people in Ancient Britain really thought that the sun and the moon were just Gods in

the sense of omnipotent beings, instead I think they were also seen as two very different worlds, one hot and the other cold. The sun and the moon look as though they are twin planets because they appear to be the same size and the same distance away from the Earth (in reality the sun is about four hundred times the size of the moon and about four hundred times as far away) and although the sun radiates heat, the moon does not. Our folklore speaks of the moon as being made of cheese, but if you think about it, the moon really looks as though it is a world of ice and snow.

We now know that the moon is a dead planet with no atmosphere, but seen from here, the dark patches on the surface at the first half moon look a bit like a face, hence the popular term, 'the Man in the Moon'. The moon shines by reflected sunlight and changes shape as it goes through the monthly cycle of phases. Sunlight is the energy that gives life to plants and in turn these sustain animals and people, and sunlight warms the Earth. So the sun was the giver and maintainer of life, whilst the moon was a cold world, similar to the mythical and legendary world of their own distant ancestors, those who had survived the last Ice Age. And because of the way that Neolithic people buried their dead in longbarrows, often with alignments towards important moonset positions, I think that many of them believed that the moon was the place where the spirits and souls of their dead ancestors lived. And many people believed, and still believe, that we are on a journey from one place to another, that our time here is limited because it is just one stop on a long journey from one world to the next. So for many ancient people the sun represented Life, whilst the moon symbolised Death.

As I said above, I think it is likely that our ancestors thought that the moon was a sister world to the Earth and if one thinks of the moon not as a satellite of Earth but in terms of this sister world, lit by the sun just as the earth is, the moon appears to show the effects of sunlight at a very different rate to the one we experience. The cycle of the different moon phases, from dark moon to new moon to full moon and then old moon, are similar to what we experience every day, as night turns to day and then back to night, but at a much slower rate. As night turns to day the first visible effect is a crescent of lighter sky to the east, rapidly brightening as the eastern sky becomes lighter than the western horizon. This is the time of the dawn chorus, when birdsong greets a new day. The sky turns progressively lighter and after a while the first flash of sunlight appears over the distant horizon.
At sunset the reverse happens, the sky to the east darkens first as the sun sinks slowly below the western horizon until the last multi-coloured hues of sunset fade and darkness descends. Seen from Space these effects mirror the phases of the moon, sunrise on Earth is like the first crescent of the new moon and as the days go by, more and more of the moon appears, until at full moon its whole surface is lit by the sun. The moon then wanes until all is dark again. In other words, a 'day' on the moon appears to last a complete lunar cycle of a month and the moon seems to have a 'night' that lasts about two days. So perhaps they saw the moon as a spirit world where a 'day' on the moon would last nearly thirty earth days, and so one year on this spirit world would be the equivalent of over ten thousand days on earth. In comparison, time on the spirit world of the moon would almost seem to stand still, giving Eternal Life. The idea of a sister world, where time stood still and where there was eternal life for the dead, would appeal to many people and it seems to make sense of the beliefs and ritual practices of the numerous observation points, monuments, burials and cremations, that took place in the directions of the extreme positions of the lunar cycle.

Reproduction and the Moon

Some African tribal people thought that the moon acted as a guide and guardian, one that would watch over their children throughout their lives and so new born babies were exposed to the light of the new moon in a symbolical ritual. The ceremony was enacted to ensure that, once they had been introduced, the moon would protect the child during the hours of darkness.
In the modern world we live in artificial environments, lead artificial lives, and because of our intellectual capabilities and our capacity to alter nature to suit ourselves we tend to forget that we are really only rather clever primates. Many of us would like to believe that we are above the mundane cycles of the natural world. The truth is very different, we are the product of millions of years of evolution and it

is really only in a comparatively short time frame that we have been able to control our environment to suit our new lifestyles. The age-old rhythms of life are still there, even if they are far less noticeable than they were even a hundred years ago. Although low levels of artificial light were of course available in prehistoric times, people were far more attuned to the seasonal changes of daylight and the monthly changes of moonlight in their lives. Their daily actions, tasks and chores were attuned to the natural rhythms of the seasons, to the animals around them and the vegetation cycle. Many of these natural cycles are governed by changes in daylight intensity and duration and by changes to the ambient temperature.

Botanical research has shown that seeds need a particular trigger to make them germinate and that this trigger varies from species to species. Studies have shown that if seeds are kept with sufficient humidity at a constant temperature they will not germinate if the level of light remains the same. What is required by the seeds is that they experience a period of low light levels, followed by a rise in levels of daylight before they will germinate. The change in temperature and light level produces growth hormones that stimulate rapid cell division but the light level must achieve a certain threshold before the response takes place. Once that threshold has been achieved the plants grow rapidly and then start to develop flowers.

Each species of plant requires a different trigger, which is why snowdrops and crocuses appear early, whilst other plants are late flowering, but for the majority of plants, growth is at its most active in spring and early summer. Moonlight is far less powerful than sunlight yet its effects can be just as effective in triggering powerful reactions. Many sea creatures are affected by the lunar cycle. They swarm, spawn or breed by the light of the full moon at a particular time of year. Other animals lay their eggs above the normal shoreline at a particular seasonal moon phase and the development of the young is regulated to coincide with the next maximum high tide when the sea will uncover the sand, liberating the young in the process.

Amongst plants, birds and animals there is usually a particular season when breeding can take place and since this occurs at a very specific time of year it seems clearly related to the sun. The internal clocks of the organisms seem to be directly affected by changes in sunlight that trigger their sexual behaviour. Amongst these organisms there is an enormous diversity of physiological differences in sexual organs and reproductive behaviour. The complex mating rituals of many birds and animals are well known and the most successful species, in terms of distribution and number, are those that have evolved mechanisms that work beyond the ordinary.

Rats for example have become such a pest because they breed so rapidly and have numerous young that quickly mature. Rare species of animal such as the giant panda have problems because they have a diet of bamboo that is not very nutritious and coupled with poor fertility they usually produce only a single young at a time. Humans are different to many other types of organism in that they do not have a specific breeding season since women are fertile for a few days each month throughout the year, until they conceive or enter menopause. The whole of human society would be radically different if women only came into season once a year, and as a species we would have been far less numerous than we are!

Across the world many ancient societies and modern cultures have a similar set of rules and customs with regard to women and their reproductive cycles. Incest is invariably taboo and there may also be religious or cultural restrictions in marrying a close relative, such as an aunt or cousin. Another almost universal restriction was that there should be no sexual contact with a menstruating woman. Menstruation was often viewed as a particularly dangerous time and many rituals and prohibitions were associated with it. In some societies women were not allowed to appear in public, or work or prepare food during their moon-time. There still exist old sayings in European folklore that menstruating women could curdle the milk, sour the wine, prevent bread from rising or cause abortions in cattle and sheep. Such magical attributes of the power of menstruating women must go back much further in time. Male hunters only bled because they were injured and in some cultures the monthly bleeding of females was seen as a threat to males, the unseen spirits that had wounded their women could perhaps weaken or cause illness, accident or death to the hunters. So in some societies women were kept segregated during their moontime.

In pre-industrial times people were far more conscious of the sun and the phases of the moon, simply because most people worked on the land. In more modern times we spend a great deal of our time indoors, either at home or at work and especially during the colder months of the year. This is because we have gas and electricity for our heating and lighting and guaranteed sources of food. In those far-off times the moon was one of the main sources of light after dark, so it is not surprising that many ceremonies and rituals, parties and feasts would be held at the time when people could travel about at night, in other words, when the moon was full. However there was more to it that, the moon was seen to be as powerful as the sun but in a different way, it caused the sea to rise and fall twice a day, every day. In addition the moon played an important role in the lives of women. In many of the world's mythologies the sun was seen to be masculine whilst the moon was considered to be feminine. One reason for this was that the moon changes its appearance throughout its monthly cycle. This is similar in some respects to the changes that take place in a girl's body as she undergoes adolescence, to become a woman and the way her belly then swells up when she becomes pregnant.

Many animals and birds have a specific breeding season and it is only then that females become fertile, are willing to mate and can be impregnated. The animals that the first farmers kept, their sheep, goats, cows and pigs always gave birth in the spring. Humans were very different; women could become pregnant at any time of the year. The moon regulated the menstrual cycle of women, and so instead of only once a year they could be fertile up to a dozen times in a year.

The change from the ancient hunting and foraging way of life, to that of a settled life as a farmer, also changed the traditions of the communities and society would never be the same again. Putting down roots and staying in the same place generation after generation altered more than people's lives, it changed their attitudes, actions and ways of thinking. In the older times, before farming arrived some six and a half thousand years ago, people were far healthier because theirs was a lifestyle with a very varied, high protein diet. People in farming communities worked incredibly hard, grew crops of wheat and barley, and ate far more carbohydrate in their diet, which had a dramatic effect on human fertility. In earlier periods women only had one child at a time, and suckling her baby for two or three years kept her reproductive cycle at a slow speed because fewer eggs were released whilst the baby suckled. Nomadic women with a very varied diet were simply less fertile than their descendants but once humans adopted agriculture in earnest the population soared because the high carbohydrate diet encouraged greater fertility, resulting in many more mouths to feed and creating a vicious cycle that continues to this day across the world.

Medical research has been conducted that shows that for modern women there is no direct relationship between their periods and the phases of the moon. However it wasn't always that way, the rough correlation of the menstrual cycle to a lunar month is too obvious to be a complete coincidence. Every month the moon has a dramatic tidal effect on the oceans and seas, so it must also have some sort of effect on the fluids in our bodies. In the modern world, many women have irregular periods, with their menstrual cycles taking anything from 24 to 40 days to complete. In some cases, doctors have prescribed the birth control pill to regulate the monthly cycle to twenty-eight or twenty-nine days. And hormonal imbalances created by a modern lifestyle can make it difficult for some women to conceive. But it was only after reading 'Lunaception', a book by American author Louise Lacey, that I finally understood the significance that the moon played in the lives of our ancestors.
Her main aim had been to discover a method of natural contraception without recourse to artificial methods, because her own body had reacted badly to the birth control pill. Her studies of the available research material over the last century enabled her to come to certain innovative conclusions about women's natural reproductive cycles. There is a risky, time based method of contraception that was used to identify the two or three days in each cycle when a woman is at her most fertile and

for the couple to abstain from having sex during those days. This is usually around two weeks after menstruation.

This technique is often known as the rhythm method of contraception, but in the past it has not always worked successfully because of the irregularity of women's cycles, the egg may be released early or late, resulting in an unwanted pregnancy. The problem lies with determining the moment when an egg has been released from the ovary and can be fertilised. Although some sperm can live for up to a week, the average is about three days, the egg also has a short life span, taking about three days to travel from the ovary, down the Fallopian tubes and into the uterus. Fertilisation usually takes place when sperm swim up the Fallopian tubes to meet the descending egg. In the uterus an unfertilised egg lasts only about twelve hours before it starts to break down. Fertilisation must take place before the egg dies and so most pregnancies occur as a result of having sex during the three days before or after the day of ovulation, in other words, a week. So it is only relatively safe to have sex a few days on either side of menstruation, not in mid cycle.

In her research into human reproduction and natural contraception, Louise Lacey was initially put off by recent studies that seemed to show statistically that there was no correlation between the date of a woman's period and a specific lunar phase. There was no discernible relationship between the gravitational pull of the moon during the lunar cycle on the menstrual cycle, women could have their period at any time of month. But Louise found an older study from Stockholm during the late Victorian era that was different and it showed that women's cycles were related to the lunar cycle. Louise realised that the difference between the two studies was that the first study had been conducted before the widespread arrival of electric light. She realised that the advent of high levels of artificial light, from such diverse sources as street lighting, fluorescent lights at work and tungsten filament lighting in the home plus the emissions from television sets, have all contributed to alter the natural biological rhythms that evolved over countless millennia and they have played havoc with women's truly ancient monthly cycle.

On doing further research, Louise found an article written by Dr Edmond M. Dewan, published in the American Journal of Obstetrics and Gynaecology in 1967, which suggested a way of regularising women's menstrual cycles by using artificial light to recreate the lunar phases. She found that if she kept her bedroom completely dark for most nights, with the exception of the fourteenth, fifteenth and sixteenth nights after she menstruated, her previously erratic cycle became regular as clockwork. During these three nights the bedroom was constantly lit with a dim, low wattage light bulb that simulated the effect of the light of the full moon. Her experiment worked well and by taking her temperature on a daily basis she was able to determine that ovulation occurred fourteen days after the onset of menstruation. A drop in body temperature on one day marked ovulation, followed by a sharp rise in temperature that continued over the next few days. (A minority of women actually feels an acute pain in the abdomen when the egg is released from the ovary.) Many modern women who have had difficulty in becoming pregnant use the temperature method to ascertain the moment of their optimum fertility. Lacey's method of contraception was different from the calendar based rhythm method because it recreated the conditions of the natural lunar cycle by using intervals of dark and light to stabilise her monthly cycle.

In other words, the natural menstrual cycle of human beings really is governed by moonlight and our ancestors were at their most fertile at the full moon. And many Neolithic women would menstruate at the opposite phase to the full moon, during the nights of the dark moon.

In her book, Louise Lacey also wrote that her body felt particularly full and receptive at the high point of each cycle, and that the full moon seemed to make her want to have a child. So clearly the ancient role the moon had on human sexuality still prevails, even though it has become far less noticeable and less powerful than in the remote past. We have become so accustomed to our modern hi-tech world that at times we forget our own truly remote origins; we tend to forget that we are just rather clever animals! What all this demonstrates is that although the irregularity of modern women's menstrual cycle is caused to some extent by the demands and stresses of contemporary life, the main cause is consistently high levels of artificial lighting. We may have banished the night but we have also interrupted a natural cycle, a cycle that evolved over countless millennia.

In addition to its effects on the menstrual cycle, the moon can also have an effect on the time of birth. Research in the 1960's by Dr Walter Menaker concerning the time of birth of over half a million babies in the New York area produced the astonishing revelation that many more children were born in the nights around the full moon than were born near the dark moon. It follows from the conclusions reached above that in ancient times the percentage of deliveries at full moon must have been even higher. The ancients did not need to know the complex biological and chemical processes involved, but simply observe the correlation between moon phase and the reproductive cycle. So it is highly likely that not only did our predecessors observe that far more children were born at full moon but also that they realised that the conceptions had taken place nine months earlier, again at full moon. The idea that human pregnancy lasted roughly nine moons is very basic knowledge. Hunting people are very familiar with length of time between mating and when the young are born, not just for animals but for humans as well. So in ancient times the moon was directly responsible for human fertility and sexuality, and the full moon, particularly in summer, was a time for travelling, having fun, going to feasts and parties.

Human reproduction was a mysterious process to them because although people could have sex at any time, it was only on some occasions that women would become pregnant. Sometimes pregnancy could result from just one sex act, whilst for other couples months and even years could go past before the woman became pregnant, but why? What was happening or rather, what was not happening? They knew that the process somehow involved a man's 'seed', and that it was only after having sex that a child could be born. So the logical explanation was that the moon somehow provided the vital link between sex and conception, in exactly the same way that the warmth of the sun germinated their crops and sunlight ripened the seeds. And whilst some women had low fertility but did eventually give birth, others never succeeded in having children at all. So the old stories of infertile women performing rituals by moonlight in order to become pregnant now make sense, because in ancient times it sometimes actually worked. If an infertile woman wanted to get pregnant she could pray to the full moon for help and expose herself to the beneficial rays that regulated her cycle and then have sex over the next few days at the moment of ovulation. There are even historical records in our folklore of local customs involving the use of standing stones to promote fertility, amongst other 'cures', barren women were told to strip naked and rub their bellies against a particular stone during the night of the full moon.

Folklore invariably contains a grain of truth that becomes corrupted over the centuries. The problem lies in separating fact from fiction, and I have found that it is only after other clues become available that it can be deciphered correctly. The truly ancient fear of the dark has been remembered in our folklore and superstition incorrectly, the most dangerous period of the month was not at full moon, but at dark moon. The long dark nights of winter lasted for up to sixteen hours and the lack of any natural light created a time of great unease and danger, when evil spirits, monsters, hobgoblins, werewolves, vampires and ghouls were out and about.

So to summarise, the dark moon was associated with danger, darkness, menstrual blood, evil spirits and forbidden sex. The full moon was associated with good times and with light, safety, beneficial spirits, conception, fertility, sex and birth. So, in addition to its role as the home of their ancestral spirits, that's why I think that the moon had such a prominent role in ancient mythology, belief and customs.

Symbolism and religious beliefs

Across the world, many ancient people saw sunrise as an allegorical representation of the birth process. This symbolism was probably based on several themes, firstly because sunrise marks the dawn of a new day and secondly because there is a period of waiting and anticipation of the coming of dawn after the darkest hours of the night, followed in turn by the crimson sky that often heralds the appearance of the rising sun. This manifestation is similar to the birthing process of humans after a long pregnancy and of the blood that accompanies the birth of a child. In contrast, the setting of the sun was often seen as being symbolic of the process of dying and death. Firstly because it marked the end of that day and the coming of night and secondly because it was often accompanied by a spectacular light show in which the ruby red glow of the setting sun was reminiscent of the bloody end of the lives of the animals that were hunted or raised for their food. (It wasn't delivered neatly cut up and attractively packaged from supermarkets!) Sunset also heralded the coming of dusk followed in turn by the darkness of night, a scary time when many people believed that spirits and ghosts roamed around outside. Sunset also symbolised death because proportionally more people died in their sleep and never saw another dawn…

The fear of dying was, and still is, universal, no one knows what happens to us at the end of our lives and so death has always been an unwelcome visitor. Just as today, many ancient cultures believed in an afterlife and so for them death was not the end of everything. Although the body died, the spirit survived because death was just another stage in the transformation of the spirit to a higher plane in the cycle and life as a human being was just one stop on the journey between this world and the next. Although the body died and decayed, the spirit lived on, and just like the sun and moon, was reborn. So in a symbolic manner, sunrise meant rebirth and new life, whilst sunset meant death and metamorphosis.

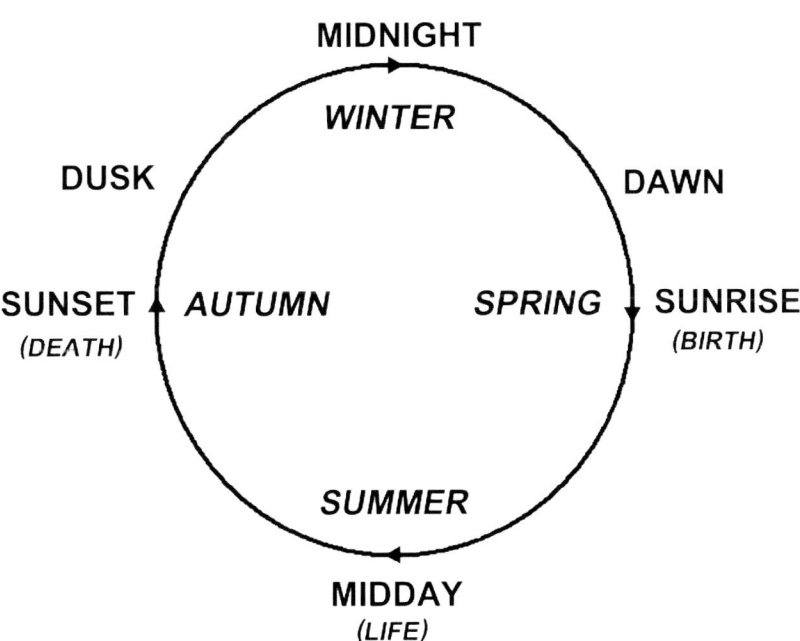

THE DAILY AND ANNUAL CYCLES OF THE SUN

In the past many archaeologists have not really appreciated the important difference that exists between sunrise and sunset at the winter solstice. They have just lumped the two together and have assumed that the winter solstice was important to the ancients because they were worried about the future. According to this theory, the solstice was seen as the turning point of the year and only when it had passed, could people be reassured that their lives would continue as before, and that the days would get longer, warmer and lighter and spring would come round again. To me, the old idea of the winter solstice being celebrated as the turning point of the year does not seem to be a powerful enough reason on its own to motivate people into building enormous monuments. Especially those that were aligned with the rising or setting sun on the shortest day of the year, places such as

Newgrange in Ireland, Stonehenge in England, Bryn Celli Ddu in Wales and Maeshowe in Scotland. So I think that our Neolithic forefathers celebrated the midwinter solstice more on religious grounds and not because they were worried about whether or not the sun would ever rise again. Like modern farmers, the ancients were far more concerned about the health of their livestock and the weather for their crops than they were about something that they knew would happen anyway, the sun always rises. So I think it far more likely that people were motivated by very powerful religious beliefs involving the rebirth of the sun, and the triumph of life after death. And in addition I think that another one of the reasons why the winter solstice was seen as a cause for celebration was because they realised that it marked the end of one solar cycle and the start of the next. In other words, it symbolised the end of the old year and the start of the New Year.

In the days after the winter solstice the sun grew stronger and more powerful, it rose higher in the sky and finally, after winter was over, the days grew warmer. As the seasons advanced the sun moved northwards until it reached its maximum position at the summer solstice, then it turned towards the south again, slowly diminishing in power until it died, only to be reborn again at the start of the next cycle. So I think that from a symbolic viewpoint, the winter solstice sunset marked the last day of the old year, and sunrise the following morning marked not just the birth of a new day, but also the first day of a new year.

So in other words, the Neolithic New Year started at sunrise on the first morning after the winter solstice. **This is important.** The symbolic rebirth of the sun is crucial to a better understanding of our ancestors and their religious beliefs because many of their open-air temples were aligned towards the rising sun and were used for ceremonies and celebrations by the living, whilst many tombs were aligned with the setting sun and were homes for the recent and ancestral dead. The cycles of the sun and the moon were eternal, for although they 'died', they were reborn at the start of the next cycle and by the construction of special temples and tombs people could benefit from the life-giving energy of the sun and the timeless power of the moon. Just as today, their religions gave people hope and a belief that there really was *'Life after Death'*. And I think that they built circular monuments to honour the sun and the moon. Throughout history people have recorded their sacred beliefs in permanent form for the benefit of future generations. However, instead of small symbols scratched into wax or clay tablets, or written in ink on papyrus or parchment, our prehistoric ancestors recorded their beliefs in a very different manner. After looking at them for several years I finally realised that the stone temples and tombs were literally written into the very landscape itself. People effectively recorded their thoughts onto the landscape, using earth and stone to symbolise their beliefs in a permanent manner, but until now we simply haven't been able to understand their true meaning. The structures they raised at their ceremonial centres represented their beliefs on a grand scale in a very physical, visual, symbolical and practical way. And because circles had such a deep religious significance to them, they often built gigantic, circular structures of earth, wood and stone. But as we shall see in later chapters, different people with different beliefs built different structures at different times for different reasons.

Just like us, our ancestors were very well aware of the fact that people could be living one minute and dead the next. Across the ancient world people reasoned that the difference between the two states must be due to a spirit that animated the body during life but was absent after death. The life force was like the wind, you couldn't see it but you could observe and feel the effects, it was an invisible spirit that made each person unique and different from everyone else. Like all of us they had dream and nightmares when they were asleep, and they must have reasoned that sometimes the strange happenings they had in their dreams were actually caused by their spirit experiencing other realities, visiting other times and places and being with other people. This would have led to the idea that the spirit or soul could travel from one reality to another and from one world to another. And just as there were good and bad people in life, so there were benevolent or malevolent spirits in death. They were superstitious people, just as many people still are today, and 'crossing your fingers', 'lucky heather' or a 'lucky rabbit's foot' are just recent examples of the sorts of charms and talismans that protected the owner from bad luck, ill health or accidents. Even today, many actors, performers and sportspeople are highly superstitious and many have specific little rituals that they have to perform before they will go on stage or before they compete in sporting events.

In ancient times, rituals seem to have been practiced that protected the living from malicious or evil spirits, bad luck or accidents and many strange rituals were acted out, often in specially built places, to ward off misfortune and to ensure that the community could benefit from the protection, wisdom and aid of ancestral spirits. The intention was to encourage the benevolent spirits to stay and of course the people treated the remains of their departed loved ones with respect, keeping their memories alive in their memories and stories and by commemorating them physically with shrines, tombs, cairns and marker stones. Other types of spirits were the mysterious causes of accidents and illness, pain and disease and so logically such bad luck could only be due to the presence of malicious, evil spirits that wanted to harm them. These sentiments seem to be almost universal and date back many, many thousands of years.

The most compelling physical evidence for the belief in malicious spirits comes from the results of Stone Age surgery. The process called trepanation was widespread across Europe throughout the Neolithic, but it declined over the following millennia and was rarely practised after the medieval period, although it is still carried out in remote parts of Africa. Trepanning involves the removal of a small circle of bone from the skull of patients who suffered from terrible migraines, mental illness or epilepsy. Amazingly, about two thirds of Neolithic patients survived the surgical technique. This is a much higher success rate than that of early Victorian surgeons, because many of their patients died subsequently from blood poisoning, usually due to the poor hygiene of the doctors. Clearly the intention of the dangerous, yet skilful, Neolithic surgery was to allow evil spirits to escape from being trapped inside the skull, like releasing the pus from an infected wound. This was a time when knowledge of the world was very different to our modern understanding, they knew nothing of the bacteria and viruses that cause virulent diseases, which could come at any time and decimate a community. They just knew that something was very wrong and if their crops failed or their herds died, starvation was just round the corner. Hard manual labour and a restricted diet meant less resistance to disease and infant mortality was high. In winter, their damp, cold, smoky houses meant that respiratory diseases such as coughs and colds, bronchitis and pneumonia were common and could often be fatal. As usual, humans developed all sorts of different strategies to cope with the fear of dying and the death of their loved ones and many different cults and religions grew up to interpret it in a host of different ways. However, an almost universal belief was, and still is, that after death there was some sort of afterlife, a place where you could be reunited with your ancestors, family and friends. In prehistoric Britain there were many different ways that the corpse, and hence the spirit, of the departed person was treated, and these were often linked to the earth and the sky.

Only a tiny fraction of the bodies of the hundreds of thousands of people that lived during the Neolithic and Bronze Ages were preserved for the future, the vast majority have disappeared without trace. The most logical explanation is that the bodies were burned and the cremated remains scattered. Of those people whose bodies were preserved, the methods used varied considerably, one method was by inhumation, where the intact body was buried and the fleshy remains returned to the earth. In other cases, people believed that the spirit or life force departed at the moment of death but the soul remained for some time and only after the last vestiges of moisture had been removed from the body was it certain that it had moved on. This was achieved either by cremation, when the soul escaped with the heat of the funeral pyre and rose up with the smoke, or when corpses were left to rot away naturally, and were laid out in special enclosures or else left on a raised platform of wood, well away from the village dogs and pigs. Sometimes combinations of these different approaches were carried out and the dried-out human remains were placed inside communal tombs later. In one respect this natural process mirrors the life cycle of plants and trees. In autumn the leaves of deciduous trees fall, leaving just the skeleton of the tree behind, this remains throughout the little death of winter, although with the coming of spring the tree is reborn and new leaves grow.

Centuries later, from around 1500 BC, many of these beliefs were replaced with other ideas about the afterlife and sometimes the ashes of cremated bodies were released into wells, streams, lakes and rivers, to be washed clean away and join with the ancestors or the Gods of the Underworld. And later still, during the Iron Age, people were sometimes sent as human sacrifices to the Gods who dwelt in peat bogs. (Some of these offerings were preserved in the peat and have been recovered. This includes Lindow Man in the UK and many other bog bodies have been found in Denmark, Holland and Germany.) Other types of offerings, of tools, weapons and implements, were given to the spirits and buried in pits dug in the ground and these sorts of rituals lasted from the Neolithic period right through to post Roman times. The basic idea seems to me that people were giving something back to the land from which all things came. However, the reasons behind the individual offerings would have been very varied. Sometimes the offering was a particularly valuable item and it could have been given in gratitude to the spirits and the Gods for an abundant harvest, or to give thanks for the birth of a long-awaited child, the discovery of a new source of metal ore, the recovery of a loved one from a near fatal illness or as a plea to the unseen spirits to avert a potential disaster. Of course some of the pits that contained such treasured items could also have been put there just for safekeeping or to hide the evidence of theft or the ill-gotten gains of a raid. Other pits were used as ground-ovens, for storage, or just for human or kitchen waste. In the late Bronze Age and during the Iron Age weapons such as swords and daggers were sometimes deliberately broken or partially melted down, in order to ensure that no one else could use the weapon after its owner had gone to the next world. At other times although they were deposited in lakes and rivers they remained intact, as though they were being offerings to the gods or sent to join their owners in the next world.

During the Neolithic period the communal tombs built to house the bones of the dead were considered to be very special places, where the spirits or souls of the ancestors dwelled or else were a familiar place where they could return to visit their descendants at special times of the year. Like magnets, the bones would draw the ancestral spirits back to the land of their origins. Strange things were done to the stored remains. Sometimes the bones were separated and grouped together in separate areas, and tombs have been found where all the skulls were in one chamber and all the arm and leg bones in another. In some Neolithic tombs the skeletons were grouped by sex and by age, so that children were stored in one place, and women and men in others. It is also likely that people believed that their priests and shamans were able to enter into a trance state and communicate with the ancestors in the spirit world, in order to get help and advice and to protect the people from malicious spirits. However, all these ideas varied enormously from one location to the next and from one time to another, changing according to the fashions of current wisdom and shifting beliefs. So I think that many of these ideas about spirits, combined with a new awareness of how the endless cycles in the heavens above affected life on the earth below, were the root cause of the development of new religious beliefs. And in turn these beliefs caused the evolution of many of the circular monuments that were built across the British Isles over a two thousand year period, from about 3500 BC to 1500 BC.

The circle was a symbol that was used extensively in the British Isles and in addition to the early large circular burial mounds, they built a wide variety of circular enclosures that were used as ceremonial places, temporary camps, fairs, stock pens and included small shrines and mortuary sites. During the course of time one site could be used for any or all of these purposes, changing its function as the years passed. One of the first types of permanent construction that they built are known as causewayed camps or causewayed enclosures. These were roughly circular sets of deep ditches with banks of earth with many gaps in them. Later on these changed dramatically to become henges, which were comprised of a high circular bank of earth on the outside of a deep ditch, with just one or two entrances into the enclosed space. Henges sometimes had rings of posts inside the area enclosed by the ditch, Woodhenge is one such example. Some of these were circle henges, they contained rings of standing stones and famous examples include Avebury, Arbor Low and the Standing Stones of Stenness, on Orkney. They also built round mounds of earth called barrows, round burial tombs and mounds of small stones, known as cairns; and of course the most famous and most mysterious of all, stone circles. In the above paragraphs we have seen how astronomy was linked to mythology and sacred belief. So I think that in the late Neolithic period, this intense fascination with the sun and the moon, and the symbolical references to human life and to the farming and agricultural cycles, was translated into religions based around the cycles of the natural world, the changing seasons, the farming calendar and the endlessly repeated rhythm of **Birth, Life and Death**, followed by **Rebirth**.

And so I think that some of the open-air temples that we know as stone circles were not just simply calendars or physical representations of the sun or the moon, but were developed as places of worship to celebrate this new ideology and a new religion: *'**The Circle of Life'**.*

However, I don't think that there was just one religion, far from it, I think that there were many different religions and many different cults and belief systems, just as there were many different tribes spread thinly across the countryside. Their ancestors had come across the Channel from the Atlantic coasts of what is now Spain and Portugal, and others came from around Brittany and the Calais area, in France, and more came from what are now Denmark, Holland, Belgium and Germany. And later on, people whose ancestors had first settled in Ireland migrated further north, to the west coast of Scotland, to the Western Isles, the Northern Isles of the Orkneys and Shetlands, and to the northeastern areas of Scotland. So a mixture of cultural beliefs and different ethnic backgrounds is not something new to Britain, there has always been a mixture of many different cultures living here, although we know little of the background and traditions of individual people.

Throughout the Neolithic, as well as in earlier times, there was a thriving trade in stone axes. These were made on an almost industrial basis, at special geological sites in Cornwall, North Wales and the Lake District, and some stone axes were even imported from Brittany in northwest France. Goods were traded with other tribes and some merchants and traders travelled great distances, even across the Channel. For example, a famous Bronze Age skeleton of a middle-aged man, known as *'the Amesbury Archer'* was found in an excavation in Wiltshire. Chemical analysis of his teeth showed that he had grown up somewhere in central Europe close to the Alps. He was buried with many grave goods, including beaker pots, a bow and a quiver of arrows, a wrist guard, and a copper knife that had been made from metal that had come from Spain. Another important burial in Wiltshire was that of a man who is traditionally seen as a shaman. He was buried in a round barrow near the village of Upton Lovell, a few miles west of Stonehenge. Amongst many curious items, that included nodules of iron oxide, boars' teeth and a collection of stones and pebbles that were found in his grave, there were also thirty-six shaped bones, each pierced with a hole at one end and sharpened to a point at the other. The traditional explanation for these is that, together with dead animals, they were sewn into the clothing of the shaman, in a similar fashion to those known to have been worn by Siberian and North American Indian shamans. But I think it far more likely that each bone point represented a ray of sunlight and that the complete set was made into a necklace and worn by a priest of a solar cult.

Previously I have written mainly about the symbolic directions of the rising or setting sun at the solstices, but for other people the most important symbolic times were at the equinoxes, when the sun rises to the east and sets in the west. Equinox means 'equal night', when day and night are the same length. The spring equinox on the 21st March is about half way between the winter and summer solstices. The summer solstice on the 21st June is half way between the spring and autumn equinoxes. The autumn equinox on the 23rd September is half way between the summer and winter solstices. The winter solstice is half way between the autumn and the spring equinox. So every major event seemed to be balanced with everything else, the solstices and equinoxes were seen as special moments in the year, when everything seemed to be in equilibrium and when time itself stopped dead in its tracks.
This was probably seen as a very special moment, a time when past and future were balanced in the present and consequently the moment when the membrane between the physical states of life and

death was thin. For many people these were the key moments of the year when magical transitions and transformations, spirit journeys and ancestral visits could take place between this world and the next. (In much more modern times such an event was thought to occur at Halloween, although another explanation is that this was just a time to remember those who had passed on.) The events that were most important to people varied according to time and place and to tribal traditions. Over the centuries society changed and with it came changes to traditional religious beliefs. The old style cults were transformed and new solar and lunar beliefs were accompanied by regional changes in ceremonies, burial practices and most noticeably, architecture.

Down through the centuries individual graves and cairns often contained people who had been buried lying on their sides, with their eyes looking out towards the east and the rising sun, whilst others faced towards the western horizon, towards the setting sun. Sometimes their feet were to the north and sometimes to the south, but what was more important was the direction they were facing, either east or west, and I think they were looking towards the direction their spirit or soul would travel, towards the place of their rebirth in the *'Land of the Dead'*. Women were often buried in a different manner to their men, and with different grave goods.

Perhaps our Neolithic ancestors thought of themselves as 'Children of the Sun', who were reborn and lived on Earth, but that for them Death wasn't the end of everything, for they would be reborn as spirits on the Moon. It is certainly an attractive idea because it ties in with many of their burial traditions, and especially since most modern religions have a belief that death is not the end of our journey, it is just the start of a new beginning. As I wrote earlier, there seems to have been a great diversity of beliefs surrounding how our bodies and minds are animated and what happens to them after death. Then, as now, there were many different ways of thinking about the body, the spirit and the soul. One complex way of thinking about this may have been that even at an early stage in the womb a developing baby became animated by a life force. This was an invisible power source, like heat, which started the infant's heart beating before it was born, then kept it alive throughout its development and growth in infancy, then for the rest of its life. But when something dramatic inter-rupted the constant flow of this life force, the lungs stopped breathing, the heart stopped beating, the brain stopped working and the person died. This life force was the spirit of the person, and in some cultures all living things had spirits. Humans were different, they had souls. Each person had his or her identity and individuality. According to some religions this was the human spirit, whilst for others this was the soul. For many people the soul was immortal and grew as the person developed from baby to child to adult, and after death it moved on and continued to develop elsewhere. This may be in a new body or elsewhere, in heaven, paradise, another dimension or another world. (One way of understanding this idea is by using a modern analogy. In a computer the 'life force' is represented by the electricity that makes it all work. The 'spirit' is the operating software that decides how it works and does the maintenance, whilst the 'soul' is represented by the new programs, data, files and im-ages that grow as the computer gets used. These accumulate over a lifetime and when the user gets a new computer, the old files are then moved to the new body!)

Ancient people studied the sky in order to understand the movements of the sun, moon, stars and planets. Once the cycles of the sun and moon were understood they could then make plans for the future, arranging the right time for key festivals and special ceremonies well in advance. And when you can make accurate astronomical predictions, you are effectively predicting the future. This must have given a lot of power to the priests and astronomers who had such knowledge. Other people had to take them seriously. In many ancient cultures knowledge of astronomy gave rise to astrology, the belief that the stars, moon and planets can have an effect on people's lives and directly influence their futures.

My issue with astrology is that modern astrologer's use the exact time and date of a person's birth to work out their star chart, and then make predictions about their future. One major problem with this is that due to changes in the earth's axis, the stars and constellations are no longer in the same positions as they once were in relation to the Earth on the same dates as before. For astrologers the starting point of the Zodiac is at the spring equinox, when the sun is said to be in *'the First Point of Aries'*, however due to precession during the last two thousand years it has moved backwards and in fact it is now in the constellation of Pisces. Oops!

Another one of the main reasons that most astronomers today have little faith in astrology is that the stars are simply too far away to have any direct effect on humans. However, we have already seen how the moon affects the tides, the reproductive cycles of marine creatures and the human menstrual cycle, and although the planets of Venus, Mars and Jupiter are far more distant than the moon, they could affect us at a cellular level. And if there are any forms of astronomical forces that can affect human destiny then it is more likely that any change takes place around the time of fertilisation of the egg and the first sets of cell division. External influences at such an early stage are far more likely to affect someone's future character and fate. In other words, planetary gravitational forces are less likely to work on a fully formed baby at the time of its birth. The revelation that astrologers are at least nine months out of synchronisation could have dire consequences for the whole astrological industry! So perhaps it's time for those who are interested in such things to look at this subject again. This would give rise to a New Astrology, based on the time of conception rather than birth, and it could certainly provoke some interesting child/parent discussions!

Death and religious beliefs

Throughout the past, there have been many different types of burial practices, rituals and traditions that have existed at the same time in the same area, and as I have said several times already, this often reflects different religious beliefs within the wider community. The diversity of religious beliefs in different ages also helps to explain why there was such variety in the way people treated the dead. These range from the sky burials of the early days, where bodies were often placed on wooden scaffolding above the ground and left to decay naturally (excarnation). Sometimes the bones were then collected and the skeletons of dozens of people were stored together in communal cairns and longbarrows. In other instances the bodies of the dead were buried in the banks and ditches of causewayed enclosures. At other times fresh bodies were just laid on the ground and a mound of earth was heaped over them. But sometimes the intact corpses were buried in a grave dug in the earth and this sort of burial is known as inhumation. At other times and places the corpses were cremated and the burned bones collected and buried in leather bags or even stored in clay pots known as urns. Sometimes the remains were enclosed in a wooden hut, which was subsequently covered over by a long mound of earth and turf. Another type of burial involved a small box-like chamber of flat, oblong stones called a cist (pronounced kist). Then from the Continent, sometime around 2300 BC, came the idea of burial in circular mounds of earth, called round barrows, these usually contained one person buried in the foetal position, with the knees pulled up towards the chest, as though they were waiting to be reborn. Women were often buried lying on their right sides whilst men were placed on their left sides. But sometimes the dead were cremated and put into pottery jars (called funeral urns) and these were then buried under a circular mound of earth.

Round barrows sometimes included grave goods of food, tools or weapons for the journey and use in the afterlife. Many round barrows were enclosed in a circular ditch and bank and the circle confines the dead inside a sacred area, perhaps to protect the living from any angry or evil spirits that may have been released. The first earth circles in the early Neolithic made a distinction between this world and the next world. The circle served as the boundary between the living and the dead, a place for the ancestral spirits to visit and where they could be revered and remembered, so that they would always have a benevolent influence on the living. Dating mainly from the Bronze Age, the most common form of circular earthen burial mounds is the round barrow, a dome of earth sometimes set inside a circular bank and ditch. There are also other shapes of round barrow such as bowl, bell, pond, cone and disc barrows. Different varieties of round barrow can sometimes be found in barrow cemeteries, particularly the Normanton Down group near Stonehenge. Logically, the different types off barrow must be symbolic representations of the sun and the moon and perhaps the planets.

I think that bowl barrows with ditches represented the setting sun and the ditch represented the aurora we see surrounding the sun. The moon does not have that glow around it and so I think that its shape was symbolically represented by a plain, unditched barrow. Disc barrows had a low, circular outer bank, which enclosed a ditch and a low platform with a very small mound in the middle, often containing the cremated remains of women and girls. So I think that it is highly likely that this sort of round barrow represented *'the Morning Star'*, the planet we call Venus.

So to summarise, this business of how the spirits or souls of the dead moved from one world to the next seems to have varied according to time and place and in accordance with different traditions and regional religious beliefs. For some societies the magical journey was thought to be easier at sunset on the last day of the year, symbolised by the construction of passageways towards the setting sun in the southwest on the 21st December. Other people believed that the journey to 'the Land of the Dead' took place at dawn on the following morning, at sunrise at the midwinter solstice, when the sun rose in the southeast on the first day of a new year. For others, the nineteen-year cycle of the moon was more important and the optimum time for spirit travel was when the moon appeared closest to the Earth, when it rose and set just over the horizon in it most southerly summer positions.

The major summer moon can seem very close because it is at its lowest on the horizon and perhaps the southern standstill point was symbolic of ancestral origins, far to the southeast or southwest. Birds fly south in autumn to pass the winter in warmer climates, so perhaps they believed that the moon carried the souls of the dead to the home of their ancestors…
Another version of these sorts of mystical beliefs involved the autumn equinox. At this time of the year the twelve hours of daylight equal the twelve hours of night time; light and dark are harmoniously balanced and in ancient times people thought that it was also a special moment when the two worlds, this world and the next, were in equilibrium and were brought close together. At this special moment the spirits of the dead, both those of the ancestors and those of the more recently departed, could move more easily between the worlds of the dead and the living. So they built structures with entrances and passageways towards the west, towards the setting sun, in a way that symbolically linked the dead with the dying sun at the end of the day. But for others, the two worlds were the Earth and the Moon and so their structures were built in line with the mysterious moon rather than towards the warmth of the life-giving sun.

In some societies the skeletal bones of the ancestors were stored in large burial mounds within chambered tombs, like those in passage graves and longbarrows. But societies changed, as time passed their beliefs altered and with the introduction of metal working, cremation became common once more. The passage from life to death paralleled the metamorphosis of the human spirit from one form to another. So perhaps this way of liberating the spirit was something akin to the magical process of transforming dull rocks into gleaming metal. The overall archaeological evidence of burial traditions seems to suggest that the ancients thought that the soul was only freed from the body at some time after death, when the flesh had gone, either by natural decay or by rising into the sky with the smoke of a funeral pyre. In many cases bodies were often allowed to decay naturally, before the final rites took place at the winter solstice. The physical remains were preserved, perhaps as tangible reminders of the ancestors for an annual remembrance ceremony in midwinter.
In nearly all the above cases the symbolism involved confirms the belief in the Birth, Life, Death, Rebirth cycle. All that differed was the treatment accorded to the dead person. Sometimes the corpse was given food, ornaments, tools or weapons for the journey to the next world, to give them a good start in their new lives. There were few such gifts for many of those buried in longbarrows, I don't think that it was because they were so poor, I think it more likely that the dead simply had no need for such things in the afterlife, only their spirits would return, but at special times of the year. Many hundreds of years later, in the Celtic Iron Age, people thought that the veil between worlds was at its weakest at the midpoint between the autumn equinox and the winter solstice, around the 31st October. This marked the end of the vegetation cycle, and the autumnal shedding of leaves and the death of annual plants.

QUARTER DAY FESTIVALS
POPULAR, CHRISTIAN and *Celtic*

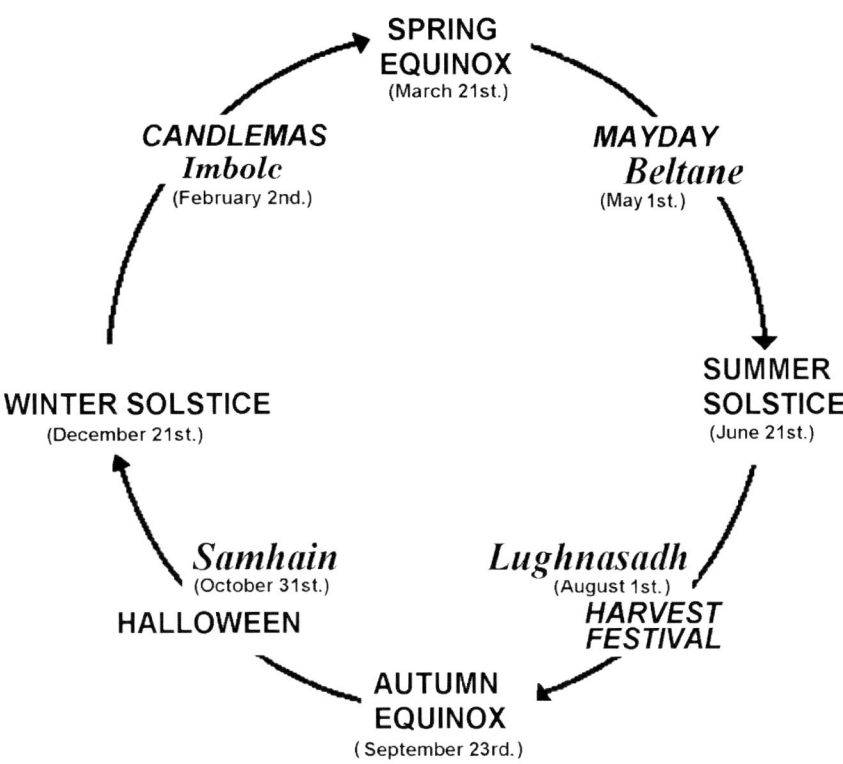

N.B. The dates of Celtic festivals to mark the cross quarter days vary considerably, the festival may even be held on the full moon closest to the calendar date. And in modrn times the calendar dates of the quarter days are not always at the mid point between solstice and equinox as they should be.

The Celts firmly believed that this midpoint was a time when ghosts and ghouls, the spirits of the dead, could visit the living and these ideas survive to the present day, although in a very much diluted and far more commercially based form. This is the time we call Halloween, the night when the spirits and ghosts of the ancestors could travel back to Earth to visit their old homes and their friends and families. The times for festivals and celebrations were often linked to the seasonal movements of the sun, particularly at the solstices and equinoxes, as well as the midpoints between the solstices and the equinoxes, known as the Cross Quarter Days. These took place in February, May, August and November. They were traditionally linked to agricultural activities such as the sowing of seed, moving the herds to fresh pasture, harvesting the crops and then fetching the herds home for winter. The main festivals of Samhain, Beltane, Lugnasadh and Imbolc were known as the Fire Festivals, and marked the turning of the seasons. Samhain and Beltane were seen as male festivals and Lugnasadh and Imbolc as female, but they were all the occasion for religious ceremonies, feasts and for lighting hilltop bonfires.

Alignments

In the preceding pages I've written several times about alignments, so perhaps I should clarify how I see them. There are several types of alignments. There can be physical, visual, symbolic, or visible alignments, or combinations of any of these. The physical alignments are the most obvious and they include structures such as the entrances and passageways into tombs and mounds like Maeshowe or Newgrange, which were aligned with the winter solstice sunset and sunrise. Other examples include long parallel banks of earth and single or parallel rows of standing stones. Structures like these can be seen as paths leading into or out of temples or tombs, but perhaps they could also be used as spirit pathways, as routes for the spirits to follow, but only at special times of the year, when the way was open. In the case of the rising sun this was a time for spiritual rebirth of the souls of the dead. At lunar sites there were often alignments towards the moon at its major rising or setting positions. And just as a moth is drawn to the flame of a candle, so beams of moonlight would awaken the spirits of the dead and lead them along the shining pathway to the next world, the moon.

Visual alignments need several points, the backsight can be one standing stone, which is then in line with another standing stone and a distinctive distant foresight, something like a notch on the horizon, or the edge of a hill where the sun or moon will rise or set on a particular day. These alignments can act as simple calendars and they are likely to be still active around a particular date. They did not have to be exactly in tune with a solstice or equinox, especially if their intention was just to give the observer a few days warning of a specific festival, such as those at a solstice, cross quarter day or equinox. We know from the pottery and trade goods that they brought with them that visitors from other parts of Britain came to such major sites as Avebury and Stonehenge. We can imagine a stream of people moving along the highways of the time, the ridgeways, heading for major festivals, just as people still do today. Other dates, such as birthdays, death days, anniversaries etc., simply cannot be retrieved from visual alignments; there is simply no easy way of knowing why it was significant to the people who raised a particular stone. Such events were as ephemeral as a rainbow, or a shadow, or the glittering path of sunlight on water, but for those who knew its significance, at least the event could be preserved and frozen in time by a particular stone or a specially built structure.

By visible alignments I mean either a beam of light or a long shadow, which could be part of a dramatic lightshow at a particular time of year. The most famous beam of light is the one at Newgrange, which appears shortly after sunrise at the winter solstice and shines down the long passageway and onto the back wall of the chamber inside. As we shall see later on, Stonehenge had many visible alignments in the form of lines of light and shadow, which were cast from the standing stones by the rising and setting sun.

An interesting regional variation of the reverence for the moon is seen in many stone circles in Aberdeenshire. Known as recumbent stone circles, the temples are noted for a special arrangement of three stones aligned with the summer full moon. Three very large stones are arranged so that the middle one is lying horizontal and flanked on either side by a vertical stone of smaller size. Such a prominent arrangement makes one think of an altar or even a stone bed, with a board at head and feet. The arrangement of stones was often aligned with the major standstill position of the most southerly moonset or less often, the corresponding moonrise. These recumbent stones are usually very long and could easily have been used to lay out the body of a deceased person for a special ceremony, perhaps inviting the powerful moon to carry away the deceased person's soul to the afterlife. From the amount of effort that went into building the recumbent stone circles it seems clear to me that they considered the major moonset a very special moment in time, when spirit travel between the worlds was relatively easy because the moon was so close to the Earth. At this special time of the year the spirits of the ancestors could return to visit their kin, and when the moon moved below the horizon the spirits of the dead could leave with it.

The recumbent stone may also have served as an altar for offerings of food, in thanks for a good crop or perhaps in the hope of a good harvest to come. Every nineteen years the full moon would set at its most southerly position but because people died at all times of the year, the altar was only symbolically set up, with the recumbent stone acting as an artificial horizon. On a more practical note, by altering his position slightly from the previous ceremony, the priest could always have observed the full moon setting behind the right hand flanker during the extremes of the swing cycle from minor to major positions, retaining the symbolical basis of the celestial events.

However, since stone circles were built over much of Britain during a fifteen hundred-year period it is important to know that not all arrangements of standing stones were circular. During the early Bronze

Age, many rings of stones were ellipses, ovals, egg shapes, or eyeball shapes (in the form of a flattened circle, a bit like the letter D). And since there were many different groups and tribes of people in the British Isles it would be unwise to assume that they all worshipped exactly the same things, some temples were purely solar or lunar. However, the concept of 'The Circle of Life' does seem to be constant for many centuries. In the area around Cork in Southern Ireland are the remains of many rings with one long, low stone set horizontally as an altar to the southwest, and the most noted of these is Drombeg. These are predominantly solar circles, and since they are often known as recumbent stone circles, they have sometimes been lumped in with the lunar temples of Aberdeenshire in northeastern Scotland. However, the Irish solar rings do not have closely-set flanking stones next to the altar stone, which is typical of the Scottish lunar sites.

Of course not every stone circle has enough marker stones to include every possible solar and lunar position, the smaller local populations just chose those directions they considered as being the most significant. But at large ceremonial centres in Wiltshire, Cumbria and the Orkneys, the local population built giant circles with up to a hundred large stones, encapsulating many more mythological, sacred and symbolical themes than at the small circles, which often date from the Bronze Age. At different times and places other types of stone circles were used to celebrate the extremes of the lunar cycle or perhaps to worship planets such as Venus and Mars, but regardless of the religious beliefs involved, most were still probably used to celebrate the rites of passage from childhood to adulthood and to mark the change of status at marriage, parenthood and death.

Many ancient and modern societies marked the rite of passage from childhood to young adulthood, often coinciding with the hormonal onset of puberty. I think that in Neolithic Britain this change was sometimes symbolised by sunset in the northwest on the eve of the summer solstice. This was the turning point, a time of transition in the solar cycle and directly opposite the compass direction of the dawn of the New Year, sunrise in the southeast. In this symbolism, sunset in the northwest on the last evening before the summer solstice, Midsummer's Eve, represented the end of childhood, then the following sunrise in the northeast, at dawn on the longest day of the year, Midsummer's Day, represented the high point of growing up, the end of adolescence and the onset of adulthood.

I think it likely that puberty rites for both boys and girls were conducted during the hours of darkness on the eve of the summer solstice. The following dawn, the rising sun would have welcomed the new adults into their new roles in the community. In most ancient cultures initiation rites were very complex and they varied considerably. The young people were often given new names, underwent difficult and dangerous tests of courage, endurance and bravery; endured periods of isolation, fasting and purification; underwent ritual mutilation or circumcision and were often given hallucinatory drugs to disorientate them and to characterise the mental, spiritual and physical transition from child to adult. Those that failed the initiation tests were rarely accepted as full adults by the rest of the community. In some societies they lived in a sort of twilight state, halfway between child and adult, without any privileges or status, and in more drastic cases they were banished or even killed and no one ever spoke their name again, because they did not exist.

3 NEWGRANGE AND NEW BEGINNINGS

The new information outlined in the preceding pages means that we can now start to look at our prehistoric monuments in a completely new light. In the previous chapter I showed how the cycles of the sun and moon influenced the development of different religious beliefs in Neolithic and Bronze Age Britain and how these in turn were responsible for the development of a whole panoply of circular monuments, including mounds and enclosures, tombs and open-air temples, all of which were built over at least a two thousand year period.

Several times in the last chapter I mentioned Ireland's foremost prehistoric monuments, the passage graves known as Newgrange, Dowth and Knowth that were built more than five thousand years ago at a bend in the river Boyne, about forty kilometres north of Dublin. The most famous of these is undoubtedly Newgrange, which is visited every year by more than 250,000 people. Newgrange is simply enormous. It is a huge, roughly circular, man-made mound of stones, turf and earth with a flattened top. It is ringed all the way round by a line of massive kerbstones that are decorated with enigmatic engravings. And along the southeastern side is a curved wall of white quartz stones that sparkle in the morning sunshine.

The chambered cairn at Newgrange, Ireland

The diameter of the cairn measures 250 feet (78.6 m) northwest to southeast and 280 feet (85.3m) northeast to southwest, giving it a circumference of around 820 feet (250 m). Inside the huge mound is a long, narrow passageway, lined on the sides and roof with large slabs of stone, which leads into a large, high-roofed central chamber. This chamber is shaped like a cross and has three alcoves, each of which originally contained a large stone basin. These basins were probably used to hold the bodies or cremated remains of people during the different ceremonies and rituals performed inside the mound.

As I mentioned in the previous chapter, passages inside tombs have often been seen as fulfilling several completely different roles. The first was purely of a practical nature - the passage provided access deep inside the mound and was used for moving human remains in and out of the tomb. Secondly, the passage could be seen as a spirit pathway, a sort of sacred road that the soul of the dead person must follow on its journey to the 'Land of the Dead'. Thirdly, the long, stone-lined passage into the chamber is very reminiscent of the tunnels inside natural caves. So they are sometimes seen as being symbolically linked to the vagina and the womb of Mother Earth. And as everyone knows, the vagina has two functions. One is to allow the fertilisation of an egg to create new life and the other is to serve as the birth canal, to allow the exit of a fully-formed baby nine months later.

For many centuries the passage tomb was in very bad condition because the steep sides of the retaining wall surrounding the mound had collapsed. As a result, the entrance to the passageway was only discovered in 1699, when a local farmer carted away stones from the mound. Since that time there were several attempts at conservation and a few small digs, but until 1962 Newgrange had never undergone a major excavation. From then onwards, intensive investigations continued right through until 1975. Much of the cairn was restored during the restoration and conservation work that followed the excavating, and a concrete framework was set up to enclose and protect the passageway and inner chamber. The significance of the passageway became even more apparent when it was finally realised by the excavators in 1967 that it faces towards the southeast, and more specifically, towards the rising sun at the time of the winter solstice around the 21st of December.

In antiquity the passageway into Newgrange could be closed off with a heavy oblong stone door, which now rests against the wall alongside the entrance. Although the entrance faces towards the southeast, the passageway was built in such a way that when the midwinter sun rose over the hill opposite, its rays could not shine directly through the doorway and down into the chamber beyond. Instead, the builders created a special window higher up, above the doorway, formed from blocks of stone and now known as *'the roof-box'*. This window could be opened and closed at special times of the year, as scratches on the base showed when it was excavated by its discoverer, Professor Michael O'Kelly.

Even after excavation and restoration of the mound and the passageway, the window still works but unfortunately it now allows less light in than it did previously. Over the last five thousand years the upright stones lining the passageway near the chamber started to lean inwards due to the colossal weight of the mound above and two of the uprights were not fully straightened during the rest of the restorations in the 1970's. The passageway is thus not quite as wide or as straight as it once was. Even so, it still produces a truly awesome spectacle every midwinter as a powerful shaft of light streams in through the window and runs along the floor of the passage. It was originally more powerful than at present and as it moved around the chamber the stream of sunlight used to vividly light up the whole of the chamber, including the basin that was originally in the end chamber and the decorations on the walls of the recesses. In modern times the shaft of light starts quite thin, but then widens to about seven inches (17 cm), although previously it was about 40 cm. wide. As a result, the intensity of the lightshow is less than it was originally but it still brightly illuminates the passageway and the chamber. As the early morning sun moves round and rises higher in the sky, the band of light narrows and then disappears and darkness returns to the chamber, the whole spectacle taking just over quarter of an hour to run through its paces. And when you consider that this fantastic light show was orchestrated over five thousand years ago, and that it still works today, you have to start thinking about our ancestors with far more respect than we have traditionally shown towards them.

However, although these extraordinary events coincide with the midwinter solstice the timing was not very precise. Five thousand years ago the midwinter sun rose a bit later and slightly further to the south than it does today and so the passageway and chamber would have been illuminated each sunny morning for at least two weeks on either side of the solstice, although the most intense effect would have been seen at the solstice. So perhaps the intention was for the experience to last throughout the month and the complete sequence of funeral rites took one entire lunar cycle to enact. For the rest of the year, the sun rises earlier and further north each day, so by the time it arrives opposite the window it is too high in the sky for a beam of direct light to shine through the window and down the passageway. Or alternatively, and this is the explanation I prefer, the window was opened just once a year, on one very specific morning.

If you read the archaeological textbooks on Newgrange you will find page after page of descriptions of the site, details of its history, the method of excavation, the carved symbols of passage grave 'art' and the finds that have been made. There are usually detailed accounts of the original methods of construction and the subsequent reconstruction of the mound in the early 70's.

But amongst all these pages of facts and figures, there are few satisfactory answers to some of the most basic questions. Why did the ancient Irish choose that part of the Boyne Valley for the site? Why did they need to build such colossal cairns containing hundreds of thousands of tons of rocks, stones and turf? And why go to all the trouble of bringing special rocks from over forty kilometres away, rocks such as the white quartz from the Wicklow Mountains to the south and dark granite pebbles from the Mourne Mountains to the north? And the gleaming white band of quartz running only round the southeastern side of the mound must have signified something very special in addition to its obvious decorative qualities, but what did such an unusual façade signify?

The window above the entrance

So what did the spectacular winter lightshow represent? Surely there was much more to the cairn than just a tomb for important people? In short, what does it all mean?

Since 1969, the conventional explanation has been that the tomb was built with a passageway that was directed towards sunrise at the midwinter solstice because this particular time marked the turning point of the year. After the winter solstice people hoped that the days would get longer, the temperature would rise and life would go on as before, with spring just round the corner followed by the long, hot, sunny days of high summer and the ripening of their crops. Life for the Neolithic farmers and their families could only go on as before if the cycles of the sun and the moon continued as they always had done and so each year they would have celebrated important solar and lunar events, to ensure the continuation of the natural cycles and guarantee their own future.

However, although the orientation of the passage is indeed towards the rising sun at the midwinter solstice, in my opinion the real purpose and symbolism of Newgrange is different to the one most people have seen. As I've said before, the idea that the ancients were worried about whether or not the sun would return at the end of winter just doesn't seem right to me, it's too feeble an explanation for such a mammoth construction. I think that the ancient Irish were far more intelligent than that and that they knew as well as we do that the sun would return, and that spring and summer would come round again, just as it already had done for countless generations before. Furthermore, what is clear from their intensive building programme is that there must have been some very powerful motivation involved, a driving force that would make them go to all the trouble of carrying hundreds of thousands of tons of earth, rocks and stones on their backs to build the cairn.

The true meaning of sunrise or sunset alignments has rarely been fully appreciated within the scientific community because the ancient builders were far more concerned with symbolism and religious belief than with scientific niceties. And to understand the real symbolism involved it is necessary to recall a few basic facts about the apparent movements of the sun. The midwinter solstice marks the longest night and the shortest day of the year. It is the most important time in the whole solar cycle, yet it is the one that has created the most confusion in the minds of our experts, they often speak of 'sunrise at the winter solstice' or 'sunset at the winter solstice', without making any real distinction about what is involved in this part of the solar cycle. In reality, the complex ancient symbolism involved the death of the sun, at sunset on the last day of the year at Year's End, (now on 21st December), followed by the rebirth of the sun shortly after dawn on the following morning, at sunrise on New Year's Day, (22nd December). This is the start of a six-month journey for the sun to reach its most northerly rising position in the northeast, at the summer solstice, which is also the longest day of the year.

According to such ancient symbolism, the beginning of the year started with the rebirth of the sun, which took place shortly after dawn on New Year's Day. In Europe we now celebrate New Year's Day on the 1st of January, but this is a relatively modern idea, in previous centuries the New Year started at the spring equinox, at that time on the 25th of March, and in Britain it only changed to January 1st in 1752. However, five thousand years ago this was neither in January nor was it on the 21st of December. The midwinter solstice occurred later on in the calendar than it does today due to precession. It means that in 3000 BC the longest night of the year was on the 13th January and the longest day, the midsummer solstice, was not on the 21st of June as it is now, but took place on the 19th of July.

The increased tilt in the Earth's axis brought the northern hemisphere slightly closer to the sun in summer, giving Britain and Ireland much warmer summers than at present. The tilt of the axis was even more pronounced twelve thousand years ago and it probably led to the end of the last Ice Age. The latest estimate by some specialists suggest that the mile-thick layer of ice, which had covered northern and central Britain for nearly twenty thousand years, melted in less than sixty years. If true, that's serious climate change!

So the design and construction of the passageway and tomb at Newgrange were geared up to mark the start of a new solar cycle. However, I am certain that there was much, much more to it than just celebrating the rebirth of the sun and the start of a new year. The regenerative power of the sun was as self-evident to the ancient farmers as it is today; after all, the sun is responsible for giving us our light and heat and it is the energy derived from sunlight that creates and maintains all life on our planet. As winter gives way to spring the increasing intensity of the sun awakens and transforms a dormant world after its long winter sleep. Spring is a magical time of creation, birth and renewal. Nature is reborn. And this transformation of the world around them gave people the hope, and the belief, that their spirit would be reborn and they too could have a new life after their death.

The three main sites of Newgrange, Dowth and Knowth were built on a ridge above the north bank of the River Boyne and the mounds were effectively enclosed on three sides by a bend in the river. On the other side of the river the rising ground above the bank provides a natural horizon close by and the height of this knoll dictated the exact positioning of the passageway within the mound at Newgrange. This is because the time and place where the rising sun actually appears depends on the height of the local horizon. A higher elevation of the skyline delays the time of local sunrise and makes the sun rise later and further south than it would do if the land were flat, as it is in Norfolk. This means that long before construction work started they must have surveyed the site and set up a temporary arrangement of posts to mark exactly where the passageway would go and above all, where the window needed to be so that the lightshow could take place. Later on in the year the sun has risen earlier and is already too high in the sky when it is opposite the window, so there is no natural shaft of light that enters and runs down the passageway. At Knowth the main mound covers two passage tombs, back-to-back, with eighteen small tombs scattered around the main mound, giving nineteen in all, a significant lunar number. The two passageways inside the huge cairn were constructed so that one faced towards the rising sun in the east and the other was directed towards the setting sun in the west. This occurs twice a year, at the equinoxes that are usually on 21st March and 23rd September.

The spring equinox marks a time of equilibrium in the annual journey of the sun, it is not just the start of spring but also represents the midpoint between winter and summer. The autumn equinox highlights the midpoint between summer and winter. In addition, day and night are of equal length at the equinoxes, so to me the symbolism of the passages at Knowth suggests a halfway stage between life and death. Were the chambers temporary resting places for the spirits, before their on-going journey to a new life? A short walk to the east of Newgrange are the ruined remains of yet another huge burial mound, now known as Dowth. Here the midwinter sun lights up the interior of the main passage as its sets in the southwest. The theoretical symbolism inherent in this arrangement is that the midwinter sunset marks the end of the last day of the year, the death of the old sun. In reality the lighting effect is nowhere near as specific as at Newgrange, weather permitting, the setting sun continues to light up the interior of the chamber for about five months, from the beginning of October to the end of February. Nevertheless I think that the intent was largely symbolic in nature, a way of linking the dead with the end of the solar cycle and the death of the old sun.

Thanks to reconstruction of the tumbled ruins it is now easy to see that the finished cairn at Newgrange must have been a truly awesome sight as the white quartz sparkled in the sunshine and glinted by moonlight. However, it no longer looks the same as it did originally, because during the reconstruction of the mound in the early 1970's, the entrance was made much wider at the front, to allow easier access into the passageway for the 250,000 tourists who visit each year. This must be far more than the number of people who built the tombs over five thousand years ago. Yet even in Neolithic times the Boyne Valley was quite heavily populated, it was very fertile land and even today the river is still one of the best in Ireland for salmon fishing. The ancient myths and legends about Newgrange, or Brú na Bóinne as it was known, speak of a *'Place for the Gods'*, and the Brú, a palace or mansion, was that of Oengus (or Aonghus), the son of a pre-Celtic God, An Dagda Mór, who had sex with Boann (the River Boyne) the wife of another god, Elcmar.

It is particularly relevant that Oengus was said to have been conceived at the break of day and born by the end of that day. Over a great expanse of time Irish mythology produced many different (and sometimes conflicting) accounts of the owners and users of the mound, including supernatural beings and gods of the Tuatha Dé Danann, the Peoples of the Goddess Danu.

A more recent myth, dating probably from the late Iron Age, said that Newgrange was the traditional tomb of the kings who had ruled from Tara, a sacred hill fifteen kilometres across the river to the southwest. However, this is a bit unlikely since the Kings of Tara postdate the construction of Newgrange by well over two millennia. In addition, rivers were often the natural borders between neighbouring tribes and a passage grave known as 'the Mound of the Hostages' was already in use as a burial site at Tara at around the same time as the three main tombs of the Newgrange group were constructed across the river. When excavated, the Mound of the Hostages contained the cremated remains of over a hundred people. Furthermore, like Knowth, the tomb at the Mound of Hostages is aligned roughly east/west, so a completely different symbolism to the winter solstice sunrise alignment of Newgrange.

The real reasons for the construction of such an important ceremonial complex at the Bend of the Boyne must lie with fervent religious beliefs. This was coupled with very effective construction and man-management skills, the pride and desire to use the best stone for the job, the knowledge of where it could be found, the experience of how to transport it, the skill to use it effectively, and the experience and expertise of the designers to know what the final effect would look like, long before work on the project started. Some of these skills may have been learned and inherited through the construction of other burial mounds, perhaps from some of the passage graves at the hilltop sites of Loughcrew, a mere thirty kilometres to the west. The top of the mound at Newgrange was flat, not rounded like the tops of so many other large burial mounds, such as those nearby at Knowth and Dowth, or Bryn Celli Dhu in Anglesey, North Wales and Maes Howe in Orkney.

The mound at Newgrange was very special. Not only was it flat-topped it had a sparklingly white southeastern side, the side facing towards the rising sun at midwinter.

> So in other words, **a big round thing that is lit up by the sun on just one side.**

Hmmm! I wonder what that could possibly be? Well, the answer should have been obvious, because it's been staring every visitor in the face since 1975…

When it was originally constructed the passage opened outwards through just a narrow doorway in the wall, which was made from a band of white quartz stones interspersed with granite boulders. But this façade was limited to just the southeastern side of the mound, and if you think about it, this curved white shape resembles something that can be seen in the sky every month.
The crescent of a new moon.

So the flat-topped, circular mound we know as Newgrange was actually built as a representation of the moon at one particular phase and the southeastern façade was deliberately decorated with white quartz to make it resemble the appearance of the moon at the start of each new lunar cycle.
As above, so below.

But can we be really certain that the intention was to represent a new moon and not the full moon?

As I mentioned in the previous chapter, the sun and the new moon rise in a similar location throughout the year but the full moon rises and sets in the opposite direction to the sun. So in winter, when the sun rises in the southeast, the full moon sets in the northwest and when the sun sets in the southwest, the full moon rises in the northeast. When the summer sun sets in the northwest, the full moon rises in the southeast.

So in other words, the full moon can only rise in the southeast in summer, never in winter. Therefore at the time of the winter solstice the circular mound of Newgrange can only represent a new moon, not the full moon.

Furthermore all of this is yet another reference to the annual cycles of the heavens above and the Earth below. The logic behind this philosophy was accurate and simple because it is exactly what happens when Nature is reborn each spring. As the new season advances, the returning sun warms the land and increasingly more powerful solar rays cause seemingly inert seeds to germinate, then the new shoots grow into plants and fresh new grass is ready to nourish the mothers of the new-born lambs and calves. For the Neolithic farmers the sun ensured that the natural world was reborn after the long sleep and little death of winter, and in turn this rebirth of nature ensured their own survival. At a time when people rarely lived past fifty, death would have seemed a lot less frightening if they believed that it was just the next step on their long journey towards eternal life.

Newgrange was all about renewal. A new dawn on a new day at the start of a new year by a new sun, which also heralded the start of a new lunar cycle with a new moon. So it is very apt, although purely coincidental, that the modern name for the ancient temple and tomb is Newgrange. In addition to this complex symbolism there is another compelling message inherent in the internal structure of the mound. I don't think that Newgrange was built as a permanent tomb for the skeletal remains of the dead, nor was it some form of *'House of the Gods'*. Instead i think that the mound was designed as a huge replica of the Moon and it was constructed with a vagina-like tunnel leading down into a chamber that was like an artificial womb. Shortly after dawn, on the first morning after the longest night of the year, at sunrise on New Year's Day in the Neolithic calendar, a beam of sunlight entered the mound through the open window. This shaft of light penetrating the passageway and reaching into the chamber is a powerful image, very reminiscent of the sex act. The shaft of light was like the mysterious, life-giving power that entered a woman's body during sex and created a baby inside her womb. And so I think that the spectacle was intended not just as a fantastic light show but also as a symbolic reference to the sex act and the creation of new life. The powerful beam of sunlight lit up the basins containing the bones and cremated remains of those who had died. To the ancient priests, and their congregations, dawn after the winter solstice was the turning point of the year. The sun was reborn and it was only at this very special moment that the highly potent energy of a new sun could revitalise the diminished life force of the dead. So in other words, they constructed Newgrange as a magical powerhouse, one with the awesome ability to help the spirits of the dead be reborn and pass onwards to the next level of existence, a new life in a new world.

And so I think that you will agree that the mystery has now been solved and that mine is a far more likely explanation for the massive construction, rather than just a simple hope that the sun would return at the turning point of the year.

We will probably never know the details of the ceremonies and rituals that were performed to mark this special occasion, but it is very likely that there were hymns of praise, and music and dancing, drinking and feasting. And it would be too coy not to expect that sex was part of the festivities of such an important festival, particularly one involving a 'Marriage of the Gods', the coming together of the sun and the moon. The winter solstice sunset marked the end of the year, and then the sun and the moon were reborn, which in turn caused the creation of life in the natural world and the rebirth of the spirits of the dead. **As above, so below.**

Many visitors have said that the reconstructed mound looks too modern to be true, but of course we are used to seeing our ancient monuments in ruins and not how they would have looked when they were first built. During the reconstruction, a retaining wall of building blocks was constructed and in front of this the wall of quartz blocks was cemented in place, so some experts have questioned the abilities of the original builders to produce a wall strong enough to retain the huge amount of earth and stone behind it. However, they had been clever stonemasons for many generations and by the time the huge cairns in the Boyne valley were built, strong drystone walls had been used for centuries to protect crops and give shelter from the wind, rain and snow for their livestock.

Tall drystone walls were used to ring other burial mounds, such as those at Loughcrew megalithic cemetery, which is only a few hours walk to the west. Although the modern wall is probably much steeper than the original one, there would have been no need for mortar in the old wall because the stones would have been very skilfully laid to interlock with each other. Further support of the mound of loose stones was obtained from layers of turf that acted as binding material and as a result the wall managed to retain the enormous weight of the mound for several centuries, until it finally gave way, perhaps when the soil became saturated after some prolonged spring rainstorms.

An alternative suggestion to a retaining wall was that the quartz blocks had been laid out flat on the ground in front of the kerbstones, to form a special path, but this was also shown to be wrong by Professor O'Kelly when an experimental wall was built, and then pushed over. The tumbled quartz blocks formed a similar distribution pattern to the one that excavation had revealed. Another interlocking technique of dry stone masonry, known as corbelling, was used inside the mound to build the six-metre high roof above the main chamber. Each new layer of slabs was carefully set a little bit further inwards than the previous layer, so that the overlapping layers of slabs closed in on themselves the higher they rose. The weight of the stones above stabilised the whole structure until just one large capstone was needed to cover the hole in the middle.

The top of the original mound at Newgrange was special in two ways. Firstly, it showed everyone that it referred to the moon rather than the sun. Secondly, the flat-topped mound referred to the New Moon at the start of the lunar cycle, like a woman with a flat belly before she becomes pregnant. The moon and the pregnant woman then become round and full, although for humans it takes nine moons (months) to complete the process of procreation and for a new generation to be born.

So to summarise, the mound we know as Newgrange was originally designed to represent the moon. The decorated white façade at the front was intended to represent the crescent-shaped part of the moon lit by the sun at New Moon. The replica of the body of the moon contained a womb-like chamber linked to the outside by a passageway, representing her vagina. This passage was orientated towards the southeast, towards where the sun would rise around the time of the winter solstice. And at dawn on the first morning of the Neolithic New Year, the light of the reborn sun penetrated into her body, lighting up the remains of those who had died, breathing new life into them, working in a similar way as it would do for the natural world over the coming days and weeks as spring approached. So the passage grave tomb at Newgrange encapsulated the following beginnings: new sun, new moon, new dawn, new day, new month and new year, in other words, all the stages leading up to a new life in the next world. But this isn't the whole story, as we shall see further on.

The kerbstone K1, in front of the entrance.

The story that Newgrange was built as the dwelling place of the all-powerful god Elcmar, and then Oengus, the son of An Dagda, looks even less likely now. The Good God, An Dagda was masculine and a sun god who was said to have mated with Boann, the river goddess. So were the annual rebirth of the sun and the creation of a new moon represented by an allegorical story about a union of the gods? Throughout history and across the globe, the moon has often been referred to as feminine and a goddess, so is it just a coincidence that the mound at Newgrange is a solar and lunar site, or was this just a way of explaining something that was already very ancient by the time the Tuatha Dé Danann appeared on the scene?

The round, grey, granite stones that were used in the white quartz façade may well have formed a spectacular series of designs or symbols, perhaps similar to those on the decorated kerbstones and the orthostats, the large stone uprights, that form the walls of the tomb and its passageway. However, the original design of the facade is probably lost forever, since over the centuries the mound held back by the dry stone walling bulged outwards and caused it to collapse in heaps, flowing over the kerbstones.

Nevertheless, thanks to a partial reconstruction of the mound some of the most dramatic decoration can still be seen on the kerbstones surrounding the perimeter and the most famous of all is K1, a spectacular stone in front of the entrance. This large oval boulder is richly decorated with swirling patterns chiselled out of the rock. The most dramatic of them is a figure of three interlinked spirals on the left side, although there are also other spirals, wavy lines, and sets of lozenges carved into the stone. The triple spiral motif is also repeated inside the tomb in a very prominent place within the chamber, as a smaller version on a wall in the end recess, on stone C10. The spiral is quite a common symbol at Newgrange, sometimes it occurs as single, other times as double or triple spirals and once even four spirals at a time, two small and two large ones on stone L19 in the passageway.

So what did the triple spiral symbol represent?
Could it have meant three days, three months or three years? Or did it represent a trinity of gods?

None of these meanings feels 'right' - they're all too vague and can't easily explain the other types of spiral designs. And so for decades people have remained unsure or have simply given up trying to decipher this key symbol of what archaeologists call 'passage grave art'. But in my opinion the answer to this enigma is surprisingly simple, as is the meaning of most symbols - **once you know the answer!**

As winter changes into spring, the sun rises each day from a different point along the eastern horizon, it travels round the southern part of the sky, reaches its highest point at noon, then as evening approaches, it sinks below the western horizon at sunset. During the night it travels onwards, to reappear the following morning on the horizon at a similar place as the previous day. As the weather gets warmer the sun rises slightly earlier each day and the point of sunrise moves a bit further north along the horizon. The path followed by the sun increases in height and length as the days go by, until by midsummer the sun seems to rise at the same point for several days, and this is known as the solstice. It is the longest day of the year and it embodies a time of harmony and equilibrium, since it represents the midpoint of the solar year and is also the midpoint between spring and autumn. So not surprisingly the warm days near the summer solstice have traditionally been a time for festivals, parties and special celebrations.

After the summer solstice, the sun rises a few minutes later and a bit further south each morning then at the end of the day it sets a little further south than the day before. As the days progress the curved path of the sun decreases in amplitude. A good way to think of all this is to imagine the sun leaving a trail behind it in the sky and that this trail winds up like a ball of string, getting fatter and fatter as the days get warmer, as winter changes to spring and spring becomes summer. After the summer solstice, the sun no longer rises so high in the sky and the days shorten, in effect the ball of string unwinds again as summer changes to autumn and winter.

In other words, the sun seems to spiral across the sky as the seasons change, growing bigger as the days get longer, and smaller as the days get shorter and colder. So I think it is must be fairly obvious from this that a spiral meant 'a season'. And therefore three spirals together meant three seasons, and since each season lasts three months, three spirals must mean nine months. Furthermore, as everyone knows, nine months is the human gestation period, the length of time it takes for a woman to produce new life and for her baby to be born.

In other words, **the triple spiral was the symbol for 'LIFE'.**

Using a triple spiral to symbolise life, rebirth or eternal life was an intelligent and elegant way of communicating quite a difficult concept. I have done it by writing a word that you recognise, but if I had to do it by using a graphic image it becomes a great deal harder to come up with a symbol or a picture that would do the job as easily and as well as the triple spiral. (In recent years the symbol has been adopted to represent ancient Celtic themes of spirituality.)

In Ancient Egypt the symbol for life was 'the ankh', an oval on top of a cross and many murals show images of Pharaohs holding this key-shaped symbol. The life of the nation was literally in their hands. I also think there was a secondary meaning to the triple spiral symbol, this time as a reference to the Past, the Present and the Future; but even this concept still refers to Life, for we are born in the past, live in the present, and we will all die sometime in the future. Birth, Life and Death. Past, Present and Future.

On other side of the huge mound, opposite the entrance kerbstone K1 with its triple spiral motif, is another very distinctive and highly decorated kerbstone, K52. This stone is positioned at the north-west, the direction symbolically linked to the shortest night of the year, Mid Summer's Eve. And again I find it simply astonishing that no one seems to be able see what it represents and then understand the significance of this stone.

overleaf, kerbstone K52

Although the carvings are now somewhat faded, (the photo has been greatly intensified), to my eyes kerbstone 52 is clearly a sculpture of some sort of symbolic bird, with its head and hooked beak on the right and its wing folded up on the left. At some point later on its history, the surface of the bird was covered in images and symbols that relate to the cycles of the sun and the moon, the four seasons and other sacred topics.

Birds are quite common themes in ancient mythology, probably because, unlike most other animals, they can fly and also because of the strange way certain species, such as swifts, swallows and cuckoos, disappear in autumn but return in spring, whilst some species of birds such as ducks, swans and geese do the exact opposite, they breed in the arctic and just spend the winter here. As the days get shorter, the sun also migrates south, returning northwards after the winter solstice. And although I seriously doubt there is any direct connection, there was a creation myth in Ancient Egypt that dates from before the time of the first Dynasty of Pharaohs, which involved the waters of the Nile and a mound called the benben. Living on the mound was the bennu bird, the mythological phoenix, a bird that was said to embody the soul of the sun god Ra and which arose reborn from the ashes of its own funeral pyre. And there are many other myths and legends about birds in just about every country in the world.

A postcard of this kerbstone, taken in different lighting conditions, shows a sculpture that represents the left side of the torso of a bearded man lying on his back, with his left arm at his side. This statue would have originally stood upright but the stone was then reused and his face and body were covered over by the engravings.

At bottom right on stone 52 is a strange face with a bulbous nose and at the top left corner of the bird sculpture is the weathered face of another creature, perhaps a sheep. I think that originally the whole stone had many other carved images on it as well, before they were covered over by the spirals, diamonds, ovals and circles that were added at a later stage. Amongst these are several sets of ovals and the two main ones each are formed from a double line enclosing three dots with a mass of loops around them. The U-shaped hoops remind me of the way that the sun and moon move from their rising positions all the way round the sky to their setting positions.

These hoops also make me think of rainbows, the fantastic coloured lightshows provided by sunlight and water. But since a spiral represents a season each of these ovals must represent something else. Each dot suggests a lunation, so perhaps an oval with three dots in it represents three months, a quarter of the year, the time between a solstice and an equinox rather than the three months in each season. The dot is a very common old Irish symbol. They are usually called cup marks and are made by grinding a circular depression in the surface of standing stones, the walls of tombs and even on natural rock surfaces. They are also very common in northwestern Scotland and northern England, and are most likely to represent the moon. Another type of cup mark has a circle around it, so these cup and ring marks are likely to be solar symbols, the ring representing the corona around the sun.

The diamond shape was another important Neolithic symbol. Together with triangles, which are half the shape, they occur on a number of stones in different ways. There are sets of diamonds that form a network of lines on the lower left side of K52 that resemble netting, whilst on the entrance stone K1 there are nests of diamonds on both left and right sides. The diamond (or lozenge) symbol has a very long history and remained a motif for many thousands of years. It is famously represented on a marvellous gold plaque dating from the late Bronze Age that was found at Bush Barrow, near Stonehenge. Diamond and motifs were also commonly used on Beaker pottery. But what did it represent? Perhaps the diamond represented the cardinal directions of the compass, not as a cross as we represent it, but by using diagonal lines to join up the cardinal points, from north to east, east to south, south to west and west to north.

However, rather than it representing the world, I am more inclined to think that a diamond shape represents a day, or rather, a day and a night. At the equinoxes, day and night are of equal length and a diamond shape can be formed from two triangles joined together. The angle at the top of the diamond marked midnight, the right corner was sunrise, the bottom was midday and the left corner represented sunset. This style of decoration is on several stones, including RS17, the last roof slab above the passage, next to the main chamber inside. The bottom row of four triangles is pecked into the surface, whilst the top row is formed from triangles that were left clear.

Another highly decorated kerbstone is K67, which is in the northeastern sector. This is a sculpture of quite a strange animal in left profile, it has a chunky body, broad head and hardly any neck and its mouth is on the far left. Things change over time and stones such as K52 and K67 show that earlier decorated images of people were sometimes covered over by host of new carvings and engravings, particularly by spirals, circles, lozenges and wavy lines. Over time the newer images have eroded and the older ones show through, making a rather blurred mixture in modern times.

Kerbstone number 67

Several of the small triangles on the left side were done on top of older pictures of bearded men's faces in left profile and each of them is wearing a conical hat or hood. There are two large interlocking spirals on K67, one flowing into the other and possibly symbolising the change from day into night and back again, or more likely, the transformation of the natural world as spring slowly changes into autumn, and autumn becomes spring. **Life/death, death/life.**

Above and below the join between the two spirals are two diamonds, one on each side, both have a wavy line in the centre, and although the top one is a single diamond shape, the bottom one is a double diamond, one diamond inside another. The half-way point between the spring and autumn equinox is the summer solstice and six months after that, mid-way between the autumn and spring equinox, comes the winter solstice. So it seems to me that a triangle with a central wavy line represents a special day, the summer solstice, and consequently a double diamond, again with the wavy line in the centre, represents the winter solstice. Ordinary diamonds represent ordinary days.

The main triple spiral on the entrance stone K1 is formed from one large spiral joined to two smaller ones of equal size, or in other words, the symbols for summer, spring and autumn. Nine months, the warmest months of the year when the natural world is most alive. (A small spiral would have represented winter.) There are other groups of spirals at Newgrange. A large spiral linked to a small one, such as the ones on C4, the northwestern sidewall of the southwestern recess, must refer to summer/ winter and life/death. So in effect, the priests and artisans were labelling special places and special stones with special information. And the power of the sacred knowledge would last forever, because it was written in stone…

To return to K1, the entrance stone at Newgrange, I noticed that in comparison with the other rough kerbstones nearby, this stone is smooth and quite an unusual ovoid shape. Its very distinctive shape makes me think of a seed of wheat or barley. When planted the seed germinates to become a shoot that ripens to become a head of new seeds. K1 also resembles a bird's egg, which hatches into a chick, which becomes an adult bird that can lay another egg. In addition, the elaborate decoration on the surface makes the oval stone resemble the cocoon of a butterfly. This is just one stage in the life cycle of butterflies and moths. The technical term for the extraordinary changes that happen during their brief lives is metamorphosis. A small egg hatches, becomes a caterpillar, which eats voraciously and grows to its full size, and then this turns into a chrysalis or pupa, which in turn transforms itself into a beautiful winged insect. The changes are simply astonishing to watch, each new form is completely different from the previous form and it must have been a source of wonder to children and adults alike, just as it is today.

K1 must therefore have been used to illustrate these forms in a symbolic way and perhaps it illustrated how much we change in our journey from helpless baby to mature adult. And perhaps this stone was a monument to the way they thought another sort of metamorphosis took place, when the body of a dead person gave up its soul and the spirit was reborn, leaving behind just the husk of the body.

With regards to the rest of the decoration on the entrance stone, two sets of wavy lines erupt upwards at the centre of the underside, and then spread out to left and right. And I think that, although one wavy line usually represents a river, this group of wavy lines symbolise the birth waters that herald a new life. On the left side they support the large triple spiral, the ancient symbol for 'Life'. To the right, the flowing lines change into a row of several inverted V's, like waves. And so I think that this part is a representation of the way that the River Boyne flows downstream and joins the Irish Sea. When the mound was excavated very few human remains were found, even though there had been a very large population in the area. So after the spirits of the dead were re-animated, was the final part of the ceremony to cast the cremated remains into the river, perhaps to wash away the sins of their previous owners?

We have already seen how the triple spiral symbol represented Life, but there are two additional spirals on the right side of K1, one larger than the other, and both spirals wind up and down in the opposite direction to the others. The symbol indicating the seasonal change from winter to spring would become larger and spiral outwards because the path that the sun travels increases from day to day, whilst a spiral symbolising the seasonal change from autumn to winter would wind inwards as the days get shorter. However, the seasons do not follow the solar cycle exactly. Due to the warming effect of the Gulf Stream, the midpoint of the cold season is not on the same day as the winter solstice, and in the same way our hottest days of summer are usually in July, several weeks after the summer solstice. So I think that although they may have used the climate and the seasons for some symbols, and they also divided the religious year into the four quarters of the solar cycle. The first quarter of the Neolithic New Year would have been from the winter solstice to the spring equinox, (22nd December to 21st March). The second quarter would last from the spring equinox to the summer solstice (22nd March to 21st June), the third quarter would be from the summer solstice to the autumn equinox (22nd June to 23rd September) and the last quarter would be from the autumn equinox to the winter solstice (24th September to 21st December). The logic behind this new idea is that it echoes the cycle of the major phases of the moon: first quarter, second quarter, third quarter and fourth quarter. Or as I prefer it: First half-moon, full moon, second half-moon, and dark moon.

One way to identify the different types of spirals is by making fists. Starting with a left fist, and the tip of the thumb, a left hand spiral curls up sunwise (clockwise), diminishing in size, as the days get shorter. Then starting at the centre of the right fist, a right hand spiral uncurls sunwise, increasing in size, as the days get longer. However, the spirals on K1 and K52 are not actually made up of single lines; instead they are doubled up, like a doubled-up length of string that is coiled in on itself. Perhaps this was to show that both sun and moon followed much the same path, and that their movements between their rising and setting positions wound up and down with time, moving from southeast to northeast and from the southwest to the northwest and back again.

K1 and K52 have far more elegant lines than the simple, single coiled spirals that are present on most of the other stones. So this seems to indicate that K1 and K52 were carved later, after the cairn was finished. The triple spiral inside the chamber on stone C10 is an intermediate example between the two different styles. It was originally two spirals, both made from doubled-up coils, with a slightly smaller spiral above a larger one, and with the lines flowing into each other, imitating the way that spring becomes summer and summer changes to autumn. Later on a third spiral was added on the left, to change the meaning of the symbol to 'Life' and it works well enough, although the new lines don't quite fit the others.

So to recap: The decorations on the entrance stone, K1, refer to the creation of life and its transitions and transformations through time. At the bottom of the stone the flowing movements of the river indicate the birth waters of a new life. And the stone itself symbolises several transformations, including those of an egg that will hatch, a dry seed that will germinate, and the changes that occur as a baby grows from child to adult, then dies, releasing the life force to pass on to the next level of our existence.

One of the enduring matters of debate concerning the decoration at Newgrange is whether some of the stones had been reused and came from another source, such as older tomb nearby. This debate started when decoration was found on the hidden sides and faces of some of the megaliths used for certain kerbstones (K13, K18 etc.) as well as on some of the uprights of the passageway and chamber. The opinion of the excavator Michael O'Kelly still carries a lot of weight; he thought that the artwork had been deliberately hidden, never to be seen by living human eyes. Many of the decorations had been pecked into the surface before the stones were placed in their final position but in some places it was clear that the engraving had been performed after they were in place because it stops at ground level. However, it should have been clear to everyone that the quality of workmanship and the style of the symbols and artwork on the hidden surfaces, such as wavy lines, concentric circles, sun symbols and spirals, is very much simpler than that used on highly decorated stones like K1, K52 and K67. We know from our own recorded history, and our own personal experiences, that people can't resist 'improving' things. As I have already pointed out, certain kerbstones were reused and redecorated and so the idea that the enormous passage grave was only built from new materials is unlikely. This idea is reinforced because the tops of some of the uprights that line the passageway have been squared off, whilst others have angled or even rounded shapes, so it becomes clear to me that many of these stones came from an earlier tomb or more likely, a stone circle.

So this revelation shows that it has always been human nature to rob earlier buildings for sources of good stone and that these stones are a five thousand-year old example of architectural reclamation! This also explains why the backs of some of the stones are decorated, even though the decorations would have been invisible once the cairn was finished. The spiral is also present at another huge passage grave a short distance to the west of Newgrange, inside the burial mound known as Knowth. This enormous cairn contains two long passages; one ends in a cross-shaped chamber (like Newgrange), with the passage directed outwards towards the east and the other just ends in a rectangular chamber, with its passage leading out towards the west. Each of the passages contains a profusion of symbols carved into the uprights of the passages and chambers. And there are over three hundred carved stones at Knowth. The symbols are usually referred to as megalithic or passage grave art, although to my mind these simple symbols and decorative motifs are more likely to represent concepts and ideas about astrological, astronomical and religious beliefs, rather than being true works of art.

The burial mounds of Newgrange, Dowth and Knowth are the most important of many burial mounds in this bend in the River Boyne, however many other small passage graves were erected in the vicinity. Over the following centuries eighteen much smaller passage graves were built around the main mound at Knowth. (Like a mother goose and her goslings.) And it seems to me that the different symbolic architecture inherent in the directions of the passageways at Knowth, Dowth and Newgrange was interlinked. East and west, southwest and southeast. Rays of light symbolically linked each of the three different passageways to one of the following themes: the equilibrium between life and death, the death of the old sun, and the birth of a new sun. And the intention was also to mark the corresponding phase of the lunar cycle, full moon, dark moon or new moon.

Originally each of the tombs contained stone basins holding the remains of the dead. It therefore seems likely to me that complex rituals would have been performed, moving the bodily remains between the different places, re-enacting the everlasting annual cycle of life, death, and rebirth of the sun and the monthly cycle of the moon. At Newgrange for example, the skeletal or cremated remains could have just been moved from basin to basin round the three side chambers in the chamber. The cross-shaped arrangement of three alcoves is usually referred to as the west, north and east recesses of the main chamber. But this is far from ideal, O'Kelly ignored the fact that the three side-chambers are actually towards the southwest, northwest and northeast, and as we have already seen, these directions had very important astronomical significance and powerful religious meaning. These compass directions represent important evidence and they may shine new light on the symbolical meaning of the decoration of the stones in each recess. It seems to me that the three side chambers had references to the birth, life and death cycle and perhaps the priests moved the bones of the departed from chamber to chamber in a ritualised sequence, magically lit up by powerful sunbeams at the start of a new solar cycle. Perhaps in an even longer ritualised sequence the human remains were stored in Knowth, moved from the west chamber (sunset and death) to the east chamber (sunrise and rebirth) and then after a time they were moved onwards to the southwest chamber at Dowth, and from there to Newgrange. Perhaps in this very elaborate sequence, retracing the cycles of the sun and the moon, the spirits of the dead were reborn and could then move on to a new existence in the next world.

Running along the edge of the lintel above the window at Newgrange is a series of eight carvings of X's, each one inside an oblong box. This suggests to me that they may represent the two solstices, the two equinoxes plus the four cross-quarter days, the days that lie halfway between a solstice and equinox. In other words, one complete solar cycle (a year). However, I also noticed that a photograph taken at the time of excavation in the 1960's shows that the far left side of the lintel is broken off and that perhaps there had originally been nine X's in a row, each one representing a month, another reference to human reproduction and 'Life'. The lintel needs to be re-examined, to see whether there were indeed eight or nine X's and whether the notation refers to the solstices, equinoxes and quarter days, or the nine months (moons) of a new life.

Ancient symbols occur on over 75 stones at Newgrange and over 300 at Knowth. The range of sacred symbols that was used will probably have included many astronomical themes of the sun and moon and perhaps the visible planets, particularly Venus and Mars. They await further decryption but many must refer to quite simple ideas, such as the ones I have outlined above. Some of these other early symbols are quite obvious. A circle with rays coming from its circumference must refer to the sun and a small sun symbol probably refers to winter whilst a large one represents summer. Simple circles represent the moon. They probably also made distinctions between important rising and setting times and positions. Further research should help us get an even better understanding of the symbols used in Irish passage graves, revealing even more about their cosmology and religious beliefs.

The main mound at Knowth, with its encircling wall of kerbstones

Although the Bend in the Boyne was a very important Neolithic religious centre in Ireland, it was far from unique. Even earlier burial sites are known. There is a very large megalithic cemetery at Carrowmore, close to the northwest coast of Ireland, near the town of Sligo. At Carrowmore there are a large variety of different styles of funerary monuments, which reveal changes in belief systems that took place over more than a thousand years and some of the burial sites are much older than the tombs along the banks of the Boyne or those on the hills of Loughcrew, twenty miles to the west of Newgrange. At Loughcrew the Neolithic farmers built several huge cairns of stones right on the peaks of three prominent hills, collectively known as Slieve na Calliagh, (the Mountain of the Witch). The best known of these burial mounds is Cairn T at Carnbane East, where the passageway was directed towards the equinox sunrise. There was originally a quartz revetment around the mound but most of the white stones have disappeared. This suggests that the mound represented the moon and was another place where the rebirthing process could take place. So the cairn was probably a precursor to the more complex design of Newgrange. Another large tomb, Cairn L, was built on a neighbouring hill at Carnbane West and there the sun lit up the decorated passageway at Samhain, the cross-quarter day that is half way between the autumn equinox and the winter solstice.

4 SYMBOLS OF POWER, SYMBOLS OF STONE

In earlier chapters I wrote at great length about the way our Neolithic and Bronze Age ancestors used symbols and symbolism in place of a written language. I have also shown that instead of using writing to communicate information to future generations, they developed specially shaped structures to convey the meaning and purpose of their buildings. At special places, such as at Newgrange in Ireland, they built circular mounds to symbolise the moon and many stone circles, particularly those in Aberdeenshire in northeast Scotland, were predominantly lunar sites.

It is also likely that a few sites were specially built to commemorate and worship the planets Mars and Venus, whilst others may have been constructed to represent constellations such as Orion - the Hunter; Ursa Major - the Great Bear or particularly prominent groups of stars such as the Pleiades - the Seven Sisters. However, the vast majority of circular monuments represented the sun, the moon, or the sun and the moon, commemorating the way that they influenced everything that happened on planet Earth. And with references to the cycles of the heavens above and the life cycles of the natural world below, the circular monuments often encapsulated in stone **'the Circle of Life'**, and its everlasting pattern of Birth, Life and Death, followed by Rebirth and the start of the next cycle.

Sometimes it is blatantly obvious that a structure referred to death, the sun, and the hope of rebirth. At a circular Bronze Age earth mound near North Mains, Strathallan, in Perth and Kinross the initial phase of construction involved the erection of a circular, wooden-fenced, central enclosure, with lines of timber fences radiating outwards. The next stage of construction involved filling up the partitions with soil, but leaving a passageway into the central enclosure that was still open to the sky. Corpses were placed in the central area and then the whole thing was covered over with earth. From the outside the overall effect was a fairly typical-looking round barrow, a round-topped mound of earth surrounded by a circular ditch, but hidden inside the round barrow the wooden fences formed a symbol of the sun. And a circle with radiating spokes was a common symbol of Irish passage grave 'art' and five thousand years later, we still use this symbol to represent the sun…

In addition to the symbolical nature of the design of ancient structures, I have also discovered that the actual stones that were used were sometimes symbols in their own right. For example, contained within the Christian cemetery at Midmar Kirk in Aberdeenshire, is a much earlier Neolithic stone circle. The recumbent altar stone is flanked on either side by thin, curved stones, which are symbolic images of the crescent moon.

Midmar Kirk, Aberdeenshire

Looking from inside the circle, the one on the right side of the altar referred to the new moon, whilst the C-shaped one on the left referred to the old moon.

Scattered across the British Isles are the remains of well over a thousand open-air temples, the famous and mysterious stone circles, which are compelling physical evidence of prehistoric religious beliefs. They have been studied for more than three centuries and some of our experts have been measuring, analysing and excavating these circles for thirty years or more, yet amazingly no one seems to have noticed some things that are remarkably obvious, once you really look.

The first of this unnoticed information is as follows: Although many megaliths (big stones) appear to be natural boulders, and have fairly natural-looking shapes, some are very different. They have been specially carved into distinctive shapes. Furthermore, these specially shaped stones are in the form of geometric shapes derived from combinations, or parts of, such basic shapes as squares, rectangles, ovals, circles and triangles. When I travelled around Great Britain and Ireland I started to notice that the same geometrical shapes of stones are present at different sites.

This is such an important concept that I shall repeat it, *"the same geometrical shapes of stones are present at different sites"*. And secondly, in view of all the studies that have been conducted, it is simply astonishing that no one seems to have appreciated that there is a connection between the shape of certain stones and their position around the circumference of the rings. And thirdly, whilst many stones on the eastern side of stone circles and rings have upwardly slanting tops, on the western side there are many stones with tops that slope downwards.

So what is the significance of these three revolutionary observations?

As the seasons change from winter to summer and from summer to winter, the sun rises at different times and different places along the eastern horizon. It travels round the sky and descends to set somewhere along the western horizon and the exact rising and setting points vary according to the time of year. The position where the sun rises is always in a broad arc between the southeast in winter and the northeast in summer, and then it sets at another point within another arc, between the southwest in winter and the northwest in summer. The moon behaves in a similar fashion, although it rises and sets in longer or shorter arcs according to the different lunar cycles. Our ancestors noticed this and decided to permanently record these important astronomical events and they did this by erecting special marker stones to map out the key rising and setting positions of the sun and the moon at different points in their respective cycles.

As a result, the significance of the sloping tops on the stones then becomes more obvious. Certain stones on the eastern side must refer to different rising positions of the sun or the moon because their tops slope upwards, from left to right. And on the western side, other specially shaped stones must refer to setting positions because their tops slope downwards. On closer investigation I found that in many cases the angle of slope on top of the stones varies according to the position of the stone, and that this angle mimics the height of the sun or moon according to the time of year. For example, when the sun is high in the sky during the summer, the angle of the sloping top is acute and when the sun is low in the sky, during the cold months of the year, the angle of slope along the top of the stone is much flatter.

There are also differences in the width and height of stones and some have angled, straight or curved sides. These refinements were often used to denote that the stone marked a particular moment in the annual solar cycle or else one of the positions of the lunar swing cycle.

It seems such an obvious thing, so incredibly simple, so very basic, yet it's true, **until now** no one seems to have noticed that there are relationships between the shape and the position of some of the stones. If these special shapes had been in the form of strange letters or signs, they would have been spotted much earlier on, and the relationship between the different symbolic shapes and their position around the circumference of the circle would have been worked out long ago. Yet even as early as 1930 it was recorded that some of the stones in the West Kennet Avenue at Avebury were oblong shapes, whilst other stones opposite them were rounded or lozenge shapes. And since then it has always been assumed that such shapes simply refer to male and female, and that the paired stones were just part of some unknown fertility cult. However, although this pairing may be true in some situations, it cannot explain the huge variety of different geometrical shapes that exist at sites across the country. Although our experts have spent a great deal of time mapping and measuring stone circles, examining the geology of the stones, excavating the ground in and around the rings, checking out astronomical alignments and recording the local folklore, the basic question of why there were so many different types and shapes of stones has been totally ignored.

Archaeologist and scholar Aubrey Burl is considered to be one of Britain's foremost authorities on megalithic Britain and he has been visiting and studying stone circles for more than forty years. He mentions many specially shaped stones in his influential books such as *'The Stone Circles of the British Isles'* and *'A Guide to the Stone Circles of Britain, Ireland and Brittany'*. These include triangular stones, rounded stones, rudder-shaped stones, peaked, rounded or flat-topped stones, rectangular 'playing card' shapes, upside down stones, guillotine shapes, tall and short stones etc. Yet despite all his hard work, he managed to miss the special relationship between the shape, position and meaning of certain stones. And all our experts seem to have forgotten that in the mythology of many cultures, the sun was considered to be masculine and the moon feminine.

The origin of the symbol stones

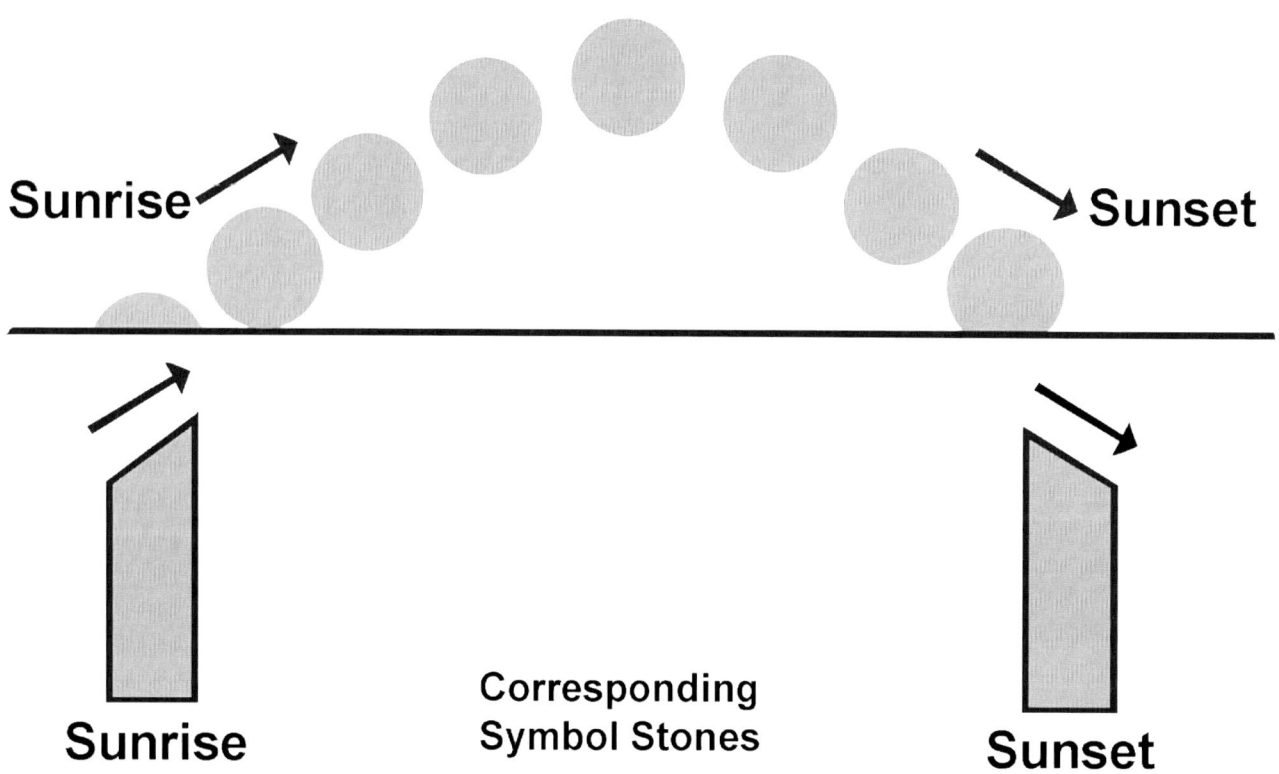

So the connection between shape and symbolism should have been obvious, the phallic-shaped columns and oblongs are sunstones and the more rounded stones are moonstones. ***It's that simple.***

In this way oblong shaped stones were often used to mark the direction of the rising or setting sun at specific times of the year, whilst other more rounded shapes would indicate the rising and setting positions of the moon during its various phases and cycles.

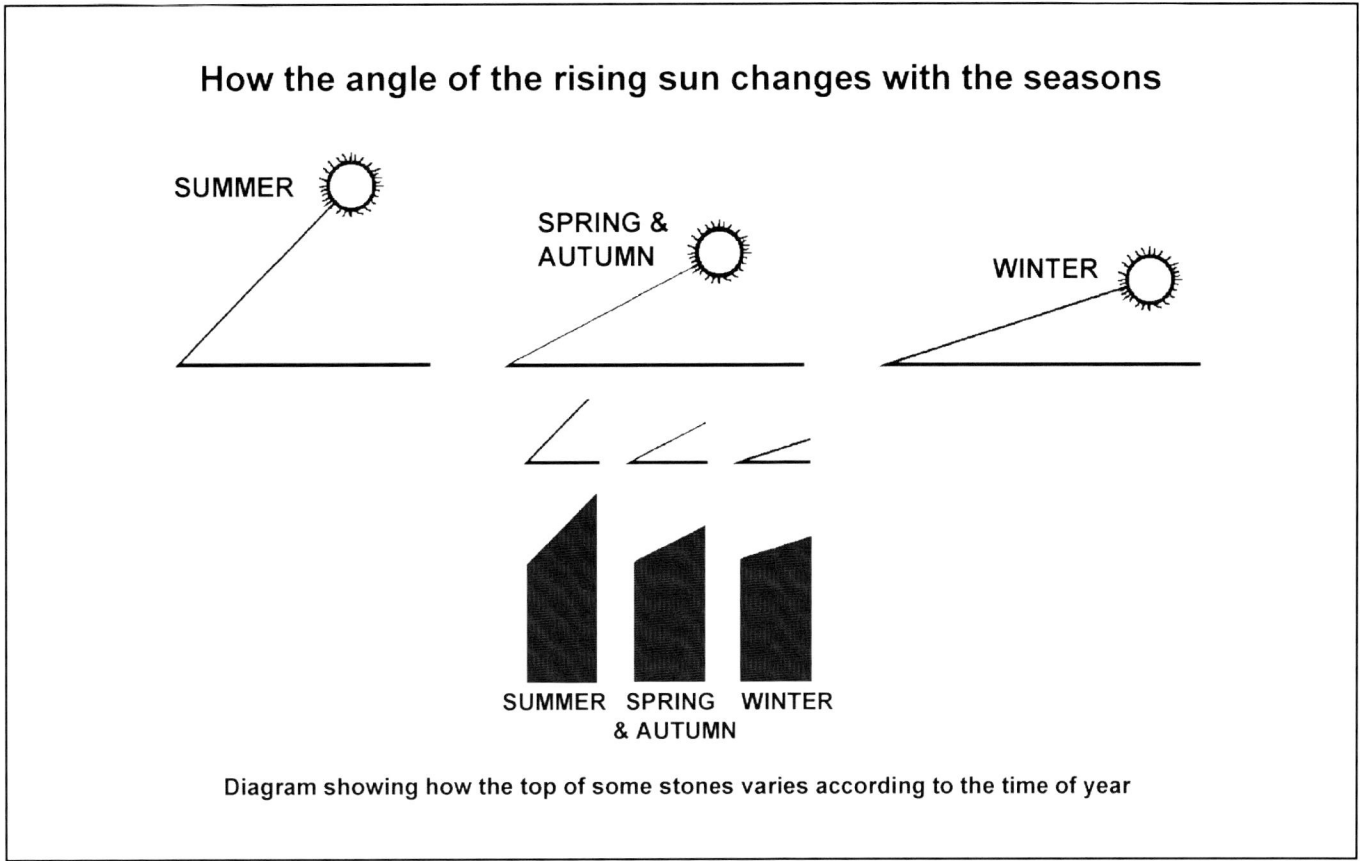

Diagram showing how the top of some stones varies according to the time of year

It is as though the stones were permanent signposts, saying for example: *"The sun will rise in this direction on the longest day of the year,* (the summer solstice)". Or a stone may mark the direction where, *"The sun will set behind here on the shortest day of the year* (the winter solstice sunset)", or alternatively, *"This is the furthest north the moon will rise* (the major northern moonrise)". Or at a point a bit further to the east, *"This is the furthest north a full moon can rise"*.

Having visited many stone circles across the British Isles, I have found that the technique of using specially shaped stones is widespread, but not universal, after all, there were many different tribes from very different ethnic backgrounds in prehistoric Britain. Their ancestors originally came from places that are now part of Portugal and Spain, France and Belgium, Germany and Denmark, and just as there were many different languages so there were many different systems in which each specially carved stone had a particular meaning. There were also local variations in size and shape according to the types of stone available. Nevertheless, the basic idea of using systems of symbolically shaped stones is evident right across the British Isles, and different systems are present at our most celebrated prehistoric sites of Calanais, Brodgar, Stanton Drew, Stonehenge and Avebury.

Similar types of symbol stones are also present at stone circles in Ireland and in the famous rows of hundreds of stones at Carnac in Brittany, northwestern France. In other words, the basic idea of using symbolic languages, written in stone, was truly international. In addition to the sun and the moon I suspect that some symbol stones refer to other heavenly bodies, particularly Venus and Mars, and in some places the symbol stones marked the seasonal direction of the first appearance of the brightest stars such Sirius or groups of stars such as the Pleiades, (the Seven Sisters) and constellations such as Taurus, Orion and Ursa major (the Great Bear, or as we call it, the Plough).

I think that the main reason that the systems of symbol stones have remained unnoticed for so long is due to the early investigators attitudes and prejudices towards the intellectual capacities of our ancestors, and then there has been a continuing belief in more modern times that anything important would have been noticed long ago. And perhaps it is this misplaced confidence that helps explain why stone circles have remained such an inexplicable mystery for such a very long time.

The symbol stones will become a rich field for new, ground-breaking research, since until now most astro-archaeological research has just been about the way that some circles and tombs were aligned with the sun or moon, rather than about the relationship and meaning of these specially shaped stones and their possible alignments. However, before you get too carried away it is important to understand that in most instances, the special stones were used as reminders, not as scientifically accurate markers for calendar events. Many stone circles are simply too small to provide the necessary sightlines and angles. In addition, most standing stones are less than the height of an adult, so they would have been of little use in forming exact alignments with the sun or moon when these were high in the sky. Therefore, apart from north and south, many alignments must have been intended for the moment when the sun or moon were close to the horizon, in other words, at rising or setting.

The whole subject of intentional astronomical alignments is highly charged with controversial opinion, a battleground of fiercely contested scientific wisdom. At one extreme are the most sceptical people who believe that no highly accurate observations could have been made using such crude methods as large chunks of rock. For them the solar and lunar cycles are so complex that much more sophisticated methods would have needed to be used to arrive at an efficient calendar, and furthermore, no stone circles were constructed as scientific observatories. For them the ancients were not scientists and any perceived alignments were more concerned with ritual symbolism, rather than scientific method. On the other hand there are those (like myself) that are convinced that although many stone structures were inspired and constructed according to religious symbolism, I think that sometimes the alignments were quite accurate, particularly those towards the cardinal directions of north, south, east and west, and the solar and lunar extreme positions. (This is pretty good considering they did not have a compass!) The problem is that many rings and circles are not very large and a sightline from the centre to a particular stone and on to a distant object on the skyline is just too inaccurate. There are only a few sites, such as Boscawen-Un in Cornwall, where there are stones near the middle of the ring. So it seems to me that the sightlines must have been from a particular stone on one side of the ring, across the centre towards another stone and then onwards to the horizon. In this way there would have been less margin of error. There were also many other places, such as at Long Meg and her Daughters, near Penrith in Cumbria, where an outlying stone gave a more accurate sightline, in this case towards the midwinter sunset. Other alignments could have produced key dates of the year, particularly the spring and autumn equinoxes when the sun rises due east and sets due west. However, it would have been a bit harder to work out the exact date of the summer or winter solstice, because the sun rises in the same place for several days on either side of the solstice. Specially shaped stones may also have marked out the quarter days, which are half way between the solstices and equinoxes, thus dividing the year into roughly eight equal parts of about forty-five days each. In addition, certain stones could have marked the extreme positions of the moon during its 19-year swing cycle, producing a long-term lunar calendar.

However, I must stress again that the majority of these special stones were not intended to mark rigorously exact alignments with the sun, moon, stars or planets. Instead they acted as a reminder and a guide, in much the same way as many of our road traffic signs just give approximate directions and distances. The map of the London Underground is a good example of what I mean by this. Unlike an Ordnance Survey map of the countryside, which is a rigorously exact representation of actual places and relative distances, the design of the Underground map was intended as a representation of the different lines, and the relationship between the stations, not as an accurate portrayal of their true locations, nor the exact distances between them.

In the same way, the positioning of stones in the circle was often more symbolic than scientifically precise. They were intended as a sort of combination compass and calendar, a way of linking the timing of important religious events with specific directions. In this way the rising or the setting of the sun (or moon) could become an integral part of the ceremony, and of course the most famous example of all is the summer solstice sunrise at Stonehenge.

So to recap, the special stones created a permanent schematic map of celestial, religious and mythological positions of the heavenly bodies at special times of the year. The very distinctive shapes of the symbol stones that our Neolithic and Bronze Age ancestors used clearly demonstrates a systematic approach to permanently recording the movements of the heavenly bodies over many months and years. They acted as horizon markers so that during the ceremonies the congregation would all be facing in the appropriate direction, towards the rising or setting point of the sun or moon. In other words, their knowledge was written in stone.

Not all stones were astronomical markers, far from it. Special stones could even have used to show the direction of a neighbouring village or the direction of a major monument. Or perhaps a particular stone was erected to mark the position of the sun when someone important died, so that a memorial ceremony could be performed each year on the same date. Many seasonal events would have been specific to that particular location and they would have varied from one part of the country to another. These could have included such ephemeral things as the first local signs of spring, the arrival of migratory birds such as the swift and swallow, the birth of red deer fawns, the salmon run, and in early autumn, the birth of grey seal pups and the arrival of geese and swans from the far north. Such timings would have been important to know, so that preparations could be made so that everyone could take advantage of nature's bounty. It should also be remembered that the symbol stones had several sides and that each side could have represented something very different.

When we talk of exact astronomical alignments and the measurement of time, we are trying to put 21st century ideas into an ancient context. In the modern world we divide time up into hours, minutes, seconds and even nanoseconds, but our ancestors had simply no need for such precision, their tools, their monuments and their way of life clearly indicate a different way of thinking to ours. Time passed more slowly for them. And we must also be wary of assuming that all their religious ceremonies and festivals were solemn affairs, we know from other early societies that sacred rites can be very noisy affairs, with drumming and chanting, singing and dancing and with the sound of babies crying and children playing in the background. At the solstices the sun seems to rise at the same place for several days, but the equinoxes are a different matter, at these times of the year consecutive sunrise positions move further apart from one dawn to the next. This would have made a marker stone a more accurate guide for the date of an equinox. And again, even if the date was not the exact Neolithic equivalent of March 21st or September 23rd, and was out by three or four days, did it really matter? Perhaps they weren't so obsessed with time as we are. (Historically, people have been quite casual about the accuracy of the date. Even the Roman calendar was hopelessly inaccurate, until its reform by Julius Caesar in 46 BC). Instead of being part of an accurate alignment perhaps some stones were erected to mark the day a week ahead of the actual event, to give time for the necessary preparations for the ceremonies and rituals.

In my opinion, what was important to the ancients was not necessarily to maintain a rigorously scientifically accurate calendar but to be aware of the complex solar and lunar cycles and have the ability to link them to their festivals and ceremonies near the correct time. The important thing for the ancients to consider was that it was a complete solar year from one spring equinox to the next and that half way between the spring and autumn equinoxes was the summer solstice. Unfortunately there is no hard evidence yet to support the idea that all of their ceremonies were governed by an accurate solar calendar, since many ancient cultures used the phases of the moon to measure time. Even in our modern, artificial, decimal world, we still count the passage of time in terms of weeks, fortnights and months, in other words, moon phases. The time between the main lunar phases is about a week, from full moon to dark moon is about 14 days and a lunation averages 29.53 days, almost a calendar month. Across the world, the lives of millions of people are governed by calendars that are tied to the moon. The Chinese, Hebrew and Hindu calendars are lunisolar, that is they have variable numbers of lunar months in a year and extra intercalary months have to be added every so often, so that every two or three years there are 13 months. The Islamic (Hijiri) calendar is purely lunar and consists of a year of twelve lunar months, lasting 354 or 355 days and so it is not synchronised with the seasons. It is however used to determine the correct day for many Islamic holy days and festivals. In the Christian faith, the festival of Easter is linked to the moon and is determined as the first Sunday after the full moon following the spring equinox. At a time when the British Isles was still mainly forest and travel was difficult, did it really matter if one part of the British Isles celebrated the summer solstice on the 21st of June and another part of the country held its festival on the 16th of June? We shouldn't expect everyone in antiquity to have had the same beliefs and the same calendar. Britain as a political and geographical entity did not exist until 1707 AD, with the Union of England, Scotland and Wales. Up until then it had always been separate countries, with different kings, different languages and dialects, and of course, different customs.

At the time of the Roman Invasion there were numerous tribes in Britain, each with their own king and later on the Romans used much of the existing tribal boundaries to form their administrative areas, the civitates or cantons of the Brigantes, Parisi, Deceangli, Ordovices, Cornovii, Demetae, Silures, Dobunni, Coritani, Iceni, Trinovantes, Catuvellauni, Atrebates, Cantiaci, Regnenses, Durotriges and the Dumnoii. What is particularly interesting is that these were probably loosely based on much, much older tribal territories and they may correspond roughly to the distribution of ancient people with very different customs and different religious beliefs, reflected in the monuments that they built. I noticed for example, that there are no stone circles in the lands of the Iceni, Trinovantes, or Cantiaci. (These territories became parts of the modern counties of Norfolk and Suffolk, Essex, Kent and Surrey.) If all this seems a bit unlikely, that five thousand years ago our prehistoric ancestors created complex systems in which small changes to geometric shapes could have complex meanings, then ask yourself this question: *Where have I seen something like this before?*

The answer is right in front of you, in the shapes we use for the letters of our alphabet, the figures and numbers of our numerical systems and the thousands of different symbols that we use in the modern world. In many written languages it is the different combinations of basic geometric shapes that form individual letters, which in turn represent sounds, and it is the changing combinations of letters that form different words, each with its own meaning. The distant origins of a written language invariably conceal a certain logical progression because of the way the basic written symbols of the language was first visualised.

We have inherited many of our letters from Latin, the written language of the Romans, who in turn poached many of their symbols from the Greeks. However the earliest symbols did not magically appear from thin air; instead I think that they were based on specific ideas, which developed into a systematic method of encoding information. For example, starting with the letter O, a basic full moon shape, divide it into two and you get a half moon shape like the letter D. Another lunar phase, a crescent moon shape, is the letter C. Add a straight line to a circle and you get P or Q, or if you make small changes to a straight line, the letter I, it can produce E, F, L, or T. And of course it is the minor differences in the shape of the letters that alter the meaning of the words they form, for example, ROOT and BOOT.

In a similar fashion, small changes to the basic geometric shapes of circles and triangles produced our system of numerals. By adding or subtracting curves to circles we get 0, 8, 3, 6, and 9; and by adding or subtracting lines to a triangle, we get 4 and 7. And it is interesting to note that eight quarters (weeks) is two moons (months), and so I think that it's likely that the symbol for two moons (circles) is the origin of the number 8. Another system of symbols that we have devised is very common; we carry it around with us all the time, though we are usually unaware of its presence since it is usually hidden from view. The system I'm talking about uses symbols made up of squares, circles and triangles, and if you haven't guessed it yet, you can find it on the labels on your clothes. It's the international system of symbols used to provide us with washing instructions!

To be fair to our archaeologists, many stone circles have been altered over the centuries, with stones having fallen down, been removed or vandalised and subsequently re-erected, not always in the original setting.

When tall stones fell over they sometimes twisted as they fell, landing on their side, front or back and on other occasions they were turned over by treasure hunters or were even temporarily removed by farmers. During the process of re-erecting a fallen stone they were usually rolled or levered out of the way, whilst the hole was emptied of loose earth and only then was the stone moved back into place. However, by this time the people had often forgotten which way round the stone had originally been, and there was less than a fifty/fifty chance of them getting it right, especially if the stone was rounded or square, rather than a broad slab. Mistakes in the re-erection of fallen stones are disappointingly common and this is certainly the case with some of the stones in the third largest stone circle in Britain, the famous Ring of Brodgar on Orkney.

An engraving by William Daniell (incorrectly titled the *'Stones of Stennis, Orkney*) and printed in 1820, in his *'Voyage round Britain'* series, shows just sixteen stones standing, with one prostrate and two broken stumps in a ring covered with grass, not hidden in heather as it is today. In 1852, Royal Navy Captain F.W.L. Thomas recorded the shapes and relative positions of the thirty-six stones out of the original sixty at Brodgar, although by that time only fourteen were still upright. During the next one hundred and fifty years, some of the fallen stones were re-erected but some of those on the eastern side were clumsily put up the wrong way round. The standing stones at the Ring of Brodgar are however some of the finest, and the most characteristic, examples of geometrically shaped symbol stones in the country. Today, twenty-one stones are upright, whilst others have fallen and await careful re-erection. In the illustration I have included the stones that were wrongly re-erected and the white versions show the way they would have originally stood.

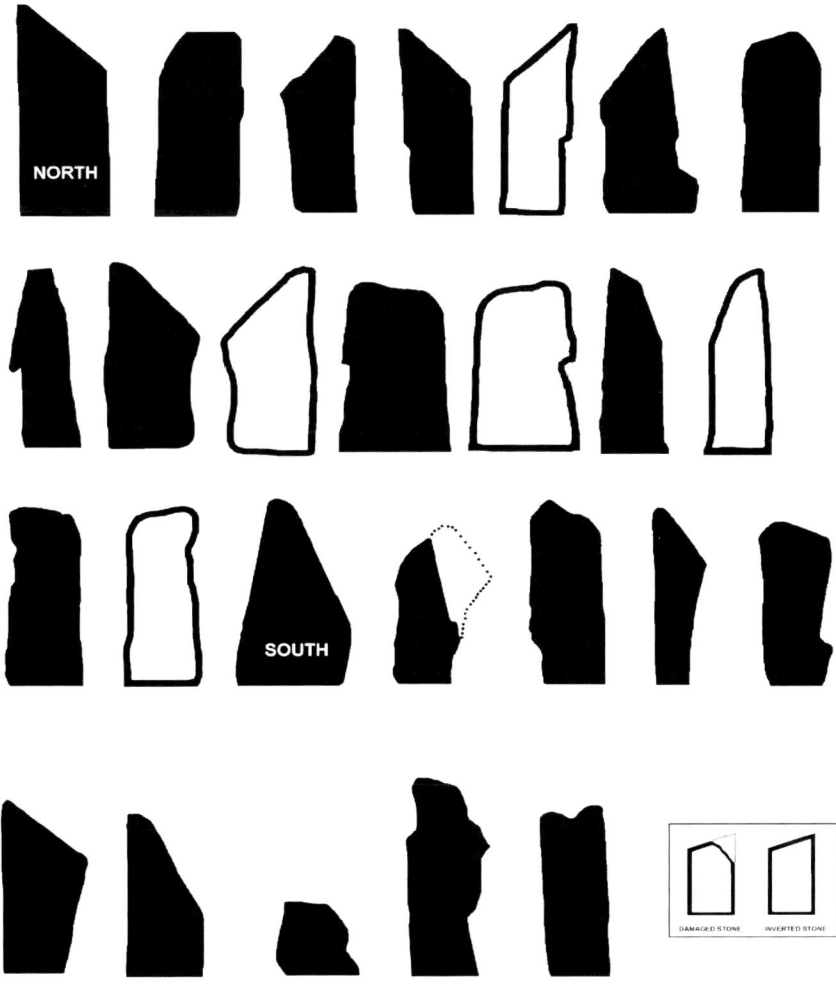

Inner faces of the Ring of Brodgar symbol stones

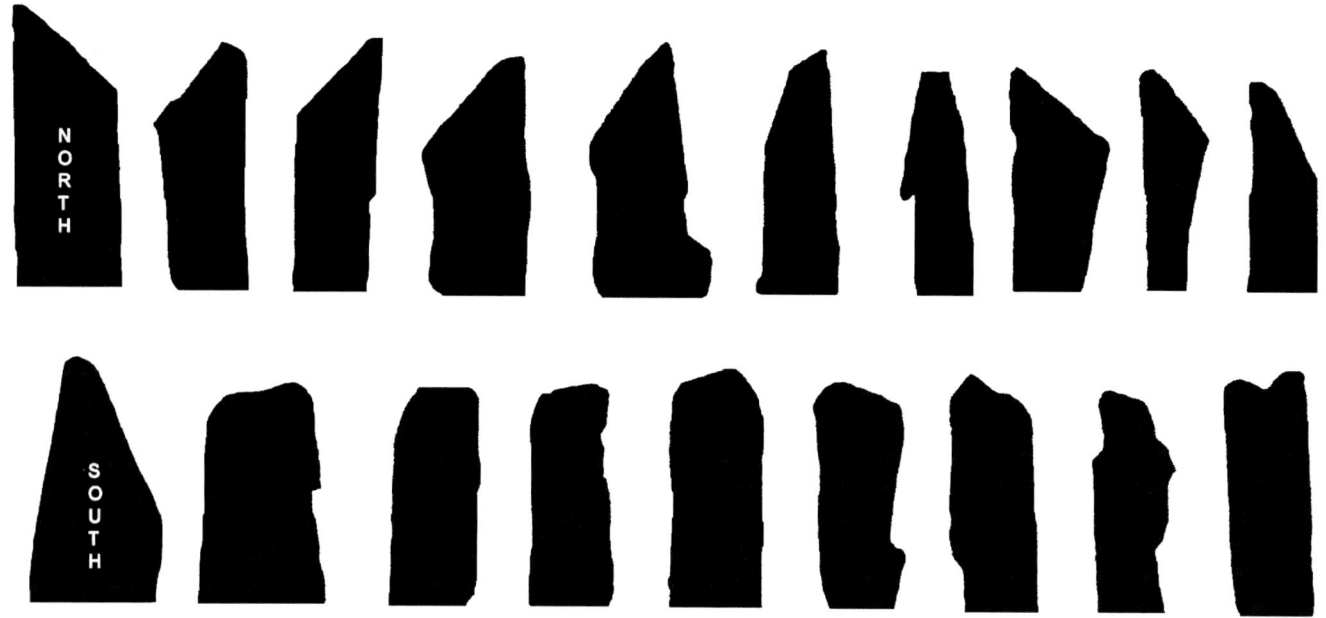

By rearranging the order of the different shapes it becomes far more obvious that there was a specific system in place. There are two distinctively different types of stone, angular stones and rounded oblongs. The angular stones (quadrilaterals) must refer to different positions of the sun whilst the more rounded stones were probably signposts for important lunar events.

The Ring of Brodgar is thought to date from around 2500 BC and is located near the end of a thin, finger-like peninsular of land that separates the waters of the lochs of Harray and Stenness. Recent scientific investigations have shown that at the time of construction, Harray was a boggy, freshwater marsh, with lagoons, rather than the saltwater loch it is today. Brodgar was a wonderful site for an open air temple since there is almost a three hundred and sixty degree panoramic view across the tranquil waters of the lochs. Such a spectacular position means that although the site is not quite level, (rising slightly to the southwest), the circle is surrounded on all sides, except to the northwest, by water. Even today there is a profound sense of peace at this extraordinary site, with just the buzzing of bees seeking nectar from the purple heather flowers and only the distant sound of vehicles to disturb the calm - until the tourist coaches arrive!

At sunrise in summer the rising sun appears over the low hills to the northeast and lights up the water, forming a glittering pathway on its surface towards the onlooker, highlighting the relationship between the three things that were so important to the early farmers: earth, water and sun. Nowhere else in Britain have I felt such an intense natural and spiritual relationship between land, sea and sky, and between past, present and future. And with Orkney's famous sunrises and sunsets and the Northern Lights in winter, it's easy to understand why it was chosen over five thousand years ago by the ancient seal hunters, foragers and fishermen who were the first to appreciate the natural beauty of the place, followed by the first farmers who delighted in the easy grazing for their animals in a relatively treeless landscape. Over time the population expanded greatly and the temple that they built was so huge that several thousand people could have sat or stood inside the ring to witness important ritual events such as the summer solstice sunrise. Prickly bracken prevents this from happening at the moment, most visitors content themselves with a hurried tour around the inner circumference of the stones, wearing down the surface. However it would make more sense to return the ring to a grassy enclosure, like the nearby Stones of Stenness, so that people could enjoy much better access and get even better views of the Ring and the beautiful Orkney countryside that surrounds it.

Part of the eastern half of the Ring of Brodgar

The sixty or so stones in the ring at Brodgar were erected at intervals around the 325-metre circumference of a huge circle, inside a ditch cut deep into solid rock. Brodgar is usually classed as a henge, but henges (Like the nearby Standing Stones of Stenness) always have a ditch surrounded by an outer bank, there is no bank at Brodgar, even though thousands of tons of stone were extracted to construct the very deep ditch. So where did the stones go if they were not used to build up a bank around the temple?

The actual times of rising and setting of the sun and the moon vary according to the latitude of where you live. So some local astronomical research was fundamental to any plans to build ritual centres where celestial events would be linked to seasonal ceremonies of great religious significance. The priests needed to be able to fix the dates of their important festivals and ceremonies well in advance, so that people had time to travel and could arrange for someone to look after their flocks and herds and to mind their crops whilst they were away from home. And someone had to organise the catering…

As most people know, at the North Pole in summer the sun never sets, it stays above the horizon for twenty-four hours each day, yet for four months of the year, during the brutal winter, the sun never rises.Further to the south, in Orkney, the local people would have known that the sun would be above the horizon for much longer in summer than in winter. At the latitude of Brodgar the winter and summer solstice sunrise and sunset positions are at about one hundred degree angles to each other. But far to the south, at Stonehenge, the variation between the extreme seasonal positions is only about eighty degrees. Five thousand years ago, the midsummer sun was above the horizon for about 18½ hours at the latitude of Brodgar. It rose at an azimuth of about 40 degrees and set at 320 degrees, but in winter the rising point was far to the south, at about 140 degrees and the days were short because the sun would set only six hours later, at around 220 degrees. So I think that before the first stones were erected, the key rising and setting points of the solar cycle must have been temporarily marked out using wooden posts. Local midday, and south, would have been determined when the sun was halfway between the positions of sunrise and sunset, at its highest point in the sky. Whilst in the opposite direction, the star Thuban would have marked celestial north at midnight. Once the major stones were in place it was just a matter of using simple measurements to fill up the spaces between them with more stones. And as usual, some of these stones corresponded to important lunar positions.

When I first visited Brodgar it seemed obvious to me that the variety of distinctly differently shaped stones had been used in the absence of written signs as a means of identification. And it is also interesting to note that the shapes of some of the Orkney stones are very similar to certain flint tools and others are like very large versions of the small flint blades known as microliths, which have traditionally been attributed to the time of our Mesolithic ancestors. Collections of these little flint tools have been found together, as though they had been carried around in a little leather bag, and I wonder if they were part of a special set of numbers or perhaps the collection of different shapes formed a sort of alphabet of symbols?

The stones in the Ring of Brodgar were set up about six degrees apart from each other around the circle. They are reminiscent of the hour and minute marks on a clock face and the time taken for the sun to move round the circle from the top of one stone to its neighbour is equivalent to twenty-four minutes. So the design of the ring goes far beyond mere decoration of an impressive sacred place; it implies measurement of time and space. Sixty stones, twenty-four minutes apart, the same amount of time as our modern day of twenty-four hours, with each hour divided into sixty minutes. (The origin of our twenty-four hour day comes from Ancient Egypt, where the night was divided into 12 portions by the rising of different groups of stars, although day length varied between 10 hours in winter and 14 hours in summer.) The positioning of the stones so that they stood about six degrees apart also infers a compass, a means of dividing the circular horizon of 360 degrees into sixty directions. This a similar method to the one that we use to mark our magnetic compasses, although we use intervals of 0, 5, 10, 15, 20, 25, 30 degrees etc. and we also use bearings such as north, north of northeast (22.5 degrees), northeast (45 degrees, east of northeast (67.5 degrees) and east (90 degrees) etc.

Since the stones were set about six degrees apart and if the north stone represented number 60, then the east stone was number 15 and the south stone number 30, west would be number 45. I think at that era the local direction of midsummer sunrise would have been at about 42 degrees, or behind stone 7. And in the evening the midsummer sun would have set at around 335 degrees or behind stone 56. As summer changed to autumn the theoretical position of sunrise at the equinox would be behind stone 15 and sunset at position 45. Then at the midwinter solstice the sun would theoretically rise behind stone 24 and set behind stone 36. In practice there would be minor variations to these theoretical positions because of an uneven horizon, and although Brodgar is close to sea level, the land slopes upwards to the south, making the winter sun set slightly earlier than it would do if the land were flat. More research is needed to verify these ideas.

In the southwest sector of the ring are four upright stones that indicate setting positions. Three of them are very angular and represent sunset positions, whilst the second from the left is a lunar marker stone.

The interval between the centres of each standing stone at Brodgar represents about twenty-four minutes and further divisions of time could have been achieved using temporary wooden marker poles set into the ground that surrounds the ring. In this way the ancient astronomers could have used the stones to help them understand what actually happens in the complex relationships between the sun and the moon throughout the year. This would include the simple changes between the hours of day and night, the seasonal relationship between the sun and the full moon and the more complex changes in timing between successive moonrises or moonsets according to the lunar phase and time of year. So, in addition to being a magnificent ceremonial centre, I think that Brodgar was the site of one of Britain's earliest scientific instruments and an observatory into some basic astronomical research. The stones could also have been used to count a two-month cycle, each cycle of twenty-nine and a half days, using 59 out of the 60 stones. The shape of the special stones would have been an important aid to memory, particularly when the long lunar cycles involving nineteen-year intervals were involved.

southwestern sector, Ring of Brodgar, Orkney

What this means in practice is that if the stones represented two complete lunar months then it would be quite easy to keep track of the passage of time and quite simple to calculate the number of days or nights until the next full moon and indeed for a long time in the future. In other words, in order to predict the timing of future events they designed a combined clock, compass, calculator, solar calendar and several lunar calendars into their temple of stone.

So although their technology of wood and stone might seem to us to have been simple, they could still have researched a great deal. Much, much more than we have previously given them credit for. Having sixty permanent marker stones meant that they could be investigate the rising and setting positions of the sun and moon, constellations, stars and planets. However, in Orkney the daylight hours in summer are very long and the twilight that occurs between sunset and sunrise would have made the observations of even the brightest stars difficult. So many of the bearings for stellar sightings would have to have been set up during the winter months, when the nights are at their longest and the skies are truly dark.

The Earth orbits the sun each year, but from the surface of our planet it appears that the sun is moving through space against a background of stars and around the band of constellations known as the Zodiac. As the year progresses, the sun appears to slowly move along its path, the ecliptic, and stars that had previously been visible at night now rise during the daytime and can no longer be seen. However, later in the year, when the sun has moved further round the Zodiac, they reappear in the night sky. (In reality, the Earth has moved on, not the sun.) For example, at the spring equinox five thousand years ago, the constellation of Orion the Hunter was no longer visible because it rose and set during daylight hours, but six months later, at the autumn equinox, it was once again very noticeable, rising in the evening and setting before sunrise. When seasonal stars first become visible again, rising in the eastern sky just before dawn, it is known as the moment of their heliacal rising and it occurs on the same day each year. The importance of this phenomenon was that the observation of heliacal risings could have formed the basis of an accurate calendar. The heliacal rising of the Pleiades, for example, was important to the Celts, Maya, Aztecs and Navajo and the heliacal rising of the brightest star, Sirius, at midsummer, was very important in ancient Egyptian mythology and religion. The paths of most of the visible planets, Mercury, Venus, Mars, Jupiter and Saturn also move close to the ecliptic, hence the use of astrological terminology, such as Jupiter being in the zodiacal constellation of Leo.

Incidentally, during Roman times, two thousand years ago, the traditional start of the New Year was at the spring equinox and it occurred when the sun was at the First Point of Aries, but due to precession the stars have moved on and the first point is now in Pisces. This has important implications for the accuracy of astrological predictions. The idea that the position of the sun, moon and planets can have influences on human traits at birth and that they can determine our future, is pure superstitious nonsense to many scientists. But it wasn't always like that, history has shown that astrology was very common in ancient civilisations and up until quite recent times it was considered to be quite respectable, for example even one of our greatest scientists, Isaac Newton, was a keen astrologer. So it is very likely that our Stone Age ancestors were also involved in astrology, divination and fortune telling.

One of the most distinctive stones at the Ring of Brodgar is an angular stone that marks south, the direction where the sun reaches its highest point in the sky, at local midday. This is not quite the same as in modern times, because Orkney is at a slightly different longitude to London and our clocks are now set to Greenwich Mean Time. When BST, (British Summer Time) is in operation the sun is due south at around 1 p.m. And since Brodgar is about 3½ degrees west of Greenwich, local noon can occur slightly later than in London. In addition, the sun is rarely due south at midday for a number of reasons including some eccentricities in the Earth's orbit around the sun, and because the Earth is not a perfect sphere, it bulges at the equator. So the midday sun is sometimes slow and sometimes fast, varying slowly over the seasons and as a result astronomers use "The Equation of Time" to work out the necessary corrections according to the date. The sun is 7 minutes slow at the spring equinox,

1 minute slow at the summer solstice, 8 minutes fast at the autumn equinox and 2 minutes fast at the winter solstice. So at Brodgar the noonday sun is 21 minutes later than GMT at the spring equinox but only 6 minutes slow at the autumn equinox (66 minutes BST). At Brodgar the sun is truly due south at noon GMT on the 13th October and again on the 22nd of November.

Two of the most important stones at the Ring of Brodgar

On the right is the south stone and on the left is another very distinctive stone, one that marks north. This is a tall oblong with a slanting top, which slopes down from left to right. Earlier on I said that these sorts of symbol stones mimic the way the sun sinks down below the horizon and that they generally refer to seasonal sunsets. However, this northern stone is a good example of a local variant of symbol stones, here at Brodgar this particular shape is directly opposite the south stone, and so it must refer to north and to midnight, when the sun is below the Earth. At the time of the winter solstice in 2700 BC, one of the brightest stars in the night sky, Vega, was very low on the horizon, and close to due north at midnight.

Near to the Ring of Brodgar is another temple, the Stones of Stenness, dated to 2356bc (±65) or about 2700 BC and sometimes called *'The Temple of the Moon'*, probably because there were originally twelve stones, one for each month of the solar cycle. However another possibility is that the stones refer to twelve constellations that were part of popular Neolithic culture, a precursor to the Zodiac.

Although the Stones of Stenness were radiocarbon dated, the date of the construction of the Ring of Brodgar remains unknown. The first attempt at getting samples suitable for radiocarbon dating was done in 1973 by Colin Rendfrew, without great success. The two ditches that he dug were reopened in 2008, with the intention of trying to use more modern dating techniques, including OSL (Optically Stimulated Luminescence) dating of sediments, but the Ring stubbornly refused to give up its secrets so easily. Another attempt, in new areas of the ditch must be made at this World Heritage Site, because we should know more about it. In my opinion, the Ring of Brodgar is probably older than the Stones of Stenness. This is simply because the Brodgar stones look far more rugged and much more eroded than those at Stenness, which are much taller, more modern looking and more perfectly dressed, often with squared-off sides and faces.

The stones at Brodgar are more than twice the height of an adult, but far to the south, at the Merry Maidens circle, near Penzance in Cornwall, the nineteen stones in the lunar ring are only waist-high.

The Merry Maidens, near Penzance, Cornwall

The circle contains a mixture of solar and lunar symbol stones. The north stone is very distinctive, it is a thin, rectangular stone that has a rather unusual top that slopes outward and downwards, from front to back, and it looks a bit like a wood carver's chisel. Several stones in the circle fell over during the long centuries that elapsed since it was built during the early Bronze Age and in the 1860's they were re-erected, but unfortunately several were put back the wrong way round.

There are the remains of many stone circles in Devon and Cornwall, mostly dating from the early Bronze Age, around 2,300 BC. One of the best areas for them is Dartmoor, where there was a large population and a corresponding number of open air temples. The remains of many of their stone-walled circular houses (unfortunately known as hut circles) are scattered across the landscape, the land became deserted later on when the pressure of farming caused intensive deforestation and major soil erosion, and the once heavily wooded landscape became covered with poor, acidic soils, resulting in the barren moorland we know today.

NORTH

INNER FACES OF MERRY MAIDENS, CORNWALL

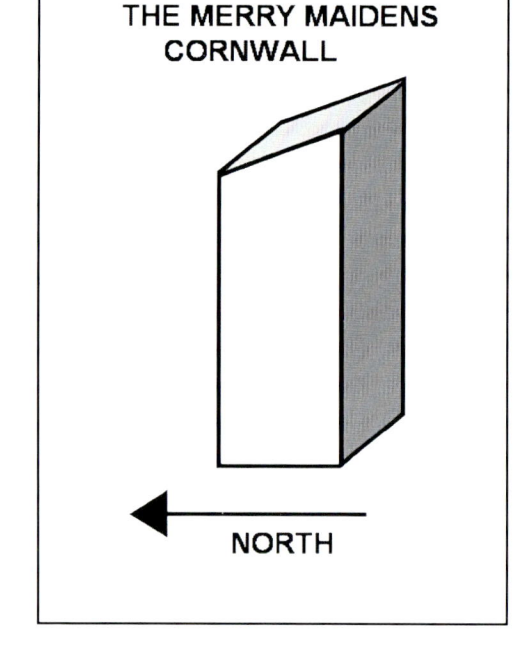

THE MERRY MAIDENS
CORNWALL

NORTH

GREY WETHERS STONE CIRCLE, DARTMOOR
inner surfaces

GREY WETHERS STONE CIRCLE, DARTMOOR
outer surfaces

One of the best sites on Dartmoor for symbol stones is the double ring known as the Grey Wethers Stone Circles, near Postbridge, Devon. Not far away from the Grey Wethers is Scorhill stone circle, which has been robbed of some of its many stones over the centuries, probably for dry stone walling or as gateposts.

Across the Irish Sea, many lunar rings of nineteen stones were built in the southwest part of Ireland. However, at the famous Drombeg Stone Circle, in County Cork, there are now only seventeen stones in the ring, and here it is the smallest of the symbol stones that represents north. Two much larger stones flank the northeastern entrance to the circle, which is in line with the midsummer sunrise. Directly opposite them is a large, oblong altar stone with a flat top and this recumbent stone is in line with the midwinter sunset. So once again, the eternal cycle of Birth, Life, Death and Rebirth was celebrated with a circle that included specially shaped and specifically orientated stones.

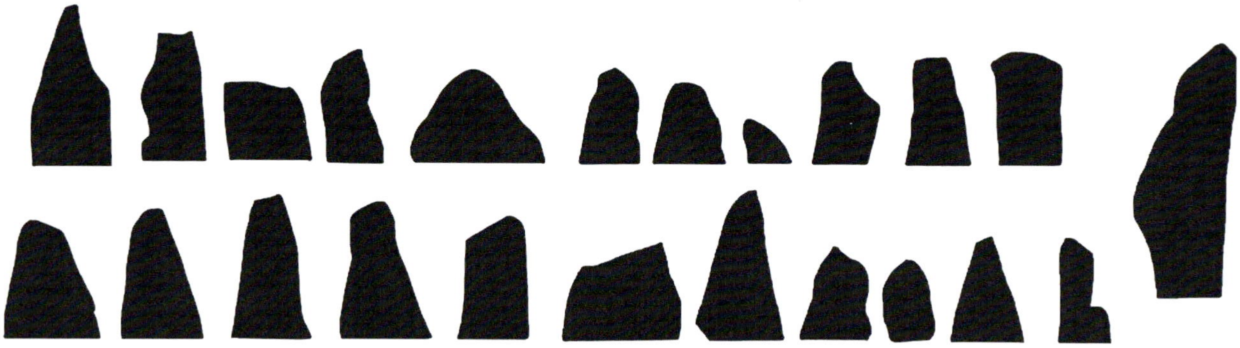

SCORHILL STONE CIRCLE, DARTMOOR

DROMBEG STONE CIRCLE, COUNTY CORK, IRELAND

5 A NEW LOOK AT STONEHENGE

Stonehenge is near Salisbury in southern England and it is now so famous that more than 750,000 visitors come to visit it every year. The traditional scientific way of looking at Stonehenge is not just as it appears today, but also in terms of its history of construction. Excavation has shown that this consisted of a long sequence of different monuments that were built on the same spot over a vast expanse of time, from at least 2950 BC to around 1600 BC.

The wrecked temple that we call Stonehenge is just the last in a long line of structures that started out nearly five thousand years ago. The initial phase started by digging a round ditch with a circular bank of earth around the inside of its perimeter. The ditch was not continuous but was dug in sections and had several gaps with causeways across it. This enclosure was eventually followed by a series of stone temples and several more earthworks. Although each of these temples was different from the ones that came before, they had one thing in common - they reused older stones and added new stones in different ways and different combinations to construct the new temple. And as we shall see further on, each new temple contained important religious, astronomical and symbolic themes that were carried forwards from the earlier structures.

The largest stones at the site are of sarsen. This is a type of siliceous sandstone that is incredibly hard and as difficult to work as granite. Many of these stones are enormous and some of the largest stones weigh well over forty tons. They were brought to the site all the way from the area around Avebury, on the Marlborough Downs thirty miles to the north. Try and imagine just how difficult it must have been to move such enormous lumps of rock such a very long way, especially since this amazing feat was done by sheer physical labour alone, without the help of any motorised vehicles or the sort of mechanical equipment that we would use today.

Despite this, many visitors to the site have commented that the monument is much smaller than they expected, but perhaps this is because we are so used to the size of the modern buildings in our towns and cities. Yet the vast majority of these buildings are composed of bricks, blocks, steel and poured concrete, not giant slabs of rock. It's only when you get really close to the sarsens that you realise that the stones are truly enormous. Even today massive stones of this size are very rarely used for construction purposes, they are simply too big and too expensive to move easily, even with modern equipment. And, despite all of our technology, it is a sobering thought that very, very few of our buildings will still be standing five thousand years from now...

The ruined state of the Final Temple, the one that we know best, does not do justice to how it used to look, nor does it really show off the engineering skills of the ancient stonemasons and their workforce. Even with modern technology it would require many months of work to build the temple, and it would need powerful mechanical diggers, cranes, flatbed lorries, tungsten-tipped drills and cutting tools, steel cables, steel scaffolding and a very large workforce. But technology in late Neolithic and early Bronze Age times was very different from today and only the simplest forms of technology were available to the builders. They used stone hammers and stone axes, fibre and leather ropes, wooden planks, poles and tree trunks and a great deal of human and animal muscle power. But this was coupled with knowledge, skill, experience and ingenuity, as well as a burning desire to build something very special. Their achievement was even greater considering that the design of the final temple included a large circle of uprights joined at the top by a ring of lintel stones. A square or an oblong temple would have been a lot easier to build because it would have used regular-sided blocks of sarsen for both the verticals and the horizontals and all the joints would have formed right-angled corners. However, the more ambitious circular design that our ancestors chose required a far greater degree of engineering skill, because the lintel ring was made up of thirty curved stones, each of which had to be connected to its horizontal neighbours with tongue and groove joints and then to the vertical uprights with mortise and tenon joints.

This complicated design was far more difficult to build since the inner curve of each lintel stone had to be precise, otherwise the final joining of the last parts of the ring would not match up and form an exact circle and the lintel ring would have been deformed. Inside the lintelled circle were other arrangements of standing stones, including a ring of the famous bluestones from southwest Wales, a much taller, U-shaped arrangement of five trilithons, (each trilithon is made up of a pair of even taller sarsen stones with a lintel on top) and inside this was another U-shaped arrangement, this time of nineteen bluestones.

The ruined temple that visitors see today has several stones lying down flat on the grass, whilst at least nine of the thirty large sarsen uprights are missing altogether and other stones lie smashed into separate pieces. Most of the bluestones are missing and most of the damage is on the southwestern side of the temple. The stones that are still standing are mainly in the eastern half of the circle and this includes a run of four stones, complete with lintels, in the northeastern sector, the part facing towards the rising sun at the summer solstice. The two middle stones in this group have a wider gap between them since they flank what was originally the main entrance. Many people think that the temple we see today is exactly how it would have looked centuries ago, but in reality several of the larger stones have had to be straightened and set in concrete and others which had fallen in autumn gales were re-erected during the last century. The temple now looks about the same as it does in the earliest known realistic drawing that dates from about 1570. However, many people think that all of the fallen stones should be re-erected, so that this memorial to the creative genius of our ancestors is restored as much as is humanly possible.

Another early illustration of Stonehenge is in the form of a manuscript that dates from the 12th Century, but the writer wasn't much of a draughtsman since to fit the design on the page he drew a rounded oblong, not a circle, of lintelled stones. Although just how many stones were still there and how much of the ring was still standing in those days is unknown, but what this drawing does show is that people were aware of the circular nature of the old temple, even if some couldn't illustrate it very well. In 1130, Henry of Huntingdon wrote one of the earliest accounts of the temple in his *'History of*

England', and he spoke of 'Stanenges', the stone gallows. Another explanation for the unusual name of Stonehenge speaks of 'the hanging stones', perhaps because the lintels seem to hang in the air, but I think the gallows version is the more likely of the two, because hanging was a common form of capital punishment for many centuries, indeed right up to the second half of the Twentieth Century. (The traditional design of a gallows was in the form of two uprights and a cross piece, with the noose, or nooses, suspended from this horizontal spar.)

The standard way of looking at Stonehenge dates back to the late 1950's and it started with the publication of the classic account of the monument by Professor Richard Atkinson. His book *"Stonehenge"* was based upon the findings and knowledge gained from excavations at the site and it included the current thinking about the lives of our prehistoric ancestors. He wrote of the structure of Stonehenge, the sequence of construction, the techniques used for its construction, the people who built Stonehenge and to a much lesser extent, its meaning. To his credit he developed new theories about the age of the site, the way that the temples had been built and how the site had developed over time. In his opinion instead of just one phase, there had been three phases and three very different Stonehenges, one each of earth, wood and stone.

We now know that this series was far too simple and that during a fifteen hundred year period the temple evolved and there were many different structures built on the same site. Although only a fraction of the detailed findings of all the countless excavations were ever recorded or published, including his own, Atkinson's book is still the basis for nearly all of the subsequent accounts of the site, including the official guidebooks, a host of scientific papers and hundreds of books and countless magazine articles.

The view from the northeast

Yet, as we shall see further on, Atkinson missed many clues that would have given us a much, much better understanding of Stonehenge. And, as we shall also see, many of his observations, descriptions, theories and conclusions were inaccurate or lacked vital pieces of information. In consequence it is hardly surprising that Stonehenge has continued to remain such a mystery for such a long time. The mistakes he made have been passed down from one generation of archaeologists to the next, and from them to us, right up to the present day.

The first temple was a simple earthen enclosure, a ditch and bank, with the bank on the inside. This is usually known as a causewayed camp and the one at Stonehenge was no different to hundreds of others that were constructed all over the country around five thousand years ago. These camps or enclosures are thought to have had a variety of uses over time, they served as meeting places, as temporary camps, as market places, and at some point in their existence they often became cemeteries. Later on at this site, known as Stonehenge 1, a series of fifty-six holes were dug around the perimeter of the bank, and these are known as the Aubrey Holes, after John Aubrey, the antiquarian who was the first to mention them, in around 1666. These holes are the subject of a great deal of debate, however it is likely that initially they were dug to hold a ring of posts, then later on they were enlarged to hold a ring of standing stones. (This is due to the way that they are of varying sizes and depths.) Later still, some of the holes were emptied of their stones and refilled with the ash and unburned human remains from cremations.

At some point a very large sarsen, the famous Heel Stone, was brought to the site and erected outside the circle to the northeast, and inside the earth circle another four small sarsen stones were erected in the form an oblong. These are known as the Station Stones, although two are now missing. Then, around four and half thousand years ago, the local people brought about sixty large Bluestones all the way from the area around the Preseli Mountains in southwest Wales, a distance of more than 130 miles (210 kilometres) as the crow flies. These were arranged in a double arc within the earth enclosure. Then about two hundred years later the bluestones were moved out of the way and they brought in a load more sarsen stones from the Marlborough Downs and erected these to form a circle of standing stones. These were joined along the top by a ring of thirty sarsen lintel stones. As I mentioned before, the lintel ring was an extraordinary achievement in its own right, especially since it called for a far greater degree of skill than the upright stones needed because nearly every surface had to curve to a precise degree. The lintels had to be carved so that the ends would interlock as tongue and groove joints, like two pieces of a jigsaw, but in three dimensions. The lintels were also fastened to each upright using a mortise and tenon joint, which consists of a recessed hole in the lintel and a raised peg on the upright, and again this work would have needed to be done accurately, so that each lintel could be slotted home. These procedures are well-known carpentry techniques but even to create the lintel ring in solid oak with just flint, stone and bone tools would have been an amazingly difficult achievement. However, the lintels were not made of wood; instead they were made of something that would last forever, sarsen stone. Each of them must have taken a very long time to create, with people pecking away at the extremely hard sarsen for hour after hour, day after day, week after week, for months at a time. And at around seven tons, each lintel weighs more than an adult African elephant!

To achieve such an extraordinary design I think that the parts of the ring of lintels must have been prepared on the ground first, before being hoisted in the air and onto the supporting sarsen uprights. This must have involved using a wooden template of some sort so that each of the lintels was the right length and breadth to join up to its neighbours. In this way only relatively minor alterations would have been required before final assembly. It is also hard to imagine them doing all this work without a model of the final design to guide them. A scale model would have been an invaluable visual aid in enlisting the help and support of the scores of people who would have been needed to bring the project to fruition. The carpentry techniques also remind us that although we tend to think of these ancient times as an age of stone, it would probably be more accurate to think of it as a time when wood was the most widely used material. Unfortunately, we have relatively little evidence of this, since the vast majority of objects made from natural materials have simply rotted away over the millennia. After the sarsen circle was complete, they added another circle of smaller stones that ran roughly parallel to the inside edge of the ring of sarsen uprights. This was a ring of around sixty bluestones. Within these circles of upright stones was a U-shaped arrangement of five pairs of much larger sarsen stones (often called a horseshoe-shaped arrangement, although this is an anachronism, since iron shoes for horses date from around 500 AD). Each pair of uprights was linked at the top with a lintel and is called a trilithon, meaning three stones. There were two sets of trilithons on each side of the U, with the tallest set, the Great Trilithon, erected in the middle of the bend in the U-shape. Then in front of this arrangement of trilithons they added another U-shaped arrangement of nineteen tall, slim bluestones.

Both the sarsen trilithons and the bluestones increased in height from each of the ends of the U's towards the middle. And both groups of sarsens and bluestones were set up so that each U stood astride the central axis of the temple, along a line roughly northeast/southwest. Standing on this axis, and in front of the narrow gap between the uprights of the Great Trilithon, was yet another stone, a large, thick slab of green micaceous sandstone, also from southwest Wales and known as the Altar Stone. Much later on, towards the end of the sequence of use, around 1600 BC, two series of 30 pits, the Y and Z holes, were dug in two roughly circular rows around the outside of the main temple. Because of their shape these pits were probably dug as shallow graves, but the site was abandoned and they were never used.

All of the sarsen stones show extensive alteration but even though the rock they chose was very unyielding, it did not deter the stonemasons in the slightest, for they were used to hard work, and construction projects that required many thousands of man-days to complete were part of the status quo. The enormous sarsen stones they used came from the Marlborough Downs, more than sixteen miles (twenty-five km) to the north, and were probably dragged to the site on sledges. The techniques that were used would have varied according to the terrain and at times the sledges were probably pulled along the ground, whilst in other places they used trackways of tree trunks laid end to end (imagine railway lines), and sometimes they would have used the tree trunks as rollers to move the sledges along. However, every single log they used represented a considerable amount of time and sheer hard work. Cutting down the trees for the movable trackways was a major endeavour in its own right, since the cutting edge of a flint axe chips off quite easily and they need to be reflaked when they get damaged. To cut down the largest trees was even more of a chore since chips of wood were detached in such a way that the ends of the tree trunks looked as though they have been gnawed at, like the work done by a beaver rather than by a saw. The overall effort involved must have been substantial but since they had been raising cattle for centuries and some were trained to pull simple wooden ploughs called ards, so they must have used their oxen to help move the logs or indeed the stones themselves.

Recent experiments have shown that in flat places even the biggest stones of fifty tons or more could have been pulled along by as little as a hundred people, or by teams of oxen. However it was done, it would still have taken months to move each of the stones all the way from the Marlborough Downs. It is very probable that they organised people into gangs, some clearing the route ahead, others laying the trackways of pre-cut timber, and others guiding the animal and human teams pulling on the fibre or leather ropes. Even children worked very hard, since many skeletons from this period show signs of osteoarthritis, caused by excessive and repetitive stress and strain on the bones and joints. And everyone had to be organised, fed and generally looked after by yet another labour force of cooks, butchers and support workers. Whilst some were grinding grain to bake bread, others were foraging and collecting firewood or fetching water for drinking, cooking and washing. It must have required extensive leadership skills and effective political, organisational and motivational ability, the same as any major modern construction site. But instead of financial reward, the main motivations of the workforce for such long-term projects must have been religious fervour and the heartfelt desire to part of something everyone truly believed in.

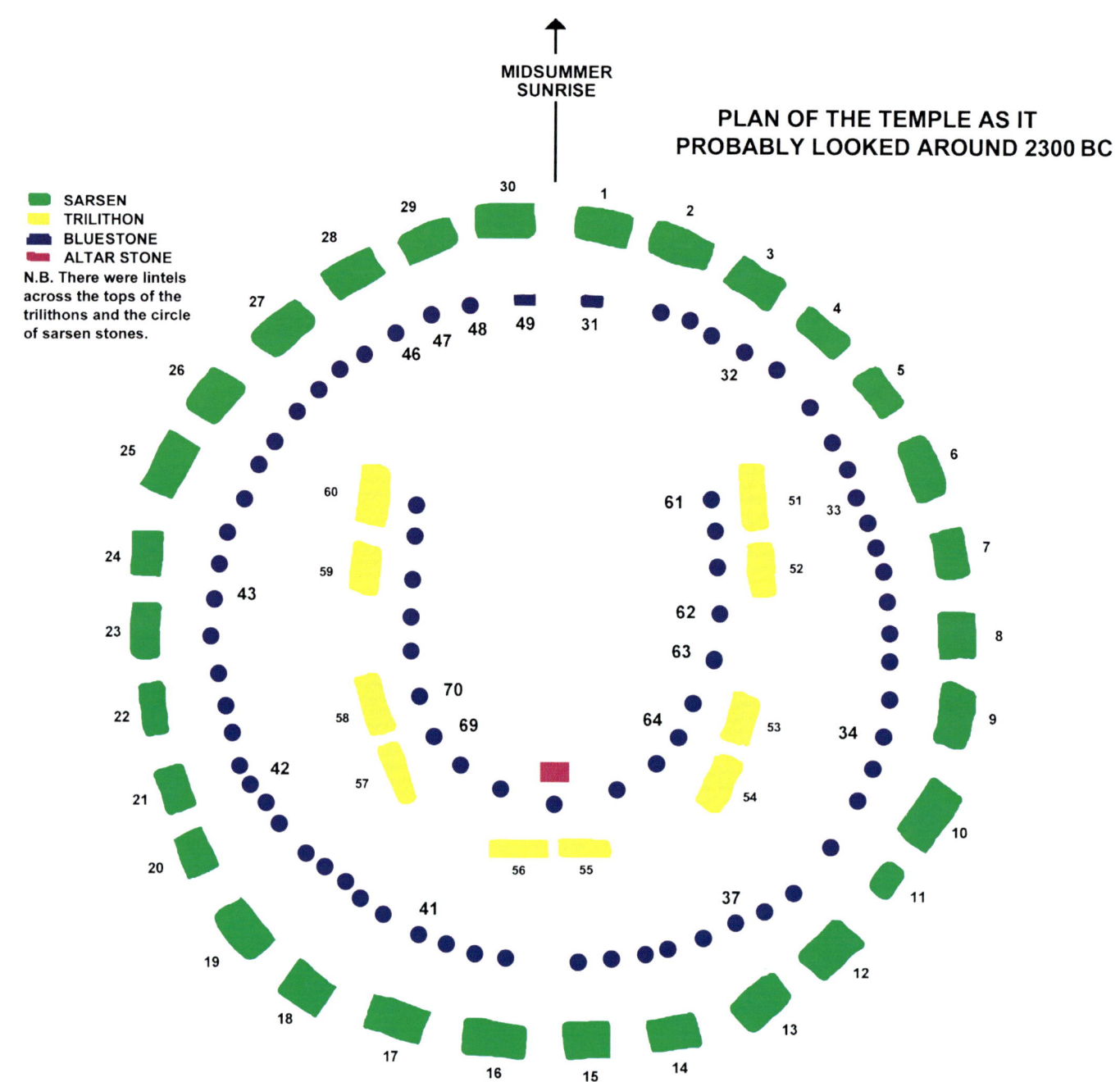

For centuries it was thought that Stonehenge had been built in one long continuous sequence. However, to his credit this all changed in 1956 when Richard Atkinson formulated his view of three main phases of construction, temples of Earth, Wood and Stone and most popular accounts of Stonehenge have slavishly followed in his footsteps ever since.

He suggested there had been an initial phase in the form of a circular earthwork, followed by some sort of wooden arrangement of posts and then by a series of stone temples. His third stage of construction, Stonehenge 3a, included the lintelled sarsen circle, the inner U of five trilithons, the Heel Stone, the Station Stones, and to the northeast, the Slaughter Stone and its companion.

In his book Atkinson wrote:

"When the centre and the axis had been fixed, the circumference of the circle on which the inner faces of the uprights of the sarsen circle were to lie must have been marked out, presumably by wooden pegs driven in flush with the surface of the ground. This operation had necessarily to be carried out at this stage, even though, for obvious reasons, the central trilithons had to be erected first. For once the latter were in position, no true circle could be struck from the centre."

And he also wrote:

"It is clear by reason of their greater weight and length the uprights of the trilithons were erected first, and the sarsen circle afterwards, the trilithon lintels being moved into the circle, though not necessarily moved into position before the latter was complete. In both settings of uprights the process of erection appears to have been the same, except that the trilithons were pulled upright from within outwards, whereas the stones of the circle were raised from the outside towards the centre."

Although on first impression it seems to make sense that the largest and heaviest stones, the five sets of trilithons, would have been erected first, it is not necessarily true. In fact Atkinson's sequence was purely a guess on his part. And it certainly doesn't make sense of the evidence from several excavations, nor of the construction techniques used to erect the stones, nor the most recent radiocarbon dates. (Sarsen hole #1, 2620–2480 BC. Trilithon hole #56, 2440-2100 BC. In other words, the trilithon hole was dug more recently than the hole for sarsen 1.) So the two excerpts I have quoted above are illogical, it as though he was saying that: *'The furniture was installed first and then the house was built around it'*.

In my opinion the sequence of construction makes much more sense of the actual evidence if the sarsen circle had been erected first and then the trilithons had been added two or more centuries later on. This revolutionary idea will be hard for many people to swallow. So what basis have I used to introduce this new approach to the phases of construction? The clues have been there for some time but no one seems to have made sense of the seemingly conflicting evidence gathered from the various digs, the radiocarbon dates and by taking the trouble to really look at the stones.

One very curious thing that I noticed about the stones was the way that the lintels simply don't fit as well as they should have done. The presence of smooth, more modern-looking stones show that the other rugged stones could have been shaped much better, since by using squared-off surfaces along the edges and sides of the uprights they would have obtained a much better fit where they joined the lintels. So why did they leave some of the stones so unfinished?

If you were the architect and wanted to arrange the construction of a temple with thirty, lintelled uprights, how would you do it?

It seems to me that the logical way would be to mark out a large circle on the ground, then carefully determine the number, the length, breadth and width of the stones needed by using a framework of wooden poles and measuring sticks. Then the builders could travel to the Marlborough Downs, select and organise the rough pre-shaping of the stones, and then transport them to the site. After a final shaping they would then need to be measured again, so that the builders knew exactly how wide and how deep each hole needed to be dug. This is because the site is not quite level, it rises to the south and for the lintel ring to be perfectly horizontal, as it was, the stones on the northern side would have to be slightly taller than those opposite. After digging its hole, each stone would then be brought as close as possible, then manoeuvred upright and dropped into the hole. Then after using a plumb line in order to ensure that it was vertical it could be packed firmly into place. After a few months the uprights would have settled down, they could then be measured again and the tenons cut to the correct size to receive the lintels, which would then be firmly secured on top.

Simple, but at the same time an incredibly difficult and complex building programme involving hundreds, if not thousands, of full and part-time workers.

Excavation has since revealed a number of anomalies to the theoretical sequence that I have outlined above. Some stones stand on the chalk in small holes, whilst others have very large pits around them. And some stones were not tall enough and had to have their holes partially filled in, so that instead of standing securely on top of the chalk bedrock, they stood on top of a fill layer of rubble made up of sarsen boulders, old stone tools, chalk and flint. In addition, some stone holes have a ramp leading upwards at an angle of about forty-five degrees from the bottom of the pit to the surface, whilst other pits have straight sides and no ramp.

So why were there so many differences in the holes? Why didn't each stone just fit perfectly inside its own hole? Why make some of the holes too deep? And why did they weaken one side of some of the holes by digging a ramp? In short, why did they make the job so much harder than it needed to be? Here was a puzzle that was waiting for a logical explanation, one that would make sense of all the apparent anomalies…

With regard to the holes for the stones Atkinson wrote:

"Three sides are steep but the fourth, towards the centre of the site in the case of the trilithons and away from it in the circle, is in the form of a ramp sloping from the base of the hole proper to the surface at an angle of about 45 degrees."

Following his lead, this is traditionally taken to indicate that the earth ramps were used for erecting the stones since they would then have slid into the holes more easily. Yet there seems to have been a major flaw with this type of building technique since over time many upright stones tilted or fell over and nearly all of them have had to be re-erected and set in concrete. For example, the fourth trilithon, stones 57 and 58, together with their lintel, fell in the winter of 1797 and all three stones were eventually re-erected in 1958. For some, such as trilithon stones 55 and 59, their positions were ultimately so unstable that they fell with enough violence to break into several pieces. And the fate of many other stones is unknown, since they are missing.

An average sarsen circle stone stands thirteen and a half feet high (4.12m), seven foot wide (2.13m) and three to four feet thick (0.91 -1.22m), and weighs about twenty-five tons. Admittedly, when it came to manoeuvring such a massive stone into its hole a ramp might well help it slide in more easily, but there was also the very real danger of weakening the hole because the packing material would not be nearly as secure on the angled side as it was on the three vertical sides. In addition, not all the stones had these ramps, about half the stone holes have no ramp at all, and they are just straight-sided pits.

These anomalies suggest to me that instead of being used to erect the stones it is far more likely that the ramps were used to remove old stones and then replace them. This is because they couldn't just pull the stone upwards out of the ground because the stones were far too heavy. So they would have had to dig away the earth on one side down to its base until the stone toppled over, hopefully slowly and safely by being held back by ropes. Then a new stone could be added and wedged in place with rubble. In addition, after studying dozens of photographs I realised that instead of bringing thirty similar sized stones to the site at the same time, they had in fact modified stones of different shapes and sizes that had come from a previously existing stone circle. What has also remained completely unnoticed is that some of them are very large geometrically shaped stones.

In other words, **they are symbol stones**.

Stones 1, 5 and 21 for example are curved moonstones, whilst many of the others, such as 10, 23 and 28, are more linear sunstones. The inwardly sloping sides of the front of sarsen 30 show that it was originally more of a triangular shape, a sunstone and that the stone next to it, sarsen 1, was originally much more curved than it is now, so probably a moonstone. Other torso shaped stones, such as 4, 6 and 7 may even represent the planets of Mars, Venus or Jupiter.

In addition to the sarsen uprights, many of the lintels that remain are not smooth, regular sided oblong shapes and as a result they do not fit squarely on the uprights. In addition to this, the top surface of some of the lintels, such as those above 1-2, 6-7 and 21-22, show signs of re-use, they

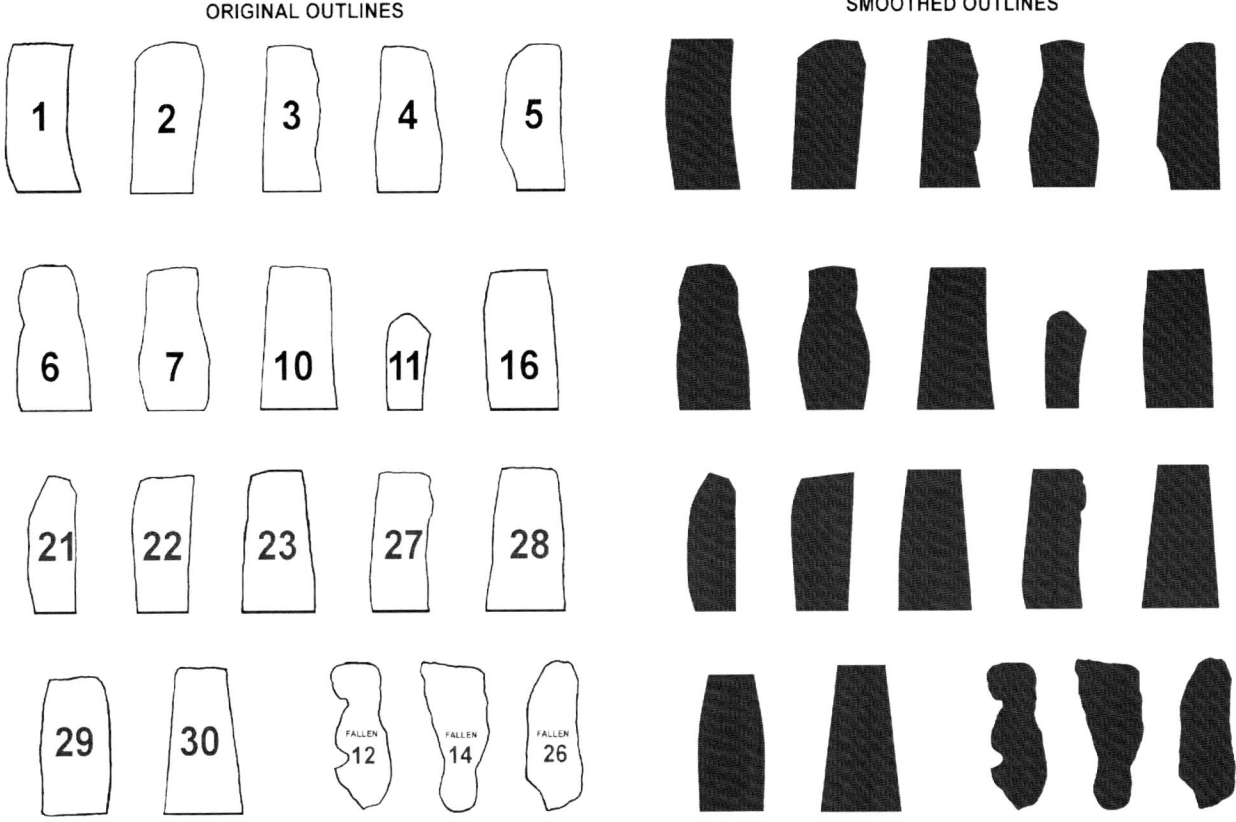

OUTER SURFACES OF SARSEN CIRCLE STONES

PLEASE NOTE THAT THE SHAPES OF 12, 14 AND 26 ARE APPROXIMATE, SINCE THEY ARE LYING IN LONG GRASS

were probably made into lintels because they were too short to be reused as uprights in the new temple.

By looking at the tops of the uprights carefully you can see that some of the oldest stones have been cut down to size and squared off in order to try and support the weight of two lintels. But moonstone 21 for example, originally had almost a pointed top and such a reduced width meant that it could not provide a broad supporting surface for both of the lintels above it. However, its partner, stone 22, was much broader at the top and so it could easily support the ends of each of the lintels it held. As a result of these issues, stone 20 and the lintel between 20 and 21 are both missing. Where a lintel rested on a rounded surface, instead of a flat one, the lintel was more unstable, and more likely to fall. Other stones were made to stand as tall as possible by precariously reducing the amount they were buried in the soil and they did this by filling in the old stone holes with rubble. Such compromises meant that in the long term the stones would not provide a secure platform for the lintels that they would support and ultimately such readjustments made them unsuitable for bearing the full weight of the lintels.

Over the millennia the sarsen ring collapsed in several places and most of the lintels fell down. Yet obviously, if the workers had known in advance the required height of the stone above ground level, they would never have dug the hole so deep in the first place. This is because it would have been simple to measure the height needed, (about thirteen and a half feet), mark this on the sarsen, and then dig a hole to the depth of the remaining length of stone. So for example, if the stone had an overall length of eighteen and a half feet, the pit needed to be dug down to five feet below ground level. Not only would there have been less work involved but also the stone would have stood on the natural chalk foundations, making it easier to pack all four sides and make the stone much more stable in the long term.

The lintel over stones 21 and 22

The lintels over stones 1 and 2 are still in place, but the lintel between 2 and 3 has fallen

Below is the lintel over stones 4 and 5 ,

The lintel over stones 6 and 7

Note the way that the left hand lintel sits badly on the top of stone 30

When a thick fill layer of rubble, chalk and stones had to be added to the bottom of an existing hole the stone became less stable, simply because the end of the stone was closer to the top and there was less support from the sides of the pit. This indicates that the stones in these holes were too short to meet the new height requirement and so in order to raise the stone to the correct level, the holes had to be partly filled in. Although some stones stand in holes that are close in size to the stones themselves, other stones sit in much larger, irregular pits. And again this seems to make little sense, especially since the builders were experts when it came to erecting complex wooden structures from tree trunks and timber posts. The significantly increased size of some pits shows that a great deal of earth and chalk had been dug away at some point and this indicates that a stone had been removed and a new stone added. In addition, if the builders had started out with the intention of producing a lintelled structure, they could have made things much easier for themselves by making all the stones a standard length before moving them from their source on the Marlborough Downs, twenty miles away to the north.

So to recap, the general design idea was to build the lintel ring as high off the ground as possible, at least twice the height of a man. However, all the compromises necessary to achieve this design affected the long-term stability of the structure. Therefore it seems to me that the logical explanation for all these inconsistencies is that the builders had added new stones (e.g. stone 16) to an existing circle of standing stones to produce a new design. This design had the previously free-standing uprights connected to each other by a lintel ring running around the top.

Atkinson mentions the way that the trilithons were erected by being pulled up from the ground in the centre of the temple towards the outside. But this could also mean that there was little room to lay them out on the other side, because the stones of the sarsen circle were in the way. He also said that the thirty sarsen circle stones were raised by pulling them upwards towards the centre; this suggests that the trilithons were not in place at that time because they would have been in the way of the hundreds of workmen pulling on the ropes.

Inner surfaces of the first trilithon (stones 51/151/52)

In addition, radiocarbon dating of the antler picks used to dig the holes shows that the sarsen circle predates the trilithon U-shape by several hundred years. (Sarsen circle stone number 1, 2618-2470 BC, average 2545 BC; trilithon 53/54, 2818-2350 BC, average 2485 BC; trilithon hole 56, 2465-2200 BC, average 2335 BC, hole 56, 2469-1642 BC average 2055 BC.) The anomaly between the dates was noticed, but ignored, because most archaeologists thought there had to be errors with dating the samples, rather than to rethink the faulty logic and then rewrite the conclusions that had been made.

Inner surfaces of the second trilithon (53/153/54)

Fourth trilithon (57/157/58)

Lastly we come to the new evidence of the stones themselves. If you look at the sarsen stones you will see that no two uprights are identical, and some stones are of a much older style than others.

The oldest stones of the sarsen circle, such as stones 27, 28, 3, 4, 5, 6 and 7, have very marked and rough textures on their sides and faces. The newer stones have much flatter, almost polished surfaces with squared off sides with right-angled corners. Some typical examples of these newer stones are sarsen circle stones 10 and 23, together with stone 16, which looks a bit like a giant version of the tip of a screwdriver.

The trilithon uprights and lintels show even more marked differences in style due to the differences between the ages of the stones. The most dramatic difference in age of the uprights is in the second trilithon, stones 53/54. Trilithon stone 54 is of the old style whilst its partner 53 is a new style stone. The same sort of differences in style can also be seen by looking at those lintels that still stand on top of their trilithons, the lintels of the first, second and fourth trilithons. The surfaces of the lintel of the first trilithon, number 151, are very rough and the inner side is corrugated and has a V-shaped hole in it. In contrast the lintel over the second trilithon, 153, has a much more modern look to it, like upright stone number 53. The surfaces are very smooth, the corners are almost at right angles and the long sides are almost rectangular.

The only logical conclusion that can be drawn from all the evidence that I have outlined above is that the lintelled sarsen circle was completed centuries before the U-shaped groups of trilithons and bluestones were added.

Clearly it has been a case of ignoring evidence or rather, altering it to fit Atkinson's theory, rather than re-evaluating and re-thinking the old theory to make it fit all the evidence. The weight of this new evidence shows that instead of just one sarsen temple, there were at least three different sarsen stone temples. Firstly there was a fairly ordinary stone circle made up of very large sarsen stones. These stones were then modified so that the lintel ring could be added along the top. Then thirdly, with the addition of the U-shaped arrangement of trilithons and bluestones, they built the final temple of stone, **Final Stonehenge.**

Egyptologist Flinders Petrie drew the first precision plan of Stonehenge in 1880, and although his method of numbering the stones did have some sort of logic to it, generations of people have adopted his method without question. He started his numbering of the stones with the sarsen just to the east of the temple axis in the northeastern entranceway and called it number 1. And the sarsen to the west of the northeastern entrance was deemed the last in the circle and so he named it number 30. (However, it would perhaps have been better if he had started elsewhere).

Directly opposite the north stone, sarsen number 26, was a southern entrance into the temple that passed through the gaps between stones 10 and 12, on either side of stone 11.

In his book *'Stonehenge'*, Professor Atkinson mentions this small sarsen stone, he wrote:

"One stone in the circle, number 11, is much smaller than the rest, measuring only four feet wide by two feet thick. It now stands only eight feet out of the ground, but presumably at some time the upper part has been broken off and removed from the site. The use of this markedly undersized stone (there can be no question of its width and or thickness having been reduced since its erection) suggests that the builders were hard put to find sufficient blocks of the requisite size to complete the circle."

This is absolute rubbish, even though many have been taken away, there are still plenty of suitably sized stones on the Marlborough Downs. Why did Atkinson not realise that the size, position and shape of stone 11 was deliberate and very important, and then investigate accordingly?

Looking south at the inner surface of stone 11

The choice of a circle of thirty sarsen stones is itself interesting, because it would have been much easier to construct a circle using 16, 24 or 32 stones. As I mentioned earlier, the significance of the thirty upright stones becomes clearer once you remember that the number of days in one lunation, from new moon back to new moon, is about 29½ days or to be more precise, 29 days, 12 hours and 44 minutes. That the ancient astronomer/priests knew the length of the lunar cycle is clearly demonstrated by the fact that stone 11 is much smaller than all the other stones of the sarsen circle. Looking outwards, the inner surface resembles a summer sunrise stone, like bluestone 49, an oblong with an upwardly sloping top, but instead of a continuous slope right to the edge, the top right corner is rounded. A slope like this usually mimics the passage of the rising sun until it reaches its maximum height, due south, at midday. And like the sun, the moon reaches its highest point when it is halfway between rising and setting, so the rounded corner of the stone must represent the moon. So I think that stone 11 represents the sun and moon at their optimum heights and it also symbolises the half-day in the lunar cycle of 29.53 days.

Although some archaeologists have noticed that the inner faces of the trilithons are often smooth, whilst the outer faces are often rough, only a few authors seem to have stopped and thought about what the trilithons actually represented. The usual idea is that because the gaps between the uprights were so narrow that a person could not pass through they were perhaps doorways for the spirits. For others, such as the late Gerald Hawkins, the trilithons were windows that allowed an observer to see the rising or setting of the moon and sun at special times of the year. I think both of these theories have merit and would add that I think that the stones resemble a very stylised figure of the lower half of the human body, with each upright being one of the legs. It is particularly noticeable that the narrow gap between the 'legs' opens up into a triangle at the top, just like the juncture at the top of our thighs. The arrangement of the five sets of trilithons and the U-shape of nineteen bluestones also makes me wonder how people might have used the setting for their ceremonies, were the sun and the moon represented by a priest and a priestess of each cult standing together in front of each of the trilithons?

The complexity of the monument and the time and effort taken to produce such a marvellous temple shows that they were devoted to their religious beliefs. There is no doubt that the main solar and lunar religions were widespread, because stone circles were built across much of western and northern Britain. Major sacred sites, such as Avebury and Stonehenge in Wiltshire, must have attracted large numbers of people from both near and far to the key religious festivals linked to the changing seasons, the agricultural cycle and above all, the high points of the lunar and solar cycles. Like any organised religion the priesthood would have required a means of measuring time and developing a religious calendar, so that the major ceremonies could be closely linked to key astronomical events of the lunar and solar cycles. In addition the timing had to be reasonably accurate, so that the public spectacles of processions, rituals, prayers, offerings and services could be linked together and culminate at the most auspicious moment, when the sun or moon rose or set. So what was needed was a way of predicting events sufficiently accurately in advance, not just for the correct day or night but also the best moment to actually start the various ceremonies.

As I mentioned in an earlier chapter, the time of sunrise and sunset changes according to the time of year and from a fixed location the position of the sun can give an indication of what time it is. During daylight hours you can work out an approximate time by looking to see where the sun is in the sky and of course that is exactly what people did in the days before clocks and watches were invented. Long before such complex artificial devices were developed people used simple sundials to give an indication of the time, with the shadow of a pointer (the gnomon) indicating the hour.

At Stonehenge there were thirty windows around the sarsen circle and viewed from the centre the positions of sunrise and sunset would have varied according to the time of year. For example, the summer solstice sun rises between stones 30 and 1, whilst at the winter solstice the sun rose between stones 6 and 7. At this latitude the length of daytime also varies according to the season, in summer there are approximately sixteen and three quarter hours of daylight and seven and a quarter hours of darkness, whilst at the spring and summer equinoxes, night and day are nearly the same length. And in winter, daytime lasts less than eight hours and the night lasts more than sixteen hours. But it should also be remembered that societies without the benefits of electricity regulate their activities in parallel with the amount of daylight available, using artificial light much more sparingly than we do.

At the Ring of Brodgar we saw how the stones could have been used as a clock and calculator to witness the times of moonrise and moonset, sunrise and sunset throughout the year. The time could have been worked out at Stonehenge using a complete day and night of thirty 'hours', each of 48 minutes In summer this would mean about twenty-one windows (21 Neolithic hours), between sunrise and sunset, then in spring and autumn it would be fifteen windows and in winter, ten windows. Obviously, the timing was not very accurate but it was better than nothing at all, and least the stones could give a rough indication of how long it would be until midday or dusk (as long as the sun was shining!).

Around 2300 BC the sun was at its maximum daily range only at the summer solstice, between rising in the northeast and setting in the northwest, and giving a time span of about 1,000 minutes, from 3.40am to 8.20pm (4.40am to 9.20pm BST). Worse still, the range of time was even less at the winter solstice, with the sun rising in the southeast at about 8.25am and setting in the southwest around 4.10pm, giving a window of sightings of about 465 minutes.

At night, the full moon could act in the same way as the sun, giving an idea of the time by its position in the appropriate window. For example, in winter the full moon rose in the northeast around sunset, at about 4pm and at midnight the full moon would be due south and seen over stone 11. Another problem is that as the day wore on and the sun rose higher and higher in the sky it would be harder to estimate its position from the centre of the circle. So perhaps some of the stones in the bluestone circle were used as a guide, with the shadow of the edge of the sarsen lining up with a particular bluestone, in the same way that the hour hand of a clock lines up with the numbers marked on the dial. But of course, the sundial clock only worked when weather conditions allowed, but it was an improvement on just a rough guess of the time.

From the earliest times of organising the ever-increasing number of modern day visitors to Stonehenge the authorities have been getting things wrong. In the early days, the old 'Department of Public Works' was responsible for displaying the temple to the public, but they did this in a poor way, with few facilities to cope with the escalating numbers of visitors. (There was not even a restaurant.) In the late 1970's the ever increasing numbers made it necessary to prevent the hordes of people from getting too close to the stones, so a path was set up around the outside of the temple. The current tour starts by looking at the western side of the ruined temple first, moving in a counter-clockwise, or anti-sunward, direction. The path then leads round the monument passing the southern entrance and ending up next to the Heel Stone with a view of the most impressive remains of the sarsen structure, the run of four lintelled uprights that flank the northeastern entrance. This was the main entrance to the temple and had the most significance for anyone approaching the temple from along the Avenue, the ancient ceremonial route from the northeast, yet in more modern times this is almost the last view the visitor sees of the temple in the organised tour.

It would have made much more sense for the millions of visitors to have their first good view of the temple from the angle it was intended, from the northeast. Then they could have followed the path round the circle to the east, then south and west, in keeping in step with the natural movements of the sun and the moon. A dim memory of ancient religious practises remains in our folklore: it was forbidden to travel 'widdershins', that is anti-clockwise, round a stone circle for *'fear of raising the Devil'*. The fact that over the decades, millions of people have travelled widdershins around Stonehenge suggests that the old black magic didn't work very well!

The Bluestones

The Bluestones take their name from their greeny-blue colouring when wet. They are made of several different types of rocks including spotted dolerite, unspotted dolerite, rhyolite, calcareous ash and two types of sandstone. For many years they were known to be foreign to the Wiltshire Plains area, but exactly where they came from was unknown. There were several ideas and one ancient myth even relates that Merlin had brought the stones from Ireland! Finally, in 1923, Herbert Thomas of the British Geological Survey established their true source. Many of the spotted dolerite stones come from just one small area on Carn Menyn in the Preseli Mountains, in southwest Wales. Recently it was shown that at least one of the volcanic rocks, a rhyolite, came from an outcrop known as Craig Rhos-y-Felin, near a bridge called Pont Saeson, close to the village of Crosswell. This village is north of Carn Menyn, and just a few miles to the west is the massive burial chamber of Pentre Ifan.
Research to discover the origin of other bluestones is on-going, many of the missing stones are only known from thousands of small fragments discovered from excavations inside the earth circle. The history of the bluestones is still a bit mysterious. There has been some speculation about whether the stones were brought directly down off the mountains and transported to Salisbury Plain or whether the stones were already in use in different settings before they were moved to Wiltshire.

The traditional explanation, dating from around sixty years ago, maintained that the stones were transported to the site in a very crude, rough, natural state and only shaped and polished at Stonehenge. However it is far more realistic to think that the Ancient Britons were not stupid and that they would have made the stones easier to transport by pre-shaping them, so that they were nearer to their final size and form. The confusion has arisen because excavation at Stonehenge has found thousands of small fragments in the earth, but these are probably the result of final shaping, of later alterations to old shapes, and from the smashing up of some of the stones in Victorian times, when people hammered away at the stones to take away fragments of stone as souvenirs. Unfortunately many of the stones from the Bluestone circle are missing so that it is currently difficult to know the original number, estimates have varied from as low as thirty to as high as seventy, although the usual number is estimated as 56 (the same number as the Aubrey Holes).

According to Stukeley, in a plan of the temple and in the text of his book of 1740, there were originally 40 bluestones in the circle, but this was a pure guess on his part, since many stones were already missing when he made his engraving of August 1722. But I think that it is more likely that there were 59 or 60 of them, the same number as the Ring of Brodgar, in which case they could have been used as a tally to keep track of two complete lunar months. (Perhaps the ancient priests had a religious calendar whereby they conducted different rituals on different days according to an eight-week cycle?)

In the final temple there were about eighty bluestones in total, so moving them all the way from Wales, to Salisbury Plain was a tremendous feat of human endeavour. Once the stones had arrived, they built a circle of about sixty bluestones around the inner circumference of the sarsen circle and put a further nineteen in a U-shape in front of the trilithons. The largest of the Welsh stones, the Altar Stone, is a huge, greenish, sandstone block that sparkled with mica in the sunlight. Previously scientists have thought that the Altar Stone came from the Cosheston beds, upriver from Milford Haven. It now seems likely to have come from more than sixty miles to the east, from the Senni Beds in south Wales, around the Sennybridge area, near the market town of Brecon. The Altar Stone weighs over four tons and is sixteen feet long, and three and a half feet wide, and a failed experiment in 2000, moving 'the Millennium Stone' from South Wales, has vividly shown just how difficult such stones were to move and just how determined and skilful our ancestors really were.

Like the sarsens, the most likely method of moving the bluestones would have been on wooden sledges, since they would be much easier to handle that way and a variety of different techniques could have been used, changing according to the terrain and the obstacles encountered. Once the stones had been brought down the mountainsides they were probably brought across country to the sea. From there they travelled by boat, probably across the Bristol Channel and up the Bristol Avon, across land to the river Frome, across country to the River Wylie in Somerset and from Salisbury, up the Dorset Avon to Amesbury, near Stonehenge. The river journeys were probably conducted in winter and early spring when the water level was high, the banks were at their widest apart and underwater obstructions could be more easily passed by the heavily laden boats. Modern experiments have shown just how difficult it is to move even one megalith a hundred metres, let alone up and down hills, through woods, across streams and valleys, on and off boats etc. Only one thing would have engendered and maintained such a superhuman effort. **Religion.**

The other, much more dangerous, route would have been all the way round the coast, passing Land's End, well out to sea to avoid the rip tides, reefs, shoals and cross currents and eventually arriving at the sheltered ancient port of Hengistbury Head, near Bournemouth, and from there up the river Avon to Stonehenge. In this way nearly all the voyage would have been by water. The problem with this theory is that no wrecks of contemporary large, wooden sea-going boats have been found, but that doesn't mean that fishing boats or rafts weren't used. They certainly had a tradition of making simple dugouts and birch bark canoes from much earlier times, and even today the traditionally made hide-covered wicker boats, such as the Irish currach and the smaller Welsh coracles still follow a very ancient method of construction. Even today no metal is used to fix the different parts together, so the original construction method probably predates the Bronze Age.

There is also plenty of archaeological evidence of fishing and of trade across the Channel with other European countries. The Neolithic immigrants of Britain came from what are now Portugal, Spain and Brittany, whilst others came from Denmark, Germany and the Netherlands. And people who had crossed over the sea from Ireland settled in northwestern and northeastern parts of Scotland. One of the famous burials in the Stonehenge area was that of a Bronze Age man, known as the Stonehenge Archer, and analysis of the enamel in his teeth showed that he had grown up in mainland Europe, in a region close to the Swiss Alps. The Orkney Islands were settled before 3700 BC and to do so the farmers must have crossed the Pentland Firth by boat, along with their families, cattle, sheep, wheat and barley seeds, and all their other belongings. They certainly didn't swim across one of the most notorious stretches of water around our coastline. Even today in summer, and travelling at fifteen knots, the ferry takes forty minutes to cross from John O'Groats to South Ronaldsay or two and a half hours from Thurso to Stromness, so the earliest settlers must have travelled with highly accomplished sailors and fishermen who had substantial sea-going boats.

Three prehistoric plank boats have been found in the Humber estuary, two in the Severn estuary and a superb 15-metre long boat at Dover, all made from planks of oak. The oldest is over 3,700 years old and they all show signs of an evolution of complex boat-building techniques far removed from those of a simple dugout canoe. The even more remote Shetland Islands were inhabited by the time the Bluestones were moved from the Welsh mountains and traders were moving stone tools, flint and pottery from one side of the country to another on a regular basis. And in some cases it was far easier to move along rivers than across the densely wooded countryside. The knowledge of local conditions obtained from such journeys would have been invaluable when it came to moving the Bluestones from south Wales to Salisbury Plain.

However, it is depressing to realise that some of our foremost prehistorians still refuse to accept the idea that it was people, not glaciers that brought the bluestones to Wiltshire. Most glaciologists are in agreement that the bluestones were not deposited on Salisbury Plain by recent glaciers. There are simply no other glacial deposits of dolerite in the Wiltshire area. If glaciers had been responsible for moving the stone all the way from south Wales there would have been a large quantity of small, medium and large rocks and pebbles strewn over a wide area, particularly along the river valleys.

But since this is not the case, there is only one possible conclusion, the bluestones were transported to Wiltshire by hard-working people, not by an ancient ice sheet.

The most frequently asked question about the early phases in Stonehenge's history is: *"Why did they bring the bluestones all the way from Wales, especially when there was plenty of sarsen stone only a day's walk to the north?"*

Clearly something very special had motivated them to perform this Herculean task. At first sight it does seems very strange that with large building stones just to the north, why would anyone want to travel to a place 150 miles away, collect stones weighing four tons or more, and then move them all the way to Salisbury Plain in England?

Until now, no one has been able to suggest a really convincing explanation for this enigma, although one of the more interesting early theories said that the stones were considered to have 'magical properties'. On the other hand, if modern influences are anything to go by, the repeated rebuilding of Stonehenge over the centuries may well have been due to periodic religious revivals. From historical sources we know that great religious building works are often the result of a religious re-awakening, causing a sudden impetus amongst a previously complacent congregation to do something special to celebrate their beliefs. A new project brings people together in a joint effort to modernise the work of previous generations, to show that they are just as good, if not better, than those who have gone before.

So what did motivate the people of Salisbury Plain to go all the way to the mountains of Wales to collect the stones for their new temple? In the modern world we are so used to goods being transported from far-off lands that many of us have not really appreciated just how difficult it must have been for them to move hundreds of tons of stone from so far away. In those distant times there were no canals or railways or motorways. No lorries, no container ships, no transport planes, just a great deal of ingenuity, know-how, skill, and a hell of a lot of muscle power. Moving the bluestones all the way from Wales only makes sense if the stones had great cultural or religious significance to the farmers and settlers on Salisbury Plain. Perhaps it was because they had moved from their Welsh homeland to new pastures far to the south. And of course many different cultures have migrated great distances, bringing with them the old traditions but adopting new ideas, new materials and new methods of construction from other areas and other cultures, in order to construct and decorate their own temples, palaces and homes. The bluestones may also have represented something exotic, a high status foreign import, as well as a demonstration of the dedication of an ardent congregation. Only a large, highly successful and well organised community, with plenty of food reserves, could afford to take the time to collect special stones from so far away and construct such grand monuments. An interesting thought is whether the stones were gifts, booty from conquest or were the result of trade. And if they were traded for, I wonder what the Stonehenge people gave as barter and what was the rate of exchange? How many cattle, or sheep, or bags of flour and grain, winter furs, stone axes or jars of honey was a bluestone worth?

However one of the real answers to the question: *"Why did they bring the bluestones all the way from Wales?"* is actually inherent in the stones themselves.

Despite the fact that Stonehenge has been actively studied and researched for more than three hundred years and that there have been many excavations, hundreds of books, and the publication of thousands of articles, in the scientific and popular press, few people seem to have noticed something that is remarkably obvious, once you really look. In many textbooks and other publications, the circle Bluestones are described as natural shapes whilst those in the in the U-shaped arrangement of 19 stones are portrayed as being of only two types, either a tall pillar shape or an obelisk. But this is simply not true. There is in fact a great diversity of shapes and sizes amongst all of the Bluestones, some stones have straight sides, others have rounded sides and some have angled sides. Some have flat tops, some have rounded tops and others have angled tops. The largest stones are more than six feet high and the smallest stones measure less than three.

Following Richard Atkinson's lead, many authors state that, apart from a couple of stones that had been dressed and used as lintels, the circle stones were just natural shapes that had been left unaltered. In contrast, the nineteen stones of the U-shape were artificial, for they had been trimmed, dressed and polished into pillars. Although previous authors had thought that the stones of the bluestone circle had been altered, Atkinson dismissed any claims that they had been artificially shaped. Atkinson also said that identical stones could still be seen on the slopes of the Preseli Mountains in South Wales. **This is also untrue.**

The confusion has arisen because in some cases the builders chose natural stones that were already close to their final form. Natural stones are just that, natural, and untreated, whereas all of the bluestones at Stonehenge have been altered and re-shaped, some more than others. In the Preseli Mountains there are several major outcrops on the summit of Carn Menyn. The western outcrop has masses of tumbled stone on its sloping western side and a few of these rocks do indeed resemble the longer bluestones of Stonehenge. But they have very irregular sides and rough edges where they have broken away from the bedrock and when I looked I couldn't see any of the large rounded shapes like circle bluestone 31 or even the smaller ones like 37, 46 or 47.

All over the Pembrokeshire area are the remains of ancient monuments and the area to the south of Carn Menyn still has several tall standing stones, some of which are singles and others are in pairs. There are also small stone circles made from local types of rock, including spotted and unspotted dolerite, and although many have been disturbed by farming or have been almost completely destroyed, there is still a circle of sixteen small stones at Gors Fawr and the remains of another at Meini Gawr. So I think that it is reasonable to believe that some of the Stonehenge bluestones were part of existing stone circles that had been transported from Wales, perhaps when local people migrated to better farmland on Salisbury Plain. The bluestones are of many different rock types, so I think that the people of a large part of south Wales were bringing some of the bare bones of their native homeland with them to Stonehenge. This is in similar fashion to the way parts of special ancestral skeletons, particularly their skulls and long bones, were moved from tombs as part of some sort of ancient sacred ritual. We still do it today; the bodies of people who die abroad are often flown home to be buried locally.

The skeletons of many of our famous dead are buried in Westminster Abbey, a very long way from where some of them died. Amongst all of the Kings and Queens that are interred in the Abbey are the remains of soldiers, scientists and scholars and other famous people, such as David Livingstone, who died from malaria in Africa in 1873.

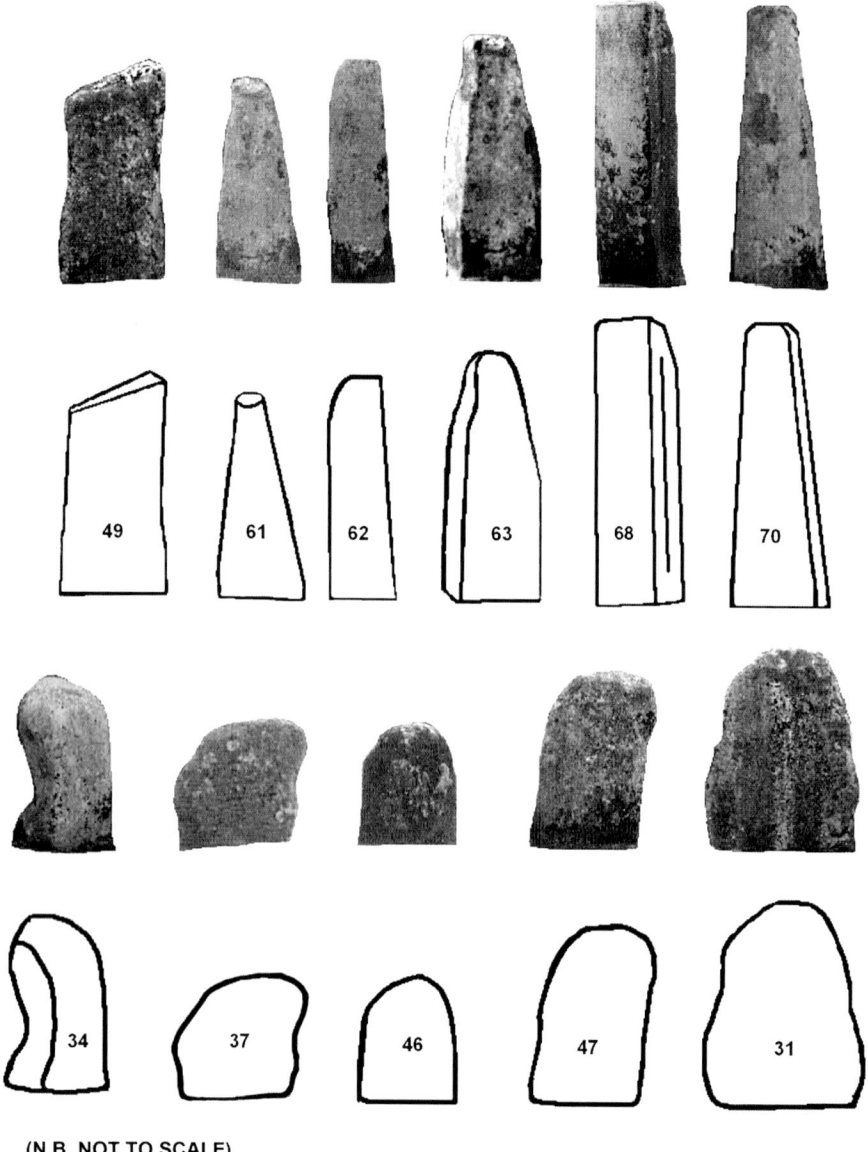

(N.B. NOT TO SCALE)

Some of the different shapes of Bluestones, stones 31 to 47 are from the circle and 61 to 70 are from the U-Shape.

The differences in shape and size of each of the Bluestones clearly shows that, like the sarsens, they too are part of a coded system of shapes and that these systems of symbolic shapes were used in the same way as we would use written signs, to store information. So I think that the information that was encoded in the shape of each stone was linked to astronomical, cultural and religious meanings. In other words, the Bluestones were part of a symbolic language, written in stone. A modern example of how special symbols can work well is the internationally recognised system that we use for our road traffic signs, which is based upon the same simple geometrical shapes of squares, triangles and circles. Small changes to the symbols on the signs alter their meaning, for example, priority from the right or the left, crossroads or a T-junction, no entry, no parking etc. We use many thousands of different symbols for our company logos and trademarks because symbols can be an excellent method of giving a lot of information in one easy-to-recognise form, once you are familiar with the symbol and its meaning.

If you are still sceptical and think that all this seems very unlikely, then it may help to remember how the Egyptians used pictures of objects, gods, people and animals in their hieroglyphs. For example, an isosceles triangle, a half moon and a star represented the hieroglyph for Sirius, the brightest star in the sky. And Sirius had a very important place in Egyptian mythology. Its heliacal rising at the summer solstice marked the advent of the annual flood of the Nile and the start of a New Year. However it should be noted that **I am in no way** suggesting that the Egyptians and the Stonehenge people exchanged information, but rather that, like many people across the globe, they invented similar concepts, derived from their own experience of local astronomical phenomena, including the direction, appearance and movements of the sun, moon, stars and planets.

Flinders Petrie's numbering system has not been successful when it comes to the numbering of the bluestones. The current system is based on the stones now visible, not as they were in antiquity. Consequently there are sometimes large gaps between successive numbers, particularly between stones 32, 33, 34 and between 40, 41 and 42.

Passing into the temple through the main entranceway, between stones 1 and 30, the visitor walks between two of the most important Bluestones at Stonehenge. Bluestone 49 is a tall column with a sloping top and 31 is an oval stone. (In the background of the photograph is the famous Heel Stone.) Only one or two authors have remarked on this pairing of contrasting shapes but even then they have invariably thought of them as simply male and female stones, belonging to some nameless fertility cult.

But as I've said before, in many ancient religions the sun was considered to be masculine and the moon feminine, so columnar 49 is a sunstone, whilst oval-shaped 31 is a moonstone. Bluestone 49 is a wedge-shaped oblong, with a sloping top, which rises from left to right. If you look towards this stone from the centre, it means that you are looking towards the northeast. Therefore stone 49 must represent the summer solstice sunrise. Stone 31 is a large, rounded stone, reminiscent of the body of a very pregnant woman, and it marks the halfway point between the major and minor extremes of the northern moonrise.

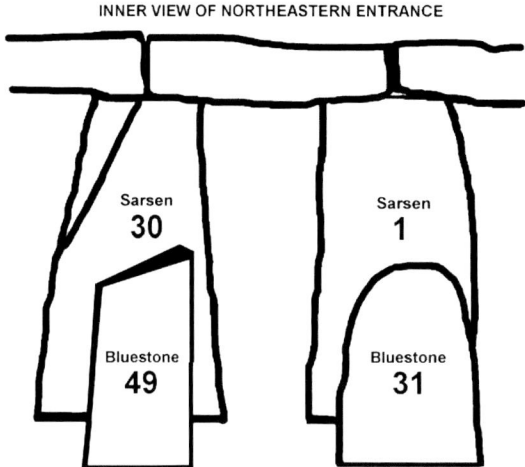

INNER VIEW OF NORTHEASTERN ENTRANCE

These two stones, 49 and 31, were set up in a very special place, on either side of the main entrance to emphasise the northeast/southwest (life/death) axis of the monument. They are representatives of the concept of duality in the natural world for they represent the pairings of male/female, man/woman, sun/moon and summer/winter. And looking at their shapes, why not the numbers 1 and 0 (one and none, or more likely, one and all)? Such basic numbers must have been used throughout antiquity, so why not here at Stonehenge? It was after all the most important religious site in this part of Northern Europe and there is ample proof in the way that they used specific numbers of stones throughout the British Isles that our ancestors could count. It would be very surprising if they couldn't add up.

The usual source for the invention of our numbers is believed to come from the Indian subcontinent, but the use of the forefinger to denote the number 'one' is very basic to many cultures, even the Romans used it as the first unit of their system. But it was clever of the Neolithic priests to use shapes that could refer to several concepts at the same time. If they had wanted to refer only to the male principle or the male sexual organ, (the Giver of Life?), they could have used a much more phallic shaped stone, such as the ones in the middle of the Boscawen-un stone circle or at Men-an-Tol, both in Cornwall or even the famous Lia Faíl at Tara, near Newgrange. As for the female/ winter/ moon-stone, number 31, if they had wanted to illustrate just the female principle then they could have used a more obvious shape, such as the large circular, holed stone at Men-an-Tol in Cornwall.

Just behind these two very important bluestones are two large sarsens, stones 30 and 1, which frame the main entrance. The inner face of sarsen 30, standing behind the male/summer/sun blue-stone also has a slope cut out of the top left corner, and again its partner on the other side of the axis, stone 1, is also quite a rounded shape. In other words, the symbolism of the traditional pairing of male/female and sun/moon shapes found in the two bluestones was copied in the sarsen circle. It is also tempting to wonder if this pair of bluestones had been installed in an earlier bluestone temple on either side of the axis, so that there was continuity down through the ages.

Bluestone 47 represents the major northern moonrise, whilst stone number 48 represents the most northerly rising of the full moon. This is a rounded stone, one that it is currently leaning so far over that it is almost flat on the ground. It needs to be re-erected. Unfortunately, like so many other stones, the Bluestone further to the east of stone 31, the one that would have related to the minor position of winter moonrise, has disappeared. In the southern half of the temple the other extreme positions of the lunar swing cycle, the major and minor standstill rising and setting points, would also have been represented by special Bluestones, but unfortunately these have also disappeared and all that remains are the holes where they once stood.

MOST NORTHERLY RISING POSITIONS OF THE MOON AND THE SUN

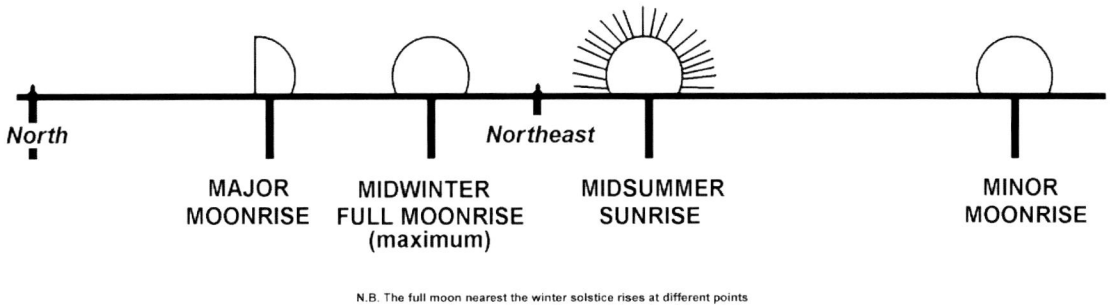

N.B. The full moon nearest the winter solstice rises at different points between its maximum position (to the east of the major rising point) and the minor rising point during the swing cycle of 19 or 18 years.

According to conventional wisdom Stonehenge was not a scientific observatory, but investigators keep making the same mistake of assuming that the ancient astronomers and priests had only used the centre of the sarsen circle as the viewing position. Previous researchers had assumed that because a central point was used for construction, a central viewpoint would have been used for every observation and hence the prediction of future appearances of the sun and moon. However, there are two ways of examining astronomical directions, either as a sightline from the observer towards the celestial body or as the light from the celestial body coming towards the observer. This simple difference in outlook explains some of the minor mysteries surrounding Stonehenge. One such mystery concerns the very narrow gaps between the uprights of the trilithons. The problem with using a single viewing position from the exact middle of the sarsen circle is that the gaps between the trilithon arches do not all line up with it. One needs to move backwards or forwards along the axis so that the horizon can be seen through the gaps between the different trilithons.

The relative positions of subsequent sunrises change with the time of year. As the sun approaches a solstice, the sun appears to slow down, rising at decreasing intervals along the skyline, until near the solstice it stays almost in the same place for each successive sunrise. Conversely, as the sun approaches the equinox position, the sun appears to rise at larger distances apart each morning, decreasing again once the equinox has passed. One way to think of this is as a series of different size beads on a necklace, the smallest beads would be at each end, increasing in size towards the largest beads in the middle. It is also like a giant pendulum that speeds up at the bottom and slows down as it reaches the highest point of the swing. In Wiltshire, it takes about 180 days to cover the 80 degrees between the summer and winter solstice sunrise positions.

In addition, the orbit of the earth around the sun is not circular but an ellipse with slight perturbations, and as a result there is a slight difference in the number of days between the two halves of the year. Because of all these different phenomena, regularly spaced gaps between the stones would not fulfil their role as windows if the viewing position in the centre always remained the same, the gaps would simply not fit in with the pendulum effect of the sun. That is one reason why the observer needed to use different viewing positions according to the event he was studying.

Nearly fifty years ago the astronomer Professor Gerald Hawkins suggested that the architecture of Stonehenge had been built to accommodate a series of alignments with the sun and moon in their extreme positions. He suggested that they had set up the first trilithon (uprights 51/52) to align with the midwinter sunrise and the second trilithon (53/54) with both major and minor summer moonrise directions. The fourth trilithon (57/58) gave alignments towards the two winter moonset positions and the fifth trilithon (59/60) gave the summer sunset position. And we already knew that the third set of stones, the Great Trilithon (55/56), marked the midwinter sunset.

The publication of his immensely popular book, *'Stonehenge Decoded'*, in 1966, caused a storm of protest from the archaeological fraternity. One of their main objections to his theories was that his alignments could never be one hundred per cent accurate simply because nearly all of the stones have been moved and replaced at some point and they were not always replaced in exactly the same place as before. Secondly, he had used certain alignments between stones that are known to have been erected at widely different times. And thirdly, he had arbitrarily chosen certain holes in the ground to line up with other stones. Although some of these holes may have contained missing stones they may have simply been where trees and bushes had grown in the circle and then rotted away. Another major problem for the Establishment was that sightings of the sun or moon through the slits between the trilithons, and through the sarsen archways, are far too rough and ready. In many cases the angles are much too wide to give the exact date of a specific astronomical event.

Although many of his first ideas were excellent, and he correctly identified that the positioning of the trilithons was of fundamental importance, Hawkins certainly upset many people by going on to suggest that the ancient astronomers were capable of predicting solar eclipses by using the Aubrey Holes as a sort of abacus, (something I am very dubious about).

This has overshadowed the validity of his earlier theories. In reality, Hawkins was very close to an even better understanding, but because he was influenced by what he had read in the archaeological textbooks of the time, he failed to take into account the next logical step, that of including the Bluestones in his calculations of lines of sight. Only the direction towards the sun or moon was taken into account and not the effects of light and shadow that are produced by them. This too is important since at the start and end of the day the temple can be a maze of light and shadow.

As the seasons change, the point of sunrise moves round the horizon and the light of the rising sun casts long shadows from the stones. And when the rising sun is directly behind the narrow gap between the trilithon uprights it forms a beam of light that shines along the ground, a bit like a laser. (Remember the winter sunlight effect at Newgrange?) I am not completely sure, but I think that not only were people able to see the sun (or moon) rise or set through a trilithon and the archway window behind, but also that some of the Bluestones would have been lit up by these special beams of light. (This is a bit like the minute hand of a clock or watch coinciding with a numeral on the dial.) Further astronomical calculation and examination on site will be required to see if this new theory is correct.

I think it very probable that Bluestone 70, which still stands in front of trilithon upright number 58 in the fourth trilithon, was a special marker stone for the spring equinox because it is a tall stone with long, equilateral sloping sides. The identical length of each sloping side could thus represent the equal number of hours between day and night at an equinox, which are also the mid-points between the winter and summer solstices. I'm not completely sure, but I think that bluestone 70 would have had a major role to play twice a year in determining the date for the equinox festivals. It may have been used to determine the dates of the spring or the autumn equinox because of the way that the equinox sun rose opposite it through the window between sarsens 3 and 4 and shone directly into the temple. Prior to this the rising sun would be hidden from view at this location by either stone 3 in the case of the autumn equinox or the stone 4 in the case of the spring equinox. For example, as the spring equinox approached, an observer standing behind stone 70 and looking towards the east, would not see the exact moment of sunrise for several days. Then one day the first flash of sunlight could be seen as it appeared round the side of sarsen 4, and a beam of light would light up the face of stone 70 in the process. For more than a week afterwards successive sunrises would be seen in the gap between 3 and 4, until one morning the first flash was hidden again, this time by the edge of sarsen 3.

As regards the midwinter sunrise, the direction and date was probably marked by fallen bluestone 71. On the shortest day of the year the light of the rising sun came in through the space between sarsens 6 and 7, and then into the inner sanctum through the narrow gap between the uprights of the first trilithon, 51 and 52, until it touched bluestone 71 on the opposite side. However, before we get too carried away with this new theory, I feel that I must repeat my earlier warning that the actual positions of standing stones are quite often just a representation of a particular direction and are not necessarily astronomically correct. They can be several degrees out because many of the stones have been replaced and then set in concrete. The stones can often represent in a symbolic manner the rising or setting positions of the moon or sun during their respective cycles and at such a major place of public worship and celebration as Stonehenge, religious symbolism was more important than pinpoint scientific accuracy. And anyway, who knew they were wrong?

Two of the bluestones from the circle (36 and 150), bear the distinctive holes of mortises, having acted as the lintels for small Bluestone trilithons, although both of them are currently partially buried. Stone 36 is particularly modern looking, like a large kerbstone from the side of a road, with carefully dressed surfaces that are very smooth and thus indicating a new-style stone. Two of the Bluestones from the U-shape show traces of tenons on their tops, so the logical explanation is that these stones supported a lintel at some point, prior to their erection in their current position. Lintel 150 is now situated towards the east of the circle and 36 is close to the southern entrance, so perhaps they are the lintels of two Bluestone trilithons that acted as gateways to the cardinal directions. Since east and south is an unusual combination, there may even have been other trilithons to the west and the north, however since so many stones are missing, this must remain as pure speculation on my part. Nevertheless it is an interesting idea that there may have been an intermediate phase using a circle of Bluestones, one that included trilithons at the cardinal points.

The stones in the Bluestone circle were not spaced regularly apart inside the sarsen circle, as they would have been if they were purely for decorative purposes. Nor are they all the same distance from the inner circumference of the sarsens. Their positions were important for the lighting and shadow effects I mentioned earlier. The difference in spacing between the stones was originally put down to the inability of the builders to measure out a perfect circle from the centre, because the trilithons were in the way. But in reality it would have been a simple job to produce a new circle of bluestones, simply by using a measuring stick placed against the inner surface of each of the ring of sarsen stones, thus keeping each new bluestone the same distance away from the sarsen circle stones.

Another of our enduring mistakes has been to assume that the Neolithic astronomers had the same way of thinking as our own scientists. But ancient people could appreciate complex astronomical phenomena through observation, without needing to know or understand the science behind it. (In the same way as so much of our modern technology can be used by ordinary people without understanding how the hardware or software actually works). The construction techniques used to create the final version of Stonehenge show a skilful use of surveying, geometry, proportion, engineering, architectural techniques and styles, and of course the equally difficult task and organisational abilities to get the new temple past the planning phase and into solid reality. So I think it is safe to assume that people who were capable of such major construction projects as Stonehenge, were also capable of the far simpler task of building sightlines into the temple, which would have guaranteed dramatic lighting effects at key times of the year. Any sunrise or sunset could generate beautiful and moving lightshows to accompany a special ceremony but the best known of these is of course sunrise at the summer solstice. But there was also other major displays using the rising or setting sun at other times of the year, such as at the winter solstice, which marked the passing of the old year and the start of a New Year.

I have written mainly about the inside of the temple, but there were other structures on the outside, such as standing stones, palisades of timber posts, and banks and ditches of earth. The first concrete evidence that Neolithic people understood the lunar swing cycle is in the accurate positioning of the Station Stones, the four sarsen stones numbered 91 to 94. A plan of Stonehenge made by Stukeley in 1740 shows all four stones still in place. Although two are now missing, these were originally arranged in the form of an oblong just inside the earth circle next to the Aubrey holes.

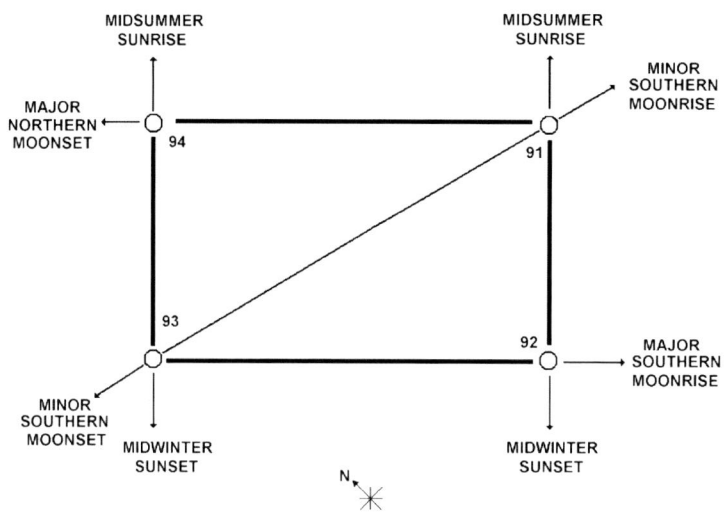

THE STATION STONE RECTANGLE

A diagonal sightline from stone 93 towards 91 pointed to the minor southern moonrise, whilst the line from 93 to 92 gave the major southern moonrise. And the line from 91 to 93 pointed towards the minor northern moonset whilst the alignment from stone 91 to 94 showed the direction of the major northern moonset. There are also solar alignments along the shorter sides, the lines from 91 to 92 and from 94 to 93 gave the midwinter sunset, and the sightlines from 92 to 91 and from 93 to 94 point to midsummer sunrise. So in effect this apparently simple combination of four stones elegantly provided the directions for many of the major and minor moonrise and moonset positions of the nineteen-year swing cycle. And it marked out the extreme positions of the annual journey of the sun, namely midsummer sunrise and midwinter sunset.

N.B. Hawkins used alignments with the position of several other holes to fill in the missing directions for the major northern moonrise (92 to hole G) and (centre to hole F) for the minor moonrise. These holes are subject to some controversy.

So clearly the Station Stones provided alignments that were associated with the solar and lunar symbolism of life and death and gave timing information for the two solstices and for the southern moonrises and northern moonsets. As the time for a special event approached, a watcher could stand next to one stone in order to observe the position of the rising or setting sun or moon getting nearer to the other stone each day. In this way it was possible to check in advance the timing for their special ceremonies, including the lunar festivals associated with important rising and setting positions of the moon during the swing cycle.
The longest sides of the rectangle were about 80 metres apart and the diagonal between Station Stones 91 and 93 was about 87 metres long. The shorter sides of the rectangle, the alignments towards midsummer sunrise and midwinter sunset, were just over 30 metres apart. The distances between the stones meant that they were far enough apart for reasonably accurate observations although by no means perfect. But did it really matter to the ancients that their solstice markers were out by a few days? I think not.

There is also the possibility that the stones were deliberately placed a little to the right, so that they would give a few days warning of the actual event, this would give people time to prepare for the ceremony and if necessary, travel from some distance away. There is plenty of physical evidence, in the form of pottery, tools and stone axes that people were travelling quite long distances to go to important sites such as Windmill Hill and Avebury, as well as visiting the large village of Durrington Walls near Stonehenge. This is where the workers, artists, priests and chiefs would have lived.

Life in rural communities is slow because it is physically very demanding and revolves around agriculture, the farming year and the eternal cycle of the changing seasons, not the precise measurement of time. At the solstices the sun rises at the same point, or close to the same point, for several days so the correct date was when the priests said it was the correct date, and the right moment for a ceremony to celebrate the swing cycle or the winter or summer solstice. The simple yet complex way that the Station Stones were arranged amply illustrates my point that ancient astronomers did not always work in the way modern scientists would, and that the sightlines they used were not invariably from the centre of a circle. In this case the celestial alignments were from one stone to another across the earth circle, even though for the solstice dates the Station Stones were much too close together to give what we would consider a scientifically accurate measurement. It was religious symbolism and the associated ceremonies and special rituals that were important, not scientific exactitude.

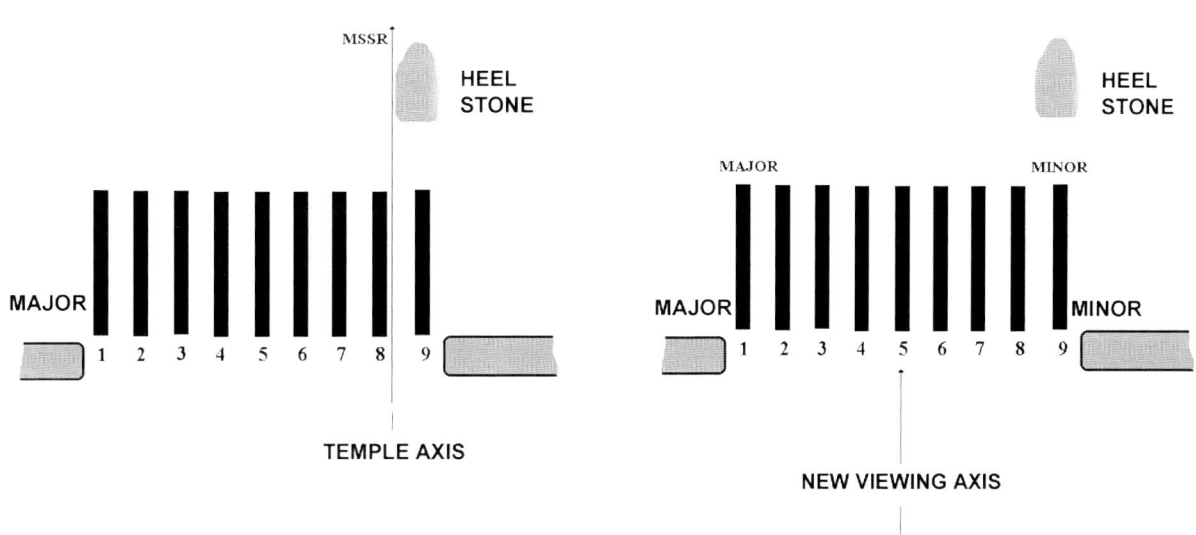

SCHEMATIC DIAGRAM OF ONE ROW OF CAUSEWAY POSTS FOR DETERMINING THE 19 YEAR LUNAR SWING CYCLE POSITIONS

SINCE POST 9 IS ALIGNED WITH THE MID POINT BETWEEN THE MAJOR AND MINOR EXTREME RISING POSITIONS, SIGHTINGS ALONG THE TEMPLE AXIS WOULD ONLY GIVE PARTS OF THE COMPLETE 19 YEAR SWING CYCLE. IN ORDER TO MARK MOONRISES OF THE COMPLETE CYCLE, FROM MAJOR TO MINOR AND BACK TO MAJOR, A DIFFERENT VIEWPOINT IS NECESSARY.

There remains one small mystery to discuss. Although the diagonal line from Station Stone 91 to 93 towards the south-east gives a summer moonset alignment, it is the other two stones, 92 and 94, which were given special status by being raised on mounds and surrounded by a small ditch and their diagonal doesn't seem to have an obviously important alignment. Both 91 and 93 are missing but I think they have just been moved and are now standing in the main street of the nearby village of Berwick St. James. These have been carved in a style contemporary to the other stones. One of these two carved stones has a very pronounced concave surface and an urban myth has suggested that this was caused by the passage of iron cartwheels when the stone was laid down in the street! In the northeastern entrance of the causeway excavators found a series of postholes in six rows of nine holes and it was proposed by C. A. Newham in 1963 that they were probably used to record the different winter moonrise positions of the lunar swing cycle over six, nineteen-year periods. To me this idea is a bit strange because the Station Stones already marked out the extreme directions of the lunar swing cycle and in addition, there would have been no need to record so many complete cycles over more than a century, they would have known that one or two 19-year cycles would be quite sufficient. In addition, the extremes of the lunar swing cycle had already been in use for hundreds of years in northern Scotland, and we know that trade was widespread between the north and south. Several scholars have made a fundamental error in their diagrams and theories because their plans show that the causeway posts were positioned to mark the northern moonrise alignments of the swing cycle. But if the viewing position was along the axis of the monument, then the right hand post was in line with the Heel Stone, however this only marks the direction of the moon at the midpoint between major and minor position of the lunar swing cycle. The complete swing cycle is from major to minor and then back again so the halfway point of the complete swing cycle is actually at the minor position.

The Heel Stone actually represents the midpoint of the moon's **return** journey between the major and the minor positions. If the ancient astronomers had been investigating the complete cycle there should have been additional posts to the right of the Heel Stone, to mark the moonrises between it and the minor standstill position. There aren't. So according to the conventional theory, only the first and last quarters of the whole nineteen-year swing cycle could have been observed and recorded by the posts. Oops!

Of course there is also the very strong possibility that the sets of causeway postholes represent something completely different, they may just have been the posts for some sort of decking, fencing or even ritual buildings erected at different times. So I think that it is more likely that they put up posts in the four 'A' holes to mark successive maximum annual moonrise positions to determine the major position, because they run in a line from the left bank of the Avenue to the Heel Stone.
Most people think that the Heel Stone indicates the position of the rising sun at the summer solstice, but it actually represents the moon. Due to the effects of precession the sun has slowly moved further south over the millennia and in 2500 BC the first flash of sunrise was even further to the left of this large sarsen stone than it is today. Weather permitting, a few minutes after the first flash of sunlight appears on the distant horizon, the full disc of the sun moves upwards, then rises over the top of the Heel Stone a few minutes later, a bit like the dot on the letter i.

Using the solstice sun as the basis for a highly accurate calendar would have been quite difficult, since around this time of year the sun rises at the same time and in the same place for several days in succession. If it did have a solar role, then it is more likely that the Heel Stone was used to estimate the time remaining before the date of the summer solstice ceremony. Each morning up to the summer solstice the sun rises slightly further to the north, and when the first flash of the rising sun was directly behind the Heel Stone the priests knew that it would be a week or so before the actual midsummer solstice. The exact date of the solstice could be determined by the experience gained from previous years, simply by counting the days of successive sunrises until the first flash returned to its position behind the Heel Stone, and then dividing by two.

In 1979 archaeologist Mike Pitts excavated a trench just to the northwest of the Heel Stone and he found a very large pit, which had once contained a massive standing stone. He demonstrated that the pit had been dug earlier than the ditch around the Heel Stone, in hole 96, and I think that there are two possible explanations for its use. The first one is the conventional theory that at one point there was another standing stone in hole number 97, near to the Heel Stone and that the pairing of the two stones provided a 'solar corridor' for the summer sun. However, if this theory is correct then I am surprised that the two stones were not placed parallel to each other, like a pair of sarsens or a trilithon. The second explanation, and the one I prefer, is that the Heel Stone had originally been in pit 97 and had subsequently been moved to its present position.
In this scenario, the Heel Stone was the very first stone on the site and when it stood in hole 97 it was a midsummer sunrise indicator for Stonehenge 1. Due to precession, the point of summer solstice sunrise moves slightly to the east over a long period, and it takes about a thousand years for it to move one degree. When the axis of the monument changed with the building of the sarsen circle, the Heel Stone was no longer much use as a sunrise marker. So it was removed and placed in its present

position in hole 96, as the marker for a lunar swing cycle position and perhaps as a timing signal for the approaching summer solstice.

Another aspect of the well-known image of the summer solstice is very phallic in nature. The Heel Stone seems to penetrate the sun after the glowing disc has risen higher in the sky. And in the very remote past of the early farmers, this sort of image may have been the symbolic theme of fertility rituals and ceremonies around midsummer's day. Human pregnancy lasts nine months, so if fertilisation took place at the midsummer solstice, children would be born near the spring equinox and with the warmer weather and fresh food supplies for their mothers, babies would have a better chance of survival. In more recent times the Maypole dance that was celebrated on Mayday, was linked to fertility. This traditional dance was based on a folk memory, the very diluted remains of ancient rites, dating back at least to the Iron Age, if not long before.

Several drawings from the 17th and 18th Centuries show that were originally four more standing stones, two on each side of the causeway. Three of them have disappeared, but lying flat on the ground just inside the entrance to the circular ditch and bank is the Slaughter Stone, which is all that remains of a pair of very large stones that were set up to frame sunrise at the summer solstice and some of the most northerly moonrises. In the final version of Stonehenge, they constructed the U-shaped arrangement of nineteen Bluestones and this is compelling evidence, written in stone, that the ancient astronomers were aware of both the swing cycle and the Metonic cycle. To remind you, the Metonic cycle is when the same moon phase occurs on exactly the same date again, but nineteen years later. This is because 235 lunar months are very close to nineteen years (only 125 minutes out). In my view, this shows that they understood the Metonic cycle as well as the lunar swing cycle and that they used the stones to keep track of both cycles, and it is yet another reason why they went to all the trouble of going to South Wales to collect the specially shaped Bluestones.

Whether the geometrical system originated in Wales is another matter, I think it more likely that it originated in Orkney, where sandstone slabs often occur naturally as long oblong shapes. Many of these long thin slabs were used in the construction of tombs and chambered cairns such as at Maeshowe, and also for building the five thousand year old village of Skara Brae. And as we have already seen, some of the largest slabs of sandstone were used as symbol stones for the stone circles of Stenness and Brodgar. The Orcadians are also the inventors of a type of pottery known as Grooved Ware, which was imported and used at Durrington Walls, the large village inside a huge henge next to the River Avon, a few miles to the northeast of Stonehenge. The size of these flat bottomed vessels varies greatly, from just a small cup to very large containers that were suitable for brewing as much as 30 gallons (136 litres) of beer at a time. Clearly a good reason to grow lots of barley!

What the Metonic cycle meant in practice was that if the full moon rose on the night of the summer solstice, the people would have to wait nineteen years before the same thing happened again. The discovery of the Metonic cycle is credited to the Greek mathematician Meton in the 5th century BC but much earlier civilisations are known to have used it extensively in their calendars and eclipse records. Civilisations that had accurate calendars often had a more scientific way of thinking, which is a result of a logical, ordered approach to life in large towns and cities. This is exemplified by the use of standard sized units of measurement, and even in the use of the same sized sun-dried bricks, baked clay or stone blocks to build homes, temples, citadels and palaces.

The Stonehenge people did not use regular sized building blocks, and we have already seen some of their reasons for doing so, some of the stones were symbols in stone and others were used for something else, which I will reveal later on. I think that the builders of the final temple at Stonehenge were close to a mathematical solution to their problems but were side-tracked away from developing the necessary means of calculation and of inventing a more compact and portable way of recording extensive data over a long period of time. Perhaps they relied too much on their traditions of remembering secret and sensitive information orally instead of developing a written language.

But we shouldn't be too hard on them for not developing writing, the Mesopotamians are credited with developing one of the first written languages but even they took many years to develop their cuneiform script, from little tokens of baked clay that had been in use as tallies for centuries for trading purposes. Other writing systems for recording information were developed as long ago as the last Ice Age, but they have not yet been deciphered.

As I mentioned earlier, the Neolithic farmers needed a calendar for agricultural purposes and the priests needed to keep track of the cycles of the moon and the sun so that people knew when to come for special ceremonies. The job of producing an accurate calendar would have been made much easier if each year was 360 days in length and the lunar month was exactly 30 days. If this were the case then there would be exactly twelve lunations in a solar year. Unfortunately none of the lunar or solar cycles are that simple. The establishment of an accurate calendar was a major problem for many civilisations. In Roman times the calendar was so inaccurate that on one occasion, the end of May occurred during the winter! A solar eclipse in 190 BC was recorded 119 days out of synchronisation with the actual season and it was not until Julius Caesar finally corrected the calendar nearly a hundred and fifty years later, in 45 BC, that the calendar became more accurate, by the addition of eighty days to the year 46 BC.

However other civilisations such as the Greeks, Babylonians and the Maya were far more adept at keeping track of time, even being able to predict eclipses from past records of the Saros cycles. (The Greek word Saros, meaning repetition, is derived from the Babylonian word 'sharu'). These patterns of eclipses occur in sequences that are repeated every eighteen years and ten or eleven days. However, even this is by no means straightforward, the Saros cycle moves forward across the globe by a third of a day and so the next eclipse in the 11 August 1999 cycle, takes place over America on 21 August 2017.

The Islamic calendar uses a year of twelve lunar cycles, in a year of 354 or 355 days. So it is also possible that the Stonehenge people used an exclusively lunar method of calculating a year. If the Stonehenge people used the same sort of lunar basis to determine their ceremonies, then it would be the night of the summer or winter full moon that was important, rather than an exact date that stayed the same each year. However since the temple is filled with references to the sun and the moon, I think they may have used a combination of the movements of the sun and the moon to determine their ritual calendar. The only other possibility of an accurate calendar is if they had great knowledge of the Metonic cycle, using this as a basis for a calendar, they would need to have used a cycle of twelve years of twelve lunar months and seven years of thirteen months. (13, 12, 12, 13, 12, 12, 13, 12, 12, 13, 12, 12, 13,12,12,13, 12, 12, 13 etc.) It certainly makes me wonder if the expression 'unlucky thirteen' comes from keeping track of this phenomenon. The more usual explanation is that it refers to the traitor Judas Iscariot, one of Jesus Christ's twelve disciples.

In the 21st century we are obsessed with time and dates, this was not the case four thousand years ago. The actual date of the solstices varies slightly when there are leap years and since the sun seems to stand still for several days, it must have been hard to say *'Today is the solstice'.* The planning of the religious festivals must have taken into account the problems of the weather and of not being able to see sunrise for several days in winter. If the solstice was close to a full moon, the actual day may have been altered so that full moonrise was followed by solstice sunrise the following morning. This alteration to the date would give the congregation a double festival, for example, summer full moon and midsummer sunrise. In the Christian calendar, the actual date of Easter is moved around from year to year, so that the main service usually falls on the first Sunday after the first full moon following the spring equinox. Jewish festivals are also linked to the moon and the Chinese New Year is celebrated on the second full moon after the winter solstice. And I have noticed that many Neopagan groups and Modern Druids, (The Ancient Order of the Druids was founded in 1781), often alter the dates for holding their seasonal ceremonies, so that they fit in with the weekend!

I have described above the sort of setting the remaining Bluestones are in today because it is easier to appreciate them in this way. However, when they first arrived from Wales, they were arranged in several different settings. Firstly they were erected in the Aubrey holes and then evidence for their removal and erection in a second setting comes from Atkinson's excavation of the Q and R holes. The part of the circle that was excavated by in 1954 showed that these were arranged in a sort of crescent moon shape, which covered the northern to the southern extremes of the moon, and were in an arc from north-northeast to southwest. Atkinson believed that the double arc continued all the way round the circle, but at that time a large part of the western side had remained untouched, so at that moment he simply don't know what it was like. Later on, in 1954 and 1956 he investigated this further and discovered that there had never been a full circle of bluestones, the arc went east, roughly from about 46 all the way round to 40c. (Two parts have not been fully investigated, an area to the north, between 43c and 46, and another to the south, approximately between 34 and 40). The Altar stone may have stood at this time in a very large pit on the axis at one end of the arc of Bluestones.

A few other pits on the western side of the circle have been found and these have sometimes been seen as some of the 'missing' parts of the Q and R arrangement. What is known is that the stones in the parts that have been excavated were arranged next to each other, so that there was a sequence that probably went 2, 2, 3, 4, 4, 3, 2, 2, etc. The gap between the central two rows of four stones was along the axis towards the solstice sunrise in the northeast. On either side of these rows of four stones was an extra, unfinished hole, as though the original design called for extra stones. I also wonder if Bluestone trilithons were arranged at head height across the two rows of four stones, so that the lintels I mentioned earlier formed a sort of covered passageway across the axis?

Atkinson's diagram shows a total of 38 stones but then, without a complete excavation, he went on to estimate that the whole arrangement of the Q and R circles would have contained more than double that, 82 Bluestones in all. There also seems to be a certain amount of confusion about this whole stage of construction, one that may only be resolved by further investigation of the northern and southern sides of the arcs of stone holes.

Atkinson called this arrangement Phase II and it included the construction of a ceremonial Avenue leading into the enclosure from the northeast. (His Phase I consisted of the earth bank and ditch of the original enclosure plus the Aubrey postholes and the Heel stone, whilst his Phase III started with the simultaneous construction of the trilithons and the sarsen circle.) The actual date of Phase II, the first Bluestone temple, is unknown at present, but it must lie somewhere between the end of Phase I and the beginning of Phase III, at least 4,400 years ago. In view of the difficulty of moving the stones all the way from the Preseli's, there is a possibility that this temple was never finished, simply because it may have taken too long to construct, with pairs of new stones only being added to extend the arc as they arrived on site. Archaeologists have found many chippings of Bluestones during their excavations, which has led some to think that all the work was carried out on site after the raw stones were imported from Wales. However, the stones of the Bluestone circle are far less worked than the tall, slim stones of the U, so I think that some of the old symbol stones, imported in a finished state, were altered to form the new style stones for the U and the lintels.

The image of Stonehenge is now iconic and millions of people have visited the ancient temple to see it as it is today, but it wasn't always a ruin. Over two days during the summer solstice in 2005, Channel 5 Television presented a show entitled *'Stonehenge - the Ultimate Experiment – Live'* that recreated and demonstrated for the public a replica of Stonehenge, as it would have been around 4,000 years ago. The show included the design and construction of the replica and contained documentaries, expert commentary and discussion, special experiments, as well as computer-generated images and re-enactments using actors and modern day Pagans. The stones were specially modelled and carved from full-size blocks of polystyrene and painted to resemble the way they would have looked when freshly carved. Some were light cream and others a light pink in colour, not at all as we see them today, battered, sadly stained, and eroded by the effects of time and the action of moss and lichen. Strangely enough the Altar Stone was put up behind and outside the trilithon U-shape, instead of in its more usual, and eminently more acceptable, position in front of the Great Trilithon.

I am not sure what archaeologist Mike Pitts was thinking about when he redesigned the temple for the show, especially since he is one the leading authorities on Stonehenge and he should know that it would have been impossible for the Altar Stone to have moved from behind the Great Trilithon to its current location, underneath stone 55. Common sense dictates that the Altar Stone must have stood in front of the trilithon and must have been knocked over and partially buried when the upright stone and its lintel came crashing down. Many of the missing bluestones were replaced by new stones for the replica but this new arrangement of bluestones varied in height without any obvious reason or pattern. However, the real bluestones that remain suggest that the stones of the bluestone U-shape originally rose in height from each side towards the centre, in a similar fashion to the trilithons behind them, and which is the case at many other stone circles across the British Isles, notably in Aberdeenshire, in County Cork and in Devon. In spite of these minor criticisms the show was generally very interesting and gave to many people a brand new understanding of the way that the old temple originally looked like and gave new insights into how it may have been used for ceremonies so very long ago.

So to summarise my insights and discoveries: Firstly they built a mortuary enclosure with a circular bank of white chalk to symbolise the moon. Next they added two series of twenty-eight posts to refer to two lunar cycles, the fifty-six Aubrey Holes. When the posts had decayed they added Bluestones for a while, then these were removed and they used the pits as a cremation cemetery, but even that didn't last, the site was abandoned for decades. Then the building of a new temple of Bluestones in the centre of the earthwork infused a new breath of life into the old site. This temple was in the shape of a lunar crescent with a solar corridor along the axis. Next the Bluestones were moved again and some very large sarsens arrived to form a circle of tall, free-standing sarsen uprights. Later on these were altered and then joined together by a lintel ring along the top. Next an inner circle of Bluestones was added, followed by the trilithon U-shape of sarsens, the bluestone U and the Altar Stone. Finally the stone version of the final temple was finished (although two circles of pits, the X and Y holes, were added later on, shortly before the temple was abandoned).

The major insights and amazing discoveries and breakthroughs that I have outlined above should help change our perceptions, and our understanding, of our prehistoric ancestors and they suggest that it is time for a complete re-evaluation of the intelligence and capabilities of our distant relatives.

For many years a small percentage of authors, scientists, and in particular, astronomers, have said that the builders of Stonehenge have been seriously underestimated by orthodox archaeology, now here is the proof, written in stone, that they were much smarter than we thought they were. So I think that we should be immensely proud of what our ancestors achieved, more than four thousand years ago.

6 THE ART OF ANCIENT BRITAIN

In earlier chapters we saw how our Neolithic and Bronze Age ancestors created and used a variety of different systems for representing information that was important to them, and we saw how this information was not recorded as a written language but was stored in the form of specially shaped stones and specially designed monuments. In this way the systems that they created gave permanent structure to their ideas, beliefs and culture and by using these techniques they could communicate valuable information to current and future generations.
But that wasn't the end of all that they achieved, far from it, I have also discovered that they had another, much more important way of communicating and recording different aspects of their lives. And they did this by inventing a wide variety of new art forms and then used these to create an extensive range of extraordinary works of art. In other words, the history of our prehistoric ancestors was not stored in the form of written records. Instead of using a written language they preserved important parts of their culture, by developing and using some radically new styles of art to form complex images, which recorded important aspects of their culture and their beliefs, and as someone once said:

"A picture tells a thousand words."

This series of amazing discoveries will lead us to a completely new understanding of the lives of our distant forefathers because the works of art that they created will give new and profound insights into their lives, their religious beliefs, their history, their daily lives and mythology. It will also fundamentally improve our knowledge and understanding of the development and history of art, and give unprecedented access into the minds of the people who created it.

At this point I have to make a slight diversion, in order to explain how I came to discover the existence of an enormous quantity of prehistoric sculptures, carvings, paintings and engravings. It all started for me in the late 1990's. Like many people I was never very interested in history at school, I much preferred science. My interest in prehistory was only awakened much, much later, through reading the wonderful series of books called *'Earth's Children'* by the American author Jean Auel, and many of you will have read her books *The Clan of the Cave Bear, The Valley of Horses, The Mammoth Hunters, The Plains of Passage, The Shelters of Stone,* or *The Land of Painted Caves.*

Her series of six novels relates in remarkably vivid detail the lives of people who lived about 30,000 years ago, at a turning point during the last Ice Age, when Neanderthals were still alive. Although fictional, the stories are very soundly based on anthropology, archaeology, geology, geography, botany and zoology. And Jean Auel brings to life the unwritten past in such an outstanding way that you feel you know and understand the lives of the characters in her books intimately, almost as well as you know your own friends and family.

The books made me want to know more about the prehistoric past, so I started to visit museums, go to prehistoric sites and read guidebooks and textbooks on prehistory. But as time went by, I became more and more puzzled, because the rich social and cultural life of Jean Auel's characters was nowhere apparent in the books that I read or the places that I visited. Everything seemed sterile, with little trace of humanity or of individual human endeavour and achievement. My local museum was particularly unhelpful. A display case showing the two hundred thousand year period preceding the end of the last Ice Age was covered by just a few stone and flint tools and weapons and remarkably little else. So much was missing, uncertain, unknown or unexplained. Millions of people had been born, lived out their lives and then died, without apparently leaving any trace of their existence. There was however in other display cases some information about our ancestors from more recent times. These displays were about people from the Neolithic period, starting from about five thousand years ago, and they showed the sorts of tools, weapons and pottery that the first farmers used, together with a few photos of a handful of their temples and tombs. But so much seemed vague or just plain missing, where was the information about actual people? Who were they? What were they like? How did they live their lives? And what were their beliefs? And I had dozens of other questions to which there seemed to be no satisfactory answers.

I started reading the archaeological textbooks in more detail and I soon discovered that there was a great deal of confusion, controversy and debate between the acknowledged experts. But sometimes it seemed to me that the explanations and the motives they gave for people's actions did not seem to tie in well with what we would consider typical human behaviour. Further studies revealed to me that many of the conventional theories, particularly those dating from before the 1960's, have been proved completely wrong! And unlike every other scientific discipline, progress in understanding our own unwritten history has been slow, tortuous and tedious, it seems to have been two paces forward and one step back, or sometimes, one pace forward and five paces back!

The three hundred year journey of archaeological research into our prehistoric past is riddled with dead ends, wrong turnings and one-way streets. Time and again conventional wisdom has subsequently been proved completely incorrect. In addition, according to our scientists, academics and scholars, our own forefathers made hardly any cultural and intellectual progress for hundreds, if not thousands of years, as though the people of those ancient times were as unimaginative and stupid as the sheep they were rearing. Yet despite all the progress that has been made using recently developed technology, what became clear to me was that, after more than three hundred years of investigation, there were still some very basic questions that remained unanswered. This is in stark contrast to the enormous scientific advances that have been achieved in every other branch of science since the beginning of the 20th Century.

What archaeologists and prehistorians have discovered over the last three centuries does not reveal very much about the character of our pre-Roman ancestors. Nor does conventional wisdom reveal much about the mentality of the people who left such obvious reminders of their way of life. This very visible evidence takes the form of the great stone and earth structures of Neolithic and Bronze Age Britain. All across the British Isles are the ruined remains of hundreds of barrows, tombs, cairns, henges, standing stones, and of course, the very famous stone circles we know as Stonehenge and Avebury. And although there have been many excavations over the centuries, what is largely missing from the archaeological record are the human stories, the details of daily life and the family histories of the hundreds of thousands of people who were born, lived their lives and died in this country. Even though there is plenty of data about the things that our scientists have unearthed, and apart from their bones there is a distinct lack of understanding about the people of the ancient world. Despite decades of investigation, the only evidence of works of art, and the artists who made them, over an eight thousand year period are remarkably few in number. From the Neolithic period onwards, the most commonplace form of 'art' was the decorated patterns inscribed on earthenware pottery. However, there are some notable exceptions to this simple decoration, such as the symbols inscribed on special stones in passage grave tombs in Ireland, such as those at Newgrange, Dowth and at Loughcrew. As I showed earlier, these symbols represent sacred themes concerning life and death, the sun and the moon, but they include a variety of other symbols, such as spirals, wavy lines, lozenges, chevrons and arcs.

There is also another variety of different decorations known as *'cup marks'* and *'cup and ring marks'* that occur mainly on standing stones and stone outcrops in Scotland and in parts of northern England. There are also a few art objects such as the curious, ornately carved stone balls from Aberdeenshire and Orkney. Further south, excavations have uncovered a few decorated chalk plaques from Wiltshire; some small, elaborately carved, chalk 'drums' from Folkton in Yorkshire; some simple jewellery; a few inscribed bones, and from the flint mines at Grimes Graves in Norfolk, came a small, poorly carved and highly suspect sculpture in chalk of a fat woman. (This is usually referred to as a representation of the Earth Mother, but no other images like it have been found and many think it is a fake). From the Bronze Age have come some finely decorated gold plaques from Clandon Barrow in Dorset and the Bush Barrow near Stonehenge; a superb ceremonial gold cape from Mold in North Wales, numerous bronze tools, weapons and other metal artefacts.

Yet in all those centuries s there were apparently no portraits, no sculptures and no paintings created, just those few simple carvings and engravings. Art, as we know it, seemed to have been completely forgotten about and only made an appearance in Britain much later on, during the Celtic Iron Age, sometime around 750 BC.

It all seemed so insignificant to me. Was this it? Was this a true and accurate reflection of the intelligence and creativity of hundreds of thousands of people? Was this the only art that our Neolithic and Bronze Age ancestors had managed to create over a span of some two thousand years? To me the absence of ancient British art did not seem to tie in with the wonderful monuments they built. Nor did it tie in with what else we know of the history of Mankind. Even during the harsh climate of the last Ice Age, when much of Britain was covered by a thick sheet of ice, the decorated caves of Chauvet and Lascaux, in western France and the cave of Altamira, in northeastern Spain, were used by generations of artists. They painted wonderful scenes of wild animals, particularly bulls, bison and wild horses, as well as giant deer, red deer, ibex, reindeer, mammoths and woolly rhinos. Some caves were decorated by artists more than 30,000 years ago and the tradition of cave painting, as well as the carving, decorating and sculpting of small portable items in ivory, antler, stone and wood continued for another twenty thousand years, until the rise in temperature heralded the end of the Ice Age, sometime around twelve thousand years ago.

This incredibly long tradition of artistic excellence represents skills passed from father to son and mother to daughter for a thousand generations or more, an incredibly long expanse of time when one considers that so few of us today continue in the same professions as our parents or grandparents. Yet even before the start of the Palaeolithic period, around forty thousand years ago, people were producing art in some form or other all across the known world. Over the ensuing millennia it was even created by small nomadic tribes in tropical rainforests, by desert people, by people in small farming communities, but perhaps the best art of all was created by the town and city dwellers of the great civilisations. In other words, people have always produced art, in one form or another, for it is one of the principal characteristics of human behaviour and self-expression.

Throughout Europe, the Middle East and Africa, and as far away as the New World, and in China and Australia, art played a vitally important role in the culture, mythology and daily lives of many different prehistoric societies. But what had happened in ancient Britain? Where were the works of art and the artists who created it? It did not seem possible to me that one of the most fundamental attributes that make us all human, the gift of creativity, was missing. I became convinced that there was something very wrong with what we have been told about our ancestors, and I realised that particularly suspect were the theories and knowledge we have inherited from the Georgian and Victorians eras, which unfortunately forms the basis for many of the traditional and conventional ideas about our distant past. Even more suspect was the propaganda of the Ancient Romans, whose written accounts classed everyone else as a primitive barbarian.

In every culture and society since we first evolved, the human spirit has been expressed through song, dance, music and most of all, storytelling. Human intelligence has been expressed through its inventions and through its creativity and art in all its forms. There is no doubt that cultural development and art go together, hand in hand. Art is symptomatic of human society, it mirrors our evolution, our thoughts and our lives and even the most basic types of human society, in the most hostile of environments, have expressed themselves artistically in some form or other, even if it was simply by decorating themselves and their weapons or making toys for their children.

Art and creativity were part of the religious as well as everyday life in prehistoric societies and ancient civilisations across the globe. In every society people have worn a range of ceremonial headdresses and masks for rituals and wearing different sorts of specially decorated clothing proclaimed their social status. Prehistoric art was present in such diverse places as Siberia and Australia, Scandinavia, Mesopotamia and Ancient Egypt, and all around the Mediterranean in countries that would later become Greece, Crete, Turkey, Spain, Malta, and art was present in the Far East, India, Japan and China. So what had happened to the cultural and artistic life of Ancient Britain? Was there really nothing here or had the first researchers, the Georgian and Victorian antiquarians and archaeologists, been unable to see anything special because they weren't looking hard enough, simply because they believed that our distant forefathers were too primitive to create works of art? (This was certainly the case for the scientific community and the general disbelief concerning the authenticity of the first Ice Age cave paintings that were discovered, at Altamira, in Spain in 1879.)

Yet the widespread belief that our Neolithic ancestors were so unsophisticated has never really made much sense, because how else could they have created such architectural wonders as Newgrange, Calanais, Maes Howe or Stonehenge? Until fairly recently many scholars tried to explain this apparent enigma by suggesting that the designer or architect of Stonehenge came from another country, instead of being the work of a home-grown expert. Fortunately this racist approach was firmly knocked on the head when much better radiocarbon dating showed that the experts had been completely wrong and that the megalithic buildings in Britain and Ireland predated the architecture of the early civilisations in Greece by a thousand years or more.

So if there were artists and works of art all over the world at around this time, then what had happened in the British Isles, where was our art? I found one of my first clues to this major enigma after a visit to our most famous prehistoric site, Stonehenge. I was looking at a photo I had taken of the Heel Stone, which stands outside the main circle.

The Heel Stone, Stonehenge

The Heel Stone is famous because just after sunrise on the summer solstice the rising sun passes over the top of this stone, a bit like the dot on the letter **i**. This photo had been taken one very wet and windy afternoon in late autumn 1998 and as I was examining the print a few days later, I noticed that some lines had been heavily carved into the surface on the east side of the stone. To me these lines on the Heel Stone very strongly resembled the lines of the mouth and the nostrils of some sort of animal, such as a wild cat, a beaver or perhaps a hare.

Yet when I looked for confirmation in various archaeological textbooks, there was no mention of any sort of art on the Heel Stone at all or indeed on any other stone at Stonehenge, apart from a few shallow carvings of Bronze Age axes and a dagger on some of the temple stones. However, I had worked as a professional photographer for many years and one of the first things you learn to do, is to really look at what you are looking at and to observe closely what you are seeing, in order to see the finer detail and to go beyond what is immediately obvious. In this way a photographer can perceive things that are not quite so evident to other people. This is also something that other artists do. They look at reality, and then use their creativity and imagination to record it in a particular way so that others can see the same thing, but this time through the eyes of the artist. Sometimes this is a pure representation of reality, and a faithful copy of the original, but at other times the work of the artist is far more creative and the art can be highly stylised, abstract, surreal and a work of pure imagination.

A visit to the enormous stone circle at Avebury in Wiltshire followed and in the South Circle of huge standing stones I could clearly see some rather bizarre sculptures, one was of the head of a white horse on a large stone and another was the head of a ram. In addition, at the far end of a long line of parallel stones, called the West Kennet Avenue, I could see another sculpture of a horse's head, a bit like the knight in a game of chess. I could see that these images were not like the accurate and realistic images of animals that Ice Age artists would have created over ten thousand years earlier - it seemed to me that the Neolithic artists had chosen naturally shaped rocks and then altered them to create works of art. And it seemed to me that they were intended to be artistic representations of the spirit of the animal, rather than just an accurate portrayal of the animal itself.

South circle stones, Avebury, Wiltshire

During the course of my early research I also read that a few other visitors to Avebury had seen similar images, but when they had consulted the acknowledged experts on prehistory, they were told that they had just been imagining things. The traditional explanation for this is that our ancestors had chosen the rocks because they had been shaped by nature into interesting shapes. However, in spite of this initial setback, I persisted with my investigations for three reasons, the first was that I had a belief in my own, trained, eyesight and that secondly, experts, especially prehistorians, are not always right, particularly when theories are hundreds of years old.

A stone at the far end of the West Kennet Avenue, Avebury, Wiltshire

And third reason was because it quite simply did not make sense to me that intelligent people would go to all the trouble of mining, transporting and then erecting hundreds of enormous lumps of rock at their religious sites for no obvious reason or purpose, but that they would do so if those rocks were going to be transformed into symbolic images, idols, statues or sculptures.

And of course that is precisely what they did.

Since that early breakthrough I have discovered that huge stones (megaliths) were quarried and then transported to sacred sites where they were transformed. Whilst some became sculptures, others became symbolical or astronomical markers, although many of these are sophisticated and highly complex works of art as well. Until now, standing stones, stone rows and stone circles have remained mysterious because we simply haven't seen them for what they really are, nor have we really appreciated just how radically different the ancient sculptures and carvings are from the Classical styles of Greek, Roman or Renaissance art that we are more used to. Instead, many Neolithic sculptures have more in common with the abstract works of art of modern sculptors, particularly artists such as Henry Moore, Barbara Hepworth and Richard Long; and it is well known that the megaliths of Stonehenge and other ancient sites inspired some of Moore's work. Like many artists before him, (including such famous painters as Constable and Turner), Moore was attracted to the shapes and textures of the stones without consciously realising what he was looking at. Like us, he had been conditioned to believe what the experts had said about the stones, that they were simply works of nature, rather the work of much earlier artists and sculptors. Yet after a visit to the painted cave of Lascaux in the Dordogne, France another prominent artist of the 20th Century, Picasso, is reported to have said: *"Nous n'avons rien inventé"* (We have invented nothing). In other words, in his opinion the ancient artists of the last Ice Age had been the true inventors of many of the styles and techniques of painting, engraving and carving that are in common use today, but were invented more than seventeen thousand years ago…

Since first observing the ancient images of horses at Avebury I have discovered that our ancestors created many other works of art that have been lost and forgotten and that they invented many styles of carving and sculpture that will be completely new to us. It will also come as a surprise to many people that most prehistoric sculptures are far more complex and far more subtle than the works of art that we are familiar with, pieces such as the statues of important people in our towns and cities, or the famous lions in Trafalgar Square, (which are large-scale reproductions of a living animal, cast in bronze by Sir Edwin Landseer). Our sculptures and statues are usually three-dimensional images that show the face, sides and back of the subject and according to your viewpoint, you can see the front, the right profile, the left profile or the back of the person or animal. This was rarely the case with prehistoric sculptures, since in most cases each of the faces and sides of large stones were used to represent different images.

There are thousands of single standing stones scattered across the British Isles and nearly all those that I have seen have been decorated with works of art of one sort or another. Although many are sculptures, sometimes they are simply boundary stones, whilst in other places they are symbol stones with directional or astronomical importance. Others are images of people or gods or animals, whilst some are memorial stones, like our tombstones. In many instances the sculpted stones were further enhanced when additional images were carved into them in later periods. Unfortunately, many standing stones have suffered extensive erosion and damage over the millennia. Thousands have been broken up and many hundreds of them have been moved from their place of origin to clear space for crops to grow and be harvested and farmers often re-used thin, oblong stones as convenient gateposts. This is particularly common in Cornwall. The observant visitor can often see large stones and panels from the side walls and roofs of chambered tombs that are now part of drystone field walls.

One of the best sites that I know of that easily and convincingly demonstrates the existence of prehistoric sculpture in Britain is the group of standing stones that were erected on what is now the second fairway of the Ladies Golf Course at Lundin Links, Fife, which is on the northeast coast of Scotland, about 40 miles northeast of Edinburgh. The three massive stones are composed of red sandstone, each is more than twice the height of a man and they are the remains of what was once an even more impressive group of four stones. They are one of the best examples that I know of that answers a fundamental question, one that has often been posed about prehistoric standing stones, namely: *"What are they?"* The answer to this riddle is ridiculously simple and with hindsight it is very obvious, as riddles often are, once you know the answer, but it has taken us simply ages to see what has been under our noses all this time.

If the stones had been erected a mere four or five years ago then we would immediately recognise them as the work of an artist, for in fact the standing stones are of course ancient sculptures and the complete group of stones is a work of art.

Lundin Links, Fife

I would guess that these stones were put up about four and half thousand years ago, at around the same time as bronze was first introduced into Britain. And they are a fine example of what was, for the people of that time, a work of contemporary art.

Once you actually take the trouble to really look at them, it becomes blatantly obvious that, although each is based on what was originally a natural piece of rock, each of the standing stones has been altered and carved. The thin one at the back, to the north, is a sculpture of a white-faced man in left profile. He is facing to the left and is wearing a full length parka with a hood with a pointed top. The stone at the front, to the southwest, looks to me like the highly stylised body of a woman, one with a long thin body and a tiny head, reminiscent of the sort of elongated shadow effect you get when the sun is very low in the sky, shortly before sunset. Such elongated forms are quite common in Bushman rock art paintings in southern Africa and more recently, in the work of the artist Giacometti.

In addition to this sculpture there is another carving about half way up the stone. This is of a rather strange, bird-like head with a beak. As for the third stone, the one covered with lichen to the south-southeast, on its broad southern side there are the remains of an eroded picture of a big man with a white face and a beard. He is in profile and is looking to the right and he too is wearing a pointed hat. There are many other images on this side of the stone, including a group of people standing at the lower right corner.

There are other celebrated groups of stones that are actually sculptures and another famous example of these is the arrangement of three stones at Men-an-Tol, near Morvah in Cornwall.

Men an Tol, Cornwall

There are three stones in a line, two are columns and between them is a circular stone with a hole through the middle. In the picture I have concentrated on just two of the stones. Together they demonstrate the two fundamental and active principles of sexual reproduction, the pairing of male and female genital organs and hence the *'Creation of Life'*. The circular stone has a diagonal line across it, to make it more reminiscent of a snake swallowing its own tail. The third stone is the sculpture of the head and upper torso of a man in left profile; he has coarse features and is wearing a round-topped hat with a narrow band running round it.

Other clear examples of the work of ancient sculptors are the burial chambers known as quoits or dolmen. One of the most obvious works of such funerary art is Chun Quoit, *(pictured above)* and it is also near Morvah, in Cornwall. This chambered tomb is composed of four vertical slabs of stone that are roofed over by a large convex capstone. The whole two metre high structure resembles a gigantic toadstool and there is even a strange face carved into the lower left side of the capstone

Lanyon Quoit, Cornwall

Trethevy Quoit, Cornwall

Similar works of funerary art in Cornwall are Lanyon Quoit and Trethevy Quoit, whilst in Wales there are funerary sculptures at places like St Lythans in South Glamorgan, Pentre Ifan and Carreg Coetan in Dyfed. (Incidentally, the heavy capstone at Pentre Ifan is balanced with great care on the nose of a leaping dolphin!)

Careg Coetan, Newport, Dyfed

Pentre Ifan, near Fishguard, southwest Wales

The artists were also busy in Ireland, organising and building similar works of funerary art, some of the best examples are at the major burial site of Carrowmore in County Sligo, and another at Poulnabrone in the Burren, County Clare. Whilst at the portal tomb near Kilclooney, County Donegal, the thin, angular capstone looks like a stylised bird about to take flight.

I mentioned earlier about how the traditional explanation for the standing stones of Avebury was that 'primitive barbarians' had simply selected interesting shapes to decorate their sacred precinct. However, once I started looking with the new insights I had gained I soon realised that the artists had indeed used natural stones, but instead of removing vast amounts of material, as a Greek or Roman sculptor would do with his iron chisels, the more ancient sculptors had used what nature had already provided, and they incorporated the natural shape of the stones into their designs as much as possible.

This style of **natural art** is quite common. The artists and stonemasons weren't stupid, they made it as easy as possible for themselves by choosing designs that fitted the rough, natural shapes of the different stones and then altered them to produce the sorts of images that they wanted. But even so, in many instances there was still a lot of hard work to do be done by hand, using quite simple stone tools. One of the most common forms of stone tools, apart from axes and knives and tools made from flint, are the hard stone implements that archaeologists have called maces or axe hammers or even battle-axes. However, although there are several instances of attack on settlements, such as Crickley Hill and Hambledon Hill in Gloucestershire, and the odd murder or two, life in the Neolithic was relatively peaceful in comparison to the millennia that followed the discovery of metals. So I think that many of these stone implements were not made as weapons but instead they were some of the tools used by the Neolithic artists and sculptors.

They also crafted special versions of these stone tools that were never intended to be used for work purposes. They were made for ceremonial use and as emblems of social standing within the community. One example is the wonderfully carved 'mace head' from Knowth, near Newgrange in Ireland. This was carved in a block of coloured flint to resemble a face, with the handle passing through the open mouth. Another stone tool, this time with swirling layers of several colours, is the *'mace head'* from one of the Aubrey Holes at Stonehenge and amongst several items of gold unearthed from the nearby Bush Barrow, there was an oval stone, originally mounted on a wooden handle. All these implements were clearly symbols of prestige and power. But were they status symbols of the master craftsmen who designed and created their wonderful temples and tombs or were they the insignia of the great artists who decorated them?

One of the outcomes of just making a few minor changes to the rock surfaces to produce **natural art** is that some of these sculptures have suffered so much erosion that they have almost completely reverted to their original forms. And it is this aspect of the megaliths that has given rise to the erroneous belief that all the stones at sites such as Stanton Drew, Avebury, Calanais or Brodgar were just shaped by Nature and simply chosen by Man, a mistaken belief by the early investigators that has persisted right through to the present day. Unfortunately the belief that the megaliths were just natural stones has had a detrimental effect in the long term because we thought so little of them and as a result we have been very careless with our heritage. Many ancient sites are now overgrown and derelict, whilst many others are lost or destroyed. Few, if any, of our most celebrated places have survived intact.

Stonehenge is a picturesque ruin, whilst at Avebury several hundred standing stones were destroyed over the centuries. Some of these were smashed up in the 1300's, others were shattered by farmers in the early 1700's and many more were toppled over and buried by local Puritans in the late 17th and early 18th Century. And it is my guess that these were the most realistic works of art, and they were destroyed by fanatical Christians because they were seen as the work of 'Devil-Worshippers'.

If you look at standing stones from a new perspective, as though you were looking through the eyes of the ancient artists, it soon becomes clear that many of the stones exhibit carvings and sculptures that reflect a world of superstition and belief in the supernatural. In addition to carvings that show various images of actual people, the pictures show images from their histories and sacred beliefs and of course, their myths and legends. They often show faces of humans and humanoids and images of strange creatures, gods and spirits.

We all know that after only two or three centuries the gravestones in our cemeteries can show pronounced effects of time and erosion on the inscriptions, the details become blurred and indistinct, until it's hard to read who the person was and when they died. Therefore one can hardly expect that after four or five thousand years the carvings, engravings and sculptures would be as fresh as the day they were created. They have been attacked by the weathering effects of acid rain, frost, ice and snow, and grit blown by the wind, and damaged by moss and lichen. Consequently the decorations are nowhere near as crisp and clear as they were when they were created forty or fifty centuries ago. Nevertheless, it is quite remarkable just how much art has survived the centuries, although the detail has become blurred over the centuries and the artwork can resemble over-exposed and out-of-focus photographs.

To help reveal the fainter images in more detail I have also pioneered the use of image intensifying computer software on photographs of the megaliths. This can help enormously with giving an idea of what the artwork looked like when it was created all those centuries ago. But there are limits to what can be achieved, because once an ancient image has become very severely eroded, little can be done to return it back to its original state. Many stones have fallen over the millennia and softer rocks that have been lying in acid soil have suffered even more than others. At some sites the stone chosen was so hard that much of the finest work could only be done in low relief and where extensive erosion has taken place, the images are only visible when they are in shadow or when they are lit from the side. Direct sunlight has too harsh an effect on the stone surfaces, the sort of 'ghost image' of the art that still remains is over-exposed by the light and only the deepest carvings are still visible. This is a bit like the effect a very powerful spotlight would have on a faded photograph. In many cases more detail can be seen when the sky is overcast, after it has rained or when the stone is in shadow.

Many of the images are now so faint that it is only through intensive image intensification that any of the decoration becomes visible again. Many images were painted as well as carved and engraved but unfortunately the paint has worn away through time and erosion, although computer software can sometimes intensify what little remains.

In some instances it looks as though the sculptors used the natural differences of colour in the stone to design the layout of the scenes. For example, a crowd scene would have darker figures at the back whilst the people in the centre were carved in a lighter shade of rock. This concentrates the eye towards the action in the middle. Sometimes these natural colour changes were used for large crowd scenes involving hundreds of tiny, individual, close-packed images of people.

One of my biggest problems has been to actually show what the art looked like four or five thousand years ago. In many instances the carving was quite shallow, owing to the tools available and the hardness of the rocks. When all that it is left is a sort of ghost image, it is only by taking photographs and using computer image-intensifying software (Photoshop) that it has been possible for me to see and show you what some of the artwork could have looked like so long ago.

All of the photographs that appear in this book have been edited, sometimes it is just to remove unwanted items from the modern era, such as cars, telephone lines, television aerials - even houses, but most of the changes that I have made were done to enhance what remains of the works of art, in order to make them more visible. Please also note that some of my photographs have needed to be much more intensively worked on than others.

It is hard to describe more than fifteen hundred years of art in just a few pages. It has taken me several years to discover the many different styles of art that the ancient artists created and used and these styles have been discovered in fits and starts, rather than in a constant flow of discovery and understanding. What I have realised is that, over the centuries, the artists developed many different styles of art that in time would become their traditional ways of working, although, as one would expect, the skill of the artist varies from person to person, from place to place and from stone to stone. The sculptures and carvings can vary considerably, from quite simple and stylised forms to very elaborate and extremely complex scenes. The most obvious images are usually the larger sculptures, although there is usually a wealth of smaller carved images all around them that can be just as interesting.

When the ancient artists first studied a freshly unearthed rock they would start to visualise the images that they wanted to reveal, the images of people, animals, or monsters 'trapped' inside the stone just waiting to appear. But unlike more recent sculptors, the prehistoric artists often used the rough surfaces of the naturally shaped stones and they incorporated the curves, lines, ridges, bumps, depressions and holes into the foundations of their artwork. In many cases it was the natural aspect of the stone that dictated what would become the final image. A Greek or Roman sculptor worked on an entirely different basis, they would use squared off blocks of marble and cut large areas away with their drills and chisels of iron, creating a sculpture that was an accurate reproduction of a person, not of flesh and blood, but of stone. Many modern sculptors work in exactly the same way, they can already see in their mind's eye the work of art that they want to realise, even before they start work on the piece of wood, metal or stone that they have chosen to use. A wood carver often follows the patterns, textures and grain of the wood to produce a carving or sculpture and a skilled artist can visualise the final form in the original piece of wood and then bring it into existence.

In the same way, the stone sculptures and carvings of Stone Age artists were works of pure skill and imaginative transformation. They used specially chosen, naturally shaped pieces of stone that could be transformed with only slight modifications to the basic shape. By subtly altering the outline, the natural look of the stone could then take on, for example, the appearance of a human face or the outline of an animal. This was just the start of the process. They then modified the three-dimensional aspect of the stone by carving intermediate sized images and then later on other artists carved and engraved more scenes of small figures of people or animals into the surfaces of the stone. Sculptures of animals are often represented as just the basic head shape, without their ears protruding over the edge of the stone, this may have been intentional or the result of the passage of time and damage to the edges of the stones.

Each site and time period had its own way of altering the basic raw material, in some cases this was only minimal because the natural shape of the rock was close to the required image and needed little alteration. However, many geometrically shaped symbol stones required straight edges and these needed much more work. One way that they would have done this was firstly to peck out a shallow line and then they would build a fire along this line, heating up the stone until it was extremely hot. They then cooled it down very quickly by pouring on water and this stress made the stone more susceptible to break along the line, helped on its way with a sharp whack with a big mallet.

Modern stonemasons will take hard stone such as granite or marble and carve it with tungsten steel chisels but in ancient times transport was more difficult, so the local limestone, soft sandstone or conglomerate near some prehistoric sites was more readily available and although easier to carve, it has been much more susceptible to erosion over the millennia. To make things even more difficult for us to understand, many megaliths were redecorated at a later stage and the new art resulted in even more complex imagery that was created on top of the older art forms. This reworking of the stone has unfortunately meant that it also became less resistance to weathering, particularly if the rock was a relatively soft type.

A good example of this can be found at the Rollright Stones in Oxfordshire where the dozens of sculptured and carved stones are composed of heavily eroded oolitic limestone. One of the pioneers of investigation into prehistoric life in Britain was the antiquary Reverend William Stukeley and in the early 1700's he described the stones as being *'corroded like worm-eaten wood by the harsh jaws of time'*. At the large sacred site of Stanton Drew, just south of Bristol, many of the stones in the three circles there are of limestone, sandstone or an agglomcrate of pustular brecchia, and the rain and snow of thousands of winters has washed away the outer surface of the images. The pasture of many sites is used by cattle and sheep, which rub themselves against the stones, hastening the process of erosion. Nevertheless some of the ancient sculptures are still quite visible, as we shall see further on.

When I first started to think of megaliths in terms of works of art I was very puzzled at first, because I thought that I could see images on some stones, yet when I looked at photographic enlargements the images disappeared. One of the first of these sorts of disappearing images that I could see was on a photograph that I had taken of the internal face of stone 16 at Stonehenge. Underneath the lichen I thought I could see the faint image of a full length portrait of a bearded man (or sometimes a bear) at the top right of the stone. On the left was a smaller person with a child clinging to his back and there were several other indistinct images of people and children surrounding the main figures. But when I tried to look at it more closely, by scanning the photo and enlarging it, much to my consternation the image disappeared. After a day or two I finally understood what was happening.

Unlike the way that most images are usually made up of finer and finer detail, this type of effect was created by an arrangement of smaller individual images that, when viewed from a specific distance, all combined to form a large, new image. In other words, large images can be made up of smaller images, which in turn can be made from even smaller images. I have decided to call this 'new' style of art **composite images**, because the main image is composed of many smaller images.

Stonehenge, inner surface of stone 16 (in the background) and on the right, a close up of the stone

Composite art is quite extraordinary. A large image, seen from a distance, dissolves into the smaller images when you get up closer. And it is this 'magical' effect that has helped keep the art a secret for so long. In the past, when people thought they could see large faces on the stones, the face disappeared as they got nearer - as the main image separated into the smaller, composite images and as a result they often thought their minds were playing tricks on them. But of course this isn't the case at all.

It is just an example of the phenomenal skill of the Neolithic and Bronze Age artists. In more modern times the same sort of effect can be seen in close ups of oil paintings, they often reveal just a mass of differently coloured brush strokes, rather than the very fine detail that one would expect and it is only when the observer stands back that the subject of the painted image becomes apparent again. Another modern equivalent of this can be seen on advertising hoardings, the giant images that we see as we drive past are intended to give us the maximum amount of information about the products advertised with just a quick glance. But if you look at these images from very close up, all you will see are a mass of small coloured dots of printer's ink, produced by the screens used in the printing process to separate full colour images into combinations of magenta, cyan, yellow and black. With images from digital cameras and scanners, the tiny squares that make up the image are called pixels and a typical photographic image is made up of hundreds of thousands of differently coloured pixels.

One of the main problems of trying to see these ancient images clearly is that the art is thousands of years old and it has become camouflaged and eroded over the centuries. When looking at these sorts of partially eroded images you sometimes need to try and look 'into' the surface, let your eyes relax and let your mind fill in the missing edges of the carvings.

As with any new art form, a shift of perception is often required to be able to appreciate the many

different images, however once you get used to making out these sorts of image it is not really that hard to do, and it's just a question of altering one's focus of attention. In some ways this 'refocusing' is like those 'Magic Eye' images, the ones where you stare at a special two-dimensional picture until a new image becomes visible, but this time in three dimensions. If you can already see these sorts of pictures it shouldn't be too hard for you to learn how to see the work of the prehistoric artists.

Sometimes the main images are more like three-dimensional paintings, rather than carved or engraved images. But unlike our modern paintings and photographs the characters in ancient images are not always distinctly separated from each other, instead they press up against each other, a bit like the individual fruit in a bunch of grapes or perhaps like lumps of clay pushed together. These sorts of scenes form such a close-knit network of line, form and texture that the images resemble paintings of crowds of people. And the individual people in the crowd are themselves composed of tiny pictures of people, all of which are pressed up against each other and packed tightly together. I think that the artists created these larger scenes by first outlining them in paint onto the rock surface and then fine lines were incised around the individual images to separate them from the background. After that, the edges were carved and chiselled away to give a more three-dimensional image. The artists were effectively carving stone as though it was wood.

In addition to the main image or complex scene, there is often a great deal of secondary decoration on the megaliths. These include small faces and isolated figures of people and a variety of different creatures, both real and mythological. Quite often the stones and the images are covered over by lichen and although this usually camouflages many images, sometimes it helps to reveal what lies beneath. The outlines of the carvings can become visible because the altered surfaces were easier for the organisms to colonise. Many images are much more obvious at a particular moment when the lighting is just right and when the light casts shadows that put the image into relief. As the sun moves round the sky, the interplay between light and shadows can cause lighting effects that make some prehistoric sculptures and carvings appear and disappear, as if by magic. They can even appear then disappear in a matter of a quarter of an hour or so and these ***moving images***, as I have called them, are often only visible when the sunlight (or moonlight) is at just the right angle.

The sculptures and carvings are hidden for most of the time and it is only around a specific time of day (or date) that the light throws them into relief and they become visible for a short time. This is quite often around sunrise or sunset, or else when the sun is low in the sky, particularly in winter. I should however stress that different ***moving images*** can be visible on the same stones at different times of the day, although they are not often visible at midday in high summer because the sun is high overhead and the lighting is too harsh.

A moving image may be visible for several weeks at a time, but it often appears around the same time of day for just a few days in succession. Where an image is only visible for a day or two, the intention of the artists must have been to link the image with a special occasion. I think that this was probably done so that the appearance of the special images coincided with special ceremonies celebrating important times of the year. As we have already seen, these were often held at midsummer sunrise or midwinter sunset, at the spring or autumn equinox or else at important times of the farming calendar, such as the celebrations held at the end of the harvest.

I shall give more examples of all the different styles of art in later chapters, each major site has its own masterpieces.

At some of the most highly decorated stone circles, usually the largest ceremonial centres, the moving images light up in sequence as the sun moves round the horizon. In high summer the first images appear on the sides of the stones facing the rising sun, this will be on the outer surfaces of the northeastern stones and the inner surfaces of the southwesterly stones. As the sun rises higher into the sky, different moving images come to life, until near the end of the day the outer surfaces of the northwestern stones show their images and the inner surfaces of the southeastern stones of the circle are directly lit up. The outer faces of northern stones are only lit by the rising or setting sun when it is at an acute angle, from the northeast or northwest, never by direct sunlight. It can be very frustrating to go to a site to look for images that you have seen on a photograph but which are not there when you visit, simply because the lighting conditions are different when you go. And as I mentioned earlier, fewer moving images are visible at midday because the light is due south and the sun is at its highest in the sky.

I suspect that the origin of this astonishing style of art came about by observing the moon. There are clear parallels with the way the moon changes shape over a month, first appearing in the sky at new moon, growing to full then ebbing away to disappear at dark moon. And like the art, the part of the moon that becomes visible changes according to the angle of the sun. Some moving images are more visible by artificial light or by moonlight, suggesting that they were intended to be seen during ceremonies at night. So another possible origin may have come about from the way that a person's face is lit up in different ways according to the direction they are facing, particularly whilst sitting next to a campfire on a dark night. With their back to the fire, there is no light to show their face. But as they turn their head round, the shadows move and change, revealing different profiles and different aspects of the same person. **Just like the art.**

The effects of light and shadow that create moving images seems to make the art come alive, as though the people and animals are about to break free from the stone. And it is these extraordinary phenomena that have persisted in our folklore down through the millennia, giving rise to tales of stones that come alive at the stroke of midnight, and stories of ghostly priests, white dogs or white horses that are only visible at the midsummer sunrise or midwinter sunset, and other myths of people transformed into stone for partying on the Sabbath. I have also found that the art is the source of some of our childhood stories, involving fabulous creatures and monsters, ogres, dwarves and trolls. The ancient images were used to record the same sort of stories, showing just how truly ancient some of our oral history really is.

Many images are visible only when you are standing in the right place and at the right time and looking from one particular angle. Some images change as you move around the stone. So for example, the face of one person becomes the shoulder of another person as you move further round to the left or right.

Many of the works of art I have found are more obvious in photographs than in their natural surroundings because of the reduced size of the image. Sometimes the main images are only visible when the stone is a particular size, which is equivalent to standing at a particular distance away but it also translates into a particular size of photographic enlargement or digital image. And so sometimes it is easier to see the overall picture when the images are only a few centimetres across, rather than on a stone measuring five metres in length. This can mean that the main image is only easily visible when it is a small sized photograph or when the digital image is at a low resolution, such as at 72 dots per inch. However, what can happen with this sort of computer file is that because you have effectively increased the size, you have moved closer to the stone. By using a larger resolution, the image disappears into the background and is no longer visible. You can also get this effect sometimes by looking at the pictures in the book from further away. Try propping the book up and looking at it from a few yards away, you might get a surprise!.

The effect of distance and size can be particularly frustrating because you can see the image of the art at one size but it then disappears when you increase the detail of the image to try and understand it better. Looking closely at the stones doesn't always help either, because you are only able to see the component parts and not the fine detail of the main image. On site, the tendency is to stand too close to the stones, rather than to stand well back and see the overall picture first. In the past, this is one of the reasons the artwork has remained hidden, what looked like the image of an animal from a distance, disappears and breaks up into composite images, as you get closer. So the person thought their eyes were playing tricks on them.

Thousands of years later certain artists deliberately created similar effects known as *'trompe l'oeil'*, literally 'fool the eye'. Some of these modern paintings fool you into seeing three-dimensional objects that can't possibly exist, for example, stairways that twist and go back on themselves ,so that you would be walking upside down or passageways that go nowhere. Victorian artists thought they had pioneered a style of art that is often used to demonstrate the way that we perceive objects. The sort of classic image that they produced is a pair of candlesticks that through a shift of perception can be seen to form the outline of a face. You can see either the candlesticks or the face, but not both at the same time Another famous illusion is the pencil sketch of either a duck or a rabbit, you can see only one image at a time. However, these are very, very simple versions of the complex forms of multiple imagery that our Neolithic and Bronze Age ancestors created.

More recently, in the 20th Century, the surrealist painter Salvador Dali used the same sort of optical illusions in his art, where a part of one image was also used to form another. In one surrealist painting, a dog with a collar is pictured as part of a large rock formation in a surreal landscape and the collar of the dog forms a bridge spanning that landscape. Neolithic artists used the same sort of magical effects, but they invented them at least 5,000 years before Dali and their images of people touch each other and blend into each other, they are rarely separate from each other, as we would paint them, as individuals in a landscape. The ancient artists were incredibly skilful, and just to make things even more complicated, many of the composite images that they created are themselves parts of other images. With this new style of ancient art the same area of rock surface can produce several different images.

These **multiple style images** are by far the most complex. They cause the most confusion to the eye because although you can only see one image at a time, there may be two, three, or even four or more different images using parts of the main image. One of the simplest examples of multiple imagery occurs where images overlap and the right eye of one face is also the left eye of the face next to it, hence the term overlapping images. One example is at the top of stone 10 in the southwest sector at Avebury. It has a strange face that is tilted and looking downwards to the left, but its left eye is also the right eye of another face looking to the right. Although the face on the left has a small bulbous nose and a slit for a mouth, the one on the right is definitely not human, just the orbits of its eyes are showing and any facial features are severely eroded.

The top left part of stone 10, southwest sector, Great Circle, Avebury

Another type of **multiple image** that can sometimes be visible on stones occurs when you change your focus of attention and you look from left to right, and then from right to left, or else when you look upwards, then downwards. Each time you look you may see a new image. In some cases you can see two multiple images in someone's face, with one image of them looking to the right, yet by scanning in the opposite direction the same area forms another face but this time the person is gazing to the left! At times it can be very disconcerting when the image seems to change as you look at it. Another form of multiple image can be even more complicated and it may show one large main image of the head of a person, yet within their hair or the hat that they are wearing is the head of another person, and there can even be a third face in the beard of the main picture.

Sometimes there can be four or five medium-sized images within one large main image. In turn these intermediate images are themselves composed of even smaller multiple or composite style images, usually of dozens of small engravings of faces or less frequently, full-length people. These tiny engravings may have well have given rise in our popular folklore to stories of 'the Little People', and the stories of fairies, gnomes, dwarves and elves and of course a great deal of the old folklore about these mythical creatures is associated with ancient burial mounds and prehistoric standing stones.

This extraordinary complexity of the carvings makes them almost supernatural pictures and the different styles of multiple and composite images are responsible for the reason why two people will often see different images in the same part of a stone, in reality they are both are correct, it's exactly what the artists were trying to show. The artists were telling stories but they were also providing entertainment and encouraging their audience to look beyond the obvious. There also seems to be a hint of one-upmanship, as though each generation of artists was trying to outdo the work of the previous generation. They did this by recarving existing images into more and more complicated forms, sometimes producing an incredibly complex mass of composite and multiple images in the same area of rock.

Swinside Stone Circle in the Lake District, Cumbria

The original photo of the Swinside masterpiece (overleaf) has been altered using image enhancement techniques to show how it would have looked many centuries ago. Just look at the incredible variety and wealth of images, including large, medium and small pictures and very complex scenes of people, often in the multiple and composite styles. This standing stone clearly shows that we have grossly underestimated the artistic and intellectual capabilities of our forefathers. This magnificently decorated stone reveals that the talent of many of our ancestral artists was truly awesome. Over the centuries they developed a wide range of new art forms, including natural art, multiple images, composite images, overlapping images, inverted images and moving images.

A standing stone at Swinside Stone Circle, the Lake District

The ancient artists were true masters of imagery and they even created astonishing optical illusions, in stone. However, the amazing complexity of this sort of art means that not everyone will see the same images at the same time. This is perfectly normal and it is due to the way that people visualise things differently. All the different versions of images are there, it just takes time and effort to see the complete range of multiple and composite images that the artists produced, but it is well worth the effort it entails. (It may help if you make a sketch of each new image as you discover it.)

Over long periods, many stones underwent a series of changes as old sculptures were recarved into new sculptures. Another thing that I have discovered is that many ancient stones, even those weighing as much as sixty tonnes, were re-used in later periods by turning them upside down. The rocks would then undergo a major transformation to produce new sculptures, these **inverted images** were then carved into yet more multiple, and composite forms or even transformed into new geometrically shaped symbol stones. The ancient artists had their own set of rules, which is why is the sculpture of the head of a white horse blends into the top of a sheep on stone 104 at Avebury. But long before this took place the stone was standing the other way up and at that time the sculpture was that of a ewe with her lamb. When the stone was inverted, the base of the sculpture of that sheep became the sloping skull of the horse's head.

At some sites, such as Avebury, many Neolithic stones were reused during the Bronze Age. And as we shall see later on, changing the orientation of stones was particularly common at Stonehenge, which went through many different phases of construction during its long history. It is also important to remember that sometimes the entire surface of a stone was covered with images, and these are all interlinked in the multiple and composite styles, so that as you study any given area, you will begin to see more and more pictures, with each new image made from an extremely complex mosaic of tiny carvings. As I mentioned before, the largest images are easiest to see under low magnification, because it is as though you are standing some distance away from the stone. Increasing the magnification, as though you are standing closer, doesn't always help because sometimes a completely new set of composite images become evident. However, it is these astonishing optical effects that reveal the true magic of the ancient artists. It is a tragedy that the techniques they mastered are lost and their art has remained hidden from us for so long, especially since so many stone circles and standing stones have been destroyed.

According to conventional theory our ancestors produced hardly any art at all, for thousands upon thousands of years, and here I am saying that not only were they very prolific but that they also created completely new styles of sculpture and carving and created works of art that in my opinion have rarely been equalled. I appreciate that all these new types and styles of art are going to be hard for many people to accept. But if all this seems a bit fanciful on my part, then it may help to remember that this was the Age of Stone, and the artists, sculptors, craftsmen and stonemasons benefited from skills and traditions that went as far back as the dawn of humanity, well over a hundred thousand years ago. And the basic techniques for producing works of art are not so very different from the skills of working a wide variety of different materials, such as stone, antler, ivory, bone or wood, to produce superbly crafted tools and weapons. It is just the end result that is different. And so it should come as no real surprise that the ancient artists copied what they saw in the natural world. They copied and improved on images they saw as the faces of people and the heads of animals in natural rock formations. What nature could do, they could do better. This technique had already been used twenty thousand years beforehand, when Palaeolithic artists in southwest France incorporated the natural curves and features of the cave walls into a depiction of several bison in the cave at Font de Gaume, Dordogne and a spotted horse at Pech-Merle, Lot.

Many other Ice Age artists carved superbly realistic representations of horses, bison, mammoths, aurochs (huge wild cattle), ibex, reindeer and even lions in small pieces of stone, bone, ivory and antler. But I have discovered that contrary to current wisdom, the skills of these artists did not disappear as the great sheets of ice melted. Thousands of years later, their Neolithic descendants took these ancient ideas and created large and extremely complex images that they used to decorate their tombs, memorials, open-air temples, and many of the standing stones that are still scattered across the British Isles. And they are well worth a visit since they are often in the most diverse and picturesque scenery in the British Isles.

As I mentioned earlier, some of the sculptures and carvings seem to come alive as the sun moves round the sky, and the skill of creating these **moving images** must have become highly developed, since at some sites the stones are orientated so that the sunlight only reveals the images at certain times of the day. The artists must have planned carefully and made the initial images using light coming from one direction only. And since the work must have taken a long time to accomplish, the source of light must have been constant, in other words under shelter and using artificial light from one direction only. Perhaps these sorts of image were prepared inside a workshop, during the winter months when it was cold, dark and wet outside and the short winter days and long nights were a good time to work on something to keep them occupied and amused. One can imagine the dedication ceremony attached to unveiling the new works of art for the first time and then the awe of the audience, when the moving image 'came to life' for the very first time.

The subjects that the artists chose to portray seem quite restricted. I have seen no pictures of landscapes, either real or imaginary. The most common subject of all is undoubtedly people, predominantly men. The next most common subjects that were pictured are animals, both domesticated and wild, then grotesque creatures and humanoids, and of course, gods and spirits. The domesticated animals include horses, dogs, goats, sheep and pigs. There also seems to be quite a limited choice of wild animals and birds that were pictured. Popular subjects are bears and wolves, with lesser quantities of wild cats, lynx, lions, hawks and eagles, storks, hares, deer and the very occasional mythical creatures, or extinct animals such as a mammoth. Some pictures may well be the totem animals of fraternities or other groups of people who revered specific animals, such as lions, eagles, red deer or white horses. The spirits they also pictured may have represented the spirit of a species of animal, ancestral spirits, or protective guardian spirits, evil spirits, or simply represent a season such as 'the Spirit of Winter'.

Many standing stones are sculptures of just the heads of people, sometimes with their chins at ground level. They usually wear hats of different shapes and sizes. Other forms of sculpture involve groups of people. To understand how some of these were sculpted, imagine a family group of father, mother, adolescent, toddler and baby. These could be carved so that the tallest was at the back, usually the man, then standing just in front of him, and slightly to one side would be the woman holding the baby and in front of her, the adolescent and the young child. Now crowd them all close together. In this way the outlines of the people hide each other, so for example, all that you can see of the man is his head and one shoulder because the rest of his body is hidden by the other members of his family. The images nestle against each other, a bit like a bunch of grapes. There was originally separation between different outlines, but over time these outlines have become softened and blurred by weathering. This can make it hard to see where one carving ends and another begins and is another reason why the sculptures have remained hidden. However, image intensifying computer software can help to a certain extent to redefine the outlines and clarify some of the detail where it has worn away unevenly.

Many of the larger images of faces seem to be those of actual people, rather than just stylised images, as though these are the records of particular people, the prehistoric equivalent of an art gallery or photograph album. Such images must have played an important role in tribal history and culture, since the myths and legends they portrayed were on the most important monuments of the age.

Many images are full-length figures of groups of people forming historical, mythological or religious tableaux. Then the smallest images are the hundreds, if not thousands, of engravings of tiny faces and people that cover the surface of some stones in such profusion that at times it is very hard to separate the different scenes from each other. Sometimes these 'little people' just seem to have no obvious purpose, as though they are there just for decoration, but at other times they participate in complex scenes. Such images are hard to illustrate photographically because these engravings were the first to have become eroded and have worn away unevenly. However one thing is clear, the styles, themes and subjects changed from one location to another and from one era to another. Although the meaning of many of the scenes is not clear for the moment, one thing is remarkably obvious; the ancient artists were creating images that would have been easily recognised by the local population. As I said earlier, many images are only visible for short periods, when the changing shadows give the sculpture or carving the necessary relief as the sun moves round the sky to produce the moving images that appear, then disappear. So if you are really interested in prehistoric art, try visiting the same site at different times of the day, you will be amazed at how the character of the stones changes as different images become visible. I'm sure that 'stone-watching' was an early form of entertainment and that people would have waited for the right moment for the hidden images to be revealed, fleetingly brought to life by the effects of light and shadow. This means that it is very likely that there were teachers and guides amongst the local population, perhaps in the priesthood, to keep the stories alive.

At many sites, the rocks were carved and recarved to produce an amazing quantity of composite and multiple images, and because this tradition persisted for such a very long time it is clear that the art was widely understood and much appreciated by the general public. Although these images were plain to see some four or five thousand years ago, nowadays they have become far more difficult to see and it requires persistence and concentration to see beyond the largest, most obvious images.

The themes of many of the scenes are hard to understand because we simply do not have the necessary background knowledge to recognise the stories that were recorded in stone and in many cases it is not easy to work out the relationships between the people that are portrayed in the scenes. At the moment this new field of research is in its infancy, but in time we will have a much better knowledge of our ancestor's history and their myths and legends, so it should become easier to make sense of more of the pictures.

Most of the human faces are of males and their ages range from adolescents to old men, with the majority in their twenties to forties with the numbers peaking at about thirty years old. Although some are clean-shaven, many wear full beards or have moustaches and goatee beards. They wear a large variety of different garments, some coats had hoods, either pointed or rounded, and hats seem to have been an indispensable fashion accessory, while specially shaped hats seem to denote the status of their leaders and priests. As one would expect, the older images show people wearing clothes made from fur and because the person is often a man wearing a beard, this combination of fur and hair can make the images difficult to see, sometimes all that shows through are the eyes, nose and mouth. The more recent images are usually of people wearing leather, woollen and linen clothes, however the exact style and details of the clothes can be quite hard to work out because the main image is often a composite or multiple image. Then extensive re-decoration makes it look as though the person was wearing clothes that were decorated with small pictures and that their skin was heavily tattooed.

There is an extraordinary vitality in many of the sculptures and carvings and they show that over the millennia, the craft of working with stone achieved an unrivalled degree of sophistication. There are many portraits and scenes from their myths and legends and religious beliefs. Sometimes there are groups of people surrounding a leader or priest and there are scenes of groups of men, women and children, sitting or standing around a central figure who looks as though they are teaching them or telling them stories. Other scenes seen to be from their ancient myths. There are scenes of large, ancient forest spirits or gods, with smaller, human figures in attendance. There are even bear-like creatures or large people wearing bearskin or red deer buckskin clothes and coats. A common scene, one that appears especially on tombs and single standing stones, is that of a large group of people standing around someone who is lying down, presumably dead or dying. Sometimes these include large, shadowy spirit people, which are lurking in the background, behind the friends and family around the deathbed. I have seen no images of the hundreds of other species of our native wildlife, particularly game birds, moles, mice, badgers and there are virtually no sea creatures such as fish or sharks, I have seen only one sculpture of a dolphin and one possibly of a seal.

There are no images of flowers or wood-land and no images of farming or agricultural activities or even manufacturing, (but that does not mean that they do not exist at other sites). There are only a few artificial constructions shown in the images I have looked at, and these seem to be restricted to chairs, thrones, beds, tables and awnings. Although there are many nightmarish images of strange creatures, awesome spirits and monsters, I have seen no images of weapons or of warfare, (just the crude carvings of axes and a dagger at Stonehenge). The most common pictures are purely and simply of people.

As I said in Chapter 1, just because people had simple technology and a simple way of life, did not automatically mean that they were stupid, far from it. The talent of the ancient artists is absolutely overwhelming. It shows that the astonishing creativity and sheer artistic vision and craft skills of our ancestors have all been drastically underestimated and that they were far more gifted and intelligent than we thought they were. It seems to me that the creative impetus of our forefathers was focused mainly on art and religion, rather than on science and technology. In terms of technology and material possessions, they were simply nowhere near as inventive (nor as avaricious) as people who lived in later eras. Apart from farming, most of their efforts were focused on the construction of their amazing sacred monuments and then producing their incredible works of art.

The many different styles of art that they created, together with the inherent symbolism of their monuments, and their works of art, all demonstrate a complex way of thinking, one that sometimes differs profoundly from our own because they were thinking in many different layers, but all at the same time. And it is this unsuspected complexity of thought that is one of the main reasons we have been unable to understand what our distant ancestors were like.

The amount of time, skill and patience required for creating their art must have been colossal, as great as the time spent on erecting very large monuments such as those at Avebury or Stonehenge. Only successful communities would have had enough spare time to subsidise and support the artists, and this may well explain why it appears that our ancestors made such little technological progress over hundreds of years.

Instead of creating a completely artificial culture, based on industrial processes, they produced works of art that were a celebration of the natural world and their artistic and creative talents reflected their society's mythology and culture, and the special reverence they had for their ancestral past and their religious beliefs. And although they had the freedom to create works of art in new and wonderful ways, much of their daily lives remained hidebound by tradition and sheer hard work.

The art of ancient Britain is very different to what we are used to. But this should not be all that surprising because our perceptions and ideas are based largely on the styles of art that were created in Ancient Greece and Rome, more than two thousand years later on. We have believed what our experts told us. We have simply not recognised and understood what we have been looking at because we have lacked the necessary training of our eyes and minds. Yet the processes of visual perception are inherent in our upbringing. As babies and infants we are taught to recognise faces and certain shapes, colours, and textures and other visual clues, such as size, distance and shadows give meaning to our surroundings.

Until now there has been no training in perceiving and understanding these new forms of art. To make the situation worse, thousands of years of weathering has camouflaged the art, so that it is quite hard to see if you are not looking for it. Be aware that other people will probably see different images at first. There are often so many images that some can only be seen by looking from left to right, whilst others can only be seen by looking from right to left. Or up and down. There are many examples of all these new styles of art in the chapters to come. And since there are megalithic sites all over Britain, there remains a great deal more to be discovered, recorded and catalogued, enough work to keep scientists, archaeologists and enthusiastic amateurs busy for decades.

It is a field of study that is wide open.

When looking at the works of art for yourself, bear in mind that a different viewing angle and a different time of day also influence which images are visible at a particular moment.

Please do not expect to see everything straight away. With no one to explain or to teach me, it has taken me many years to fully appreciate the amazing complexity of prehistoric imagery. At times, these images are so complicated that it takes a lot of effort to see all the different permutations, but that's what makes it a challenge and a source of wonder and enjoyment.

All the photographs in this book have been subject to image intensification and manipulation, and this was done in order to undo the erosion of many centuries, to try and show you the complexity of the wonderful works of art that our ancestors created. Consequently, please take time to really look at the photographs, because there is *always* far more to see than those parts of the pictures that I have selected for description.

7 Stonehenge art

In the previous chapter I explained about how I came to make the momentous discovery of the existence of masses of prehistoric art at the ancient stone circles, tombs and standing stones of the British Isles. Now it is time to look at how the many different styles and techniques of sculpture, carving and engraving that I described in the last chapter were used to decorate the most famous prehistoric site in Europe, the open-air temple we know as Stonehenge.

According to conventional wisdom the only decorations on the whole of the temple are some simple carvings of a dagger and a few dozen bronze axes. Yet even the dagger and axe carvings were ignored for centuries. This is what Richard Atkinson wrote in his book after he discovered the first carvings in July 1953:

"... the carvings present us with an object-lesson in the fallibility of human observation. Few people who have seen the Stonehenge dagger will deny that, once one knows where to look, it is perfectly obvious; indeed when the sun is shining across the face of the stone, it can be seen from the gate of the Stonehenge enclosure, over 100 yards away. Yet during the past three centuries, hundreds of thousands of visitors must have looked at the dagger (to say nothing of the other carvings) without actually seeing it. Nothing could demonstrate better that one sees only what one is expecting to see."

Prophetic words indeed, however it is a great shame that his observational skills were not as good as he thought, because it has ensured that all the *thousands* of other decorations on the stones have been completely ignored and have remained unnoticed ever since!

As a result of my own investigations and observations I have discovered that during its lifetime Stonehenge was covered with carvings, paintings and engravings and that many of the larger stones are in fact sculptures and some are even statues. These large sculptures are quite obvious once they are pointed out to you. Yet for years people have not really understood what they have been looking at, perhaps because we have had such faith in our experts and believed what they told us when they said that apart from the simple carvings of axes and the sword there is no other art to see.

Yet it has never made any sense that the ancients went to all the trouble of constructing Stonehenge, working so hard for hundreds of thousands of hours, and then couldn't be bothered to decorate it with anything more elaborate than a few simple symbols. Yet throughout the ages, and across the world, decoration has been present at every other place of worship, whether it's a sanctuary, shrine, church, cathedral, tabernacle or temple. To me the crude carvings of the axes and dagger seen by Atkinson are just ancient symbols of death and destruction, that were added like graffiti long after the main construction work was finished. The real works of art at Stonehenge are far, far more complex, far more skilful and much more interesting than a few simple engravings of bronze weapons…

As I mentioned in the previous chapter, the height and direction of sunlight has a great impact on the way certain sculptures and carvings become visible, and then disappear as the sun moves round the sky. And different moving images such as these become prominent at different times of the day and at different times of the year, and their visibility is affected by different lighting conditions according to the weather. So the descriptions of the images in the following pages should not be taken to be the only images that exist, but rather, they are a sample of the major images that can be visible under certain lighting conditions. The descriptions that follow will just give a broad outline of the art and act as an initial framework to start from. Researchers with more sophisticated techniques and much better equipment will be able to fill in a far more detailed account in the years to come.

If one is observant, the silent stones can tell their own story.

Just by looking at the shapes and textures of the different stones it becomes obvious that some stones are much older than others. And as I mentioned previously, the newest stones are generally regular-sided oblongs with flat surfaces and straight edges, often with right-angled corners.

The older stones show considerable variation in texture and shape, and they have grooves, bumps, ridges and hollows, and these natural features were often used to produce the carvings and sculptures. Once the first group of huge sarsen stones were brought to the site they were then sculpted into the shapes of animals, people, symbols and some bizarre images from Neolithic mythology and religious belief. As I explained earlier, in Neolithic art each side of a megalith could be used for many different sculptures, and the artwork could be created in a variety of different ways. This includes the composite style, where large images are composed of a host of small images, and multiple images where parts of one image were used to form other images. Different images can also be seen

according to the way one looks, for example, one image can be seen by looking horizontally from left to right and another image can be seen by looking from right to left, and sometimes even more images can be seen by scanning vertically.

Although much of Stonehenge is ruined, we are very lucky that the most important stones at the front of the temple are still in place. Looking at the run of four lintelled stones in the northeast sector, the stones are numbered, from left to right, 2, 1, 30 and 29 with the stones flanking the entrance and axis numbered 1 and 30. As at Calanais, the traditional method of numbering the stones is far too cumbersome and it demonstrates a complete misunderstanding of the significance and symbolism of many of the stones. In my opinion it would have made far more sense to use numbers and letters, rather just numbers, because there were more than eighty stones in all.

The northeastern entrance in early morning light

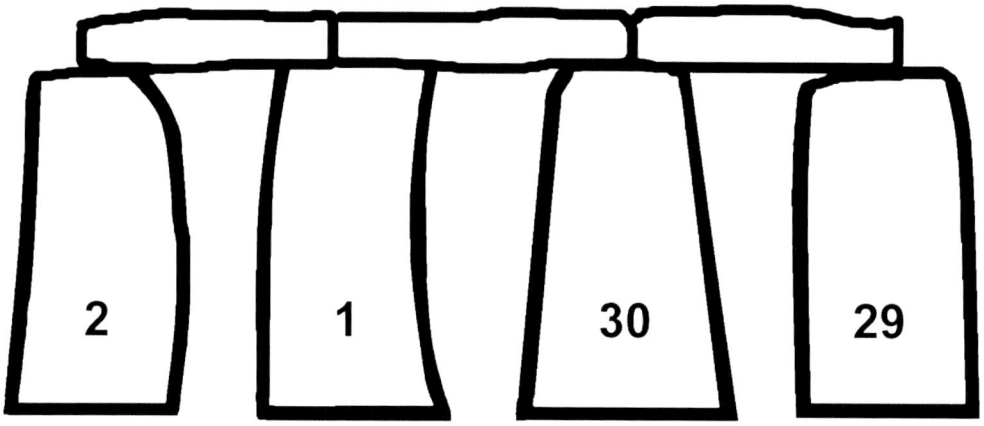

The sarsen circle could then have been numbered S1 to S30, their lintels L1 to L30, and the upright trilithon stones would have been T1 to T10, so that the stones of the Great Trilithon would be T5 and T6 instead of 55 and 56. Their lintels would be numbered TL1 to TL5. Then if the sequence of sarsen stones of the circle had been numbered like a clock, the fallen northernmost stone (26) would end the sequence as S30. The first stone in the run of upright stones in the northeastern sector would then become number S1 (instead of 27). In this way the northeastern entrance stone, (currently stone 30), would be then be called S4 and stone 1 would become S5. In other words, the axis of the temple passes between S4 and S5. And the small sarsen stone, number 11, would then have the more significant number of S15 since it is half way round the circle of thirty stones and is due south. You will remember that this is where the sun is at midday, half way between its rising and setting points. Inside the circle the two most important bluestones flanking the axis, bluestones 49 and 31, could now be numbered B4 and B5, and the nineteen bluestone pillars in the U-shape in front of the trilithons could then be numbered U1 to U19, instead of 61 to 72. Unfortunately there is probably far too much literature that has been written about Stonehenge to change things now…

However, this might be a good time to remind you that different images become visible according to the magnification of the image, and this is because it is equivalent to moving nearer or further away from the stone. Different images on the stones can be seen according to the time of year, the weather conditions and the time of day. Apart from the problem of erosion there is also the camouflaging effect of lichen, although sometimes this does help when it follows the outlines of the carvings beneath. The colour of the sarsen stones varies dramatically from a light yellow to dark green according to the time of day and the weather conditions. As we saw previously, the wedge-shaped stone 30 referred to the sun and curved stone number 1 referred to the moon.

In early morning summer sunlight, from around 5.30 am, the most noticeable image on stone 1 is on the bottom left quarter of the stone. This is a full-length picture, over a metre high, of a young man standing face to face with a strange, bear-like creature. They seem to be holding each other, as though they are dancing. There are also some large images of people near the top of the stone, although these are very faint and outlined by lichen. One of them has rather a beaky nose and is looking to the left and is holding up a smaller person who is wearing a hat. I don't quite know what to make of this scene since there are multiple and composite images all over the surface. The sizes of the two heads are quite different, so does this picture represent a woman holding her son or is it a moon goddess holding up a bearded man? In view of the symbolic lunar shape and position of the stone I'm inclined to think that the latter makes more sense. In the left corner is another person, a woman wearing a sort of bonnet on her head.

To the left is stone number 2. By around 08.30 a.m. a strange carving becomes clearly visible from the bottom of the stone to just over half way up on the right hand side. This image will certainly cause a great deal of interest and controversy. It is a full-length image of a cloaked man wearing a long, pointed hat or hood. I think this is the image of a high priest, but others will undoubtedly see it as someone from our folklore, such as a magician or wizard. It shows once again that, like the composite images of little people, our folklore is sometimes based on figures that have incredibly distant origins. It seems to me that this conical hat was most likely to have been the trademark of a priest, since the pointed, triangular outline resembles the rays of the sun… And as we shall see later on, this is not an isolated image, there are other pictures of people wearing pointed hats.

If you're thinking: **"Wizard hats! - He's definitely lost the plot!"** then rest assured that there is firm archaeological evidence that I'm right. Three late Bronze Age conical hats have been discovered in Germany and another in France. The most notable is *'The Golden Hat of Schifferstadt'*, which is a tall, conical hat made from one sheet of gold and decorated with hundreds of circular symbols that represented a variety of lunar/solar cycles.

Sarsen Circle Stone 2

The pointed hood or hat of the man is also part of the main sculpture on the stone. In the multiple style, his hood also forms part of the mouth of a strange creature that is facing down to the right. This creature has a long oval head and a very beaky mouth. The back of the head of this bird-like creature is formed from the top edge of a groove, which has a rounded end, and the bottom edge of the groove forms the shoulder or wing of the creature. Taken on its own, the outline of this groove looks very phallic in nature. Part of this groove is also part of a faint image of another man wearing a long pointed hat that has a band around the brim and this points upwards along the groove, and the lower edge of this groove forms the man's right shoulder. He is wearing a long fur coat, has a sparse beard and is looking to the right.

Later in the morning several faces, including one very large face looking downwards, appear on the top left part of the stone. This time the main moving image is formed from what was the lower part of the back of the head of the bird-like creature. This seems to me to be an image of a giant figure, perhaps a god, bending down towards the figure of a man whose head and body is on the edge of the stone. This whole area was covered with a profusion of tiny images in the composite style but the details aren't very clear because the area has suffered quite a lot of erosion. In strong sunlight, on a fine summer's day, the moving image of the hooded man is visible until about 9 a.m., by which time the light has moved round and the shadows have changed.

The bottom third of stone 2 is largely composed of a complex scene that is heavily encrusted with lichen. It seems to be a group of people, some standing and others kneeling who are clustered around, or paying tribute to, someone with a child in the centre right. To the left is a full-length image of a bearded man in the composite style. He is wearing a sort of helmet and is looking to the right, towards the group. However, this is an area of many composite and multiple images so that other scenes appear and disappear according to the time of day and the lighting conditions. On cloudy days some images may not be visible at all, simply because there are no shadows, whilst others become visible because the weak sunlight does not overexpose the details, which can happen when direct sunlight shines strongly on the sandy coloured stone. Incidentally, it's one of the curious things about Stonehenge how the colour of the stones varies so much, between light yellow and dark green, according to the time of day, the season and the weather.

In bright summer sunshine, a new moving image starts to appear on stone 1 from about 9.30 a.m onwards. This is a very large sculpture occupying the entire upright sarsen stone. It is the head of another strange creature in right profile, with its eye just over halfway up the edge of the stone. Its mouth curves round on itself into a groove. Part of this sculpture forms another image in the multiple style in which parts of the lower eyelid of the main image also form a diagonal image of a face with two slits for eyes and a strange nose.

Sarsen circle stones 2, 1 and 30

There is also a third image, this time of a wolf looking straight ahead to the left, his muzzle is outlined by two black lines that were part of a white horse that was visible earlier in the day. By about 11 am, the strange head on stone 1 has become very pronounced, the surface of stone 30 has become ridged and it now shows the head and body of a bearded man in left profile he is wearing a tall head-dress and he has a beaky nose. Sarsen stone 29 is now lost in shadow.

There is also another complex scene below waist height along the bottom of the stone, but unfortunately the lichen makes it hard to work out what is going on. I think that there are several dozen small figures, some seated, with larger figures behind them.
Above the four stones that frame the axis and entrance into the temple are three lintels that are also decorated with small carvings, but they are covered with lichen and quite faint. Although they are

quite simply carved they may represent some quite important images due to their prime location. They seem to be mainly the heads and shoulders of people plus a few strange creatures that are difficult to describe.

Flanking the right side of the northeastern entrance is stone 30, a wedge-shaped sunstone. When the early morning summer sun shines upon this large block of sandstone it does not reveal many clear images since large parts of the surface are heavily eroded or covered with lichen. Only a few large pictures of people are partially visible near the top and even then these are just barely outlined by some scattered patches of lichen. Then from about 9 a.m. onwards the shadows caused by the sunlight coming from the left start to create an abundance of moving images in the multiple style. By 11 a.m. many different images have appeared and disappeared, including one very large, but faint image of a man's face that can be seen in the upper part of the stone. He is wearing a loose cap perched on the top of his head, has a thin pointed nose and a long beard, showing up as white hair on the left side of his face. In addition, there is a very large face of an older man, who is looking outwards towards the north or the north-northeast and he too has a bushy white beard.
There are also two other carvings of men that occupy most of the right and left sides of the front of this stone and both of them have beards and wear fur hats, whilst standing in front of them, about half way up the stone, is a group of smaller figures. The central figure is a man with a bulbous nose. He is wearing a hat with a fur brim and is looking to the left. He is amongst quite a crowd of images of people wearing furs but he is the most noticeable since his left arm is bent and his elbow is quite visible.

There is another large face of a man in profile in the top left quarter of the stone. He is looking across the entrance towards the stone opposite and the outline of his face is carved into the edge of the stone. On the top right corner of the stone is the carving in profile of a large wolf cub that is standing upright and looking down to the left. Just below the middle of the stone, towards the bottom left quarter, is a large image of a white face looking outwards, it is the face of a man with thick lips and a goatee beard. He is flanked on either side by groups of full-length figures, each group is in side view and the people are looking towards the man in the centre. On the right is the large head of a man with very pronounced features and a long beard, he looks a bit sad. Next to this sad face are

two people wearing long coats. One is wearing a round fur hat, whilst the other has a pointed hat. To the left of the white face are three people of different sizes, and the middle one is wearing a hooded cloak and he looks a bit like a dwarf. Along the bottom part of the stone is yet another group of smaller images of people, some are sitting down, others standing. Next to this stone is sarsen stone 29, (*pictured on the left*)

The most visible image on the lower half of stone 29 is in a very different style to the more usual forms of early Bronze Age imagery and I suspect that this is all that remains of some painted graffiti from a more modern era. The image is a very fuzzy picture of a hairy man. He is quite stocky, has a beaky nose and is pictured in three-quarter left profile, sitting on a ledge with his legs hanging down. His left arm in his lap and his legs are simply shown as two thick black lines, whilst above his right shoulder is a broad horizontal line going backwards from left to right, and it is attached at the front to a vertical line. This image seems to me to be the remains of a very crude picture of a man holding up something with his right hand, perhaps a flag or a scythe?

Outer surface of stone 29 at around 9.00 am

On the right side, just above and to the right of the seated man, are much older images of two people face to face, both of them are in profile and are wearing hats. There is another much larger figure, with a smiling face, just above them. On the left of the seated man is an image of a face in left profile but with its deep set eyes it does not look quite human. Different images appear on circle stone 29 according to the time of day and the weather. However from about 8.30 a.m. until 10 a.m., stone 29 can be transformed by bright summer sunlight. The shadows on the whole stone can then reveal the moving image of a giant sculpture of a cat-like creature in left profile. Its head is tucked onto its chest, as though it is standing upright. This is a very curious multiple image because it seems as though it is combined with another animal with horns, possibly a goat.

There is another image about a quarter of the size on the top right corner of the stone. This is a carving, in left profile, of a woman riding a horse. A band around her head keeps her long hair back and her left sleeve is clearly visible, as is the shoulder pad of her coat. However by 11 a.m. on sunny days the outer surface of this stone is lost in shadow as the sun moves further round to the east.

The next stone to the right is sarsen 28, which has lost its lintel. It is a curious sculpture. The top third of the stone is heavily carved to form some sort of stylised animal in right profile but the most obvious feature is the smooth area that occupies the bottom two thirds of the stone.

Outer surface of sarsen circle stone 28

Carved into this smoothed surface is a curved face with a bulbous nose, pronounced chin and heavy eyebrows. It is best viewed from the right side and then the face looks as though the whole stone is a picture of someone wearing a fur hood made from an animal's head. This animal is a cat-like creature, with a slitted eye and open mouth. On the right side of this stone is a strange image. It is a bear-like creature in right profile, standing upright and holding something like a rod up to its nose. Just below the creature's chin is a man wearing a hat. He is in left profile and has a pronounced chin and a bushy moustache and beard and is looking at someone to his left. This area has several multiple images and a composite image, made up of many smaller images.

In the sequence of stones framing the entrance the last stone to the right is sarsen number 27 and it stands next to stone 28 and close to the fallen remains of 26, the north stone. Stone 27 is another strange sculpture. The main image reminds me of those pottery spaniels that often stood on either side of the fireplace in Victorian homes. This is a multiple image and the top third of the stone is also of two heads side by side. They are quite strange; I think that the one on the left is female and the other is male, but they don't look quite human, the male in particular is a bit dog-like. Further down the surface of the stone is quite smooth and on a panel to the left is the head of a cat. This whole area is covered with small and medium-sized composite and multiple images.

The right side and edge of this stone is only about half the length of the rest of the stone but it is a sculpture of a young man with long hair. He is in left profile and being held up to look face to face with a huge sculpture of someone wearing an enormous fur hat.

Sarsen circle stone 27

This giant sculpture must be that of a god, and by now you have probably realised from the descriptions and the photos that many of the sculpted stones are depictions of Neolithic and early Bronze Age gods. Some look like large versions of people, whilst others look much less human. And some of these other deities are in the form of animals or strange mythical or imaginary creatures.

So clearly Stonehenge was more than just an extraordinary piece of architecture dedicated to the celebration of the cycles of the sun and the moon, it was also an incredible art gallery, in which the complex decorations showed important images concerning their religious beliefs. In its day, it must have been truly awesome to visit the *'Temple of the Gods'* and to marvel at the powerful religious images and to look at stories and scenes from well-known myths and legends. Sadly, four and a half millennia later, many of the sculpted stones are lost and the decorations are blurred and have become eroded with time and many are hidden from sight because they are covered with lichen.

Retracing our steps to the left, and to the east of the axis, is another curious stone sculpture without a lintel, sarsen stone 3. The broad outer surface of stone number 3 is composed of two major sculptures. Looking straight at the stone, and scanning from right to left, one can see the left profile of a face that is looking eastwards. Its left eye is formed by the deep groove in the rock. Then by moving your perspective a few metres to the right and looking in the opposite direction, from left to right, you can see a curious sculpture of an animal in profile on the right edge of the stone. This is a stylised horse's head. It has a very compact face with its muzzle flattened downwards against its chest. In certain lighting conditions a rather curious image of a man with a long face is visible in what was the nose of the horse.

Sarsen Circle Stone number 3

Along the left edge of the bottom half of the stone is the carving of a grinning woman in right profile, she is holding a wrapped-up child close to her face, with the child's left arm holding onto her around the neck. Her hair is piled up in a spiral on top of her head or perhaps she is wearing a sort of turban. Below her, on the bottom left-hand side, there is a large bear-like figure with a group of bearded men standing in front of it. On the bottom right side of stone 3, there is another group of seated figures including two women. Like many of the stones at Stonehenge, this is by no means a definitive list of the images that exist. There are many other carvings of faces and of people scattered over the whole surface of stone number 3. Previously, this stone (like several others) stood the other way up, and at that time many carvings were done along what was the base but is now the top of the stone. At that time, there was a group of several dozen standing and seated people. The tops of some of these images were cut off along the edge when the stone was ground away in order to make the stone ready to bear a lintel. This reinforces the idea that this stone was originally freestanding and was then re-erected the other way up…

The next two sarsens around the circle, stones 5 and 4, still share a lintel. The outer surface of stone 4 is now very faded and covered by a layer of light green lichen. The whole stone was originally carved to form one giant image of a man's head and torso in left profile. He has a well-trimmed whitish beard and has longish hair down his back. He has a small mouth that is about a third of the way down the edge of the stone however the top of his head was flattened to make way for the lintel above. (Seen from a distance stone 4 is also a multiple image and can show a different head and upper body of someone wearing a hat.)

At the top of the stone, in the middle, are the very faint profiles of two people standing face to face. The most obvious decorations on the stone occupy the bottom half and are quite heavily encrusted with lichen. Standing in the bottom right corner is the metre-high image of a man in left profile wearing a fur hat. He has a very pronounced triangular nose. This hat is in the multiple style of a wolf and bear's head and is also composed of other smaller images. Standing next to him is a slightly smaller figure of a bearded man. They are looking towards the centre where there is a group of several strange, very hairy people, and by hairy I mean that they have long straggly hair, unkempt beards and wear thick furs. The smaller, central figure however is clean-shaven, has his hair pulled back and is holding out what looks like a dog in his arms. This dog looks a bit like a terrier.

Stones 5 and 4

The rest of stone 4 is covered by a maze of small and medium sized pictures, in the multiple and composite styles, and these were often carved into scenes or form vertical lines of images. In the top right hand corner is the head and torso of a large bear in left profile. Opposite him, below the top left corner, is a much smaller image of a bear cub with its mouth open and its right arm hanging down at its side. The bear in the top right corner is a multiple image and when looking at it from left to right you can see a rather strange triangular-shaped human face with a goatee beard, and whose nose runs down the edge of the stone. Just below this is another strange face in profile that is looking outwards to the right and is wearing a hood that forms into a sort of thin cylinder at the back. The images that I've just described are just a few of the hundreds of large, medium and small images that are on this highly decorated and extremely complex stone.

Stone 5 is a semi-circular moonstone, shaped like an inverted letter D and probably refers to the third week of the monthly cycle. It was originally more curved than at present but it too has had the top cut down to receive a lintel and at an earlier point in its history the stone was upside down. It is a stone with a very rough, granular surface. Powerful image intensification of the stone reveals some extraordinary and quite beautiful decorations that were originally carved and then coloured and it reminds me that in ancient times many of the carvings would have been painted, to make them stand out far more than they do today. There are splashes of relatively modern orange paint on this stone and these have helped to camouflage a very large piece of decoration that forms a large 'S' shape.

It is formed from a host of images and the curve at the bottom of the 'S' makes me think that this part of it represents a boat, since a crowd of people are sitting and standing on it. The whole of stone 5 is covered with small and medium pictures, including faint images of some animal heads including a wolf and a bear above the centre of the stone to the right.

Further round the circle, in a sunwise direction, are stones 6 and 7, which are still connected by a lintel, although the lintel between 5 and 6 is missing. Sunstone number 6 has a similar shape to entrance stone number 30, whilst stone 7 has a different shape to its partner.

Sarsen uprights 7 & 6 with their lintel

These stones, like so many other sarsens are very old, some of the oldest in the temple and their surfaces have been worn down by the grit in the strong winter winds that sweep across the Downs. As a result of this erosion, the surfaces are now so rough and granular that the decorations are hard to see clearly, even with image intensification. Nevertheless, stone 6 as a whole is a sculpture of the head and upper torso of a man in right profile. The outline of his face is set back from the edge of the stone. He has a white face and wears a beard and has a domed hat on his head. At the top of the stone are two animals standing facing each other.

The animal on the right has lighter fur on its belly, like a stoat or weasel. The one on the left is mole-like and it is also a multiple image within the man's hat. The rest of the stone is covered by several medium-sized pictures and a host of small images in the composite style. Running along the bottom of the stone is a vivid scene, with small images of people galloping from right to left on horseback. Behind them is a larger image of an old man with white hair and a beard and he is wearing flowing robes.

Most of the top of stone 7 is occupied by two full-length figures facing each other, and there is now a dark area between them in the middle of the stone. This is a full-length image of a man in right profile. He has long wavy hair and a small moustache. Just below this is a larger, medium-sized image of a man in profile who is looking to the right. He is wearing a fur hat, made from a small animal with its tail intact and hanging down over his right shoulder. The tail is part of a multiple image and is also the right arm of another man, so I think that this is a good moment to remind you that the images that are visible at any one time depend to a great extent to the time of day, the weather and the season.

Moving on round to the south the next stone, number 8, is broken and lying down in the grass. Next to it is stone 9, which is also lying down on its outer face and could be re-erected. The next upright stone is sarsen number 10, which is similar in shape to stone 30, though more rectangular, with slightly less sloping sides. Next to this is a small upright stone, number 11, which has a sloping top with a rounded corner, and as I've mentioned previously, this stone indicates south and midday.

The smaller circle stone 11, with stone number 10 on the right
(note also the eyes of the face in the middle of trilithon stone 53 in the background)

From a distance stone 10 shows one large sculpture of the left profile of a hairy man with a fur hat and long beard, his mouth is in the centre of the stone and he is facing outwards, towards the south. Closer up, there is a second large sculpture of a man wearing a big, baggy hat on the right side of the stone, the top of this hat has been cut off so that the stone could bear a lintel. The man has a beard and long, shoulder-length hair. He is in right profile with his nose along the right edge of the stone and he is gazing outwards, towards the east. This is also a multiple image and several other figures, including another sculpture of a larger face looking in the opposite direction, to the right. This picture is of an older man with a beaky nose and a pronounced lower jaw (visible in the centre of the stone). He is wearing a round fur hat.

Facing this man is a smaller image of another man; he has a goatee beard and wearing a sort of crown, with the points framing his upper face. However, since this is a composite image and a multiple image unfortunately there are other pictures that obscure the finer details of the main image. Just to the right of the centre of the stone is a rather strange face that is looking straight out of the stone. It has piercing eyes and a long triangular shaped nose and a droopy white moustache. It is only a small picture but even so it doesn't look quite human, it looks a bit like a weasel dressed up as a man. Below this, in the bottom half of the stone are several medium-sized, full-length images of people that are facing towards the southwest. There are also full-length images of two people standing face to face. They are also parts of an overlapping image, the right eye of the person on the left, and the left eye of the person on the right, are the eyes of another large face that is looking straight out of the centre of the stone. All in all, this is a very complex stone containing many moving images in the multiple and composite styles of artwork.

Sarsen 11 is the small south stone and it too was decorated with a large variety of images, the most noticeable is in the top right corner, below the slope, it is the head of a man wearing a band around his forehead, perhaps to keep his hair back. To the left is the image of a brown bear standing upright with its mouth open; it seems to be smiling rather than appearing dangerous. The next stone in the circle is stone 12. This is the sculpture of a dog (or a wolf) sitting down with one paw raised, and it is no longer upright but is lying down in the grass. This stone was re-erected upside down, so that the older image of the dog then resembled a face (and also the number 3).

Stone 13 is missing. Stone 14 has fallen down. Aerial photos show a strangely shaped stone with a flat base and a long curving edge that becomes thinner near the other end, something like a comma. Its current position is to the right of the Great Trilithon, well away from the outer ring of other sarsens and its current shape is such that it could not easily bear the weight of a lintel on its own. Stone 15 has been broken up and all that remains is a lump of rock next to sarsen 14.

Sarsen circle stone 16

The next stone still standing is number 16, which is a new-style sarsen stone, shaped a bit like the end of a screwdriver. From inside the temple an observer could have seen the midwinter sun set in the window between this stone and its missing neighbour. Sarsen 16 was decorated with thousands of tiny images in the composite style and shows a profusion of multiple images. The main images on the outer surface are two large pictures of men standing face to face, one on each side of the stone, and about three quarters of the way up. The man on the right seems younger and has a peaked hat with a fur rim that slopes downwards to below his neck. His chin is covered with a beard. Facing him is an older, stockier man with a beard and shoulder-length hair. He has a grumpy expression and a pronounced nose. About half way up on the left side is a small, image of a girl with long hair, wearing a band around her head and playing with half a dozen very small people holding hands and dancing in a circle around her. For want of a better description, I think of these sorts of tiny images as representations of the 'Little People', since they are so much smaller than the girl. - A full sized adult is about the same size as her head. At the bottom of the stone are scenes with several seated adult figures with children of different ages sitting and standing around them. (I described the inner surface of stone 16 earlier, when I was writing about composite images.)

Sarsen 16 is also one of the key stones that were mentioned by Atkinson in his description of the techniques used to dress the stones to shape, he noted that small areas were ground off the side of the stone and he suggested that this 'tooling', as he called it, was one way that the rough texture of the natural rock surface was removed.

However, I think that in this particular instance the coarse pounding and then grinding away was done to remove older images that had been censored by a new priesthood. Other sarsen stones, such as 23 and 28, have quite flat, smooth, polished outer surfaces and this also suggests the removal of earlier, unwelcome images.

Further round the sarsen circle to the west is a large gap, with stones 17, 18 and 20 missing. 19 is broken in half and lying outside the circle. 21, 22 and 23 are still upright and 21 and 22 are joined together at the top by a lintel, but the lintel between 23 and 22 is missing.

Sarsen 21 has a thin inverted D-shape and is another very obvious lunar stone. It originally had a more pronounced curve to its top but this was subsequently flattened to receive the ends of two lintels. However, because the top of this stone is so narrow and unsuitable for load bearing, it is not very surprising that the lintel to the right, between 21 and 20, fell down.

Left, stones 22 and 21

Sarsens 21 and 22 are old stones, with very rough surfaces and as usual each stone was originally covered in a multitude of carvings of groups of people, however most of the surfaces are now covered by thick lichen on this western side of the temple. The side of the battered lintel over the top of these stones shows a peculiar bulge in the middle, showing that this is a recycled stone. In the more diffused light of an overcast day, stone 21 shows that it is a sculpture of a bearded man's head in left profile. He has a thin face and is wearing a tall hat.

The top right corner and edge of stone 21 is the head of a bear looking southwards, to the right. Stone 22 is roughly rectangular with the top left corner sliced away. On the right side is a very large image of an elderly man who is wearing a fur hat and fur coat. With the right lighting, the curve of his left sleeve is quite obvious and the top of his hat supports the lintel. He is in left profile and has a long, bushy white beard. He looks a bit grumpy because his lower lip curves upwards so that it is just under his rather bulbous nose. He is looking downwards to the left, towards a smaller figure that is rather indistinct. This stone is also covered with multiple and composite images. At the bottom of the stone is a large group of people, some are sitting down whilst others are standing around them in the background.

Sarsen circle stone number 23

The surface of stone 23 is quite unlike its neighbours - the lower two thirds are very smooth and worn away. Perhaps the reason for this smoothing out of the surface was to make way for the large face of a very unusual creature seen in right profile. With its flat face, tiny nose, gash of a mouth and flat head it is definitely not human, it looks a bit like a gorilla but without the pronounced nostrils that these apes have. The sides slope inwards and upwards and the corners are square, indicating a new-style stone. It also resembles stone 30, the sunstone on the right of the main entrance.

Stone 24 is missing, and stone 25 has fallen outwards and sideways. Sarsen 26 is the north stone and only a lump of it remains.

That completes the tour of the outer surfaces of the stones in the sarsen circle, but of course it is only a preliminary indication of the sort of decorations that are on the stones. A full and complete catalogue requires far more time, personnel and finance - together with much more advanced photographic and image-enhancing techniques than those I have at my disposal. This will include laser depth measurements, ultra-violet and infrared photography as well as hundreds of pictures taken at different times of the day under different lighting conditions.

In time, the significance of the images, and the stories they tell will become better understood.

Further out from the main temple are several other stones that need to be looked at, particularly the famous Heel Stone. This is without doubt one of the earliest and most important stones on the site and as such, it has suffered from very extensive decoration and redecoration over the centuries. It has become a badly-weathered, extremely complex sculpture of animals and people in the multiple and composite styles. The Heel Stone stands in the Avenue just outside the earth circle, and may have had a twin, or more likely, stood more centrally in the past, in hole 97. It also indicated the path of the rising sun at midsummer, several minutes after the first flash of sunrise, like the dot on the letter **i.** However, four thousand years ago the midsummer sunrise rose a degree or so even further to the left than it does today, so the Heel Stone was never a very accurate indicator of the midsummer solstice. Later on I think the Heel Stone was moved to hole 96, to line up with the winter moonrise at the midpoint between the major and minor northern moonrise positions during the long nineteen year swing cycle.

The Heel Stone, view from the western side

Near the top of the stone are several overlapping multiple images (just to remind you, these are where the right eye of one animal is also the left eye of another image). Looking back along the axis, outwards from the circle, towards the northeast one can see that the principal image on this huge stone was originally a statue of a large, rather angry-looking, bear standing upright, with his head leaning over to the side. Pressed up against his left cheek is the face of a bearded man who is wearing a domed hat with what looks like a white fur rim around it (although it may be a crown). These two pictures are part of a group of at least four overlapping multiple images (where the left eye of one face is the right eye of another). They consist of medium sized animal and human faces in the multiple style and they include several bears and the head of a wolf.

The symbolic image of a bear seems to tie in well with the way that the stone indicates an average position of the midwinter moon (rather than the exact position of the midsummer sunrise) and even today we still think of bears hibernating inside their northern caves during the winter months. In addition, in many ancient cultures the easiest pattern of stars to identify in the northern night sky was the group of seven main stars that form part of the constellation of Ursa Major, the Great Bear, although most people in the UK now know it as the Plough, or in America, as the Big Dipper. The Great Bear would have been very useful as a guide five millennia ago since at that time the constellation moved closely around the north celestial pole throughout the year, however in those days the pole star was Thuban, not the brighter star we call Polaris.

There are many carvings and sculptures of people wearing long fur coats at Stonehenge (and other sites) and the brown bear was the most obvious candidate to supply them with really warm winter clothing. The fur from other animals such as red and roe deer, seal, otter, beaver, stoat and even lynx would also have been used to keep people warm during the winter months. Öetzi the Ice Man, who's frozen, 5,300-year old body was found high up in the Alps, was wearing a waterproof cloak made from woven grass and he had warm clothing including a coat, leggings and a loincloth made from sheepskin and he wore a bearskin fur hat. His feet were protected by wide shoes that were made from bearskin soles and deerskin uppers. They contained a sort of woven net which went around the foot. This held dried grass in place and reconstructions have shown that the shoes would have kept his feet warm and they were suitable for walking on rocky ground, but were not very water resistant.

The lower two thirds of the Heel Stone form another strange creature, an animal with a diagonal gash for a mouth, a triangular blob of a nose that overhangs it and an oval eye. This animal has a very wide mouth, although since its eyes are on the side of its head it is unlikely to be predator, (they mainly use stereoscopic vision and their eyes are next to each other, like ours,) so it is perhaps the picture is of a young bird still in the nest. After looking through a book on British birds I was struck by the way the wide mouth and lips of the bird resembled that of a swallow chick. Swallows are migrant birds that fly huge distances each year, they arrive from Africa and lay their eggs in late May and the chicks hatch in June, then when fully grown in early autumn, they fly all the way to South Africa for the winter.
If I am correct in identifying the carving as a young swallow then it gives an interesting insight into the range of images shown in this view of the Heel Stone. At the top of the stone are several images of the heads of bears and below them is the mouth of a young bird, symbolising two of the extreme aspects of winter and summer, the hibernating bear and the insatiable bird chick.

Near the top left, is an upside down U-shaped depression. This is the famous heel that gave the stone its name, although perhaps a more fitting name for the stone would be the Great Bear. (Some authors have disputed that the stone bears this mark, perhaps because the heel is upside down.) The head of the bird chick uses this U-shaped mark to give shape to its forehead, it is where one would have expected its right eye to be, but all that is there are two small round holes. It has a down-turned, partly open mouth and to the left there is a diagonal, oval hole that looks more like an eye.

The 'heel' is also the rounded top of a large domed hat worn by a man who is in left profile and who is looking to the left, he is seated and his left arm is bent and resting on his lap. The large oval hole is cut into the side of his head, where his ear should be. The bottom left quarter of the stone shows the partly eroded head and upper torso of a man wearing a sort of parka with a narrow rim; he is in profile and is looking towards the temple.

Just below the mouth, half way up on the right side, is a carving of the head of a young wolf in left profile. This is part of a multiple image since just above the head of the wolf is the head of bearded man in left profile. The collar of his coat is defined by part of the large diagonal cut and his left arm forms the wolf's left ear. (The wolf may in fact be a dog, sitting next to its master.)

From close up the texture of the Heel Stone is very rough and in some areas it's covered with tufts of lichen. Looking from more to the east the stone shows a very different sculpture. Just to remind you, this is the image that started me on my amazing journey of discovery, into the minds and the lives of our prehistoric forefathers.

This sculptured stone has many multiple images, including a hare and a wild cat. On the surface are many eroded carvings, including the head of a horse in right profile, this is just to the left of centre in the top part of the stone, above the diagonal gash. There is also a picture of a man on a galloping horse (in left profile) on the bottom half of the stone. These images give credence to the old idea by Stukely that the nearby Cursus was indeed a racecourse. Recent dating of an antler pick that was used to dig this enclosure gave a radiocarbon date of between 3,300 and 3,600 BC, meaning that people were coming here at least five centuries before the causewayed enclosure was built at Stonehenge.

The image of a wild cat on the Heel Stone becomes much more pronounced on a sunny summer afternoon around 16.45 p.m. (BST), but it is even more noticeable in midwinter, when the sun is low and close to the time of sunset around 16.00 (GMT). Diagonal lines of light and shadow produce markings reminiscent of our native feline, although to our eyes it probably looks a bit like a domestic tabby cat! (Genetic studies have shown that all domestic cats are descended from an African species, *Felis silvestris lybica*.) The territory of our own powerful, fierce, untameable and fearless wild cat, *Felis silvestris grampia*, is now greatly reduced from its ancestral woodlands and they now live in the Highlands of Scotland.

8 INSIDE THE TEMPLE

A *full* description of the complex artwork on the inner faces of all the stones in the sarsen circle will have to wait for another time, since I have been unable to take photos of all of the standing stones. However, a few of the more obvious sculptures and carvings are well worth describing, starting with the inner surface of sarsen 27, the first upright in the run of standing stones in the northeastern sector.

Inner surfaces of stones 27 and 28

Sarsen 27 is a truly ancient standing stone and over the millennia the surface has become very eroded and broken up. However, one image that is sometimes visible on the southern aspect is that of the left profile of a stocky man with a bushy white beard, his chin and the edge of his beard are delimited by the curve in the cut about half way up the left side of the stone. He is wearing a sort of loose fitting coat or tunic that is open to the waist. His inner clothing is tied around his bulging waistline with a corded belt. This is also a multiple image of several other people. With strong lighting, from above and from the right, the southern surface of this stone can also show a very pronounced, partial outline of a man's face in left profile. His chin, frowning mouth and bulbous nose can be quite obvious, whilst several smaller images can be seen below his mouth. The line of the mouth is also the outline of the top of the head of a man in right profile. He has a bushy beard and seems to be sitting on a small horse. With more diffuse lighting, when the western side of this stone is no longer in deep shadow, the thinner side shows a sculpture of the head and upper body of a person with neat, shoulder-length hair, in profile. And there are secondary carvings of people within this hairstyle.

Below this, from about half way up the stone, are carvings in the multiple style of a man and woman standing next to each other, the man (or god) is the most visible, he has a wavy moustache and is wearing what looks to be a horned helmet. He is holding a baby close to his face. Below them is a host of other small, medium and large characters, the smallest ones are clambering over each other, and all these form several very confusing scenes of multiple imagery. In late afternoon, when the sunlight is from the west, two large moving images of people can be seen. They are standing face to face. And the man on the left has a goatee beard and is wearing a floppy hat with a wide brim.

The next stone to the east (to the right) is sarsen 28. This has no lintel either, but the inner surface does show a very distinct sculpture, a moving image that is most visible when the light is from the southwest. I think that this is a stylised sculpture of another horse, with its head pressed downwards against its chest, although it's also possible that it represents a sculpture of a wading bird, with its long wavy bill pressed down against its neck. In diffused lighting the right half of the stone shows a full-sized carving of a bearded man, sitting down with his hands on his knees. He is wearing robes and has a tall hat on his head. The outline of his face and chest is also the wavy line of the horse's jaw. In the top right corner is a multiple image of another man, who is wearing a sort of fluted hat or feather headdress. Like all the stones in this run of sarsens, the surface is covered with hundreds of subsidiary carvings and the surface is rough and very pitted, covered over and camouflaged with lichen. Next to it is sarsen 29, a stone that has a diagonal crack running down the bottom half of the inner surface. In some lighting conditions the top half shows a very large head in right profile, with their nose running down the right side and edge. He is wearing a round cap, with a wide band around the rim, perched on the back of his head.

Looking from inside the temple, sarsen 30 is the sunstone that forms the left portal of the entranceway. The top left corner of this symbol stone has been sliced off, so that the resulting slope mimics the path of the rising sun. As one of the most important stones in the temple it must surely have had some of most meaningful decorations. Most of the published photographs that include this stone show the view looking outwards, towards the northeast and the summer solstice sunrise. However, this is not the best time of day to light up the decorations; it is much better when sunlight is from the western side and the surface is more in relief, from about 4pm onwards.

The inner northeastern part of the circle with standing stones 27, 28 (hidden), 29, 30, 1 and 2. In front of them are the smaller bluestones 46, 47, 48 (leaning), 49 and 31. In the foreground is fallen sarsen 25, with a piece of stone 26 behind it, together with lintel 126. Lying horizontally on the right is fallen bluestone 45, in front of trilithon stone 60.

The main image seems to be of several adults standing around the central figure of a baby or a child that is being held up by a person on the left. Behind and to the right is a larger, very bulky individual wearing furs and it is difficult to say at the moment if this is human or a bear. And in the same way, an individual standing to the right looks decidedly foxy. The problem with identifying the images at the moment is that this whole area is a maze of large, medium and small images in the multiple and composite styles and I simply don't have a good enough photo at the moment to give better descriptions. To make things even more difficult, the stone is heavily encrusted with lichen. Nevertheless, what I have been able to see is that there are some small images that are carved vertically in lines on top of each other, a bit like the images on a totem pole, and these stacked images are usually in the multiple style and form parts of other pictures. Next to this is the right portal stone, number 1. This curved upright is an obvious moonstone. In the top left corner of the inner surface is the head of a man in profile; he is wearing a hood that comes down below his shoulders, almost to his waist. He is looking at some other people to the right. A bit lower down the stone and further to the right is a very hairy man, almost bear-like, and he is standing next to a bearded man wearing a small conical hat.

Near the centre, in the bottom half of the stone, at the same level as the top of the bluestone in front of it, is a very curious face. Centrally it looks a bit like the head of a wolf, but as a multiple image it is also the hat of a person in profile who is looking downwards to the left, and the right side of this hat is also a tiny man wearing a hat with a wide rim, he looks a bit like a gnome. This is a classic combination of multiple and composite images.

There are many other faces on the stone, both human and animal. Just above the central image is a curious picture of an animal with the long, broad head of a lion but strangely it has the left foreleg and hoof of a horse. Above and to the right is a white face with frizzy hair. Most of the bottom half of the stone is one very large picture of a seated man. He seems to wearing very long bushy hair or an enormous headdress, one that reminds me of the sort of wigs that were worn in France during late 17th Century, at the time of Louis XIV, the Sun King.

As usual, the main picture is covered in secondary images and there are many additional pictures all over the stone. On the left lintel above sarsen 1 is a very clear outline of the head of a bearded man. He is wearing a headband to keep his ragged hair out of his eyes. This is also a multiple image, one is the bearded man looking down to the left and there is another face looking to the right. Further along, towards the end of the stone, where one lintel joins the next, is another head, this time it is the left profile of a man with a very angular jaw and a big, beaky nose.

To the right of stone 1 is stone 2, the last in the run of four stones that have lintels. The surface of this stone is very heavily covered in lichen and it is difficult to see the images, nevertheless I think these are quite interesting since their subjects are in a different style. The major decorations on the stone give the impression that they consist of older images. In the top half of the stone is a row of three or four medium sized people wearing furs. In the centre of the stone is a medium-sized, three-quarter view of the head of a wolf that is looking to the left.

Inner surfaces of stones 2 and 3 with bluestones 49 and 31 in front

As we saw already, the outer surface of stone 3 is a stylised sculpture of a horse but there is even more of a stylised image on the inner surface, it's just an outline. It is made up of a wavy line that runs from about halfway up on the right side down to the left, outlining the rounded nose of the horse. The stone is also a huge statue of a woman's head and body in right profile. Her flattish face is along the top right edge of the stone, she has a small nose and her long hair is pulled away from her face and runs down her back, as though it was in a hairnet, and delimited by the wavy line. Just below her jaw is a large hole. As usual the whole surface is covered with a network of hundreds of small images in the composite style.

Further round the circle are stones 10 and 11, and as I pointed out earlier, number 11 is the small stone that represents midday, south and the half day in each monthly lunar cycle. The inner surface of this stone is yet another masterpiece of multiple and composite imagery and extensive image intensification shows a variety of different mythological scenes. The top of the inner face slopes upwards from left to right, in a straight line, then it curves to form a rounded corner.

Inner surfaces of stones 10 and 11, with bluestone 34 in the foreground

The stone is encrusted with scaly lichen, although two main images are visible, a large head of a lion is standing in right profile along the left side of the stone and this animal is looking downwards but is facing towards the slightly larger figure of a man standing on the right side of the stone. The left eye of the man is particularly noticeable as a hole in the stone and he has a triangular nose, a pronounced chin and is wearing a floppy fur hat. The nostrils and mouth of the lion can be seen as a Z-shaped line, thicker at the top and bottom, about half way up the left side of the stone.

The image of a lion is relatively rare, and although we tend to think of them as cats of the African plains, their distribution was far more widespread in ancient times, they are known to have lived right across Europe and of course during the even more remote period of the last Ice Age. There were several species of lion that preyed on the large herbivores of that period, including a very large cave lion. At what time the last lion was exterminated in the British Isles is unknown, although they are known to have still existed in southeastern Europe in Roman times. There used to be several other native species that are now extinct in Britain, including the lynx, beaver, wolf, brown bear, tortoise and the formidable aurochs, a type of wild cattle that was twice the size of our domestic bulls. Twelve thousand years ago, just after the last Ice Age, there were still reindeer and musk oxen in northern Scotland.

As usual, sarsen 11 was covered with secondary decorations, including a short man in the bottom right corner. He has a squat body, a white beard, and a green pointed hat with a broad band around the brim and is wearing a green coat. All that is missing is a fishing rod and he could then be described as a garden gnome! It shows that once again our ancient folklore contains a grain of truth, but only in the respect that some of our folk mythology and traditional bedtime stories, about elves, dwarves and fairies, are very, very ancient indeed. However it should be remembered that dwarves are not necessarily just mythical creatures, it is also a rare medical condition.

As I mentioned earlier, sarsen 12 is lying down in the grass. As a result it is hard to see, but I think that this was originally a vertical sculpture of a dog, with its right paw raised and bent under. At some point it was turned upside down and the base was flattened ready to receive the lintel. The next stone that is still upright is sarsen 16. The inner surface of this stone was a key element for me in understanding the complexity of our ancient art. When I first looked at this stone I could clearly see the head of a man with white hair the top right corner of the stone. He is standing a bit hunched up and looking over his right shoulder. Yet when I looked again, more closely, this area became the head of a strange bear-like creature. But when I looked at the image under greater magnification even this disappeared.

As I mentioned in the previous chapter about prehistoric art, it took me a while to understand what was happening, later on I realised that the main image of the man was a multiple image, which when looked at in a different way became the picture of a bear. Then in close up the picture dissolved into its component parts of much smaller individual images, in other words, this was a composite image. With the benefit of a great deal more time and experience I can now reveal that the man is just standing in the background of the main image, which is a very complex scene involving hundreds of small images as well as several medium sized ones.

On the right side is a small, stumpy man who is sitting down on a chair. Further down, along the bottom of the stone, to the right, is a picture of a bear with a white muzzle and an open mouth. (The mouth looks like a triangular notch in the edge of the stone.) The lower part of the body of this dumpy person is a multiple image and it shows the left profile of the head of a man with a bushy beard. The seated figure is wearing some sort of helmet and he is holding out his left arm to touch a child that is held out to him by a small, grinning figure on the left.

Unfortunately I have not been able to photograph the internal surfaces of any of the remaining sarsen circle stones, this will have to wait for another time.

The trilithons

Just to remind you, there were originally five sets of trilithons, each of two uprights with a lintel across the top. These were arranged in a U-shape, with two sets of stones on each branch of the U. In the middle was the third set, the Great Trilithon, and this stood astride the axis of the temple. The trilithons increased in height from each of the two ends towards the centre. Although the midwinter sunset occurred behind the Great Trilithon, there was a very tall bluestone, number 67, in the way and although it is now missing it would have blocked the view from the centre of the circle. This is because it was standing in the gap in front of the Great Trilithon. In front of this bluestone stood the wide Altar Stone, number 80. The first trilithon consists of the two upright stones 51 and 52, which are still standing and they are surmounted by lintel 151. And from inside the temple, although not quite at the centre, the midwinter sun could be seen to rise through the narrow gap in between these stones. Four thousand years ago this would have been a degree or so further to the south (to the right) than it is today, this is due to precession.

The first trilithon, stones 51, 151 and 52

The second trilithon comprises stones 53 and 54 and these stones are still standing, along with their lintel. Around midsummer the full moon could sometimes be seen to rise through the narrow gap between the two upright stones. Further round was the third set, the Great Trilithon, but only stone 56 is still standing, the other upright, 55, is broken in two and lying next to their lintel, across the Altar Stone. Next around the U-shape comes the fourth trilithon, upright stones 57 and 58 together with their lintel, and in some years the midwinter full moonset could be seen through the gap between these two stones. On the same side of the U-shape stood the fifth trilithon, upright stones 59 and 60, and behind them could be seen the setting sun at midsummer. (Stone 60 and the lintel are broken and lying on the ground.)

So to sum up, the five different sets of trilithons were linked to the moon and the sun at different times of the year. The first trilithon was linked to midwinter sunrise; the second to the midsummer full moonrise; the third (Great Trilithon) was linked to midwinter sunset; the fourth to midwinter moonset and the fifth to midsummer sunset. All in all a very neat bit of architectural design work, although perhaps not as accurate as some scientists have believed, (remember this was a temple and not a laboratory). It was an observatory only in the sense that with the correct timing, derived from daily observation, ceremonies could be linked to important astronomical events, and the sighting of the rising or the setting of the sun and the moon was a visual aid that helped emphasise important moments during the ceremonies and festivals. However there is no clear evidence, at the moment, which clearly demonstrates that mathematical precision was an important part of the Stonehenge peoples' religious beliefs, although the discovery of all their new art forms clearly demonstrates that we have seriously underestimated their abilities and their culture.

From inside the sarsen circle, the inner faces of the first trilithon, stone 51 is on the left and 52 on the right, and they are without doubt truly awesome works of art. (Remember this set was particularly important because it was linked to the midwinter sunrise, it marked the end of one year and the birth of another.) The decorations on these stones are some of the best on the site, they are extremely complex, but unfortunately most of them are eroded and camouflaged by lichen and therefore the details can be hard to make out. This is particularly difficult with stone 51. Even a negative image of the photograph reveals a confusing mass of hundreds of small pictures.

Nevertheless, I have managed to make out some of the large images on this trilithon stone. In the bottom half are four medium-sized images of some rather strange-looking people standing almost in a row. These figures stand a head taller than the bluestone (61) that is in front of them. They seem to be wearing masks and headdresses. Below them is a smaller central figure, this is a man with a beard who is surrounded by several other people who are holding up some sort of large circular object. It is as though they were going to place a large ring, wreath or garland around his neck.

Higher up the stone, to the right of centre and near the top, are some very strange images. One of the pictures shows the head of a young man in left profile, his left eye is the deep rounded hole in the middle. Above, and a bit to the left of this picture, is a man with a long beard in right profile. He is wearing a tall fur hat, has a black beard and is looking to the right, towards another person in the top right corner of the stone. This person is wearing a spiky hat, has raised their right arm in the air, whilst his left arm is bent downwards. In the extreme top left corner is the angled head of a cat-like creature with big round eyes (formed from holes in the stone) and has an open mouth. Below this the rest of the stone is covered with a mass of multiple and composite images.

Stone 52 has several large images and one very large image on the right side, occupying most of the surface. This is a person in profile, who is looking downwards, towards a rather strange creature on the left. This strange animal has its mouth wide open and it is threatening to engulf the lower face of the person on the right. The eye of this creature stands proud of its face and a thin curved line marks the eyebrow. The man is wearing a tall domed hat that forms a multiple image of the head of a young man in left profile. This younger man has a goatee beard and is looking straight ahead to the left. His left eye is marked by a deep hole in the surface and he is wearing a close-fitting cap that covers his long hair. There is a deep hole just below his chin, which forms the eye socket of the main character, whose left shoulder is formed from a deep-set, curved line in the rock. He is wearing a coat and is holding his left arm raised and slightly bent at his side. The back of his head and his neck form a second image, of the head of a wolf looking down to the ground. In the bottom half of the stone are several tall figures on the left, one wearing a fur parka. There is another person in the centre who is looking towards a seated figure on the right, close to bluestone 62. The seated man is in the background, almost on the edge of the stone and he is surrounded by other people. Just in front of him is someone wearing a special hat and he is bending over towards what looks like a boy and his dog, although perhaps it's a lamb, the covering of lichen makes it's hard to sure.

Behind the seated man are some much larger images of strange creatures, including one whose head is very skull-like. It has large eye sockets and a wide-open mouth. All of these images are hard to see properly because the whole area is covered in secondary decorations, in the multiple style and composite style, these small images are composed of hundreds of small people, children and animals. One of the most intriguing pictures is quite small. It is of two men with long white beards who are riding on the back of a very large animal that may be some sort of huge sea creature. It has a wide-open mouth with pointed teeth and the people are holding onto it just behind its eye. The man at the back is wearing a hooded coat pulled up over his head, whilst the other old man on the right is bare-headed. This eroded picture runs right the way along the curved line of rock, starting on the left about two thirds of the way up the stone. The mouth of this huge fish is on the right, close to the right edge of the stone and the hooded man is on the far left. This area is also a large image of a rather strange flat face with a prominent chin, which was carved at a 45-degree angle. Above the two uprights is a lichen-encrusted lintel, so there are just a few images that are easily visible on this stone, and they are mainly faces of people in profile.

Other small images show that this lintel was originally a standing stone and at that time it was a sculpture of a wolf that was standing upright, with its muzzle tucked under. (To see this you need to rotate the picture). Later in the day, under different lighting conditions, the lintel over the first trilithon shows a series of grooves cut into it, a bit like vertebrae. The sculpture is now of a cat-like creature with oval eyes, which are set high up its face. I think this is a very old stone, since in this orientation there are scenes of an archaic style engraved into the rest of the stone. There is a host of tiny carvings of people that are distributed in horizontal layers, with each layer forming its own little story.

Inner surfaces of the second trilithon, stones 53 and 54

The second trilithon comprises stones 53 and 54, together with their lintel 153, and in comparison to the other lintels this is a very modern-looking stone. It fits squarely on 53 but overlaps the top of 54 at the back, suggesting that 54 is an older stone than 53, which is more rectangular and has smoother surfaces. 53 is a grey-blue colour, whilst 54 is a sandy yellow and brown colour. 53 is quite a famous stone because on the inner face it has the carvings of a hilted dagger and the four axe heads discovered by Atkinson in July 1953. It also bears an inscription that looks like IOH:LUD:DEFERRE, which is only a few hundred years old, possibly from the 17th century.

About a metre above this inscription, about half way up the stone, on the left edge is a rough carving of a curious face with a sharp, thin nose and sunken eyes. And below this, at the height of the top of bluestone 63 on the left, is another face with quite crude features. I don't think that these carvings are contemporary with the building of final Stonehenge since they are so crude. However, the older carvings on stone 53 are quite subtle and not very deep, the surface is so smooth that this stone was most likely engraved, then painted and indeed spidery lines of yellow are visible under high image intensification. About a quarter of the way down from the top, near the left edge, was a yellow semicircle, possibly a representation of the crescent moon or a partially eclipsed sun.

On the outer surface of trilithon stone 52 there is a curious U-shaped image that is not covered with lichen. On extreme image intensification this resolves into a sort of ornamental boat with people sitting in it. The prow of the little boat consists of a pair of creatures that I think represent sea horses, although it's hard to make much out since the picture has suffered from erosion. I'm not sure about this image. I'm not convinced that it is contemporary with the other images and decorations on the rest of the stone and it may even date from the Iron Age.

Below this boating scene, at the bottom of the stone is another picture, this time it is of several people including a man and a woman, who are sitting down. These are multiple images and the most noticeable figure is in the centre, it is a man wearing a round fur hat that is worn on the back of his head. Next to him, to the right, is a strange face, with very angular features. It is not human but has a sharp nose, jutting chin and spiky hair. This brings to mind a figure from our folklore, that of Jack Frost. Further to the left is an indistinct mass of small figures. Further on up the stone, above the centre, is a series of small faces and people that are stacked vertically one above the other.

Detail of inner surface of trilithon stone 54

With regard to its decorations and artwork, stone 54 is a very different proposition. Looking at the inner surface of the stone, from slightly to the left, the main image, occupying three quarters of the stone, is the giant sculpture of the head of a dog-like creature. As usual there are several other quite large images carved into other parts of the stone and a host of smaller decorations, although many are covered in lichen. In the centre of the top half of the stone is a multiple image scene involving some strange-looking people holding hands and it looks as though they are dancing in a circle. Covering this sculpture is an amazing engraving/painting, but because of erosion and the covering of lichen, it's hard to see what's going on, even with image intensification. The original colours were blue, yellow, red, green and brown and the picture shows a variety of scenes, including a hairy, almost bear-like person at top right. Just below, and superimposed on top of this image, is another face also in left profile. This is also a multiple image showing a group of people in line. In the centre of the stone is the head of a deer in left profile. Further down, on the right, is another very large faded head, this time in right profile, its nose is right on the edge of the stone. Below this are several people and a man wearing a hat, the brim of which is clearly visible, it looks a bit like a bowler. Next to him, on the left, is a large seated figure, again in right profile. I think that this person is wearing a yellow symbol of the sun, a golden crown. Just above and to the left is a greeny-yellow snake that is rearing upwards, and curling around the recess that marks the mouth of the main sculpture pictured above. I am not 100% confidant about some of these descriptions, this is due to the erosion and the lichen and because of the hundreds of tiny images in the composite style, which together form the much larger images. These are also in the multiple style, so the whole surface becomes incredibly complex. This stone will need to be investigated a lot more because the trilithon marks the major southern moonrise at the heart of the temple, so the images will be very important.

On the outer side of stone 54 is some even older art that shows nowhere near the same degree of expertise as the inner surface. High up on the left edge, just below the lintel, is a carving of a chunky man with a rather squashed nose. The left side of his face has been ruined by the addition of some secondary artwork.

Outer surfaces of second trilithon, stones 54, 53 and lintel 153.

A very enhanced detail of top left of stone 54

The original piece of art was a sculpture of a big man with a long beard, sitting on a sort of chair or throne, set into the rock. The bottom of his chair is marked by a horizontal line, about half way up the side of the stone. He is wearing a round hat with a flattish top, a bit like a fez.
To the right is another person wearing a flowing robe with a hood or a headdress that has material all the way round their head and down to their shoulders. It's difficult to be certain, but I think this is a woman. Her arm in its wide, left sleeve is stretched out, as though she is giving something to the man. These images are moving images and are only visible when the sun casts deep shadows on the bleached surface. Image intensification shows that the whole area was covered with hundreds of tiny, painted images in the composite style. Just below the mouth of the man is a smaller image of a bearded man wearing a pointy hat. His right sleeve also forms the cap of a smaller standing figure. A large image in the centre of the stone is the face of a cat-like creature with wide set eyes, small nose and a tiny mouth. At the bottom of the stone, to the left, is a flat area that is marked by a path of coppery coloured discolouration. I suspect that closer examination will show that this hides a picture of a host of people sitting down, with a pole in the middle. It is perhaps a raft or boat. At about the same height, but on the right edge of the stone, stand two more men with pointy hats.

In contrast to the wealth of imagery on this stone, the outer surface of neighbouring stone number 53 has relatively subdued decoration.

As I mentioned earlier, the Great Trilithon is wrecked and only stone 56 is still standing, although in the last century it had to be straightened because it was leaning badly and only held upright by bluestone 68. The tenon at the top is easily visible. This is a marvellously shaped stone, the longest prehistoric stone in Britain, and it was a fitting tribute to the stonemason's craft. It stands around 22 ft high (7m), with at least another six feet (2 metres) underground.

The inner surface of Great Trilithon stone 56, with bluestone 68 on the right.

With its fallen partner, 55, it marked the midwinter sunset, the longest night of winter and the end of the Old Year. We can therefore expect that the decorations on the inner surface were highly significant. Unfortunately these are far from clear, since the stone is covered with such a thick coating of moss and lichen. However, the most obvious decorations are two large heads of strange creatures about three quarters of the way up the stone on the inner surface. The creature on the left is standing square on but is hunched over, with its head looking downwards. The one on the right looks a bit more bear-like and is standing more in profile. Between them is the faint image of another creature, vaguely human, but with strong image intensification one can just about make out a horn coming out of the top of its head. Above this is the face of a cat-like creature. To the right is a full-length image of a slightly larger person in left profile. He has a full beard, a triangular nose, and manages to look quite stern.

All the pictures on the stone are carved into multiple and composite images, and they include several medium sized images of animals, including wolves and bears, and hundreds of small people, some with children and babies. Further down on the left is a picture of a young man in three-quarter profile, he is sitting down, looking to the right and he is wearing a hat with a wide brim and holding something in his hand. About half way down the stone is another set of large images. This is a group of six or more people (?) wearing furs and standing around another figure in the middle. What they are actually doing is unclear at the moment, due to the covering of lichen. Photographs taken with ultra violet and infra-red light and using special film may reveal more details.

I have managed to just about make out a few images at the top of stone 56. In the centre is the head of a young woman. To the right, close to the edge of the stone is the profile of a man wearing a crown with triangular points. He is also wearing a fur coat with a wide white collar, probably ermine. The whole area is covered with images of little people and there are pictures of the head of a wild cat and a dog or a fox. Interestingly even the tenon on the top of the stone has been decorated, suggesting that the surface of the stone was decorated just before the lintel was added. It would certainly have been easier for the artists to work at ground level but it was also a risk, the thin stone could have broken during the erection process. So I think the artists must have had scaffolding and indeed it would have been needed anyway, in order to put the lintel in place.

The outer surface of the stone (pictured on the left) is even more camouflaged by lichen than the inner surface. However, near the top of the stone is a series of lines that radiate outwards, like our symbol for the sun. And although it looks like the small central figure is that of a man wearing a fur hat, the whole area is covered with tiny images of people that are concealed by the lichen. His bearded chin forms a multiple image of the top part of a skull. He is close to the edge and the top of his head is outlined by a wavy crack in the rock. His left arm and sleeve are visible, hanging down at his side, right down the edge of the stone. He is in left profile and is looking towards a much more enigmatic figure on the left, and I'm not even sure if this is a human being, it has such a strange, beaky nose. Further down the edge of the stone is a pronounced V-shaped mark. This is the nose of an animal, perhaps a bird. The secondary decoration demands a much closer inspection because I think it looks like some sort of wheeled vehicle.

Like the rest of the stone, it is covered with images of tiny people, and another picture in the multiple style looks as though they are riding on the back of an animal's head, one with pronounced eye ridges, like the head of a snake perhaps. At the bottom of the stone is a picture of a dozen or so people who are sitting down, bent forwards and crowded together. Some of these characters look very odd and not quite human. The other upright of the Great Trilithon, Stone 55, is broken in two and lis lying on the ground across the Altar Stone.

The fourth trilithon (below) is composed of upright stones 57 and 58 and lintel 157.
Standing in front are bluestones 69 and 70, and in the foreground are fallen parts of the Great Trilithon.

The inner face of stone 57 was originally decorated with marvellous pictures and stone 58 shows a variety of sculptures on both the inner and outer surfaces. The inner surface of trilithon stone 57 has a multitude of very faint pictures of people. These were originally engraved and painted and include two large images of a white-faced man and a woman in the top half of the stone and a crowd of people in the bottom half. However, the whole stone was covered with secondary scenes and images, and decorated with hundreds of small images in both the composite and multiple styles.

One of the strangest and most impressive scenes on trilithon stone 57 is in the top right corner and shows some people riding on the back of a large, but strangely dog-like, creature. However, these wonderful images are sadly faded and eroded and most of them are only visible with very powerful image intensification. What are easier to see is a series of faces, some human, that are carved vertically above each other into the right side of stone 57. (Incidentally, many of the little holes that you can see in the surface of sarsen stones are actually the eyes of the hundreds of people in the small carvings and engravings.)

The outer surface of this trilithon stone, number 57, *below,* is quite flat, although it has been battered at some point in antiquity. The most interesting image is the faint picture of the head and chest of a lynx that runs from right to left across the middle of the stone, with the animal's nose on the left edge and its front left leg curved around the right edge of the stone.

Very enhanced detail of the outer surface of stone 57

The bottom right side and corner looks as though it was smashed off, but since the rough surface has been decorated with images, this must have occurred in antiquity, and the damage was not done in Victorian times by souvenir hunters.

One of the other images is that of a full-length picture of a person wearing a pointy hat. He is standing in profile and facing towards the stone, looking towards a much larger face that is carved on the rough, broken edge of the stone. The face of this person is leaning towards the smaller man, and he too is wearing a long pointed hat. There is a crack in the rock that goes from his nose up past his right eye and onwards up to a hole in the stone. It was the drilling of this hole that must have made the stone crack. There are also two other larger holes, and these are the eyes of a very faint image of a triangular animal face, which is tilted at an angle. Just above this, and to the left, is another strange image of a mass of people riding on some sort of sledge or a boat. At the back is a man wearing a big hat with a band and a floppy brim. He is standing up, as though he is steering. However, as I mentioned before, images like these are very faint and they need powerful image intensification to be seen.

The inner surface of stone 58 is one very large multiple sculpture of two heads, one to the left and the other to the right. The most obvious image is the one on the left side, it is a strange face with a bulbous nose and a gaping, down-turned mouth, but it is not a sculpture of a human.

Inner surface of stone 58

By looking from left to right you can see the second giant sculpture. This is a long, thin, stylised face in right profile, his eyes, nose and mouth are reduced to fit in along the edge of the stone and he has a bushy beard with sideburns that meet up below his chin and descend almost to ground level. The hair on the right side of his face is a multiple image, it is also a strange caterpillar-like creature, and yet another image shows a picture of a long, thin face and neck, its nose is close to the corner of the mouth of the first very large sculpture.

On the right side of the stone are two smaller, individual sculptures, one overlapping the other. At the top is the head and left shoulder of a man who is in profile and is looking to the left. Next to him, and a bit lower down, is a proportionally bigger but very long and narrow head of a man wearing a beard on his chin. He is wearing a domed cap on his head. This particular image is a bit strange since, depending on the lighting, it can also look like a caterpillar. In the top left corner is another carving of two heads, each of them looking at the other. The one on the left is wearing a parka with the hood up and since he is also in right profile, we can only see a bit of his face. The other individual has a white face and is wearing a fur hat and bushy coat, and I think this is a young woman. Just above the woman's head is a white patch and around it are four or five small figures in a circle, they may be holding hands and dancing. This then forms into another much larger multiple image, that of a bushy-bearded man with a sort of circular headdress.

Perhaps the most extraordinary feature about this trilithon stone is that in a previous era it stood the other way up and at that time the main sculpture on the inner side was a big happy face with a big nose, in right profile. However, I don't think that this is a human being, since the mouth turns upwards, directly below the nose, and there is no gap between nostril and upper lip. The rounded edge of the nose forms a secondary image in the multiple style. It is the left side of the top of a head in three-quarter profile. This head is that of a dog-like individual that looks a bit like a King Charles spaniel. The animal's left shoulder is formed from the top of the chin of the large happy-faced sculpture, and the mouth of which cuts into the dog's left eye. The man on the left, the one wearing the parka, is also a multiple image and now becomes a man in three-quarters view. He has a neat, pointed beard and is wearing a special hat that is wide and baggy at the sides, then curves round and upwards to a point at the top. As usual the whole of the stone is covered with additional decorations, some which are now upside down.

Further proof that the stone has been turned upside and re-erected comes from excavation evidence. The hole for this stone has been extensively dug into, to allow its safe removal, especially considering it weighs about forty tons. It was reburied to a depth of only about a metre and a half, and although it survived for over three and a half thousand years, it fell over in January 1797. Nearly two hundred years passed before it was re-erected again, this time in 1958. Just in front of the gap between 57 and 58 lies bluestone 69, a tall, thin rectangle. Next to it, towards the north-northeast, is bluestone 70, a tall stone with sloping sides. At the top of this stone, on the right corner, is a picture of the head of a wolf. Next to it in the top left corner is the head of a man who is wearing a fur hat and a parka. Further down the stone are several other images of animals and people, with the different scenes stacked vertically above and below each other. As well as the decoration, the difference between the two shapes must be significant. According to Hawkins, the gap in the fourth trilithon has sightlines towards the two extremes of the setting moon around midwinter.
And twice a year the sun could be seen to set through this gap on several days, about two months on either side of the summer solstice. (It is difficult to give precise dates since few of the stones are in exactly their original places, and this limits the sort of the accuracy needed to calculate the ancient astronomy precisely.)

The outer surface of trilithon 58 is also formed from two massive sculptures, one of which is now upside down, like the inner surface. Looking from slightly to the right of the stones, and under the correct lighting, the sculpture resolves into the massive head and left shoulder of a bearded man who is in profile and looking down to the ground at a forty-five degree angle. He has a pronounced triangular nose and jutting forehead and a beard on his chin and has sideburns. The point at the bottom of the man's beard is also the head of a bird, probably a swan. (You can see a good version of this sculpture on the front cover of the best-selling paperback version of *'Stonehenge Decoded'* by Gerald S. Hawkins) From a central viewpoint, most of the top half of the stone becomes a gigantic head, but one with only a hint of facial features on the right edge of the stone. This is not a human being, its face is flat with only a tiny nose and triangular eyes, and its neck slopes backwards and downwards from the point of the chin.

There is a very distinctive scene on the front of this stone, which is very different in content to any other images that I have seen. Near the top of the stone are two parallel holes, with a wavy white line above them. This marks the eroded carving of the top of the head of a sheep or goat, probably an ancestor of our old breed of Soay Sheep, the sort that now roam the slopes of the Cheddar Gorge.

Enhanced detail of trilithon stone number 58

Outer surface of fourth trilithon stone 58

To the left of the eyes is a strange sort of beak, and then further left, there is the arm of a strange creature with a curved nose and jaw, like the beak of a parrot, this is definitely not a human; and this figure overlaps another that is slightly to the right. Below its arm, right on the edge of the stone is the head of a strange bird with a ferocious beak. This part of the rock surface then curves round and down, to about a quarter of the way up the stone. This becomes the head of a snake-like creature with a broad, triangular head with big oval eyes. (This head is turned through ninety degrees.) At sunset around midwinter the stone is lit up by the setting sun and takes on a golden colour. The light from the right side turns the top half of the stone into a carving of the head of a dog-like creature with a narrow muzzle. This can only be seen by turning the stone anti-clockwise ninety degrees, suggesting that it is an earlier sculpture. As I mentioned earlier, this stone was originally the other way up, and at that time the whole of this surface was the sculpture of the head and body of a bird with a long beak. However, the top of the head of the bird is no longer visible since it is below ground level, so the rest of the head starts just above the level of the bird's eye, which is now only a few inches above the grass. The beak is tucked up against the bird's breast and the shape of the beak suggests that it represents a fishing bird, such as a heron, an egret, a stork or perhaps even a kingfisher.
In view of the ancient stories in our folklore about storks, and how generations of kids were told that

Fourth trilithon stone number 58, inverted

they were the bringers of new-born babies, I'm inclined to think that this is what the sculpture represents, a stork. However, although common on the other side of the Channel, white storks are no longer summer migrants to Britain, probably because the Victorians shot so many of them and they stopped coming here.

Below the level of the bird's throat is another curious image, which is the eroded head of a rather cross-looking animal with a short muzzle, a bit like a cross between a wild cat and a wolf. Below this is the triangular head of another strange creature, which has a long thin nose overhanging a square jaw and a wide mouth. The head sits on a very squat body with muscular shoulders. Secondary decoration has made the area rather confusing to the eye since someone has added a composite image of the face of a bearded old man wearing an enormous hat, thus turning the squat shape into a man wearing a coat with wide lapels. The composite image of the old man's head is faint but is composed of about six or seven small images of people. Below this and towards the right, almost on the edge of the stone, are several strange faces stacked in a vertical formation. On the left, below the bird's bill, is a medium sized image of a rather cat-like person wearing a large tubular hat. (A horizontal crack in the stone goes right through its eye.) At the bottom of the stone (now the top) is a group of rather sinister looking creatures/people that are partly covered by lichen.

The reason why the stone was turned upside down is a minor mystery at the moment, but since the older artwork was no longer suitable it must have had something to do with a change in cultural values and beliefs. And just to make things even more complicated, at one point the stone was carved when it lay on its side, perhaps prior to being erected. The lintel on the fourth trilithon is quite interesting. Aerial views show a deep notch in the top of the southern end of the stone, indicating that it was used previously and then reused in the new temple. In some lighting conditions the lintel looks a bit like the body of an otter with its head to the left and there is another animal head at the other end.

The fifth trilithon is ruined. Stone 59 lies in pieces on the ground, as does the lintel, but stone 60 still remains upright because its base is filled with concrete to keep it stable. The inner face of 60 is often hidden in photos taken from the eastern side of Stonehenge because it stands behind the first trilithon, as well as circle stones 6 and 7. And this gives an insight into the way that the design of the inner temple made sure that certain decorations were hidden from view to people outside the temple. However, trilithon stone 60 does show a faint scene in the bottom half of the stone when the light is from the southwest. On the right side is the seated figure of a person with a white face and very angular features.

Outer surface of the fifth trilithon stone number 60

Opposite him (or her) are two smaller images of people, both standing up and the one at the back is the taller of the two. I think these are two children of different ages. Both are in profile, as is the person on the right, who is wearing a domed cap or hat. In some lighting conditions there are big patches of a whitish discolouration that cover this whole area. The outer surface of stone 60 is easier to see since there are gaps in the northwestern sector of the sarsen circle. This is the north side and it shows how the bottom of the stone has fragmented and broken off and how it has needed the internal support of a big chunk of concrete. It is a very rough stone, at the back it was formed into a slightly tapering oblong, whilst in front of this, but still part of the natural rock, is a sort of irregularly shaped domed section of rough stone with a gap at the bottom where it is broken off. This is a very old stone.

Although still abundant, the decorations are relatively sparse in comparison to other flat-surfaced stones that are highly decorated. However, there is a certain degree of secondary imagery that was added at a later date. As usual the art that is visible changes according to the time of day and the direction of the lighting. In the early morning one of the most noticeable images is an overlapping image. At an angle across the top left quarter of the stone is a triangular, not-quite-human face; the left line of the jaw is outlined by a wavy, roughly horizontal crack in the stone and there are heavy ridges above the eyebrows. It shares its left eye with the right eye of another triangular face that is looking out of the stone square on, but this has just a stub of a nose, a bit like that of a very young wolf or perhaps a bear cub.

This is also an overlapping image, making three in a row, this time the left eye of the cub is the right eye of another face further to the right, the face of a wolf, whose left eye is closed, and this is illustrated by the wavy line. There is another face a little further down the back of the stone and to the right. This is the right profile of a rather hunched-over man wearing a parka, with the hood pulled up over his head. He is in profile and the top edge of the rounded lump of rock at the front of the stone becomes the lapel, shoulder and back of the big, thick parka he is wearing. The top of his hood is outlined by a curved crack in the top right. This crack also runs through the middle of another animal face that is at a forty-five degree angle in the top right quarter of the stone. The crack makes an inverted V-shape across its nose. This face looks more like that of a cat than the others. The right ear is just behind the clearly visible, round, right eye but the wild cat's left eye and ear have been badly altered by subsequent artwork.

At first I underestimated the skill of the artists who worked on this stone but as time went by I began to appreciate their craft further, since the more I looked, the more I saw. One of the best visual illusions on this rock was specially created using the face of a wolf. The head of the animal is on the back of the oblong stone whilst the long muzzle is carved into the rounded surfaces in front of it, the whole piece of art is only visible if you are looking from exactly the right height and angle and only then do the two parts join together, to form the whole head of the wolf. Although the bottom of the rounded part is no longer there you can still make out that it was the sculpture of a large head of someone looking to the right. He is wearing a round cap that covers his hair, although the features look decidedly ape-like. Without doubt the secondary decorations on this part of the trilithon stone are very strange indeed.

One of the main images is the massive sculpture of the head and torso of a man in right profile. He is wearing a bearskin hat. He has deep-set eyes and is hunched up. His right shoulder forms the curved part of the stone, with his face two thirds of the way up. His forehead and the edge of his hat are outlined by a wavy line. There is also an image of quite a triangular face, tilted at an angle, on the upper left side.

Powerful image intensification of the eroded surface reveals a very bizarre scene on the whole of the curved part of the stone. It looks to me like a lot of small people and animals riding on the back of a very large animal or in some sort of vehicle, with others riding on top. The problem with these sorts of scenes is that sometimes the artists added so much elaborate decoration on top of the original images that it makes it very hard to separate out the different elements of the original parts. Just below the pointed top of the rounded part is the head of a young dog with floppy ears and below that is a charming picture of a cat-like creature with wide eyes and pointed ears and this makes it look almost human. Just above the curved part, where it is broken off at the bottom, is a scene of several humans, and some other creatures, riding big animals, and they are all galloping from left to right. Maybe this is a hunting scene of some sort or perhaps it represents a chase or a joy ride?

Art on the Bluestones

With regard to the art that was created on the bluestones, I have only a few close-up photographs of them and the two most important ones, 49 and 31, on either side of the entrance, are covered with layers of lichen. The phallic, male, sunstone, bluestone number 49 is one of the oldest stones in the temple. One large image is partially visible; this is the face of a young man looking to the right, towards the oval, female, moonstone number 31. He is wearing a sort of headdress that is tubular in shape, a bit like a bonnet, and although it is very hard to make out, I think it has a band of feathers around the top rim. The outer surface of the stone has been carved along the left side and a big scoop taken out of the edge. Stone 31 is also camouflaged by lichen and all I can make out is several people standing in a line. One of these is a man with a thin face and a goatee beard. The major image is a sculpture of a head in profile, with the outline of the face along the right edge, and it is carved in such a way that the rest of the stone is the rounded part of the head.
Although all the bluestones were decorated to some extent, one of the stones in the U-shaped arrangement of nineteen stones is particularly interesting because it is an eroded statue. This is bluestone 63. It stands in front of the space between the first and second trilithons, roughly southeast of the centre. The northeast side is the most interesting. It's very curious, at first I thought that it was a woman wearing a long dress that reached down to the ground. Then I noticed the beard… In fact it is quite a complicated little sculpture; it is a group of several people of different sizes standing very close to each other. At the back is the tallest person, the bearded man, his long hair hangs down his back and he is wearing something on his head, possibly a crown. He is holding a small person up to his face and the top of their head is level with his mouth. This small person is also part of a large secondary multiple image of a bear. It forms the muzzle, whilst the head of the man is the back part of the bear's head. There is another tall person standing slightly sideways on, in front of the taller bearded man. There are one or two other minor images, then lastly another large image of a person standing sideways on at the edge of the stone. This person is looking to the left, towards the second trilithon. He is wearing a helmet with what looks like a gold rim and has a dark face, a short beard just on his chin and has short curly hair on the side of his face. There are also additional images all over the stone, but these are a bit hard to make out from the photo I have. However, most of the stone can also be seen as the sculpture of the head and upper body of an animal with a long face and a square nose, possibly a horse but it is more likely to be yet another bear, standing upright.

The other bluestone columns of the U-shape will also be the source of a great deal of interest, since these stones are more recent than most of the circle bluestones. Excavation of the earth inside the circle has shown that it contains thousands of small chips of the various geological types of bluestones. This suggests extensive reworking of the surfaces of older stones, in order to give them the flat surfaces typical of the bluestones in the U-shape.

The most intriguing stone of all within the temple is the altar stone, number 80. It now lies half buried under the top half of the broken Great Trilithon stone number 55. When this came crashing down it knocked the altar stone over, the lintel fell off and part covered the altar stone as well. The altar stone is of Welsh sandstone, about five metres long it was originally a beautiful pale green stone, with flecks of sparkling mica and grains of ruby garnet. It faced out along the axis and was lit up by the rising sun at the summer solstice on the longest day of the year and by the winter full moon near the shortest day of the year.

Yet in its current position, face down in the grass, the Altar Stone can reveal very little to us about what must have been the most important and most scared decorations in the whole of the temple.

In my opinion, the Altar Stone, the Great Trilithon and many other stones must be re-erected. We owe it to our ancestors, the extremely talented designers, stonemasons and artists, together with all the other dedicated people, who created and then decorated the most extraordinary temple of the ancient world.

9 THE SYMBOLISM AND MEANING OF STONEHENGE

Stonehenge is without doubt the most visited, the most studied and the most highly excavated prehistoric site in the whole of the British Isles. So after three centuries of scientific investigation one would expect that there is very little that has not already been observed, recorded and understood, yet despite all this work, the great mysteries surrounding Stonehenge remain largely intact. There are many enduring mysteries about Stonehenge, but for many visitors the most commonly asked questions are probably: *"What is it?"* and *"Why was it built?"* and *"How was it used?"*

In spite of all the research that has been done over the last three hundred years the answers to such basic questions remain unresolved. But as I explained earlier, and as I shall show in the following pages, the reason why Stonehenge has remained such a major mystery is simply because vitally important clues have been missed, wrongly interpreted, or simply ignored by generations of our 'experts'. Correctly interpreted these clues would have revealed an enormous amount of new information about the series of monuments that were built on this site over a period of some fifteen centuries. Our long-term inability to understand our most famous prehistoric monument is, in my opinion, an absolute disgrace, an insult to our forefathers who built a marvellous temple, or rather a series of temples, more than two thousand years before Julius Caesar and his legions came to these shores.

The simplest way to answer those basic questions is to say that Stonehenge was a temple and that it was built as a place of worship. However, even this is a very simplistic view of something that becomes surprisingly more and more complex the more you look at it. And it took me a very long time to have my **'*Eureka!*'** moment, and finally understand what has been perplexing prehistorians, archaeologists and scientists for centuries, namely:

"Why is this stone circle so very special, so unique and so different from all the hundreds of others that were built across the British Isles?"

Nearly everywhere else the stones stand separately from each other, around the circumference of a ring, but here in Wiltshire the stones stood close together in a circle and were connected to each other at the top by lintels. So why was this temple so different from all the others and what did such a special and unique design mean?

Although he was a classical scholar, and experienced field archaeologist, the author of the classic book on Stonehenge, Professor Richard Atkinson, understood very little about the minds of the Neolithic and Bronze Age people he was investigating. His generation of academics were far more concerned with the traditional sorts of archaeological 'facts', namely what an excavation could reveal of the architecture, methods of construction, and particularly the tools, weapons, bones and pottery found during their digs, rather than the intellect of the builders. As a direct result of his background, education and training, his attitudes reveal an arrogant and blinkered way of thinking and he looked without seeing things that should have been obvious to someone of his stature and reputation. In his 1956 book Atkinson asked a series of rhetorical questions about the structure, origins and meaning of the different temples that were built at Stonehenge, with each question beginning with the word *'Why?'* and he answered them as follows:

"To all these questions beginning 'Why?' there is one short, simple, perfectly correct answer: We do not know, and we shall probably never know."

Such a depressingly pessimistic attitude would no longer be acceptable in our society, because we want answers to the big questions. But his generation of archaeologists felt that any speculation about prehistoric religious beliefs was simply a waste of time since any conjecture could never be proved, just because there were no written documents dating from such a remote period. And so

Atkinson and his colleagues thought that any form of investigation that did not deal exclusively with the physical evidence resulting from their scientific excavations was pointless. In their opinion, any speculation about prehistoric belief and religion just encouraged 'the lunatic fringe'. But I think they were embarrassed, because they didn't know the answers to even the basic questions. For theirs was a more scientific way of looking at an ancient building, in terms of its archaeology, its engineering and architecture, rather than as a physical representation of human thought and culture and of religious belief and philosophy. Although he did suggest some pretty tame ideas about the meaning of Stonehenge, his generation of archaeologists wanted to know more about 'who' and 'how' and 'when', rather than 'what' and 'why'. (This probably explains how they managed to miss so much…) Even the basic shape of the structure itself remained a mystery to them, an enigma that has stood the test of time.

And Atkinson wrote:

"There is no need to labour the point that the sarsen structure of Stonehenge 3 is unique. As such it is all the more hopeless to try and interpret it in terms of belief and ritual."

But he might just as well have said: *'Since I haven't a clue what it all means, someone like you shouldn't even bother to try…'*

That was fifty years ago. Since then things have improved in a number of important ways. Firstly our attitudes have changed and we are much more likely to challenge the views of the 'experts'. Secondly, major surveys of the surrounding area, further excavations and a multitude of improvements in our science and technology have provided us with a great deal of new information about the distant past and they have solved many minor points. But despite all the progress that has been made in gathering more and more scientific data about the ancient environment, by using the latest techniques, such as soil sampling, snail shell analysis, forensic science, improved dating techniques and many other modern procedures including genetic research and geophysics, the basic questions that Atkinson posed have remained stubbornly unanswered.

So what does it all mean? The most popular explanation was that Stonehenge had something to do with the rising sun at the summer solstice, but beyond that simple idea the precise reasons why the temples were built, and what they meant to the people who built them, have remained a seemingly unsolvable mystery. Atkinson was one of the first to suggest that the sarsen temple was a representation of the framework of a roundhouse, but built in stone rather than in wood. A 'Home of the Gods', perhaps. The way that the designs of the different buildings changed over time suggested to him that changes in religious belief were the root cause of the alterations, with the final temple a compromise between different religious factions. But beyond this simple idea, expert opinion remains divided.

For many academics the sarsen temple was built to celebrate the most northerly rising of the sun, which you will remember usually happens at sunrise at the summer solstice on the 20th or 21st of June, the longest day of the year. But other scholars have thought that the temple was built to commemorate the exact opposite. According to them it was built to commemorate the winter solstice, the shortest day of the year, usually on the 21st of December. Yet to me neither of these arguments seemed to be a powerful enough reason to have inspired thousands of people into building such a complex monument. When I started to think about it in more detail, I felt that there had to have been a much greater motivation to justify using such enormous blocks of stone in such an ambitious project.

To make matters worse, the difference of opinion between two different sets of experts has simply confused the overall picture for decades. In my opinion, it says more about the people who have been studying our prehistoric past than it does about the priests, designers, engineers, artists and builders who actually constructed the temple. The idea that Stonehenge was built to celebrate just the summer or the winter solstice seems far too simple. Were our forefathers really so unsophisticated that they were incapable of having more than one concept at the same time?

I don't think so. I am certain that, like us, there was a wide range of different types of people and that many of them were very intelligent. They proved it time and time again in the design and construction of earlier major monuments, such as those at Calanais, Avebury, Newgrange, Maes Howe and a host of other temples and burial sites across the British Isles. Even if their technology was not as advanced as contemporary civilisations in other parts of the world, it should have been obvious long ago that many prehistoric monuments were the result of the creative work of designers, artists and stonemasons, allied to the demands of the priesthood and the expectations of society. The monuments that they built were not crude constructions of earth, wood and stone dotted haphazardly around the landscape, far from it, they were designed and built to become a part of the landscape itself.

Their monuments fulfilled a deep spiritual need, coupled with intense emotional meaning for the people who built them and used them throughout their lives. Their most famous temple, the place we call Stonehenge, was the result of the labour of hundreds, if not thousands, of people and decades of hard and sometimes dangerous work. If they had wanted to, they could have produced a temple in which the blocks of stone were the same shapes and sizes. But they didn't. Instead, they used specially worked stones to build a temple in which religion, astronomy, symbolism, art, history, myth and legend were all combined to form a glorious whole. What has also coloured our perceptions of our distant ancestors, in such a negative way, is the fact that many of their ancient buildings are now in a ruined state. But if we were able to see these temples and tombs as they once were, then our perceptions would be dramatically altered, and we would think much more highly of them and the people who built them, especially when we remember that they were all laboriously constructed by hand, just using simple tools and quite basic equipment.

So to be able to understand the symbolism and meaning of the different Stonehenge temples we need to be able to visualise how the structures would have looked shortly after they were constructed more then four thousand years ago. And as we shall see, each new temple that they built contained important religious, astronomical and symbolic themes that were carried forwards from earlier versions. In its earliest form, Stonehenge was indeed a *'House for the Dead'*, a place to lay out corpses until their flesh had returned to the land. Over recent centuries numerous digs of the central area of the earth circle have found unknown quantities of human and animal remains from these earliest times. They have included many bones, both human and animal, as well as the skulls of cattle (both the domesticated variety and the huge, wild aurochs) and many red deer antlers. Few of these 'excavations' were recorded in any detail since many were undertaken by treasure hunters. However, a proper excavation by Lieutenant-Colonel William Hawley in the early 1920's showed that the large, circular ditch had been dug in sections, with the chalk spoil piled up on the ground to form a bank, again in a circular form.

The axis of the circle at that time was slightly to the left of the midsummer sunrise position and the view through the wide gap in the bank in the northeastern part was towards a variety of rising positions of the moon, and to a lesser extent, the sun. The most northerly sightline was towards the major rising point of the moon during its nineteen-year swing cycle. A bit further round to the right, and to the east, was the midsummer sunrise position. This suggests that the moon was of greater religious importance than the sun at this time. Further references to the moon include the erection of the fifty-six posts or stones in the Aubrey Holes, a highly probable reference to the 19-19-18 year sequence of the swing cycle (or perhaps two lunar months of four weeks each). Later on, before the site was abandoned for a while, the Aubrey Holes were reused for burying partially burned pieces of bone, the sparse remains of over a hundred cremations. However, of all the references to the moon, the most important is one that is still partially visible, yet it has remained overlooked and unsuspected.

Stonehenge is unusual in that the bank was erected on the inner side of the ditch. But true henges, like the ones at Avebury, Stenness and Stanton Drew, always had the bank on the outside of the ditch. So why was this bank on the inside of the ditch? The answer is that this form of earthwork was intended to represent something different. But what was it? To understand this you need to be able to visualise how the bank would have looked to someone from outside the circle, when it had been freshly constructed. (It is now very low, because the bank has washed into the ditch, filling it up in the process.) From either the eastern or western side of the circle a person would have looked across the deep ditch and would have been confronted by a wall of glistening white chalk. This high bank curved round to the left and to the right. In other words, a white crescent.

This is similar to the crescent we saw at Newgrange, in other words, an arc of the moon. But by walking all the way around the circular ditch an observer would have seen an almost unbroken white wall, with just two entrances, one to the northeast and the other to the south. In other words, the full moon. So in honour of this early form of ancient shrine, I have named this lunar temple and burial place: **'Moonhenge'**. Later on a modification involved digging the 56 Aubrey Holes, in order to set up posts around the circumference of the enclosure, some of which could have marked important moon and sun positions. These may have been the temporary precursors to the next phase of **Moonhenge** after it was it was abandoned for a few centuries until it was given a new lease of life by the arrival of the first lot of Bluestones from Wales, which were set up in the Aubrey Holes and replaced the wooden posts. But even this arrangement didn't last. The Bluestones were removed and set up in a new arrangement in the centre of the henge. The Aubrey Holes were not abandoned completely, they served as the receptacles for cremation burials. The second setting of Bluestones was in the form of a double semicircle of stones, with a corridor of more stones in the northeastern entranceway, perhaps with lintels. This new temple, **Bluestonehenge**, was predominantly a lunar site, due to the arcs of stones, but it did have some solar alignments.

Like many people today, their beliefs would have been central to their existence and their faith would have governed their lives in the same way as the sun governed the changing seasons. In turn the sun controlled the success of the harvest and the health of the livestock, and all this had a great influence on the lives of the farmers and their families and friends. The omnipotent power of the sun was something anyone could appreciate, it was something seen and felt and trusted, for sunlight kept the terrors of the night away and evil spirits at bay. Sunlight was the regenerative force of the world, because each spring the natural world was reborn. As a result of such clear and direct evidence, it must have seemed logical to them that there was indeed some form of life after death, that death was not the end of everything, but just one more stage in everyone's journey to another life. The different ways that the dead were treated suggests a wide variety of different religious beliefs. But although their time on this world may have been brief, there was always the hope that they would be reborn and have an afterlife, if not here, then certainly in *'the Spirit World'*, on the Moon, or perhaps on planets such as Venus, Mars or Jupiter, or out along the Milky Way and amongst the stars.

As I explained earlier, at a time when there were no written means of passing on information, our ancestors used other ways of communicating their thoughts and beliefs to future generations. One of these techniques involved the use of systems of geometrically shaped stones, another method was the creation of complex works of art, whilst yet another method, one that has been known about for decades, involved the specific orientation of entrances and exits of tombs and temples so that they would line up with the direction of certain exceptional astronomical events.

From the time of Moonhenge, some five thousand years ago, the axis of each subsequent temple ran along a line roughly northeast/southwest. The entrance into the sacred enclosure was positioned so that in each funeral procession the remains of the deceased travelled on their last journey from the northeast to the southwest, symbolically passing from Life to Death. And as I have said previously, the direction of southwest symbolises Death, because the setting sun marks the end of each day and because southwest is the furthest south the sun ever sets. To remind you, this takes place on the shortest day of the year, at the winter solstice, which is also the longest night of the year, and therefore, from a symbolical viewpoint, marks the end of the annual solar cycle.

At the winter solstice, the old year dies with the setting sun, then at dawn the following day the rising sun represents the rebirth of the sun and the start of a new year. From then onwards the position of sunrise moves further and further north, until six months later it reaches its maximum position, in the northeast at the summer solstice. We are all more active and feel much more invigorated, more alive, during the long hot days of summer, and throughout history the midsummer solstice has been a good time to celebrate being alive and of enjoying the life-giving and life enhancing power of the sun.

Confirmation of the life/death symbolism inherent in the northeast/southwest axis can also be found at the nearby site of a large wooden building called Woodhenge, which dates from around 2300 BC.

This structure was probably an enormous roundhouse, with the roof supported by concentric oval rings of tall posts and massive tree trunks of oak. Like the more famous stone temple nearby, the wooden building was erected within a henge on a roughly northeast/southwest axis. But what makes this site particularly interesting in terms of ritual and symbolism is the grave of a child in the centre of the building. This grave was situated across the axis but to the southwest of the middle of the building. The burial is famous because the skull was in two parts, and to some this has been cited as evidence of child sacrifice, however it was a young child and the bones of the skull do not fuse together until the head has arrived at its final size, when the body has stopped growing at the end of adolescence. So it is just as likely that the skull had separated along a natural line. Whether the child died from natural causes or something more sinister, it was the final resting place of a life cut short, and as such it is a very clear reference to 'Death'.

The Life/Death axis was something of a tradition, since it featured in many other important tombs and temples around the British Isles. One of the most famous is the chambered tomb known as Bryn Celli Ddu, on Ynys Mona (Anglesey), in North Wales. Here the long stone-lined passageway opens out towards the life-giving rays of the midsummer sunrise. And inside the central chamber was a tall, very phallic-looking column, another clear reference to the male principle as the giver of Life. Whilst the chamber was the womb of the mother.

Every ancient culture has had its own stories to tell of legendary figures, its own mythology and a set of philosophies, and in many cases, important information was hidden within these histories, stories and parables. Some of this was recorded in their works of art, in the form of complex sculptures, carvings and engravings. Our Neolithic ancestors had their own versions of philosophy and mythology, some of which were based on their insights into the natural world. Their particular vision of the earth beneath their feet and the sky above their heads gave them the basic insights to develop their own brand of natural wisdom. One aspect of this philosophy was the realisation that nearly everything in their worldview was cyclical and kept in balance and that there was a harmony to the natural world. They would have noticed that pairs of things are not just simply opposites of each other; the contrasting pairs demonstrate the basic dualities of existence.

Sometimes these dualities revealed opposite viewpoints of the same thing, like the two sides of a hand, but they invariably showed that you couldn't have one without the other. They realised that duality could be seen everywhere and there were many paired opposites, such as day/night, light/dark, hot/cold, sun/moon, birth/death, spring/autumn, summer/winter, old year/new year, male/female, man/woman, husband/wife, father/mother, boy/girl, youth/elder, left/right, up/down, earth/sky, good/evil, bull/cow, ram/ewe, sow/reap, etc. etc., the list is endless.

Without a written language the Stonehenge people demonstrated this concept in the design of their temple in practical ways. The relationships, balance and harmony that exists between the sun and the moon were demonstrated by a multitude of symbolical references, including sunrise and sunset, moonrise and moonset, day and night, summer and winter, summer sun and winter moon, as well as northeast and southwest but above all else, by references to Life and Death. Death and Rebirth. The choice of the axial layout, that is, the line from the northeast to the southwest, illustrates how they simply, but elegantly, incorporated the concept of duality into the basic design of many of their tombs and temples.

There were many symbols of power inherent in the design of the stone structure, for the stones themselves represented the major forces that governed people's lives, the sun that ruled by day, bringing heat and light, caused the seasons to change and ripened the grain for their daily bread. And the moon, which ruled the seas, divided time up into weeks and months and regulated women's menstrual cycles. To maintain harmony and balance everything in the natural world seemed to need a partner, a complementary side that was sometimes its exact opposite. In other words, their monuments imprinted the duality of the natural condition onto the landscape itself, for their religious beliefs were the driving force behind the building of monuments that celebrated and testified to their faith in a very physical, yet practical way, one that they thought would last forever. And they were right to do so, since stone is permanent, whilst wood is not. And although they and their wooden homes are long gone, the remains of their temples and tombs have endured the march of time.

At Stonehenge, the fundamental principles of the duality of their world were embodied into the design of the final temple. They did this by creating new themes and new ideas and adding them to older examples borrowed from previous temples. Inside the final temple, symbols of the sun and moon had pride of place along the axis; these were the old male and female Bluestones, 49 and 31, which also represented summer sunrise and winter moonrise. Whilst on the outside, flanking the main entrance into the inner sanctum, sarsens 30 and 1 were examples of solar and lunar symbol stones. In addition the U-shaped arrangement of five trilithons produced an imposing example of the nature of duality. Each was erected as a pair of tall, closely set stones, joined together, at the top, by a lintel.

To some prehistorians, Stonehenge was a temple to the sun, whilst for others it was a temple to the moon. But beyond this, few scholars have attempted to try and explain the unusual arrangement and symbolism of the trilithon stones. Some have just said that U-shaped arrangements of stones have their origins in Brittany and are not unknown in Britain. Take for example the henge at Arminghall in Norfolk, dating from 3150 BC, it had an arrangement of massive posts inside two ditches and a bank. The bank was set between the two ditches. And some scholars think that the post arrangement may have been the precursor for the trilithons but with wood changed to stone and a change in the meaning, since the focus was outwards, towards midsummer sunrise, rather than to the midwinter sunset, as in Norfolk.
According to Dr Terence Meaden, the U-shaped arrangement of trilithons at Stonehenge was symbolic of the womb, and that at the summer solstice the shadow of the Heel Stone caused a symbolic penetration of the womb, mimicking a *'Marriage of the Gods'* of the Sky Father and Earth Mother. This may have been the case when the Heel Stone was installed in its first position, just after the earth circle was erected, but it doesn't seem to fit in with the complexity of the stone temples that were built later on. And the shadow is not very obvious at sunrise because the ground is already lit up by the dawn sky; it was only obvious during a re-enactment that was filmed for television using a powerful arc light.

I am not convinced of this penetration of the womb theory for several reasons: The first is that the Heel Stone was not really lined up with the position of midsummer sunrise, and secondly, if a symbolic womb was intended, with all their design and construction skills they could easily have produced something far more realistically shaped than five pairs of upright stones in a U-formation. To me, the trilithons seem more like a symbolical device to 'capture' the summer sun, like a pair of cupped hands catching the glowing ball of the golden sun (ten stones, ten fingers). Perhaps this design was created because there was a real concern that the weather could worsen, and by symbolically capturing the sun, it would guarantee that their crops would ripen and life could continue as before. For farmers, then as now, the right amount of rain and sun meant Life, for without this balance their crops would not ripen correctly. Excessive rain or severe drought meant the crop would be poor and life would become very hard for everyone.

Although the majority of us see the final temple as a construction built to witness the rising sun on the longest day of the year, some scholars prefer another explanation. They think that the temple was built to observe sunset on the shortest day of the year, and they have said that one would have been able to witness the setting of the winter solstice sun between the uprights of the central trilithon.

But there are major problems with this theory.

The view to the southwest is now an artificial situation, because trilithon stone 55 has fallen and broken in two. So the setting sun at the winter solstice can, weather permitting, be clearly and dramatically seen in the space to the left of the remaining Great Trilithon stone, number 56. But when the Great Trilithon was intact, the stones would simply not have been wide enough apart to produce such a highly dramatic effect of the setting sun. To make matters worse, the view towards the setting sun from inside the circle would have been completely blocked by the Altar Stone. When upright this was by far the tallest and broadest of the Welsh stones, it measures sixteen feet long, three foot four inches wide and one foot four inches thick. (4.8 x 1 x 0.4m). It stood about twice the height of a man and was located just in front of the Great Trilithon on the northeast/southwest axis, facing outwards across the circle towards the summer solstice sunrise. The Altar Stone stood in front of the gap in the Great Trilithon, and just behind it was the tall, central bluestone, number 67. In addition to all these issues, there is yet another problem with this winter sunset theory, because unlike the clear view through the entrance and down the Avenue to the northeast, the high circular bank of earth and chalk behind the sarsen circle would have partially blocked the view of the horizon because the land rises to the southwest... Oops!

If indeed the midwinter sunset had been of key importance for viewing purposes then the Altar Stone would probably have been placed nearer the centre of the temple, and without the bluestone and the central trilithon behind it, thus allowing greater access and a direct view towards the southwest.

The position of the Great Trilithon before its collapse

■ TRILITHON LINTEL
■ TRILITHON 55
■ ALTAR STONE

Clearly, if the architects had really wanted to highlight such a dynamic and dramatic image as the setting sun, then it would have been quite a simple matter to construct a wide doorway or a passageway to the southwest. In complete contrast, the gap in the sarsen circle to the northeast, between stone 30 and 1, is wider than the norm and so the rising sun at the summer solstice can easily be seen from inside the temple. The view to and from the northeast is along the Avenue, which at that time was very visible and consisted of a bank and ditch on each side of the passageway that formed a sort of solar corridor. In addition, the summer solstice sunlight came into the temple through the entrance and would have shone directly onto the Altar Stone.

One of the usual criticisms about *'the northeastern view towards midsummer sunrise'* theory being the correct version is that, generally speaking, a congregation never enters a temple, then turns round to focus their attention back the way they have come. Consequently for some academics the correct direction was to look forwards, into the temple, towards the gap in the Great Trilithon and onwards to the setting sun in the southwest, the direction of the midwinter sunset.

However, at the start of a marriage ceremony in the Christian Church, all the congregation turns to watch the bride as she arrives and then makes her way up the central passageway, usually on the arm of her father, to join her future husband near the altar. What has also been forgotten is

that although the congregation in a Christian church looks towards the altar, the priests look in both directions! In the modern Church the priests look towards the congregation for much of the service, especially during the sermon and during the hymns, but when it comes to special prayers and dedications to God, they turn and face the altar, which usually has the symbol of Christianity, a cross, placed upon it.

Of course at the time of the winter solstice people could have watched the dying sun on the last day of the year from outside the temple. Whilst from inside the temple, a few people could have stood with their backs to the Great Trilithon at sunset and looked outwards through the gap between stones 15 and 16 of the sarsen circle, towards the southwest. However, unlike the summer sunrise celebration, this would probably not have been a grand public spectacle since travel was difficult and dangerous in the winter months. But in high summer, travel was easy and many people would have come from far and wide to stay at Durrington Walls then walk uphill, along the long processional way of the Avenue at the time of the Festival of the Summer Sun. However it is likely that only the privileged few would have been allowed into the stone temple, there simply is not enough space inside the centre for more than a few dozen people at a time.

The view from the southwest is across the ditch, over the bank, through the sarsen circle, between the Great Trilithon stones, across the centre and out through the northeastern entrance, towards the rising sun of the midsummer solstice.

Once the procession had passed between the flanking stones of the sarsen circle, 30 and 1, their attention would have been immediately been focused by the architecture of the U-shaped arrangements of trilithons and bluestones towards the Altar Stone. And then, once inside this U-shaped setting, their attention would have been briefly focused outwards, turning expectantly towards the northeast to welcome the rising sun. Once this had happened they would then turn round again, towards the spectacle of the life-giving sun, lighting up the most important stone in the whole temple, the Altar Stone.

But at the winter solstice sunset, there was not such an obvious and dramatic visual effect from inside the temple. The spectacle would have been reduced to the appearance of just a part of the sun's glow above the Altar Stone. It is only today, in a ruined temple, that the dramatic effect of the setting orb is readily visible at the winter solstice. So this must mean that the temple was designed and constructed so that the main view would be towards the northeast, and it confirms that midsummer sunrise and midwinter moonrise were more important to them than the direction of the setting sun on the shortest day of the year.

Forensic evidence from ancient burials show that malnutrition and famine were regular spectres in the lives of many Neolithic and Bronze Age people and few people saw their fiftieth birthday and many people were dead by the age of forty. At a time when life expectancy was so low, Death was the enemy of the living. Therefore, I see the very specific placing of the Altar Stone in front of the Great Trilithon gateway as a dual design, welcoming the summer sunrise but obstructing the last sunset of the year, in other words, a symbolic way of holding back Death. The whole focus of the U-shaped arrangements of trilithons and Bluestones is towards the northeast, they seem to reach outwards, like a person standing with their arms outstretched in front of them, welcoming and embracing the life-giving light and heat of the summer sun. Since Neolithic and Bronze Age mortality rates were so high, the religious symbolism inherent in the final temple may have acted as a sort of 'prehistoric life assurance policy'. The temple was built to keep the spectre of premature death at bay, by honouring, welcoming and celebrating Life, symbolised by the warmth of the rising sun on the longest day of the year.

The designers of the different stone temples that followed on from Bluestonehenge used a similar symbolism, the circle, for their designs, but over time each new temple became more complex and more sophisticated than the previous one. The final version was the most complicated of all, and the most difficult to achieve, since it required outstanding expertise in planning, surveying, man-management, stone working and construction. Such techniques had taken a thousand years to evolve and, just to make things even more difficult, some of the key astronomical alignments that dated from the earliest phases had to be incorporated into later temples. As I mentioned earlier, I think that some of the Bluestones were used to mark and predict astronomical phenomena that were an important part of their religious calendar.

When the sarsen temple with its trilithons was finished, the traditional explanation is that an oval of dressed Bluestones was added, and then some were removed to leave just nineteen stones in a U-shape. I am not very happy with this explanation. There are three stone holes (labelled J, K and L, in the English Heritage plan) in the rounded end of the 'oval', which is the part nearest to the northeast entrance. These pits are usually said to have contained the missing stones of the Bluestone oval, yet the position of the stones does not look right, the arc looks too flat and the spacing between them looks too wide. So I think it more likely that the extra three were from an earlier period and had been part of some other arrangement flanking the entranceway. From a symbolic viewpoint, an oval of twenty-two bluestones doesn't make much sense, it makes far more sense that they set up a U-shape of nineteen bluestones to copy the U-shape of the five sarsen trilithons. And indeed bluestone 61, the first on the east side of the U-shape, lines up well with the edge of the first trilithon stone, number 51.

These U-shaped structures probably had several meanings, including representations of the visible movements of the sun and moon. This is because both arrangements, sarsen and bluestone, grow in height from one end, reach a maximum at the centre, then decrease in size towards the other end, copying the vertical movement of the sun and moon as they rise, reach their zenith, then descend, to disappear from view, only to rise again the next day.

In addition, the tallest stones were placed in the centre and aligned with the winter sunset, and so the horizontal arcs formed by the five trilithons and the nineteen Bluestones seem to represent symbolic journeys, from life towards death, and from death to rebirth. The nineteen stones also illustrated two of the most significant rhythms of the moon, namely the nineteen-year swing cycle and the nineteen-year Metonic cycle. In addition, someone standing with their back to the Altar Stone, and looking outwards to the northeast, would have seen nine bluestone pillars to the left and nine to the right (with the nineteenth bluestone hidden behind the Altar Stone).

And as everyone knows, nine months is the amount of time a new life remains in the womb before it is born.

The builders of Stonehenge encapsulated their myths and legends in a form that would endure forever, stone. The decoration of the temples, the sculpting, painting and carving of the stones provides a real insight into the minds of the leaders of the ancient farming people. The decorations show pictures of their myths and legends, of important historical events, thousands of images of actual people, as well as representations of their religious and cultural beliefs. Sometimes the images are quite alarming, the images of strange monsters and horrible creatures seem to represent evil spirits associated with the living and the dead. Stones that had been used in one temple were uprooted and transferred to a new arrangement. Sometimes old images were erased or the stones turned upside down and new carved paintings were done on top. The complexity of the imagery shows they were not simple-minded people, but in fact their artists produced some of the greatest works of art of the ancient world. They created composite pictures, which seen from afar, represented huge images of well-known themes. As the observer got closer, the large images disappeared as they sub-divided into smaller and smaller images. In addition many images shared common areas, which produced a new set of multiple images. The sculptors used the sun and the effects of light and shade to produce shape-shifting images that appeared and disappeared, which seemed to come alive and were in effect the first moving images. To them, the carved and sculpted stones were the ancestors. The images, portraits and symbols on the stones were as evident to them as our statues are to us. In the same way as our more immediate ancestors are enshrined in the marble and bronze statues of kings and queens, soldiers and sailors, statesmen, scientists and explorers that populate the centres of our towns and cities.

Stonehenge is without doubt one of the most complex sites of the Ancient World. Much of it is subtle but that does not mean that it had to continue to remain a mystery for so long. Although the ancients used an oral tradition to pass on secret knowledge, they also used more mundane methods of recording and passing on information in the structures they built. They registered their knowledge in stone, so that it would endure for eternity and yet many people could understand the symbolism involved. The last version of the sarsen circle brought forward, and combined, the accumulated knowledge and experience of those who had gone before and in the end Stonehenge became a marvellous blend of astronomy, art, architecture, symbolism and religion. The best minds of the day were to incorporate much of their knowledge, skill and experience in an extraordinary feat of engineering and scientific prowess. In addition, the work force would have needed to be fed, housed and properly organised and this in itself would have been a major project, and only possible because of good social organisation, successful agriculture, trade and a common purpose that everyone believed in.
The new temple was to become the wonder of the age and the success of its design was due to the combined talents of planners, architects, mathematicians, astronomers, engineers, stonemasons and artists. All of them worked together to create the combined equivalent of a cathedral, calendar,

calculator, observatory, national art gallery and museum, all rolled into one. And so it is no wonder that our scientists have been unable to decide which single one of these roles fitted the design of Stonehenge.

With so many references in stone and earth to both sun and moon, to circles and to U-shapes, to the cycles of nature and to life and death, it is clear that the final temple had many roles to fulfil and one single, simple, explanation for its existence was never enough. In the past, our scholars have been unable to agree upon the meaning of Neolithic and Bronze Age symbolism, simply because each expert only saw one part of the whole. They based their opinions on what they had learned from their teachers about the different burial traditions and the simple artefacts that our ancestors produced. And they completely overlooked the evidence of enormous landscape symbols and huge works of art in the form of twenty-ton blocks of stone…

In the 15th Century the world was a very different place to the one we know today. In the late 1480's Christopher Columbus was seeking money from the King and Queen of Spain to finance a trade expedition to the Indies. He needed financial backing for his revolutionary scheme that proposed travelling west, across the mysterious and unknown Atlantic Ocean. At that time the traditional route to the Far East was to sail south to Africa, round the Cape of Good Hope and then on to the Spice Islands of Indonesia, via the Indian Ocean. His revolutionary theory was that it would be far shorter to travel due west, rather than to go all the way south, around the tip of Africa and then east across the Indian Ocean. The Royal Court was very sceptical of this idea and some of the courtiers were particularly cynical of his plans, saying he was mad or that it that it was far too difficult and anyway, since no one had ever done it, no one ever could do it.

But once he had Royal support Columbus was finally able to set sail and managed to prove that part of his original theory was true; there was indeed land far to the west. And although he did not discover a route to the East Indies, he did become the first European of his era to find a New World on the other side of the ocean, landing in the Caribbean in 1492. Later on, the story goes that after his return home from the West Indies, one of a group of courtiers was still very dismissive and sceptical, saying that Columbus hadn't done anything very special, anyone could have done it… But Columbus replied to this by saying something like: *'Everything is easy, once you know how to do it.'*

To prove his point he challenged them all to solve a simple puzzle. He asked them to try and make an egg stand upright on the table. Of course everyone tried and they all failed miserably, since even if they spun it very fast, the egg just overbalanced each time. So once they had all admitted defeat, Columbus showed them how to do it. *But like many puzzles, the solution is very simple, once you know the answer.*

Columbus simply picked up the egg and squashed the end down on the table so that it stood upright! Of course there were howls of protest that he had cheated, but he had proved his point, the answer is very simple, but only when you know the answer. (As for sailing to America in 1492, Columbus was by no means the first, because according to research done by author Gavin Menzies, a Chinese expedition, led by Admiral Zhou Wen in 1421, beat him to it by more than seventy years.

However, even this early voyage was bettered by the Vikings, who sailed across the Atlantic to America and a group of Danes even settled for a while in Newfoundland. But even this is much too recent, since it was some Ice Age Europeans who were the first to arrive in America, around 16,500 years ago, they did this by crossing the Atlantic along the ice shelf, which was much further to the south than at present. They would have travelled in canoes or kayaks from what is now western France.

Now back to the major enigma surrounding the meaning of the design of Stonehenge.

The original sarsen temple was once viewed as a circle of thirty upright stones, joined together at the top by lintels, thereby producing a series of doorways in a circle. But a more modern view is that the stone circle, with its lintelled structure, represents a ring beam, the circular timber framework of a roundhouse, which supports the roof. In other words, the temple was a monumental version of the skeleton of the builder's homes, but instead of wood it was made of stone, so that it would last forever. This is a very good theory, one that fits nicely into the social background of the builders, but as we have already seen several times before, our prehistoric ancestors often expressed more than one concept at a time.

But I prefer to think of this open-air temple in a very different way to the traditional viewpoint. Instead of a circle of uprights linked together at the top, I see this version as *a circle of uprights that was erected in order to support a ring of solid stone that was perched high overhead.*

This fundamentally different viewpoint was the key for me to get a better understanding of the symbolism of such a unique design. Now imagine for a moment that the lintel ring had been squashed down on the ground, with the thirty uprights splaying outwards around it. The lintel ring would be resting on the grass and the uprights would still be touching the lintel ring but they would now be horizontal instead of vertical. From above, the effect that one would get is that of a circle with lines radiating outwards from all around the circumference, just like the symbol we use to draw the sun…

One of the major enigmas about Stonehenge has finally been solved.

Like many enigmas the answer is incredibly obvious, once you know what it is. It's so simple that you may feel that there must be a catch to it and wonder why no one has thought of it before.

We should have seen this a very long time ago and understood that Stonehenge is not just a temple to the sun; it is also a physical representation of the sun itself, a religious symbol that was built in solid stone, so that it would last forever. The sarsen circle was a cleverly designed piece of religious architecture that encapsulated the idea of 'home', and the symbolic form of the sun. And I think that a new name, **"Sunhenge"**, fits the lintelled design of this temple very nicely.

The circular structure of Sunhenge also makes me think of a closed-up flower, such as a daisy (day's-eye), with the petals hanging downwards, ready to open up in the sunshine of a new day… It's also an intriguing thought that such a commonplace flower, with its multitude of white petals surrounding a golden yellow centre, could have been the initial stimulus for the design of Sunhenge. The fact that the flower opens and closes as the light changes is just one of those casual miracles that Mother Nature provides us with on a regular basis, but as so often happens, one that we hardly pay any attention to. However, as children many of us will have made daisy chains, necklaces, bracelets and crowns on long summer afternoons, although perhaps in antiquity this activity had more of a religious aspect. One can even imagine a bride with a ring of yellow wildflowers woven into her hair. Many wildflowers resemble the sun, including dandelions, buttercups, coltsfoot, fleabane, lesser celandine and ragwort, and most of these yellow-flowered plants have medicinal properties that have been used for centuries, if not millennia.

The moon also had an important role to play in the design and meaning of Sunhenge. A drawing of a circle with rays coming from it has often been used to represent the sun, whilst a simple circle was commonly used to represent the full moon (It is still used in weather forecasts and in tide tables). And as I revealed earlier, the lintel ring was a circle of stone, supported high overhead by the sarsen uprights. So the sarsen uprights supported a representation of the moon and were themselves part of the symbol for the sun. In the final temple, the ring of thirty sarsen stones contained twenty-nine stones of about the same height, with one stone to the south, number 11, much smaller than its neighbours. The number twenty-nine and a half must therefore refer to the days of a lunation, which is a synodic month of 29.53 days, so in effect, in addition to circular representations of the sun and the moon, Sunhenge also cleverly incorporated a lunar month in its design.

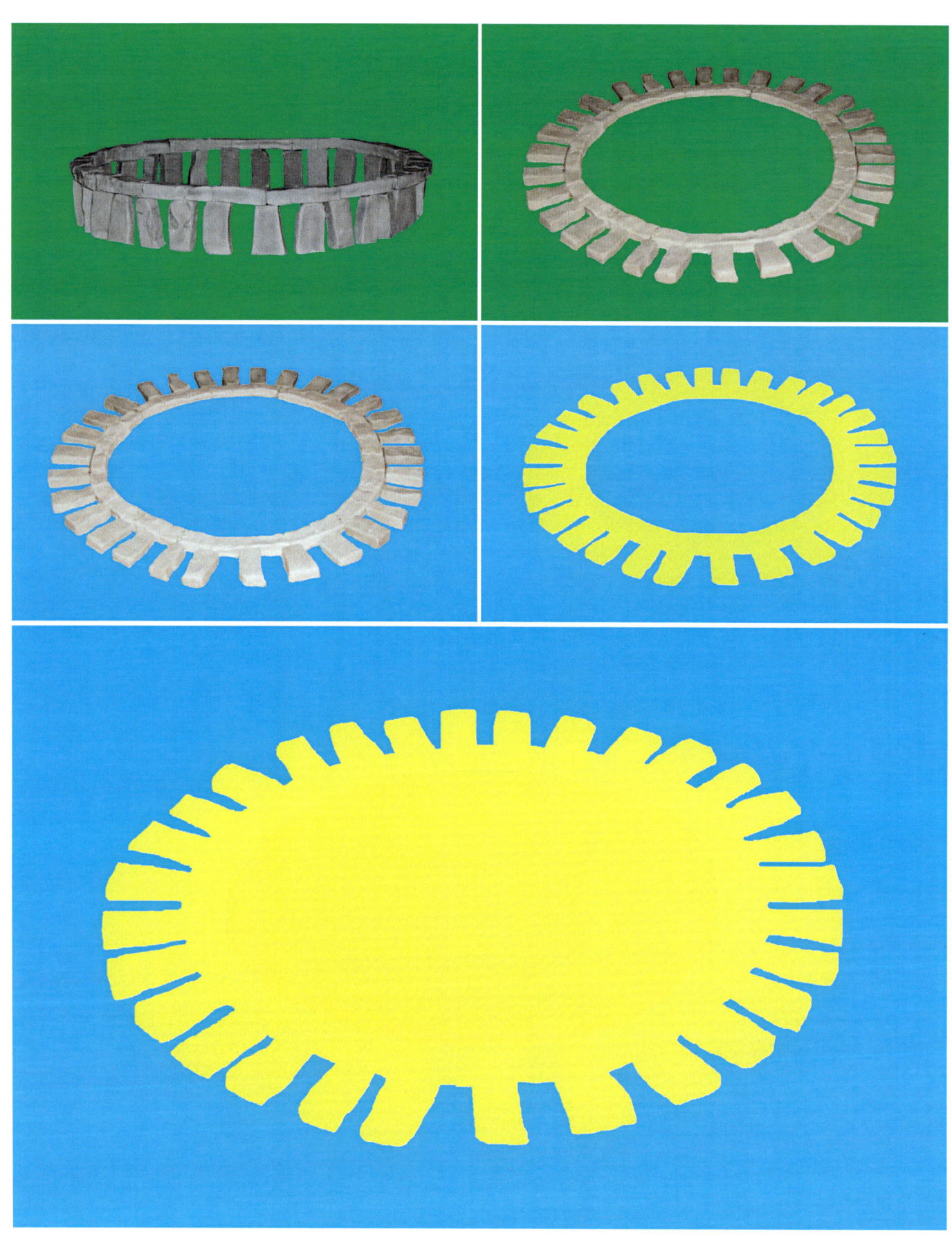

The symbolism inherent in the design of Sunhenge

In the preceding chapters we looked at Stonehenge, and the world of our pre-Roman ancestors, through fresh eyes. We also looked at how prehistoric mythology and astronomy created religious belief and we rediscovered a forgotten world through the eyes of the ancient artists. We have also seen how they developed and used symbolic shapes and symbolic structures to store information about the world that they lived in, so that this knowledge would become available to their children and to their children's children and all the generations that would follow after them. This information, stored in stone, enshrined their awareness of the natural cycles of the world around them and the eternal cycles in the heavens above. Their mythology and philosophy showed how the sun and the moon were the father and mother of all life on earth. Their awareness of the never-ending cycle of birth, life, death and rebirth was permanently recorded in the circular structures that they built, not just in the design their open-air temples, but even in the way they built their homes and graves. The design of many of the monuments that they built actually stored information about the movements and cycles of the sun and moon in stone, showing their awareness of how the heavenly bodies synchronised the rhythms of their own lives. And in turn this must have given them a sense of harmony, position and permanence in a world over which they must have felt that they had little control. They were at the mercy of the gods and evil spirits and their crops could become the victims of such elemental forces of nature as high winds, thunderstorms, torrential rain, sleet and snow and summer drought.

As farming people their crops, and hence their lives, depended on having the right proportions of sun and rain at exactly the right times of year. A poor harvest would be just the start of a miserable tale of hardship, hunger, starvation, disease and even death for themselves and for their friends and families. And in addition to the vagaries of the seasonal weather they must have believed that they were dependant on the whims of the gods and the will of the spirit world.

Death was a frequent visitor to the neighbourhood, and far too many people lived brief lives, particularly women and children. There was a high level of infant mortality and frequently death in and around the time of childbirth. Much of this would have been down to poor diet and bad hygiene and although this may sound particularly bad, it is in fact very similar to what happened to us in quite recent times, particularly in the overcrowded slums present in many Victorian industrial towns and cities.
However, despite all their problems, the Stonehenge people celebrated their place in the natural world in a way that made sense to them and some of them developed an amazing range of artistic skills by working with stone and creating extremcly intricate works of art. And as we have seen, these were in the form of statues, carvings and sculptures and over the centuries they developed many different and complex styles of sculpting, carving, engraving and painting. Nevertheless, the memory of exactly what they achieved has almost died out with them, since apart from the physical ruins of their culture, all that is left is a few vague whispers of the distant past enshrined in our folklore, within stories about the ancient tombs of stone and earth, and of dancing at the rings of standing stones. And of the people themselves all we have left with are the mythical stories of fairies, dwarves, giants, trolls and elves, and many pictures of 'the Little People', and all that remains of the history of their shamans and priests are a few tales of witches and wizards.

The situation is very different in Ireland, where there is a very rich mythology and oral history of legendary times. Ancient Irish and Celtic Mythology and history are well known, much appreciated and eagerly studied. Sadly, the Roman occupation of England and Wales, followed by centuries of Christianity, must have done a lot to kill off the oral histories of the ancient past. However, as we have already seen in the wonderful art that they created, that these stories were not dead to the Stonehenge people, they were very much alive, and they must have played an important part in their daily lives. The pictures and complex scenes that the artists created in stone came from the traditional tales told around the fire as entertainment for young and old alike. They pictures would have come from stories about family and tribal history, chronicles of their distant origins, the sagas of legendary people and the accounts of spirits and gods, and all the hundreds of other mythical tales that enriched their lives and produced wonderful bedtime stories for their children. This great oral tradition was preserved in stone, forever. Or so they thought… It is only now that we can really start to appreciate their story through the works of art that they created, their equivalent of a written history.

The more modern-looking stones at Stonehenge, such as trilithon stone 56, show that, had they wanted to, they could have produced a temple using identically shaped oblong building blocks for the uprights, the same sort of curved stones for the lintels and regular pillars for the bluestones. However, they didn't want such unnatural look, it was alien to their way of looking at the world. Nature is natural, not contrived and everything is similar yet slightly different to others of its group, in the same way that every tree in a pine forest is different, yet all the differences come together to form a whole. So they designed and constructed a series of temples that followed their artistic temperament and fulfilled their beliefs and values. Like all those that had come before, the final temple would astonish, educate, entertain and inform. Yet throughout all its different transformations Stonehenge was always a temple built to worship the sun and the moon, the spirits and the gods, and later on, to celebrate 'the Circle of Life'.

It was Atkinson who suggested that the lintelled circle was a stone replica of the ring beam in a roundhouse, which supported the roof. Many people think of roundhouses in terms of the Iron Age or the Bronze Age, but this distinctive shape of home is one of the easiest to build and their ancestors, the hunters, fishers and foragers of Mesolithic Britain, had built permanent roundhouses thousands of years beforehand. As time went by the surrounding area was increasingly cleared for pasture, and more and more trees were cut down to make way for crops, homes and of course, for firewood.
The landscape became home to thousands of people, and many of them would have helped in the major construction projects. Although most lived in small settlements and isolated farmsteads, sometimes people lived together in large communities and they built enormous roundhouses to house themselves. However, little trace of the smallest buildings has survived the intensive ploughing that the area has suffered in recent years, in many cases all that remains are a handful of broken pottery and a few bits of worked flint. Excavation of some longbarrows has revealed that they were sometimes built on the site of an old house, which had been changed into a mortuary enclosure. Then many years later this was covered over by a long mound of earth, chalk and stones. In some cases I get the impression that the old bones were being buried by newcomers to the area, to prevent the restless spirits of the ancients from disturbing the living. The West Kennet longbarrow, for example, was completely filled in then sealed off permanently by toppling the large entrance stones to prevent any further access. Such an act of desecration can only be the result of a fundamental cultural shift, perhaps by a new ruler or else from a drastic overhaul of religious belief and practise. (During the reign of Henry VIII, the power of the Roman Catholic Church in England was drastically diminished and most monasteries were emptied and abandoned when the Protestant faith came to power.)

By the time the final Stonehenge temple was finished the population in the surrounding area had swollen to very large numbers of people, and many of them were the descendants of the earliest builders and some could probably see images of their direct ancestors in the pictures that the artists had created on the stones. Whatever you think of our ancestors, you have to admire their spirit and belief in doing a job well. The amount of work that went into creating such a fantastic piece of engineering, particularly at a time when there was no complex machinery available and everything was done by hand, is simply unimaginable. The total time needed to bring the megaliths from so far away and then create a temple that was so intensively decorated must have run into many hundreds of thousands of hours of hard work.

When a new building programme was taking place, everyone for miles around would have been involved in one way or another, even very young children and the elderly and infirm. For every person engaged in moving, erecting, building and decorating there must have been many, many more who were involved in what would we call administration and support, because everyone who worked on the project needed to be looked after, they needed to be fed, clothed and housed. They would have had to have regular supplies of grain and meat. So in turn this meant that other people had to look after the herds of goats, sheep and cattle, which would then have to be milked to make butter and cheese, whilst the fattened calves, young rams and bullocks, and the oldest animals would be driven from far outside the local area to be turned into fresh meat at the site.

Hunters would have gone out to pursue wild cattle, red and roe deer, hares and wildfowl. Fishermen would have supplied fresh fish from the river Avon, as well as seafood and salted, smoked and dried fish from the sea only thirty miles downstream to the south. The grain for bread, beer and the soup-like potage would have needed to be grown and that required a seasonal supply of labour, to clear and till the soil, plant the seed, weed the growing shoots, harvest the ripe grain and bag it up, ready for transport to Durrington Walls and Woodhenge, the main dormitory sites for the army of workers. It was not really surprising that Durrington Walls was sited close to the river, since the demand for fresh, clean water for such a large working population would have been immense. Just as today, water was needed for drinking, cleaning and washing but it had to be carried by hand. It was also needed in large quantities for the treatment and dying of hides and skins to make clothes of leather, linen and buckskin. In addition to all this there would have been a constant demand for firewood, for heating and cooking and for drying out wet clothes when the weather was bad.

As time went by the firewood had to come from further and further away as the nearest sources were used up. There was also a demand for timber for housing and scaffolding and a need for masses of leather thongs and ropes and cords, for moving the big stones. Although some ropes were made from lime tree bark, string from nettle fibres was used for fixing the scaffolding poles, and of course there must have been an army of butchers, cooks and kitchen helpers, as well as many potters to make the cooking pots, storage jars and beakers. There would also have been site carpenters and joiners, who made the framework for the buildings to house everyone and the furniture inside. (The mortice and tenon joints and the tongue and groove joints used for the lintel ring shows basic carpentry techniques were already widely used. The stone furniture in the houses of Skara Brae, the dressers, cupboards and beds were replicas of wooden furniture.) Many other hands would be needed to gather wild food, such as berries, fruits, nuts, vegetables, herbs, roots and mushrooms in the woods, hedgerows and pastures. Someone also needed to care for the sick and injured, since construction sites are always risky places, where accidents are common, and the transport and erection of the huge stones were particularly dangerous tasks. This must have led to many crushed fingers and flattened toes, as well as broken wrists, broken arms and legs and even the occasional death when ropes gave way or a stone moved unexpectedly.

Skeletal evidence shows that, even from the time of the earliest farmers, six thousand years ago, many people, both young and old, suffered from excessive wear and tear on their bodies from carrying heavy loads and working hard in the fields. Many suffered from osteoarthritis, a painful disease caused by friction and stress on the cartilage around the knee, elbow, and hip joints, as well as the wrists, fingers and spine, this was widespread amongst the young population, and affected even quite young children. Everyone seems to have worked really hard. As time went by the general state of health of the population became worse. Although the ancient hunting and foraging lifestyle had been very healthy with a varied diet, by 2000 BC most people worked very hard and had a very restricted diet, based primarily on grain. Skeletal evidence and special patterns in their teeth show that malnutrition amongst the farmers and their families was a regular occurrence.

This suggests that many of the old bushcraft skills of hunting and gathering had been forgotten. The fragmentary skeletal evidence from round barrows shows that many people had poor dental hygiene and suffered from tooth decay and abscesses in their jaws. Apart from being very painful, an abscess could easily lead to blood poisoning, followed by death. An increase in child mortality and generally high death rate must have caused a corresponding increase in people's concerns for the future and any help that religion that could bring towards a lessening of their pain and suffering, and for the hope of a better future, would have been warmly welcomed.

We've seen religious revivals in historical times whenever society is under severe strain due to plague, war or famine, people turn to anyone and anything that might be of some help. If the person concerned is already quite religious then the stress of an adverse situation will often reinforce their beliefs. In the historical past, religious revivals have been the cause of a flurry of construction work and have resulted in the building of grandiose temples, churches and cathedrals. It's as though people were trying to do a deal: "Look Gods, we'll do something special for you, but we expect something in return for all our hard work, so you'd better do something nice for us! Give us plenty of lambs and calves in spring and grant us a bountiful harvest in summer! Keep our families safe and well!"

All this construction work and associated activity needed constant organisation to get the work done in a cooperative and friendly manner and the leaders and priests would have needed special abilities to cool people's tempers and right injustices. During the different construction phases it is likely that work gangs were organised according to kinship ties, and with extended families working together. But however the labour force was organised, it speaks well of everyone's abilities and desire to keep doing the work, day after day, year after year and, despite only having very simple technology, they managed to create a truly impressive series of monuments.

Whether slave labour was used is highly debatable, I think it more likely that people worked on the temples because they wanted to do so, in exactly the same way as the Egyptian farmers worked hard to build the pyramids for their god-like Kings, the Pharaohs, working with stone during the off-seasons when they could get away from their farms.

The final temple at Stonehenge must have meant many different things to many different people. To the local chieftains it was a source of position, wealth and influence. To the priests it was a place of status and power, a special place where the gods were portrayed, worshipped and celebrated. To the artists it was a place where their skills and talent could be displayed for all to see. To the designer it was a tribute to his skill of combining many different elements to form a marvellous whole but to the actual builders it was a lot of very hard work. However to everyone involved, Stonehenge was a fabulous temple that expressed their culture, their beliefs, their mythology and their history. It was also the ultimate symbol of their appreciation of the everlasting cycles of the sun and moon and the perpetual rhythm of Birth, Life and Death.

> I think that there is yet another symbolism inherent in the design of Sunhenge.

As I showed earlier, the uprights and lintels are a representation of the sun, whilst the lintel ring on its own becomes the circle of a full moon. So this ring of stone perched on the uprights high overhead is a representation of both the sun and the moon at the same time. It is reminiscent of one of nature's greatest spectacles, an annular solar eclipse. Solar eclipses occur when the dark moon (new moon) hides the sun from view. When the moon completely covers the sun the light is cut off and we get a total solar eclipse, and these are quite rare, far more common are partial eclipses, which occur when the path of the moon doesn't quite match that of the sun. Sometimes when the moon is further away from the earth the two discs don't quite match up in apparent size and the disc of the moon doesn't quite cover the totality of the sun, and you get a very spectacular ring of light, an annular eclipse. Such an image would be the very embodiment of their most sacred symbol, the circle. It would also be a very graphic representation of the coming together of the sun and the moon, in an act of divine sex. So the design of Sunhenge, the sarsen circle with its lintel ring, was a very clever way of embodying a number of different themes all at the same time. It had symbolic references to the sun and the moon at different times of the day and season. It showed the number of days and nights in a month, it was a physical representation of the sun with its rays of light. In one brilliant design it showed their understanding and appreciation of the natural cycles of the world, embodied as *'the Circle of Life'*; and it demonstrated the mating of the sun and moon, a *'Marriage of the Gods'*, this is something our astronomers call an annular solar eclipse.

The rings of standing stones that our Neolithic ancestors designed and built contained coded messages in the shape, position and above all, the decoration on each stone. So instead of just having numbers or letters for every stone, each of them had its own meaning and its own story to tell. In this way a typical ring of standing stones would have had different stones that related to different themes, not just moonrise and moonset, or sunrise and sunset, but other themes as well, for example, to a direction, a spirit, a celebration, an animal, a special time of year, a number, a person, or perhaps a god.

In addition it seems likely to me that sometimes the stones represented astrological themes. At Stonehenge there are images of lions, horses, bears, dogs or wolves, and even a goat and a hare, all of these animals are constellations and some appear in astrology as parts of the Zodiac. In the same order they are Leo, Pegasus, Ursa Major, Canis Major, Aries and Lepus. However, these constellations originated in Mesopotamia and were developed by the Greeks, who counted 48 different constellations or pictures in the sky, (since then a further 40 constellations have been added to the list). What is certain is that the ancient Britons would have had their own constellations, yet I suspect that some of the myths concerning these pictures in the night sky go back into the very distant past, and, since most Europeans have the same distant origins, why not right back to the last Ice Age and beyond?

So instead of numbering the megaliths as we have done using labels such as 1, 2, 3, and 4 or A, B, C, D etc., The ancients erected rings with different shapes of stone, each of which related to something different. For example, one stone could mean North, another stone could refer to the Spirit of Winter; another to midwinter full moonrise; or Life; a constellation; the spring equinox; a famous person; midwinter sunrise; midday; a god etc., etc.

Across the British Isles, each ring was different from others because the meaning changed locally, from priest to priest, stone to stone, and from artist to artist. And that is why we have never been able to make sense of the hundreds of small and large stone circles that were built across the countryside. They are far more complicated than we thought they were. But although each ring is a different work of art, there were similarities between the different types and in the way in which the rings could have been used. Some sites, such as Calanais, Midmar Kirk and the Merry Maidens, were primarily lunar temples, whilst some of the other recumbent stone circles of Aberdeenshire were primarily solar sites. Stonehenge, Stanton Drew, Brodgar and Avebury combined both lunar and solar worship in their design and function.

These ancient stone temples all give the visitor a sense of being somewhere different and special, a place created for marking and celebrating those unique times in a person's life, whether it was their birth, passage into adulthood, marriage or death. In addition to such milestones it seems very likely that as well as religious ceremonies there were also times that the rings were used for special community meetings. Perhaps the stone circle was a special place that was used for making decisions, giving judgements, electing leaders, or more mundanely as a place to barter and trade and to do deals, and all the other things that a community needs to do to make it run smoothly. Incidentally, some localities had a variety of rings that were built quite close together, and they were probably used by different groups of people to fulfil all sorts of different functions. (A good example of this is on Isle of Arran, off the northwest coast of Scotland. On Machrie Moor, a mile or so inland from the west coast of the island, are the remains of six megalithic rings that are set quite close together, although each one seems to have had a different purpose, since each is distinctly different to its neighbours.)

One of the many intriguing puzzles to do with prehistoric sites is the question *'Why build it there?'* Many sacred sites in other parts of the world mark the birthplace of a spiritual leader or a special event or even a miracle. Although sites such as Durrington Walls and Stanton Drew are near to rivers, many stone circles are in open countryside and Stonehenge in particular was originally in an unremarkable part of the ancient landscape, a woodland clearing, yet its heritage goes back ten thousand years, to the site of a meeting place in the ancient wilderness marked by special posts. The Cursus had already ben in use for centuries before the first ditch and bank was built, so the area already had a special history and exceptional meaning, even before the Heel Stone was brought to the site.

Over the decades many theories about why Stonehenge was built in this very unexceptional part of Wiltshire have been suggested, some more bizarre than others.

A small number of people believe that the ancient priests were in tune with Nature and were sensitive to the earth's natural energies, not only of wind, sun and rain, but also of a more subtle energy that they say flows through the earth in currents along definite paths. This is quite an unusual idea, one that few scientists would give time to because they can't detect it or measure it. Yet some people are sensitive enough to such unseen energies that they are able to dowse for water or even minerals. And although the Chinese have used acupuncture for thousands of years with continuous success, until fairly recently, orthodox medicine in the West refused to acknowledge that it worked. According to practitioners of acupuncture there is a subtle energy called Ch'i (or qi), which flows through the body along meridians and this life force can be harnessed, balanced or corrected. In the physical world, the Chinese developed Feng Shui, literally wind/water, a science of aligning and harmonising buildings with cosmic forces.

New Russian research into death has shown that low level energy fields survive clinical death, diminishing in time for up to three days, in the case of suicides, the life force is said to decay more slowly, taking up to a week before the energy is reduced to zero. This new research ties in with the energy Ch'i, and the auras that mediums see. According to them, people have a pulsating aura around themselves; a bright red aura indicates that the person is healthy whilst a weak, blue aura indicates ill health. And in the same way as martial artists and practitioners of acupuncture can use the power of Ch'i, dowsers can sense natural earth energies. Sometimes these earth energies flow in straight lines but they are more like streams and rivers, twisting and turning, merging and diverting. Some people think that this arcane knowledge was the basis for the location of many ancient monuments, the infamous leylines. According to some dowsers many prehistoric sites were located on 'hot spots', areas where the energy currents surfaced or crossed over. In Medieval Christian times, the battle of religions between pagans and the true faith was symbolised by images of St. Michael slaying dragons, and some people think that the dragon represented the old ways and beliefs, including a paranormal sensitivity to nature and earth energies.

I'm fairly open-minded but not entirely convinced about leylines and mystical earth energies, however trying to make sense of cultures that were intimately linked to nature is hard to do if only a rational, coldly scientific approach is used. It is hard to gain insight and understanding of people that lived in a weird, mystical, mythical reality just using a 21st Century framework and clinical mind-set. And how can one really understand the life of a superstitious hunter or a worried farmer from the warmth of a university lecture room? I think that what is needed is a better appreciation of the eternal cycles of nature from a more practical experience, rather than just on a purely intellectual basis. In other words, to feel, to sense and observe the natural world. However, I am not suggesting that our scientists should go completely New Age, but rather that they should not automatically dismiss everything non-scientific as superstitious nonsense. History has shown time and time again that when it comes to understanding the actions and emotions of human beings, and particularly within the weird and wonderful world of mythology and cultural beliefs, a strictly scientific approach is not enough. People have always been strange!

To summarise, the final version of Stonehenge incorporated many different layers of symbolism, some of these incorporated the symbolism of the sun and the moon, whilst others were concerned with the birth, life and death cycle. There are also circles wherever you look, the banks and ditch, the sarsen uprights, the lintel ring, the Bluestone circle and the circles of various holes that were used for posts and cremation burials. Circles within circles within circles, the same as in the movement of the heavens above and in the eternal cycles of the natural world below, and in Sunhenge, the continuous ring of lintels supported by the circle of sarsen uprights, they built the ultimate symbol of all, the Circle of Life. Then later on, with the creation of the Final Temple, they were able to include a multitude of references to Life and Death.

The male and female bluestones flanking the entrance were symbolic of the creation of new life. Then the cycles of the sun and moon were encapsulated in the sarsen uprights and the lintel ring, a reference to the Birth, Life, Death and Rebirth cycle. The axis of the temple, northeast to southwest, was symbolic of the journey from Life to Death, followed by Rebirth. The orientation of the temple and the U-shaped arrangements of trilithons and bluestones were towards the northeast and to the rising sun at the summer solstice, symbolically linking everything to 'Life'. The Altar Stone, the central bluestone and the Great Trilithon all acted to mask the setting sun at the winter solstice, symbolising the act of maintaining Life, by keeping Death at bay. The two sets of nine bluestones, visible on each side of the Altar Stone were references in stone to the creation of a new Life and the nine months of human pregnancy. And finally we have the very dramatic sight of the rising sun passing over the top of the phallic-looking Heel stone, another symbolic reference to the sex act and the creation of new Life.

All these symbolic references to the sun and the moon, and more importantly, the human life cycle, were permanently recorded in stone, so I think that the final temple at Stonehenge could have been called *'The Temple of Life'*.

Stonehenge was never just one thing or another; it has always been complex, with layer upon layer of symbolism and harmonious blends of astronomy, religion, art and architecture. And it is a tragedy, that all we see today are just the ruins of a monumental masterpiece that represented thousands of years of human evolution. For two millennia, the Ancient Romans, the Christian Church and many prehistorians and archaeologists have dismissively called the original inhabitants of these islands as peasant farmers and sun worshippers, when in reality they were astronomers, mathematicians, philosophers, artists, craftsman, architects, builders, in short, people. It's just that they were different to us, a very spiritual and artistic people and their way of life was based on what they knew of the world around them. This included the natural flow of the seasonal cycles, of life, death and rebirth, the earth below and the sky above, as well as their stories of myths, legends and spiritual beliefs. So they were always much, much more than simply sun or moon worshippers. Their way of life was based around things that they could see, live and experience, things that they felt deeply within themselves and this gave them a real sensitivity to the natural world and its cycles and patterns. These concepts were encapsulated in a theme that any of them could understand, the Circle of Life.

There remains one other important question.

Why have all the *'experts'* who have studied Stonehenge been unable to see the works of art and the complex symbolism inherent in the stones? The answer must lie in suppression, a term that psychologists use to describe the denial of facts that do not conform to the status quo. The other term is cognitive bias, used to describe the way that we see what we want to see, not what is actually there. Generations of archaeologists and prehistorians have followed their Georgian and Victorian predecessors in 'filtering out' evidence that has been right in front of them all the time, refusing to see what their eyes have told them because it does not fit in with current wisdom. They have relied on those that came before to guide them and this has resulted in a form of intellectual blindness, to see our ancestors only in a certain way, as a series of tools, bones, artefacts and ruined buildings, rather than as people. In the case of our ancestral art, no one seems to have seriously questioned its absence, even though our ancestors, the Palaeolithic artists, were carving antler, bone, flint and stones and painting wonderful images inside caves for well over 20,000 years during the last Ice Age.

For well over three hundred years, Stonehenge has remained almost a complete mystery. The new evidence I have discovered, including the development and use of complex symbolic shapes and images, and the many works of art, together with the insights gained from a re-examination of traditional ideas, has enabled me to make sense of what we can see and helped me to develop the ideas and theories that I have outlined in the preceding pages.

All this represents a major breakthrough in appreciating and understanding Britain's most extraordinary prehistoric monument, Stonehenge.

SEQUENCE OF CONSTRUCTION OF THE DIFFERENT TEMPLES AT STONEHENGE.

(THE DATES ARE VERY APPROXIMATE BECAUSE NEW RESEARCH KEEPS AMENDING THE RADIOCARBON DATES)

3100	**The mortuary enclosure.**
3000	**The Aubrey Circle of posts** (The holes then contained bluestones and then cremation burials and were used for over five centuries.)
2700	**Moonhenge,** including the first ring of Bluestones around the ditch
2600	**Bluestonehenge,** including the lunar arcs of Bluestones in the centre
2500	**A Circle of Standing Stones**
2400	**Sunhenge,** the lintelled structure
2300	**Stonehenge,** intermediate stages included the addition of the circle of bluestones, the erection of the five trilithons, the addition of the nineteen bluestones and the Altar Stone.
1600	The Y and Z holes, unused graves.

N.B. The long periods needed to accomplish the major construction work of the stone temples would have also required a great deal of time for the artists to create the wonderful decorations, once the stones were in place.

10 CALANAIS AND BRODGAR

The accurate prediction of extraordinary lighting phenomena at special times of the year would have impressed the local population to such an extent that the astronomers and priests would seem to have magical qualities, to seemingly control the heavens and be the masters of time. Their power was expressed through the construction of their unique architecture, and even today, such power is still vaguely remembered in our folklore, in tales of the occult and of magicians, wizards and witches. The folklore surrounding standing stones and stone circles suggests that some of the megaliths are 'people turned to stone', in other words, what we would call…statues.

Many stone circles have local names such as the Pipers, the Merry Maidens, the Wedding, Long Meg and her Daughters, the Hurlers, the Nine Ladies, the Three Kings and even the Twelve Apostles. But as we have already seen, many of the large stones are in fact complex sculptures of people, gods, spirits or animals. In this chapter I'd like to talk about some of the other works of art that were created at a few of the many sites that I've looked at, and photographed, over the last fifteen years.

More than five thousand years ago people voyaged even further north than mainland Scotland, they found new habitats and started new lives by crossing the sea to the Western Isles (Outer Hebrides), the Orkneys and going even as far north as the Shetland Isles. To do this they must have had quite large seaworthy boats because they needed to take not only their families with them but also all of their livestock, their cattle, sheep, pigs and goats. They grew emmer and einkorn wheat for flour and potage (a sort of thick soup) and raised barley for bread and beer. Once they were settled, the population increased through their own efforts and by attracting new families from further away. They made a good life for themselves and for their families.

This increase in population was also due to the food they ate. More dairy products and more carbohydrates, in the form of bread and gruel, meant that women became more fertile and more children were born, but that meant there were more mouths to feed, so the pressure was on for these children to work hard, to make sure that more land cleared for more fields and pastures, then more bread became available and more children were born. Agriculture became a runaway 'success' story, in view of the huge number of people that now inhabit this planet. (In mid 2012 this was estimated at 6,928,198,253 people).

Calanais (Callanish) viewed from the northwest

Our forefathers were a deeply religious people, or rather set of peoples, because there is great variation across the Orkney Islands in the sorts of burial mounds and cairns that they constructed for their dead and they also built many other different types of monuments and open-air temples. And as we shall see further on, there is also a great deal of variation in the way they decorated the standing stones that were a vital part of their customs, ceremonies, history and sacred beliefs.

Some of the earliest and best artwork in the Neolithic world was created at Calanais (Callanish) on the Isle of Lewis in the Western Isles, off the northwest coast of Scotland. The sort of stone that the artists used is a type of gneiss that dates back an incredible three thousand million years, the oldest rocks in Scotland. The standing stones are particularly pleasing to the eye because of the very distinctive wavy layers of rock, making the standing stones look as though they were carved from fossilised tree trunks. (Fossils of animals and plants have sometimes been found at ancient human burial sites. The most notable is the large fossil of an ammonite that is embedded in the western upright of the entrance to the longbarrow at Stoney Littleton, near Wellow in Somerset.) The Lewissian gneiss that the artists used was formed in the same way as marble. The original sedimentary rock was part of a Continental Plate that became subjected to incredible pressure when it collided with another Continental Plate, but instead of being forced upwards, to form a mountain, it was forced downwards, towards the molten interior of our planet. This combination of intense heat and intense pressure created metamorphic gneiss from the sedimentary rock. Unfortunately much of our prehistoric art has suffered from thousands of years of erosion and neglect. But because gneiss is such a very hard stone, a great deal of the artwork at Calanais has survived. But which of the partially eroded images are visible to the observer depends on the lighting conditions of the moment because, as usual, different images can be seen according to the weather, the time of day and the season.

As I have already mentioned several times in earlier chapters, Calanais is famous for its celebration of the major southern moonset of the swing cycle. However, in addition to the astronomical aspects of this monument to the moon, the whole arrangement of standing stones is also an enormous work of art, a religious and symbolic sculpture made of stone. The inner part of the lunar temple is formed from a ring of tall standing stones, many of which are more than ten feet high. There are also three short rows of stones, radiating outwards from the circle, one to the south, one to the west and one due east. There is also an avenue to the north-northeast comprised of two almost parallel rows of stones. And although there are other instances of an avenue of stones leading into a circle, notably at Avebury and Stanton Drew, in England, the design of the Calanais temple is simply unique. This arrangement is often referred to as a sort of Celtic cross (a cross with a circle in the middle) but this just confuses the issue because of course the lunar temple was built long before Celtic Christianity arrived, by well over twenty-five centuries.

Calanais is very different from the other temples nearby, such as Cnoc Ceann a' Gharraidh, Na Dromannan and Ceann Thulabhaig, which are more in keeping with the design of many other rings and circles of standing stones across the British Isles. The acknowledged authorities on stone circles have no convincing opinions to explain the strange architecture of Calanais and calling it a Celtic cross hasn't really helped in understanding the basic idea behind the temple. The anachronism just confuses the religious sentiment that was expressed in the original design.

There is a very old story associated with the cyclical astronomical phenomenon we sometimes know as the lunar nodal cycle or as I prefer it, the swing cycle. According to the first century BC writer Diodorus of Sicily: *"There is an island to the north of Gaul (France), beyond the north wind, whose inhabitants are called Hyberboreans and who worship the sun god Apollo. Leto, wife of Zeus and mother of Apollo, was born on this island"*. And that there was *"a sacred precinct dedicated to Apollo… on an island not smaller than Sicily. They say also that the moon, as viewed from this island, appears to be but a little distance from the earth and to have upon it prominences, like those of the earth that are visible to the eye. The account is also given that the god visits the island every nineteen years, the period in which the return of the stars to the same place is accomplished."*

The writer also mentioned that on this island was *"a sacred precinct and a spherical temple decorated with many votive offerings."* The god was also said to *"play the cithara* (a small harp) *and dance the whole night through, from the vernal equinox to the rising of the Pleiades".*

This rather garbled account is typical of stories where myth, legend, fact and fiction become blurred and blended together over time, space and alcohol. There are references to a sun god, a moon goddess, the lunar swing cycle and the Metonic cycle, and probably Avebury, Stonehenge and Calanais. This text is quite controversial since some people see the sacred precinct as referring to Avebury, but when Diodorus speaks of *"a spherical temple decorated with many votive offerings"*; many people, myself included, think he is referring to Stonehenge.

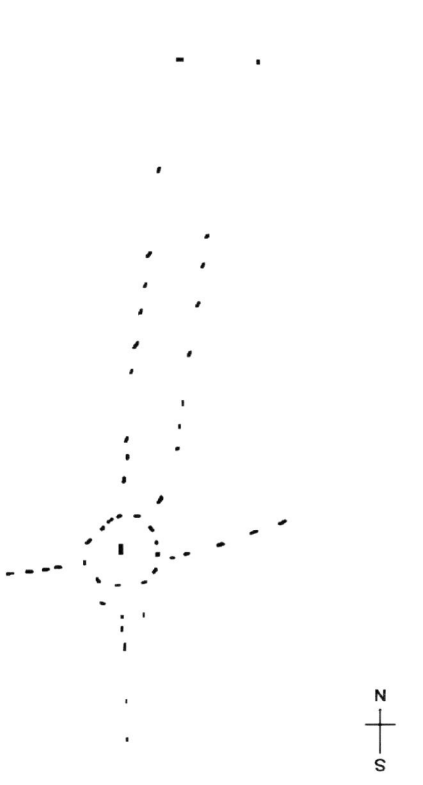

Moreover, since the sun does not have a nineteen year cycle, it must therefore be a reference to the lunar swing cycle or the Metonic cycle and the reference to the nearness of the moon suggests that the 'sacred precinct' was somewhere much further north than Wiltshire. He also makes a comparison of the relative size of the islands, which suggests that the temple was not on such a large island as mainland Britain. To my mind this entire story suggests that the island he refers to is the Isle of Lewis and the sacred precinct refers to Calanais. And such a renowned spherical temple, decorated with many votive offerings, can only have been Stonehenge. Diodorus may never have visited these places; his mixed-up account is based on other people's stories, gleaned from travellers to distant lands. In ancient folklore, the heliacal rising of the Pleiades was simply a calendar reference to the onset of spring. The Pleiades are in the constellation Taurus and at the spring equinox five thousand years ago, they rose heliacally in northern latitudes and consequently they were only visible for a short time, just before sunrise. In other words, if you saw these stars you knew that the night was nearly over and that dawn was only a short time away. It was time to have something to eat and then to go and check on the livestock.

Another of the many other myths and legends concerning Calanais is a tale of how the stones are a race of giants that were turned to stone by St Kieran for opposing Christianity. In the early 17th Century the stones were known as 'Fir Brhrèige', the false men. Then sometime around 1680, John Morisone recorded another legend:

> *"It is left by traditione that these were a sort of men converted to stone by ane Inchanter"*.

For nearly three millennia the stones were partially buried in peat, up to a depth of five feet in places. The peat was eventually removed from around the stones in 1857, but by then the bottom half of the stones had been bleached by the acidic waters of the peat and this had given the stones a peculiar two-tone look. This was duly recorded in postcards and even appears in an engraving by Sir Henry James published in 1867. This illustration was subsequently turned into a cartoon that was entitled "Turusachan Callernish, as seen under the influence of spirits". The picture shows the stones as ranks of bearded men, some holding staves with prongs and others with hooked sticks. In the picture the whitened, bottom part of the stones becomes the men's trousers, whilst the top parts are their jackets. They are all wearing hats, some with angled tops, others rounded. In the air above are skeletal bats and some other rather strange, flying creatures. On one of the smaller stones on the left is a seated man playing the fiddle, whilst to the right, another playing a pipe. In the foreground are two 'devil' children, complete with horns and tails. And coming out of the small burial chamber inside the ring is an animated skeleton. (I have not included details of this chambered grave in my description of the temple. This is because it was added to the ring during a much later period and to include it in the plan would just complicate and confuse the original design.)

It is a shame that our scientists, prehistorians and scholars have taken none of these stories, myths and legends very seriously, since as I have said before, people that are said to have been turned to stone are known as 'statues'. And in fact many of the standing stones are eroded statues of people, whilst others are sculptures of animals and strange spirits. The artists of Calanais selected interesting pieces of stone to produce their works of art. This was in much the same way as a wood carver would have used an interesting piece of gnarled wood with a swirling grain as the starting point for his or her work of art. Nature had already given them a major helping hand but it was up to them to modify the existing surface according to their particular skills and abilities. The sculptures they created seem to me to be pictures of actual people, important people, some of whom may have been their ancestors whilst others were more contemporary leaders and priests. The stones or parts of stones that were buried in peat are also those that have preserved their artwork to a greater extent than many other standing stones, not just at Calanais but across the UK.

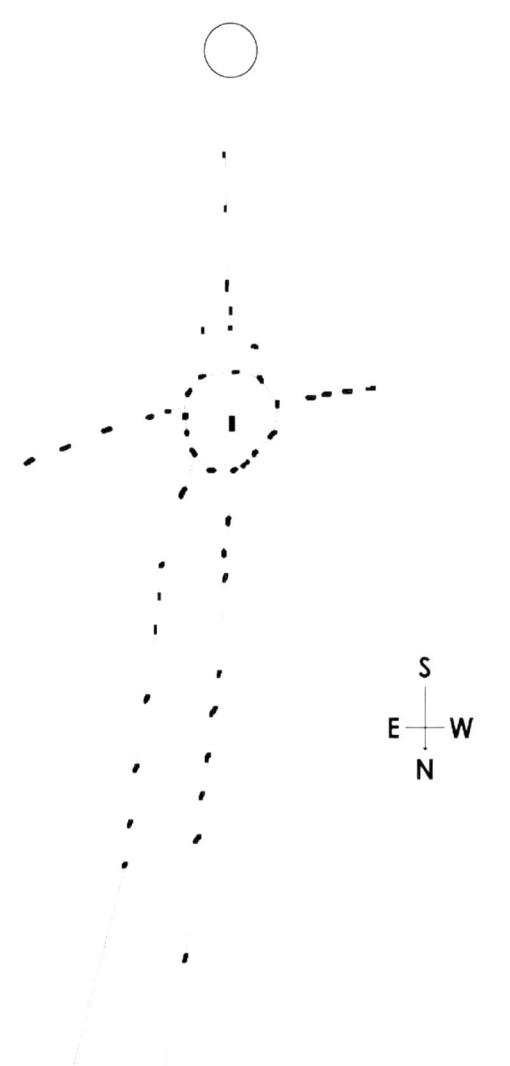

The land on which Calanais was erected is a bit like a backbone that rises out of the ground in an area of low-lying land and lochs. To take the analogy of a spine of land further, and looking down from above, from the northeast, the layout of the temple seems to me to resemble a sort of 'stick figure' of a person lying on their back. The outline of this reclining figure was created in my mind by inverting the traditional plan of the stones so that we now look to the south and then join up the dots embodied by the rows of standing stones. The body is then represented by the central ring of thirteen tall stones. The line of five stones to the east is the outstretched right arm, the left arm is formed from the row of four stones to the west and the legs are represented by the two lines of stones from the north-northeast. Most of the avenue stones are positioned so that they stand in line with each other but the stones at the end of each leg are positioned broadside on, like feet. The figure's elongated neck points due south to a nearby outcrop of stone known as 'Croc an Tursa'.

This outcrop has a particular role to play every nineteen years when the major southern moon rises from the hills to the southeast, an arrangement sometimes known as 'Sleeping Beauty', but locally as Cailleach na Mòintich (Old woman of the Moors) because the hills resemble the profile of a woman lying on her back, the moon then seems to skim the earth, passes above the left side of Croc an Tursa and then sinks down as it sets, apparently within the circle.

This is a truly awesome natural spectacle enshrined in stone. But it seems that the intended design of the temple needed something special to complete the outline of the stick figure, and they achieved this by using the glowing orb of the full moon as its head. In this way the temple at Calanais was designed to represent the body and womb of a lunar goddess who visited her temple every nineteen years.

I think that the traditional system of numbering the stones at Calanais is strange and completely illogical. It is extremely difficult to visualise which stone goes where without constantly referring to a copy of the plan, derived from the first diagram drawn by Somerville in 1909. Due to the unnecessary complexity of Somerville's 'method' I have devised my own numbering system, one that is far simpler to use, far easier to visualise and at the same time, far more logical. This new system should also help make it easier to make connections between the position, shape and direction of each stone and I predict that it is going to be essential in the future to have such a system, since many of the stones will be at the centre of considerable interest and debate. This is because each of the sculptured stones had its own significance and meaning within the overall structure. The stones had been placed carefully so that there were astronomical sightlines between them and the significance of the direction would have been recorded as a specially carved and shaped stone.

My system uses letters and numbers, with different letters to denote the central ring and the five rows. In this new diagram, the most southerly stone in the circle of thirteen stones is C1.

This is because it is shaped like an index finger, number one.

The circle stones are then numbered sunwise (clockwise) from C1 to C13. The idea behind this revised plan, and the changed view towards the south, is because that is the direction where the spectacular lunar event takes place. (The direction of north had relatively little interest to the designers.)

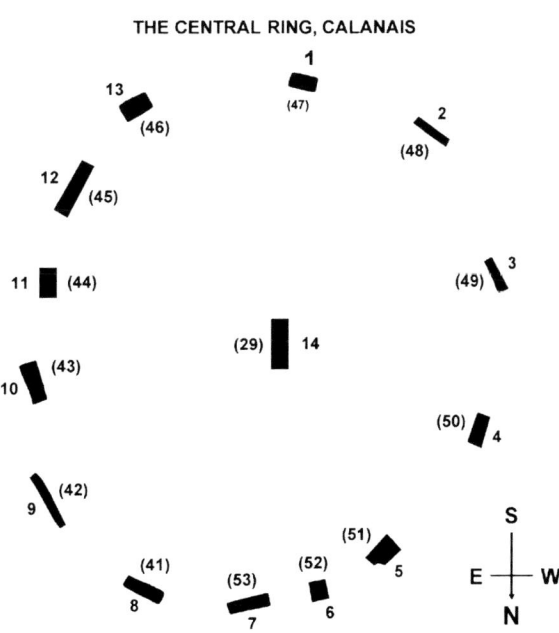

Inside this ring of a thirteen stones is the tallest stone at Calanais, C14, which is slightly off-centre to the west. (In Somerville's plan the stones were numbered 41 to 53, with 29 as the central stone.)

The central stone C14 is tall and slim and it is accurately positioned on a line from north to south, so one of its broad, flat surfaces faces towards the equinox sunrise in the east, whilst the other faces

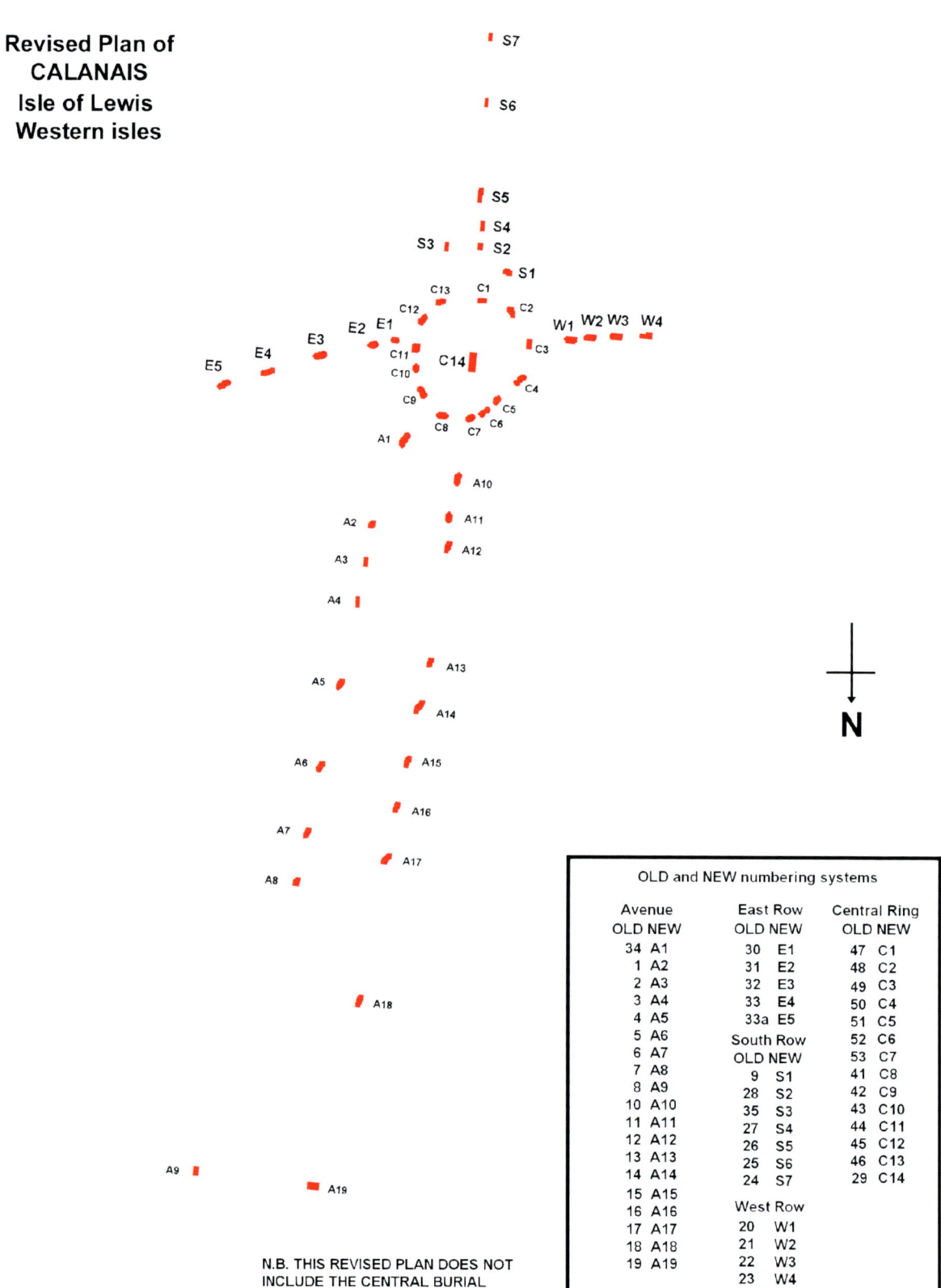

N.B. THIS REVISED PLAN DOES NOT INCLUDE THE CENTRAL BURIAL CHAMBER BECAUSE IT DATES FROM A MORE RECENT PERIOD

towards the equinox sunset in the west. The slanted top of this central symbol stone is also very distinctive, because it rises upwards to the north or slopes downwards to the south.

The ring of thirteen stones around C14 does not form a true circle, it is slightly flattened on the eastern side. Calanais is well known for being a lunar site and looking from north to south, this flattened circle is shaped like the moon a few days before full moon. Although we now use a year of twelve months, the ring of thirteen stones must originally have referred to the maximum number of lunations in a tropical (solar) year. Just to remind you, some solar cycles have twelve moons and others have thirteen, so perhaps the stones were used as some sort of abacus to keep track of the different lunar cycles. The priests would certainly have needed to predict the date of the next major ceremony well in advance, in order to allow distant travellers the time necessary to make the arduous trek to the site by land and sea. Nowadays it is a lot easier to know about such events, because we have newspapers, radio, television, mobile phones and the Internet and we can travel very easily. In ancient times the word would have gone out very slowly, and only at the speed of traders, travellers and priests travelling by canoe, boat and on foot or if they were wealthy, on horseback, although in those far-off days their ponies were quite small. As we shall see further on, some of the stones at Calanais show pictures of people on horses, and the southern side of one stone (E4) in the eastern row is a multiple image that includes the stylised sculpture of the head of a horse. These pictures are some of the first hard evidence that, five thousand years ago, our ancestors had domesticated horses and that they were riding them as well.

Looking down the southern row towards the circle, with the western row on the left and the eastern row on the right.

The row to the east (actually east-northeast) has five stones, E1 to E5, and the numbering now starts with the stone nearest to the circle, E1, (previously number 30). The southern row of stones, S2, S4, S5, S6 and S7, is very close to true south. The other two stones, S1 and S3, are not in line with the rest but it is easier to include them with the southern row, rather than to re-number them as arbitrary figures. S1 may well be part of a special alignment across the circle towards A1. The true position of stone S3 is not certain, since when it was excavated in 1981 it was found that it had been set in concrete, probably in Victorian times. The stone may even have come from further along the row, in the big gap between S5 and S6.

The western row is aligned very slightly south of west, towards the equinox sunsets and it probably consisted of five stones, one of which is missing. In the old plan they are numbered 20 to 23, but I have renumbered them W1 to W4, with W1 the stone nearest to the circle.

The avenue to the north-northeast (hidden) consists of two rows of stones, the spacing suggests that about half the stones are missing, and it is possible that there were originally many more stones in each row, but this has not been confirmed by excavation. The rows of stones are traditionally numbered 10 to 19, and then stone 34 and 1 to 8, but to make it a bit simpler I have renumbered them, from A1 to A19.

Looking down the avenue, southwards, towards the circle, with the Cnoc an Tursa in the background.

Symbol stone C1 (old 47) marks south. This is another very distinctively shaped moonstone, a thin oblong with a rounded top, like the side profile of your right-hand forefinger. I think that this particular shape must also refer to a local moonset position because the temple is on a high ridge and much

Stone C1

of the view to the south is blocked by the large stone outcrop of Cnoc an Tursa. As a result, the moon sets much further to the left than it would do if the horizon were lower and flatter. It also suggests that the site was deliberately chosen (even though people were already growing crops on it) so that the rocky outcrop would form a local horizon that could be used in ceremonies at the major point of the swing cycle, when the very dramatic moonset would happen. Perhaps the priests would stand on the Cnoc an Tursa, waiting for the moon to appear just behind them, and perhaps bodies would be left up there, waiting for the moon to take away the souls of the departed at a time when she was so close to the Earth?

Circle stone C 2 (old 48) is a wide, oblong stone with a rounded top and a lump on the western side, a bit like a left-hand fist with the thumb just peeking out of the side. The stone can also be seen as the right profile of a strange bear-like animal, one with a very snub nose, but a massive head. The southern side of this stone is a very complex work of art. The bands of swirling pink, grey, white and black layers of stone lend themselves to an impressive work that is included within the major image of the head of a bear-like animal that is in left profile. The bulge on the left side of this main sculpture is a secondary image that has been changed into the left side of a head that is looking downwards.

This is another strange image. The head does not look entirely human, yet it has a long chin with a heavy jaw, the left ear is quite prominent and it has a whitish line above the nose and it is wearing a sort of hat that has a red band running from front to rear.

Inner surface of circle stone C2   *Outer surface of circle stone C2 (very enhanced)*

It is as though the person is wearing a cap made from the body of red squirrel. Above and to the right of this bump on the side of the stone is another strange image, this time it is the head and torso of a reddish animal with a long thin snout, like that of a shrew. Although because of its relative size to the heavily built, bearded man to the left, who it seems to be attacking, it probably refers to some sort of giant mythical animal.

The bottom half of the stone is composed of several large scenes involving a variety of quite strange-looking people and weird creatures. I'm not sure exactly what is going on in these scenes, but it doesn't look good for the humans… When the light is from the east some other images can be seen, the main image is the head of a dog, with the wavy line at the top forming his eyebrows. The bump on the left becomes part of the head of a wildcat or perhaps a lynx. At the bottom of the stone is the head of an owl. This is quite unusual, since I don't remember seeing any other pictures of owls in Scotland. It is a multiple image since the right side of the picture is also the head of a man with a dark face, white beard and wavy moustache.

The southern edge of stone C3 is a rather angular and stylised face of someone wearing a tall, conical hat with a flat top. In the centre of the stone is another face, this time of a man with a bushy beard wearing a hat with flaps on the sides. There is no obvious marker stone for due west, that role was taken by a row of five (now four) stones. This row works in both directions and so it is also aligned with the direction of east. Further round the ring is stone C4, which shows two main images. Near the top is the head and torso of a bearded man in right profile, wearing a hooded parka. Below him is a larger image of the face of a man wearing some sort of helmet. Next to this stone the inner surface of Stone C 5 makes it a very phallic-looking stone. Half way up the stone is the right profile of someone wearing a sort of cap, with a thin strap running down in front of their ear. Stone C6 (old 52) is a very thin, D-shaped moonstone with a flat top that probably symbolises the direction of the major northern moonset. The right side of the top of stone C 6 is the head of a dog that has rather a squashed appearance. It looks to me a bit like a bulldog. The whole stone from a three-quarter viewpoint is an image of a man wearing a sort of headdress. This is a multiple image and a host of smaller images of

Circle stone C3   C4   C5   C6

people are visible carved into the wavy lines of rock. The northern stone in the circle, C7 (old number 53), is a thin isosceles triangle. The inner surface of this stone is also the eroded right profile of the head and torso of a man wearing a tall conical hat. He has a long beard and is probably a priest. Included in the swirling layers of rock on this side of the stone are many secondary scenes showing images of people, animals and spirits.
Next to this sculpture is one of the most distinctive stones in the central ring, stone C8 (old number 41). This stands between the two stones (C7 and C9) that frame the avenue to the north-northeast. This crescent-shaped stone is a clear reference to the moon and it probably represents the major northern moonrise that happens every nineteen years. Unfortunately, the hills to the north behind this stone would have hidden the moon from its most northerly rising point, the major moonrise position, and throughout every year of the swing cycle it would have delayed the actual appearance of the moon until it was well to the right of its theoretical bearing. However, an observer standing in a central position at the other end of the avenue, between A9 and A19, may have been lucky enough to witness the moon setting in the opposite direction at the time of the major southern moonset. So the inner surface of C8 represents the major northern moonrise, while from the other direction it marks the major southern moonset.

The inner surface of stone C 8 is another extremely complex work of art containing a wide variety of different images. At the top of C8 is the head of a thin-faced man wearing a parka with the hood up, his face is at an angle and tilted to the right. The edge of his hood is also the outline of a woman's head in left profile, she has a beaky nose and her long, wavy hair hangs down past her shoulder. WithIn her hair is another image of a woman. In another multiple-style image the thin face of the hooded man becomes the head of a wolf. And below this is another wolf's head in left profile, although this time the muzzle of the animal is quite rectangular. Just below this, about half way up the stone, is another peculiar image, a sort of cartoon character of a hound with a big mouth who is wearing a floppy hat. The gap between the top of the dog's muzzle and the bottom of his hat also forms the gaping mouth of a multiple image of a strange, mythical creature with a broad, blunt face and a heavy lower jaw.

Inner surfaces of circle stones C7, C8 and C9

Left and below, details of Stone C8

The inner surface of the next stone, C9, is another very complex work of art involving several multiple images. Depending on the size of the photo that one is looking at, one can see different figures, and as I've mentioned previously, this effect is the equivalent of looking at the stone from different distances. A small-sized image reveals two people in left profile who are standing side by side. The one at the back is clean-shaven with a small moustache and he is looking to the left. He is wearing a cone-shaped hat. His companion at the front is very bulky, as though he is quite fat and wearing very thick furs. We are looking at his back and his head is turned slightly downwards to the left. Each of the men is holding up a child.

A larger image of the same stone shows a different scene. This time it is of two people in right profile, with a tall man wearing a hood holding someone who is slightly shorter. They are standing with their faces pressed close to each other. Looking at it as a slightly larger image this scene changes, so that the hood of the man becomes the head of a dog in right profile. *Below are stones C10, C11, C12 and C13*

The dog has big floppy ears, a bit like a spaniel and is standing upright. Below his nose is a round area that is composed of several human heads squashed up close together and the dog seems to be pressing these people up to his chest with his right paw. This part of the stone is yet another multiple image and the dog can also be viewed as a bear standing upright. All of these are in the top third of the stone, but there are many other partially eroded scenes and faint images of people and animals on the rest of the stone, including a large image of a cat-like creature in profile that is looking to the right and whose pointed ear is also the dog's paw.

Further round the ring to the right is another triangular sunstone, number C10, (old number 43), but this time the distinctive shape refers to the cardinal direction of east, as well as sunrise at the spring and autumn equinoxes. (The eastern row of five stones aligns more to the east of northeast.) This stone is almost a perfect right-angle triangle.

The northern edge of C10 is nearly vertical whilst the sloping southern edge is at an acute angle of about 75 degrees to the horizontal. Next to it is stone C11, which is very peculiar. This fine-grained column has an upwardly sloping top ending in a sort of sort of knob. And this lump is actually a small image of boy who is riding on the back of a man wearing a fur hat and a thick fur coat, probably a bearskin. Stone C12 is a larger stone that is the stained and eroded statue of two people in right profile standing next to each other. On the left is a bearded man wearing a rounded hat. His face is stained white, and he is looking towards the person to his left, our right.

The distinctive, vertical bands of coloured stone were used to produce lines of stacked carvings and engravings, with each figure separated from its neighbours by the lines separating one band from another. A good example of this is on the outer surface of stone C 12; the swirling lines on this southeastern side make the surface look as though it is the petrified bark of an oak tree.

The artists have very cleverly used the natural patterns of the Lewissian gneiss to produce work of an outstanding quality. The many small subjects that were also carved into the stone are usually of people, although some carvings are of animal heads, strange creatures and spirits. It really looks to me as though the images are those of tree people, perhaps woodland sprites or elves.
The main subject is a three-quarter right profile of a bearded man wearing a bulky hooded coat. The bottom two thirds of this stone is made up of a scene of a dozen or so very tall, thin, wraithlike people, and I wonder if they are meant to be woodland spirits? Looking at the stone from more to the left, the image of the bearded man disappears and is replaced by a host of carvings of tiny figures.

One of the most obvious sculptures in the ring is on the inner surface of stone C13 (46). This is a moonstone and facing towards the centre of the ring is the eroded remains of a statue of a woman wearing a cloak and hood, her head is bowed and she is a bit hunched up, perhaps from the winter cold. However from a viewpoint more to the left, her face becomes the face of an adolescent young man. As usual the stone shows other multiple images. These include a bearded man in three-quarter right profile, he is wearing a strangely shaped hat that looks like the head and body of a fox. Sitting on his lap are several children.

The most important stone at Calanais is also the tallest. Although it stands 16 feet tall (4.90m), C14 (old 29) is not the largest stone on the island because that honour goes to another massive standing stone, the tallest in Scotland, which was erected about twenty miles to the northwest. This is known as 'Clach an Trushal' and at 19 feet high (5.8 m) it is more than three times the height of a tall man.

Circle stone C14 is the thin, central stone that stands slightly off centre within the ring of thirteen smaller symbol stones and statues. And, as I mentioned before, it is accurately aligned north/south, with its broad sides facing east and west. As with all the other stones at Calanais, there are images on both sides of this megalith. The images that are visible on C14 change with the lighting but when the stone is lit from the south one can sometimes see that about half way up the east side of the stone is the battered and eroded outline of a long face. This is a woman with long, straight hair cascading down over her right shoulder.

She has a very long neck and I think she looks quite young, in her late teens or early twenties. She is sitting or kneeling down so that her lap forms the bottom right edge of the stone and the outline of her back forms a ridge along the lower left side. She is looking slightly downwards and to the right and, although the stone is quite eroded, it looks to me that she is wearing some sort of a headdress that rises upwards, almost to the top of the stone. On her lap is a young man in left profile. He is sitting on his knees, with his face pressed against her chest and he is wearing a conical hat with no brim. The young man's left arm and shoulder are outlined in red. His face is smaller than hers but I don't think that this image represents a mother and child, I am inclined to think that the picture is that of a goddess with a young acolyte, a novice priest. Since this picture is on the east side of the stone, she may well have something to do with spring.

Stone C14, view from the west and from the east

As the bearer of New Life, *the Goddess of Spring,* was a recurrent theme in communities and cultures across the whole Continent. In parts of mainland Europe, the Goddess was sometimes depicted in three of her ages, as the Maiden, the Mother and the Crone.

This unusually large image of a woman also highlights the fact that the vast majority of images of humans that were portrayed on standing stones, across time and right across the country, were of men, suggesting that for thousands of years much of ancient society was organised for, and run by, men.

The western side of C14, the central stone, also has many other complex decorations. When the sunlight moves round from the south it forms shadows and these create several large faces in profile. The largest is that of an old man who is looking north. His head is a bit squashed up to fit within the width of the stone, he has a bulbous nose and a beard and he is wearing a strange hat on his head. The whole western surface of C14 is covered with many smaller images of people, both of faces and full-length pictures, although these become more evident when the light is not directly on the stone. An image in the centre of the stone shows two people, perhaps a man and a woman, standing under some sort of an arch.

The lower part of the stone can be visualised as the profile of a dog sitting down, it's looking upwards and has a broad squat look, with its nose and mouth on the edge of the stone. It reminds me of a Scottish terrier. The wide variety of different breeds of dog that are pictured at Calanais, and at other sites across the British Isles, suggest that some of our most familiar breeds of dog have a very long pedigree indeed and may well go back more than five thousand years. There are many other intriguing sculptures at Calanais.

The northern and southern faces of the western row of four stones are particularly interesting. But since my camera malfunctioned at this point, the major images on the northern side of these stones will have to wait for another time... *The southern surfaces of the western row of stones - W4, W3, W2 and W1*

Stone W1 *(above)* is the tallest on the right and nearest to the ring, it is an eroded and bleached stone. However, there are many multiple and composite images on this superb sculpture. The main image uses most of the stone to produce just the head and torso of a bearded man in right profile, he is wearing a large hood, his nose forms the slight bump along the edge and a wave in his hair covers most of his right cheek.

The stone is also the head and torso of a man in right profile who is looking to the east. His moustache and beard form diagonal white lines. It is difficult for me to decide if a secondary image represents a young woman with a hooked nose, wearing a rounded hat or if it is some sort of non-human creature. Just below the figure's chin is a tiny imp-like creature with curved horns that stand up from its head. There is a third multiple image that shows two people standing close together, with a taller, third person standing behind them. The head of this man is in the top right corner and is tilted at an angle. The other two people are a man with a long, dark, bushy beard and on the right is a woman wearing a bonnet. The man and woman are looking at each other face to face.

There are several other quite large images and a multitude of images of little people carved into the vertical bands of gneiss, but judging from the style, these were added later on. Looking at the stone from right to left produces two other large images. The first of these images is the head of a man in left profile. The more prominent picture is the head and body of a strange animal standing upright. It has a rounded head, a bit like a beaver or perhaps a squirrel. Its left forelimb is part of a Z-shaped line of white stone.

Western row, stone W2

To the west of stone W1 is a short, oblong stone, which has a top with two slopes that rise and meet in the middle. This sculpture has also suffered the bleaching effects of time and the decoration is now quite faded. This is a great shame since this work was originally an amazing piece, a true masterpiece of multiple and composite imagery. One of the larger images of the main scene is in the bottom right quarter and it shows the head and body of a man wearing a thick fur coat. He is in left profile, has a hooked nose, a bushy black beard, and is wearing a fur hat. He is looking to the left, towards a young woman with large round eyes, long blonde hair and a snub nose. Above her is the head of a very strange-looking individual, his mouth looks distorted; he is clean-shaven, has little hair and is wearing a cap on the back of his head. The secondary decoration near the bottom of the stone shows a scene that is very weird, I am not sure what is going on but I think it shows a variety of humans in some sort of spirit world, because some of the creatures with them look very bizarre.

Next to this stone is a very distinctive, tall, almost hexagonal stone, W3 (old 22). The south side shows a full-length figure of a big man on the right half of the stone; he has a reddish beard and is wearing a bearskin coat with big sleeves and has a hat made from a squirrel on the back of his head. His right arm is outstretched to the left, his wide sleeve hangs down and his hand is raised towards something, as though he is giving it a drink from a flask. Just behind and to the left of this man is second, smaller individual who looks older.
This man has a blobby nose and is wearing a rather squashed hat, a bit like a trilby. Just below the man in the fur coat, and to his left, are three or four other, slightly smaller people. Then along the bottom of the stone are several groups of seated figures. Up along the left side of the stone is the torso and head of a man in right profile, he is seated and has a bushy beard. He is wearing a coat with lapels and three buttonholes (!) and has a strange sort of hat on his head. This area is a multiple image, it also shows another man with a triangular nose, a goatee beard and he is wearing a hat. The next image starts about half way up the left side of the stone. It is very eroded and hard to make out the subject. It looks like some sort of young animal that the red-bearded man on the right is feeding. Perhaps he is giving a bear cub or more likely, a lamb, some milk from a leather flask.

Southern surface of stone W3, western row

The top of the stone is also heavily eroded and faded and one can only just make out the very large head of a hairy and bearded man in the left half. In comparison to the other figures on this stone the man is a giant, the right side of his back and his bent right arm are very noticeable, as is his white fur coat. This coat was probably made from young sealskins. In the right corner is the much smaller head of a woman with a prominent nose and jutting chin. Her hair is bunched up at the back and she is wearing a white, sun hat with a broad brim. There are also many other secondary decorations on the surface of this side of the stone.

What is also very interesting is another picture that runs down the left side of the surface of the stone. This area shows several strange multiple and composite pictures of groups of people of different sizes. At the far left, and at the back of some smaller people, is a bearded old man wearing a domed hat This looks as though it is tied down and around his chin by a scarf going over the top of the hat. Just below him is a younger man wearing a round cap on the top of his head. Then there is a row of people who are arranged around something on the ground, which they are all looking at. I think that it is a baby, but I'm not sure. The main central large image is of some sort of large animal in right profile. It has its mouth open, and looks a bit like a stoat or weasel. It is following another animal that has its head turned to look over it shoulder, as though it is being hunted.

(If you are looking at the stone, you need to turn your head through 70 degrees to see this picture!)

The last stone in the western row, W4, has a faint image of an old man in the middle of the stone. It also shows the heads of two people above this image. Unfortunately this is where my camera malfunctioned, so I can't illustrate this with a picture for you to see.

On the other side of the central ring, at the start of the eastern row, is stone E1. It is now faded, but the quality of the art was originally quite exceptional since it is a maze of multiple and composite imagery. There is a multitude of large, medium and small images on this stone. At the top are two medium sized images of people that are standing face to face. In the top right corner is the head of a man in left profile. He is wearing a fur hat and is looking towards the other individual, who is also wearing a fur hat. The stone also shows a major multiple image of the left profile of a man's head. He has a short white moustache and a small brown and white beard on his chin and he is wearing a domed hat. This is a multiple image since by looking from left to right you can see another head, this time of a bear-like animal with a snub nose and a white incisor showing in the corner of its mouth. Below this, near the bottom of the stone, is the head of a horse in right profile, it is wearing a halter that is visible as a black band across the end of its nose. Also part of this image are two seated figures, a woman and a man with a very hairy beard in the bottom left corner. The woman is wearing a white dress and she has her hair pulled back and covered by a small round bonnet that sits on the back of her head. My picture of stone E2 is also missing.

Eastern row, stone E1

The next stone in the eastern row is E3. This stone is another very interesting work of art. It represents the head of a dog with a broad head and a rounded muzzle. It has a very shaggy coat and only one ear is visible at the top. In the centre of the top part is the left profile and upper chest of an old man with a reddish face, wearing a cap towards the back of his head.

Eastern row, stone E3

Along the right edge, just below the end of the dog's nose is a full-length figure of someone wearing a hooded fur coat. In the middle of the bottom half of the stone is a complex scene of strange people.

Towards the end of the eastern row of five stones is stone E4. On the northern side of the stone is a highly stylised sculpture of a young horse's head and neck. The southern side of E4 also shows the head of this horse, but within this image is the picture of a young, clean-shaven man in right profile who is wearing a patterned conical cap. His head is tilted backwards due to the shape of the stone and his right shoulder shows that he is wearing a cloak over his clothes. Above his nose and peeking out from under his cap is a mass of hair, which is also the image of an animal's head. Within the main image there is also the three-quarter left profile of the head of a cat-like animal with a broad nose and a triangular chin.

above is Eastern row stone E4, its outer (northern) and inner surfaces
below is Avenue stone A11

It is not my intention to describe every single stone at Calanais but there is a particularly interesting sculpture in the western side of the avenue to the north-northeast, it is on stone A11. One side of the stone shows a curious image of a man's head in three quarter left profile. He is wearing a peaked hat that rises steeply at an acute angle. He has a beaky nose and is grinning. At the top, and just to the left of the crack in the stone, is the face of an older man with a long white beard in three-quarter right profile. He is wearing a close-fitting hat that narrows at the top. The bottom two thirds of stone 11 is made up of a couple who are sitting down and looking to the right. The figure on the left is wearing a thick full-length fur coat with a large hood. To her right is a larger figure of a man with long hair and a cloak. There is a multiple image of another man within his beard. Facing him on his left side is a smaller figure of a girl with long hair.

There are also several other images on the lower part of this stone, in particular there is a picture of a seated old man with a very long white beard at bottom left, facing him to the left are two other young men who are kneeling down. Stone A11 clearly demonstrates the clever way that the artists used the natural, wavy lines of the Lewissian gneiss to give texture to the clothes that people wore. The shape of stone itself looks like the perfect symbol to demonstrate an astronomical direction such as north. It also reminds me of the outline of a hunting dog, such as a Pointer, that is looking sharply upwards into the air.

There are many extraordinary works of art at Calanais and about half way along the eastern side of the avenue is another stone that deserves a special mention, this is stone A6 (below). The eastern side of this astonishingly complex work of art is roughly triangular, although the top has been dramatically altered. The layers of rock swirl upwards on the left like smoke, twisting and turning in the wind. The top left corner shows the head of a man wearing a hooded parka.

However, this is also the right ear of the main image on the left side. This is a multiple image of a cat-like animal in right profile. This is also a carving of a broad-faced man in right profile who is wearing a hooded parka. A third image in the same area shows a fish in left profile, its open mouth and round eye are very noticeable. This multiple image can also be seen as the head of a horse, with its eye set further back, this is the same eye as the main image. The area to the right is also a very complex set of images. The main picture is a smiling man wearing a sort of tall hat with a fold, a bit like a bishop's mitre. He looks happy, although his head does look a bit too big for his body. Above his left eye a part of his hat forms a multiple image of another individual in left profile, possibly a human, but who has a very long, thin nose. This is also the right profile of a man with a goatee beard. He is wearing a fur hat that slopes up to the right-hand corner of the stone.

There are also multiple images all over the bottom half of stone. The main scene shows several overlapping animals in left profile, with one that has a gaping mouth. Their outlines and front legs form the series of wavy lines. Further to the right is a burly man with a short dark beard who is wearing a bulky fur coat and a flat cap. The bottom right corner of the stone shows a man on horseback, galloping to the left. In the middle of stone A6 are many other multiple and composite images, one image stands out on the left edge, it shows a man wearing a hat with the brim turned back, a bit like a sailor's sou'wester. He seems to have a rope tied round his neck, although I think this is actually just the collar and edge of his sheepskin coat where it overlaps. Just below the chin of the cat-like creature is the face of an old man with a bushy white beard.

Just below the centre of the stone is a fascinating scene that is superimposed in the multiple style onto the heads of the group of animals that are moving to the left. The general impression I get from this is that it is a deathbed scene, consisting of a group of a dozen or so people who are standing around a child who is lying down on a platform, or some sort of bed that is formed from a tree trunk. The curving roots of the tree grow upwards, from the middle of the bottom of the stone. Above and to the left of the child is the head and body of a woman who is wearing a brown bonnet. She has a white face and quite a beaky nose. She is wearing a fur coat that shows a white trim up the middle, like a sheepskin coat with the inner fleece showing where it is turned outwards. Behind her, and to the left, is the figure of a bearded man wearing a similar sort of coat and a fur hat with a white brim.

Calanais is an ancient site and its geographical position begs further thought and discussion since it is situated on the unsheltered northern coast, to the west of the modern cultural centre of the island, the busy coastal port and town of Stornoway. The northern side of the island bears the brunt of the ferocious winter gales that sweep in from across the Atlantic. The remote and isolated position of Calanais suggests that it was settled by immigrants looking for a place of security. Five thousand years ago the climate was better and there were pastures and small fields and woods in areas around Calanais that are now under water. Judging from the art and architecture of the site I think that it was settled by a group of people with a different religious background to those who lived further to the east or those on mainland Scotland.

There are of course many other wonderful sculptures and carvings at Calanais and also at the other circles of standing stones on the Isle of Lewis, including Cnoc Ceann a' Gharraidh, Cnoc Fillibhir Bheag and Cean Hulavig, to name just a few. But it is now time to move about a hundred and forty miles across the sea to the northeast and look at some of the works of art at another very important Scottish site, one that I have already mentioned several times, the extraordinary Ring of Brodgar on the Mainland of the Orkney Islands.

ORKNEY

Western half of the Ring of Brodgar, Orkney, and below, House 1 at Skara Brae

We saw in earlier chapters how many of the uprights at the temples of Brodgar and Stenness are symbol stones made from the local Old Red Sandstone. The long, thin, slabs of this sedimentary rock were also used for building houses in villages such as the one at Skara Brae and for the walls and structural supports of large tombs, such as those at Maes Howe, Cuween Hill, Unstan and Isbister.

The surviving houses at the small village of Skara Brae are quite amazing. Built and used five thousand years ago, the village boasted a covered passageway connecting the houses together. Each house featured stone furniture that included a central hearth, a dresser, built-in cupboards, querns for grinding wheat and barley, boxes for food and most extraordinary of all, a toilet that was connected to a drainage system! The sophistication of the design, the construction and the furniture and facilities should have sent alarm bells ringing in the ears of our archaeologists. They should have realised that something was very wrong with the idea that our distant ancestors were stupid barbarians. The Neolithic was the New Stone Age, but it was also a time when our ancestors were using a great deal of wood, and not just to burn it. They were using wood in much the same way as the Orcadians were using stone, to build their farms, houses and furniture, because, unlike the Northern Isles, there were plenty of trees and plenty of timber in mainland Britain. The age-old tradition of building wooden houses still persists in Scandinavia, although the furniture might now come from a well-known Swedish store!

At the time of construction, the houses of Skara Brae were not isolated examples of stone houses that were built on the islands. There must have been many hundreds of others, scattered across the landscape. Over the following centuries, many of the stones from the ruined houses would have been recycled for newer dwellings or simply used for field walls. An earlier pair of houses were found at the Knap of Howar on the small island of Papa Westray. These date from 3,700 BC and were in use for over a thousand years.

Other houses have been excavated at the settlement called Barnhouse, which is very close to the Standing Stones of Stenness. Its location suggests to me that this was once a religious community of small roundhouses with a large communal meeting hall. The entrance into this meeting hall is unusual since it was built to the northwest and facing the symbolic direction of midsummer sunset.

The farmstead at the Knap of Howar, Papa Westray

One of the most notable sculptures at the Ring of Brodgar is a tall stone on the western side of what was originally a perfect circle of some sixty megaliths.

This is a complex work of art, but the main sculpture shows the head and neck in right profile of a humanoid who is looking to the north. I say humanoid because this picture doesn't look quite human and it is probably the image of a god. He has a long, thin face with a beaky nose that has a pronounced bump in the middle. He has a down-turned mouth and beard. The top of his hat slopes backwards and upwards to form a multiple image of another person in left profile who is wearing a large, baggy hat. His left cheek forms a smaller image of a bearded man in right profile.

There is another small secondary image of someone in right profile standing next to the main person's right shoulder. This is another multiple image and shows several other pictures, including, on the left side, a rather strange face with round eyes looking slightly upwards. Another image, running down the bottom left side of the stone, shows a rather grumpy-looking, bearded man wearing a parka with the hood up. There is also a large scene along the left edge of the surface, but you need to turn the image through 90 degrees anti-clockwise. Just below the middle of the stone is a man riding a horse at full gallop and another image of a horse's head is formed from part of the god's beard. There is yet another horse and rider in the bottom left corner.

The images change according to the lighting, the time of day and the season. There is a multitude of moving images, composite images and multiple images. This incredibly complex stone was a true masterpiece when freshly carved, but it is only thanks to modern technology and image intensifying software that we can get even some idea of just how incredibly talented the ancient artists were. Very unusually for a standing stone, each side of the stone shows the same face in profile, the right profile for the inner surface and the left profile for the outer.

Which is why I chose pictures of this extraordinary sculpture for both the front and the back covers of this book.

Also at the Ring of Brodgar is one of the strangest sculptures that I have seen over the last few years. This extraordinary stone marks a southwesterly moonset position and just behind it, to the right, you can see a notch in the landscape where the moon would set at a particular point in one of its cycles. This strange sculpture is the second of the four standing stones that mark the southwestern sector of the circle. It is shaped quite differently to its neighbours, which are a variety of winter sunset symbol stones.

Ring of Brodgar, southwest sector

The main inner surface shows a weird-looking face, which is definitely not human. The face seems twisted and distorted, with just one eye, a triangular nose and a gash for a mouth. The creature is looking over its left shoulder, towards the west. The stone is covered with many images of people and some strange creatures, particularly at the bottom of the stone. There are several other images to be seen, the most notable is at top left and it shows a person in right profile who is wearing a sort of helmet that covers his ears. In the top right corner is another person wearing a domed hat. This is a multiple image because by looking from right to left you can see another face, with a beaky nose and they look distinctly gnome-like!

I described the symbolism and architecture inherent in the design of the Ring of Brodgar in an earlier chapter. The two main symbol stones for north and south both have carvings on them and of course all the other symbol stones at Brodgar are decorated, but perhaps not to the same extent as the ones that I've already described. Brodgar was part of a great ceremonial landscape that included the nearby circle known as the Stones of Stenness, but only three of the original twelve very tall pillars are still intact. The stones were originally enclosed within a henge, a circular bank with an inner ditch. These are all huge symbol stones, but it is known that at least one of them (5) fell down in 1814 and was re-erected in 1907, it measured 5.5 metres in length and weighed nearly 10 tons. The tallest stone (3) is a whopping eighteen feet nine inches high (5.75m). The inverted Z-shaped stone is number 7 and this is all that remains of a much larger stone that snapped off. The surfaces of the stones have become quite eroded over the centuries, so the carvings and engravings become more visible with dramatic side-lighting.

The Stones of Stenness, Orkney and below, detail of stone number 2 (on the right)

The stone with a jagged edge (#2) has a top that slopes upwards at about forty degrees. Together with symbol stones made from squares, oblongs, triangles, pentagons and parts of circles, this is proof indeed that our ancestors were well aware of basic geometry. The lower half of this jagged-edged stone has a picture of a man in left profile. He is wearing a large, rounded fur hat, has a triangular nose and has a short tufted beard on his chin. Above and to the right is a broad skull-like face, which is part of a multiple image of a large animal in left profile, its left front leg is also the outline of the man's nose. There is also another large image of a man with a bushy beard. This stone is best viewed from a distance, since there are least four large multiple images in this area of the stone.

Above them, in the top right corner, is a small skull-like creature with large eyes and an open mouth. It is in three-quarter right profile and is also part of another image below it. This is the head of a man with a long, narrow beard who is wearing a fur headdress

that incorporates part of the skull-like creature. Seen from a distance, this stone resembles the right profile of a bearded man; he is a bit hunched over and is wearing a coat with a pointed hood, which forms the tip of the megalith.

The main picture on the tallest stone (the one in the centre of the photo) is the head and body of a bearded man, with a bulbous nose, wearing a floor-length cloak with a pointed hood. He has wrapped the cloak around his body with his arms tightly folded inside, thus the whole surface of the stone is used in this one image. He must have been famous. There is also a multiple image of two people standing face to face and many medium-sized composite images. This, the broadest of the three tall stones, has a twenty-degree slope along its slightly dished top whilst the narrowest stone has a top that slopes upwards from left to right at a perfect forty-five degree angle.

All the Stones of Stenness were decorated with thousands of tiny carvings, in the composite style. These formed into a crowded and dense mass of medium-sized multiple images of people and animals. Unfortunately the sandstone has become eroded over the centuries of fierce winter gales and the carvings are worn down and far less visible today. But I think that on the southern side of the top of number five, the narrowest stone, they carved another image of a man wearing a cloak and hood. The hood comes to a triangular peak just above the man's head. And since the temple was erected around 3,100 BC, perhaps these images, like the ones at Calanais, were precursors to the sun priest's tall conical hats that are visible at Stonehenge, far to the south. However it does seem a bit strange that the Stones of Stenness were known in local folklore as '*the Temple of the Moon*', because it originally had twelve stones. Perhaps the stones were a reference to the number of months in a solar year, and the priests had a dual role. An excavation in 1975 suggested that one stone hole (#12) may never have been used or at least not for a big stone. But this remains unclear because the surface of the enclosure has been ploughed on many occasions and traces of the ditch and bank of the henge are hard to make out.

I noticed that many of the people whose portraits feature in the works of art, in both the Western Isles and the Orkneys, are wearing furs, fur coats or parkas. This is quite surprising really when you think about it, since bearskin garments must have been difficult to obtain and also because the weather was better than now , so they were only suitable for wearing in the colder months of the year. This suggests two things, firstly that fur clothes were 'expensive' and so that they were a sign of prestige, and secondly, not everyone had the luck to have been the subject for one of the artists. It suggests that most of the people that were recorded for posterity were the leaders, particularly the priests, chiefs or perhaps kings. In addition, many of the best-dressed people were men, mostly wearing full beards and wearing fur hats. This also suggests that it was a male dominated society since they were the ones who were portrayed the most often. And although many people would have had their winter clothes made from red deer furs, imagine how difficult it must have been for ordinary farming people to get hold of a fur coat made from a bear, lynx or even a wolf. So there must also have been a thriving trade in sealskin furs, and particularly desirable would have been the soft white coat of young pups. But even so, not everyone would have had the luxury of having a thick fur coat to keep them warm in winter. Most people must have had to make do with sheepskin, buckskin or leather for their coats and parkas, but for the fashion conscious, these were probably trimmed with squirrel, ermine, hare, otter, seal or beaver fur.

Unfortunately the remains of such ancient clothing have rotted away over the millennia, with one notable exception. Ötzi, the Iceman, whose frozen, five thousand-year-old body was found high up in the Italian Alps, had a bearskin cap to keep his head warm. He was also wearing a deerskin upper garment and deerskin leggings, both originally worn with the hair still on, fur side out. But instead of a real fur coat he was wearing a thick cloak made from woven and plaited grass. However, this garment would have been very effective for shedding rainwater and of course the insulation properties of thatch are well known. So even in very wet weather he would have kept warm and dry. His clothing has given insights into how some early Bronze Age people lived in the mountains of southern Europe and further study of the art at our own prehistoric sites will give fresh insights into the clothes and fashions of Ancient Britain. Hats were very commonplace, some, such as the conical varieties, suggest they were worn by the priesthood whilst others shapes were for the social elite. Simple caps worn on the back of the head, were probably just everyday wear for those who worked hard for a living...It is worth thinking for a moment about the energy and resolve that went into erecting the enormous slabs of rock that were used to build the Stones of Stenness and the Ring of Brodgar. The amount of effort needed to cut these huge stones from out of the bedrock, move them from their different quarries, drag them to the site and then erect them must have been simply phenomenal. And it was all done without any complex machinery. Just by people working together and using their knowledge, strength and determination to build temples that represented their thoughts of who they were and what they believed in.

In the summer of 2008, Historic Scotland allowed the excavation of two parts of the Ring of Brodgar, with the intention of obtaining a confirmed date from the ditch and hence the date of construction of the circle. The idea was to re-excavate and extend the two ditches that had been dug in 1973 by Colin Rendfrew, this time by a team led by Dr Jane Downes of ORCA (the Orkney Research Centre for Archaeology), who is quoted as saying:

"Although the excavations 35 years ago were undertaken to obtain dating material and establish chronology, they failed due to the limitations of available dating techniques at the time. The advanced new techniques now at our disposal mean that this time our investigations should establish when the Ring of Brodgar was built and help us learn a great deal more about it."

One of the aims of the new excavation was to get a better understanding of the architecture of the circle, since even the original number of standing stones was a mystery, and it has always been assumed that the circle contained sixty megaliths spaced regularly around the inner perimeter of the ditch. The plan was to do geophysics research to determine if there had indeed been sixty stones or if there had been any more. Work on this geophysics project was started by Adrian Challands and his wife Norma, using an electrical pseudosection surveying technique to locate the position of the sockets of missing stones.

Between the 25th and 27th July 2008 the couple were able to survey just over half of the perimeter around the eastern side of the circle and they discovered the positions of 49 sockets. These sockets are a mixture of currently upright megaliths, stubs of broken megaliths and empty holes. Some of the empty sockets still contained packing material. The figure of 49 sockets does however include the remains of a façade of 13 closely-set slabs, set within a sort of trench and flanking the southeastern causeway, the thinner of the two causeways leading across the ditch and into the circle. Although they were not regularly spaced, the thirty-six post holes suggest that the ring may have had more than sixty standing stones. What was particularly interesting to me was the revelation that many of the single stones that were missing had been in quite shallow and narrow holes, suggesting that they had contained slim stones or even posts that had been removed at some time, perhaps even before the temple's design was finalised. One possibility is that they were astronomical markers, set up to temporarily mark horizon events of the rising of the sun and the moon during their respective cycles.

However, due to a lack of time and other constraints, the Challands were unfortunately unable to finish their survey of the circle, so there is still no definitive total for the original number of standing stones at the Ring of Brodgar...It was shortly after my second visit to Orkney, in July 2011, that I started to think about the results of the 2008 excavations in more detail. I contacted Dr Jane Downes because I couldn't find any published details on the internet about the results of the dating of samples taken from the ditch, in other words there was no published change to the estimated date of the Ring of Brodgar at 2500 BC. (This date is loosely based on other sites, in particular the nearby Stones of Stenness, which dates back to around 3200 BC.)
As a result of my enquiries I found that in terms of obtaining a confirmed date for the ditch, the excavation was not a great success. There were no radiocarbon dating results and according

to Doctor David Sanderson of SUERC (Scottish Universities Environmental Research Centre), luminescence profiling and 'single aliquot regenerative quartz OSL' dating procedures were not able to pinpoint a fixed date. This was partly due to the way that samples had to be obtained from the exploration trenches that had been dug previously, by Rendfrew in 1973. Therefore I think that a new excavation, in unexplored areas of the ditch, would probably be much more successful in finding out the true age of this iconic World Heritage site.

The Ring of Brodgar is often described in textbooks as a henge, which is a circle or an oval area of land enclosed by a circular bank with an internal ditch. The ditch at Brodgar measured up to three metres deep, nine metres wide and 380 metres in circumference (10ft x 30ft x 1250ft). However, there is no trace of a bank surrounding the ditch at Brodgar, this is quite strange given that the ditch was cut from the underlying bedrock and hundreds of tons of rocks and stones were removed during its construction. A clue to solving this little mystery was revealed when I read about the site of a major archaeological discovery at the Ness of Brodgar, about half way between the circles of standing stones at Brodgar and Stenness. The first discovery was made in 2002 when a geophysics survey revealed a mass of structures buried beneath the soil. Test trenches were dug in 2003 and the remains of a house, similar to one at the settlement of Barnhouse, near Stenness, was discovered. Subsequent excavations each summer thereafter revealed more and more details about a complex of thick walls and large buildings, including the massive Structure Ten, which had an outer wall that was an astonishing five metres thick. By Neolithic standards this building was huge. It measured 25 metres by 20 metre wide (82 feet by 65 feet) and it was surrounded by a paved passageway.

Excavations in 2010 discovered traces of painted stones inside some buildings and at least two of them were roofed with slates, made form thin sheets of sandstone that were trimmed to a standard rectangular shape. There was also a massive stone wall, four metres thick, which seems to have run across the width of the peninsula. The whole religious community complex seems to have been in use from as early as 3,500 BC and right through to the Bronze Age, 1500 years later.

Ness of Brodgar excavations July 2011

So have you guessed what happened to all the missing stones that were dug out of the Ring of Brodgar's ditch and where they were used?

Although completely unnoticed, this small, exquisitely carved and engraved stone is standing upright, just behind the archaeologist on the right. (*It's behind you!*) The main image is the head of a dog, or perhaps a wolf. There are a host of multiple and composite images and at least three pictures of horses. The most noticeable is the one with its head and body that runs along the top of the slab and facing to the right. Below, and to the left, is another horse that is rearing up and behind it in the left corner is a third horse. Looking from right to left you may be able to make out the head and body of a wild cat occupying most of the stone. Its head is in the top left corner and the cat is looking over its shoulder and to the left. In the middle of the picture is the image of a seated man who is looking to the left, towards another man who has a dark beard and is wearing fur robes.

11 Stanton Drew

The next major site that I want to illustrate is in the county of Somerset, in the southwest of England, and a few miles south of the outskirts of the city of Bristol.

At one end of the Chew Valley lies the small village of Stanton Drew. Although quite close to the city, it is in a secluded area, well away from the main A37 road to Shepton Mallet and Yeovil. This is probably one of the reasons the stone circles are less well known than those of Avebury and Stonehenge. Another reason is that at first sight, there is not much to see, apart from a few dozen rocks and boulders lying in a large field. However, at the height of its authority, Stanton Drew must have been as important as those better-known religious centres just a day's walk to the east.

Although Stanton Drew was first studied over three hundred years ago, until now most recent authors have contented themselves to repeat what other scholars have written before, mainly about the folklore relating to the site. The three stone circles at Stanton Drew were first recorded in 'Monumenta Britannica' by the antiquary John Aubrey after a visit he made in 1664. However, at the time of his visit the crops were high and barley was growing all around the stones. Since he could not get close to them he seems to have confused the actual arrangement of the stones and so his sketch leaves a lot to be desired. The next historical visitor of note was Dr William Musgrove in 1719, followed by William Stukeley in 1723. Stukeley went on to become an expert on prehistoric sites and visited many stone circles, barrows and graves and he wrote a series of articles on Stanton Drew, Avebury, Stonehenge and many other sites in his book 'Itinerarium Curiosum', published in 1776. Other visitors who recorded their visit included the Reverend Samuel Seyer in his 'Memoirs of Bristol', in 1821, the Bath architect William Long in 1858 and C.W. Dymond in 1877. Then in 1956, L.V. Grinsell, a local archaeologist, wrote a more technical account in the Ministry of Works guide: Stanton Drew Stone Circles, Somerset and in his private publication: The Megalithic Monuments of Stanton Drew.

Stanton Drew has three open-air temples: the Great Circle and two small circles, the Southwest temple and the Northeast temple, as well as two short Avenues and other outlying features such as *'Hauteville's Quoit'* and *'the Cove'*.

The Northeastern temple, *pictured below*, is quite small. It is about a hundred feet across (44.2m) and had eight large stones, three are upright, one emerges at an angle, three lie on their backs and one is in pieces, mixed up with the broken remains of other stones from a short avenue close to the circle. The smaller southwest temple is further away from the main site and on higher ground in a field of its own. It has thirteen stones but not a single one of them is still standing, all of them lie scattered around the mound on their sides, backs or fronts.

The stones of the religious and secular complex at Stanton Drew vary considerably in size and shape, from some quite small stones in the southwest temple, less than three feet long, to the giants of the northeast temple measuring up to 12 feet high and weighing in excess of fifteen tons. The stones that make up all three temples are of several different types of rock, including pustular brecchia, oolitic limestone and a red sandstone, possibly from the Avon Gorge, five miles to the northwest. When freshly worked, the white limestone would have glowed by the light of the full moon and the sandstone would have looked even redder by the light of the setting sun.

The largest of the three rings, the Great Circle, is the second largest stone circle in Britain. It is simply enormous, with a diameter of more than a hundred paces across, (368ft., 112.2m). Originally there were at least thirty stones in the circle, there are reports that some stones were smashed up and others buried but in a plan dated 1858 only 14 stones are marked, the others were buried or missing. We currently know the positions of some twenty-seven stones, about twenty of these are plainly visible, whilst the rest are wholly or partially buried in the ground. Only a few are upright, most of the stones have toppled over and many have been moved about by generations of farmers.

In 1997 a team from English Heritage used geophysics to survey the area and they discovered that the Great Circle had originally been surrounded by a circular bank and ditch, with at least one opening, to the northeast. The ditch of the henge was about 20 feet (6 m) across. The scientists also discovered something far more unusual, for inside the circle of standing stones there had been a series of nine concentric rings of pits, each of which had once contained a very large post. However, none of this is visible today, since long ago farmers filled in the ditch with the earth from the bank and then ploughed up the soil for their crops. As late as the 1660's the main field, containing the Great Circle and the Northeast circle, was still being used for growing wheat and barley, but by the early 1700's it had become an orchard. Nowadays the fruit trees are long gone and it is used as pastureland for cows and sheep.

Extraordinary as the rings of pits are, they are not unique, similar structures have been excavated at Woodhenge, Mount Pleasant and at Durrington Walls, near Stonehenge and again at the Sanctuary, near Avebury. The metre wide pits are all that remain of the foundations for huge posts made from the trunks of hundreds of large trees.

Print based on Crocker's survey of 1826

STANTON DREW.
1858.

In my view, the posts would have been decorated with the same sort of highly complex images that were created on the surfaces of standing stones. But however they were treated, the amount of effort required to erect so many hundreds of heavy posts must have been immense.

The site of Woodhenge near Stonehenge is similar but a lot smaller, and with a diameter of about fifty paces it may well have been roofed, certainly there were some massive beams that had been erected in the dozens of postholes, and these were capable of bearing the weight of many tons of timber roofing struts and thatch. Woodhenge is very likely a domestic site since excavations in the 1920's by the Cunningtons found that the ground was littered with broken Grooved Ware pottery and old meat bones. As for Stanton Drew, we'll just have to wait and see what turns up, because it will certainly become the focus of a great deal of renewed interest once the discovery of its art is revealed. It wouldn't surprise me greatly to find that the circle had once contained an enormous roundhouse, as big as the reconstructed Globe Theatre in London.

Some archaeologists are quite sceptical about the existence of these giant roundhouses and they prefer to see the pits just as the remains of rings of short posts, open to the sky with no roof, like a forest of tree trunks with no branches or leaves. But this doesn't make much sense to me, why would they go to all the trouble of cutting down hundreds of trees and then not use the timber to build a house or a temple? One reason for the scepticism of some experts is that there is no evidence of water runoff from the eaves of the roof. They say that the rainwater from such an enormous expanse would have left deep gullies in the soil. But if people like them could construct Newgrange, Maes Howe, Calanais, Silbury Hill and Stonehenge, could they not have included some form of wooden guttering in their design to cope with the heavy autumn downpours and let the water run off safely into the surrounding ditch?

Unfortunately until the site is excavated we will not know for certain if the rings of pits were just circles of free-standing posts in some sort of ritual setting or if they were the vertical supports for a truly massive circular roof. Nevertheless, I do think that the number of rings is particularly significant since nine is a key figure in human biology. If each circle of posts represented a complete moon cycle, then there would have been nine months in all, the same length of time that a human foetus develops in the womb, in other words, the nine rings symbolised **'Life'**. For the moment it is not clear about the precise position and arrangement of the pits in each circle. Were they aligned with each other so that they formed lines radiating out from the centre, like rays from the sun?

If there really had been a roundhouse here then the labour required to produce such an enormous building would have been immense. Over a thousand large trees would have had to be felled, trimmed, cut to size and hauled to the construction site. Then holes would have had to be dug and the trunks set up as uprights and the branches trimmed and jointed to form the joists and struts, all in order to form the skeleton of the building, which then needed to be thatched. The thatching alone would have required a mountain of straw or reeds and all this would need to be cut and carried to the site and then stored ready for the thatchers working high overhead. Once the roof was finished, the interior could then have been divided off into private and communal rooms, probably on several levels, with storage space, animal stalls and barns. Such a huge building could easily have been home to three or four hundred people, living and sharing together as one community, and the interiors would probably have been furnished with wooden furniture and partitions and then decorated with carvings and painted scenes on the walls.

All this work would need to be accomplished with the use of simple stone, wooden and flint tools and a great deal of hard labour. Even with the help of teams of oxen, sledges and packhorses the task would have been enormous. In addition, much of this work would have to have been seasonal, to allow time for ploughing, planting and harvesting. The whole site would have required years of work by a dedicated population of hundreds of labourers, carpenters, toolmakers, carvers, sculptors, architects and thatchers, as well as all the people required to feed and look after them.

Such a magnificent building speaks volumes about the organisational capabilities of their leaders and priests. How long would it take and how much would it cost to do the same today?

Local folklore says that the site was known as *'The Wedding'*, and the stones were supposedly wedding guests who had continued to make merry throughout Saturday night and into the following day and were then turned to stone for dancing on the Sabbath. Like so much of our folklore, I think this is probably a garbled version of a distant memory of the sculptures and carvings of people on the stones. The art is quite interesting since many of the stones have been sculpted to emphasise their natural shapes and to transform them into animal and human figures, some of which look as though they are emerging from the rock. But as so often has happened with limestone and the softer varieties of sandstone, the sculptures, carvings and engravings have become heavily eroded over the last four to five thousand years and it is best to look at the stones from about twenty paces away. Looking at them from close up, the large sculpted faces and other images tend to disappear into a mass of broken and eroded stone covered in lichen. This wasn't always the case, since many of the larger images were covered in smaller carvings in the composite and multiple styles.

THE NORTHEAST TEMPLE

The northeast temple is made up of eight stones and most are huge, roughly rectangular blocks except for one that is totally different in shape to the others. It is roughly triangular and was buried in the ground so that it is pointing upwards at such a sharp angle that it looks as though it could fall at any moment. At the Cornish stone circle of Boscawen-un, there is also a stone that points out of the ground but it is near the centre of the circle, rather than on the circumference. I have renumbered the circle, with the most northerly stone as N1 and called the triangular stone, N5, the Southstone and like the Obelisk at Avebury, or the Heel Stone at Stonehenge, the Southstone is one of the keys to this temple and from there to the whole site of Stanton Drew.

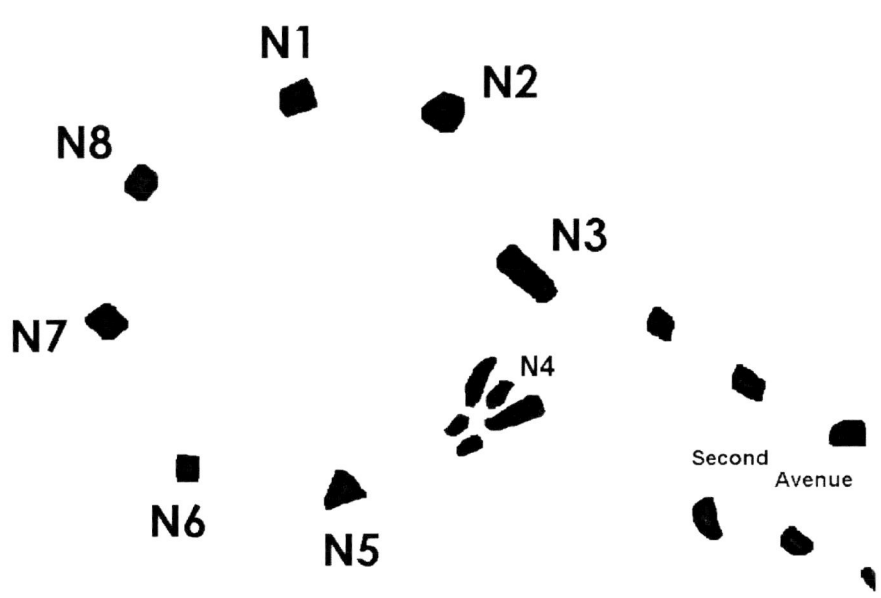

The Northeastern circle

The Southstone, N5, is clearly the most important stone in the northeast temple because of its unusual orientation, position and triangular shape. It is quite a complex sculpture, and, as with other 'moving images', in late afternoon the sunlight from the west can make the side view of the stone

Western side of northeast circle stone N5, the southstone

looks like the nose of a wolf pointing upwards into the air. (A magnetic compass bearing gives the stone as south of southeast, a major moonrise position.) This is important, because if you look at the photograph of the northeastern temple and follow the line of sight provided by the edge of this slanting stone, it shows you where the midsummer sun will rise over the local horizon, just behind the seventh or eighth tree in the long line of trees to middle right. (In modern times this point will have moved a degree to the right.)

On the west side of N5 are several eroded images of people and animals. The most visible image is that of a woman near the centre of the stone. She is wearing a hat or perhaps a sort of tiara. She is sitting at an angle, surrounded by other people and children. Looking at the stone from a very low viewpoint on the other side, the eastern side, the stone resembles the hunched up figure of an old man with a beard. To his right is a shorter, full-length figure of another man standing close to him and his face presses into the older man's shoulder. This was a complex piece of art since the overall sculpture also looks like the body of an eagle but there were many other multiple-style images on the stone, including the head of a hawk. The problem with seeing these images is that the stone has suffered quite a lot of erosion, but with the right lighting and image intensifying software you can get some idea of how the sculpted stone would have looked, all those centuries ago.

The Southstone stands on the southern part of the circle and is aimed towards the centre and then northwards, on towards Maes Knoll, which centuries later became an Iron Age fortified settlement, overlooking the hill between Stanton Drew and Bristol. Stanton Drew is my local site and it was the first prehistoric site that I really looked at in detail and it gave me the first clues into new insights that would subsequently transform my understanding of the ancient world and the lives of our distant ancestors. It was here that I started to REALLY think about what I was seeing and what it could represent in terms of prehistoric religious symbolism, and in particular, the purpose of the standing stones at this and other sites.

Northeast circle stone N7

One of the first things that I noticed was that several of the large stones of the northeast temple weren't just boulders in their natural state; instead they display some of the most visible works of art at Stanton Drew. For example, when viewed from the south, one stone in the northwest circle, N7, shows a very large grotesque face in left profile on the left edge of the stone. This face has its chin at ground level and its tongue partly protrudes from an open mouth.

On the right side of this stone are some other faces, particularly visible is the head and upper body of a stocky man in right profile, again on the edge of the stone. He has dark hair and a bushy black beard. When the stone was previously upside down it showed two large faces on the southern side, back to back, but these are now heavily eroded. Next to this stone is a reddish stone, N8, the sculpture of another strange head that is partly covered in green lichen. This image is not that easy to see at first, but it occupies the lower two thirds of the stone, on the right. It is in left profile, and the nose and chin are quite prominent but in the full length photo overleaf the eye socket of this face is lost in shadow

from another overhanging face. This new face has very angular features and is wearing a floppy hat, a bit like a turban, with a sort of tassel that is hanging down on the left side, but I don't think this is a picture of human being, the face doesn't look right. Below this figure are several eroded, full-length images of people. One of these, on the lower right side of the stone, shows the head and upper body of a bearded man, who is also looking in the same direction as the main image.

All of these sculptures are covered with the remains of hundreds of tiny, multi-coloured carvings of little people, but unfortunately erosion has taken quite a toll on all of this artwork.

As is so often is the case, the lighting conditions can influence which sculptures and carvings can be seen at any one time, so it is a good idea to visit Stanton Drew at different times of the year and at different times of the day.

Northeastern temple, the southern surface of stone N8.

In very bright sunlight the finer artwork can become quite difficult to see because the rock surfaces are reflective and the art becomes overexposed, like a photograph that has received too much light. One of the best times of day to see these smaller images is when the sky is overcast and the deep shadows are not so pronounced.

The southern side of this stone, N8, is also very interesting, because the stone was originally lying on its right side. The surface of the stone was then covered by artwork including a large scene involving dozens of seated and standing people, clustered around a central figure. There are also a few animals, including several terrier-like dogs. The main image in the picture shows some other people sitting in a boat. This is also a multiple image, in the bottom left of the scene (now the right corner and right side of the stone) there is someone lying flat on their back, perhaps on their deathbed. I think this is a woman dressed in white. Next to her lies another figure of a man who is also lying down on his back. He has a yellow hat and a goatee beard. At the other end of the stone (now the top right corner) is a seated man who has very angular features, a white face and a short, curly beard and he seems to be laughing.

Western surface of stone N8

This complex scene deserves more study, since it seems to be telling several different stories at the same time. By tilting your head and looking from the other side, as though the stone was lying on its left side, another set of images can be seen.

At the midsummer solstice the sun rises over a flattened, tree-lined hill to the northeast but since the northeastern circle and the Great Circle are surrounded by hills on three sides, one does not see the sun rising or setting at the same time or place as one would if the horizon was lower and flatter. So although the day is already well advanced, sunrise comes later and sunset earlier than it would do if the land were level.

From the Celtic Iron Age come many accounts of the old myths and legends, folklore and festivals associated with the seasonal activities of the farming calendar. The stories told people when to plough the land, when to sow seeds, when the first lambs would be born, when to harvest and when to cull the herds of cattle and sheep towards the end of the year. These events were often celebrated with special days in the social calendar.

There were eight special moments during the year; these included the four major highpoints of the solar cycle: the spring equinox, the midsummer solstice, the autumn equinox and the midwinter solstice. Then halfway between each of these four highpoints came four more special days, giving the rather strangely named Quarter Days. The Celtic quarter days were Imbolc, Beltane, Lugnasadh and Samhain, and festivals were held on special days near the beginning of February, May, August and November. But it is likely that long before the development of iron casting these seasonal festivals were already very ancient.

Therefore I think that each of the eight stones in the northeastern temple represented a different time of year, namely the four quarter days plus the two equinoxes and the two solstices. The eight stones of the northeast temple could also have symbolised the eight milestones of a human lifetime, those of birth, childhood, adolescence, adulthood, marriage, parenthood, old age and finally, death.

There is also another function that the northeast temple may have represented, that of a calendar linked to the cycle of the planet Venus. We know from historical records that the Aztecs celebrated and recorded the fact that every 584 days the planet Venus has a heliacal rising as a morning star, (its first appearance at dawn just before the rising of the sun). Five of these Venus cycles correspond to eight solar years. In European classical mythology, Venus was often linked to a goddess, such as Artemis or Diana the huntress, so it is equally probable that Venus had a special place in Neolithic religious culture. Other heliacal risings of stars or groups of stars, such as the Pleiades, have also been used in antiquity to calibrate quite accurate calendars. However, the positioning of the northeastern circle at Stanton Drew suggests more of a symbolical significance, rather than providing scientifically accurate sightlines to important calendar events on the skyline. As with many stone circles, the arrangement of the standing stones of the northeastern temple was probably intended as a sort of map of celestial and seasonal events during the year, rather than reflecting any scientifically precise astronomical alignments. (However the southwestern temple at Stanton Drew would have provided a much better observation point for the annual risings and settings of the sun and those of the moon.)

Close to the northeast temple are the remains of two short avenues, one leads into the northeast circle and the other, the longest, joins the Great Circle from the northeast. As usual, the stones in the avenues are a mixture of sculptures and symbols. One of the more interesting ones in the longer of the two avenues is shaped like the rounded head of an animal, probably a wild cat or possibly a red squirrel. Although now faded and eroded it was originally a very complex work of art. There were many small and medium sized full-length images of people, including a scene along the bottom of the northern face of the stone that showed a group of adults and seated children. Just left of the centre is a picture of a man wearing a hat with what I think are feathers at the back, he has a very bushy beard jutting out of his chin and he is looking to the right, towards a smaller seated figure of a man in left profile. Just above this man's right shoulder is the head of a wild cat, or perhaps it's a lynx. It is also interesting to note that the short second avenue goes uphill and joins the northeastern

temple at such an angle that it would be quite natural to enter the circle in an anti-sunwise direction, this is quite unusual and it may suggest that the avenue was the exit rather than the entrance. In Christian terminology travelling anti-clockwise is called 'widdershins' and must not be done 'for fear of rousing the Devil'. This is probably a garbled reference to an old pagan tradition of moving around sacred sites in the same way as the sun. It is probably a bit of propaganda handed down to us by sanctimonious people who did not appreciate the fact that pagan rituals were still being re-enacted in some rural areas!

Many of the prehistoric sites that still exist in the British Isles are in quite remote areas and one sometimes wonders why they were built there when there was so much space to choose from, perhaps they are just the survivors of far more sites than those that still exist today. Stanton Drew has always been an excellent location. The Chew Valley would have been a prime spot for agriculture since the rich soil could even have given two harvests a year in Neolithic times, when the climate was warmer than it is today. The site is also close to the third largest estuary in Europe and is only a few miles from the River Avon, which was the main route to the east by canoe. In winter, the Bristol Channel and the Severn Estuary are home to tens of thousands of migrant wildfowl, including game birds such as geese, swans and ducks. But throughout the year the estuary was a haven for seafood, with over twenty varieties of fish available. In addition to all the wildfowl, fish and shellfish, the nearby sea provided another precious commodity, salt. This was needed not just to enhance the taste of food but also to act as a preservative of meat and fish. In addition, the wooded valley would have been home to a variety of game, including wild boar, red and roe deer.

All this potential food meant that the area could support a relatively large population all year round. But life for the farming community was not always easy, since many were trapped in a never-ending, backbreaking cycle of plough, sow, weed and harvest. But it didn't end there, once harvested the grain had to be dried, stored, processed and then ground up for flour. (The true origins of the phrase, 'the daily grind'.) The lives of farmers and their families have been governed by this routine since agriculture first started in the Middle East around ten thousand years ago. As a result, farming people became highly sensitive to the cycle of the changing seasons. In addition there were the life cycles of their livestock and the animals and birds of the natural world: courtship, mating, birth, growth, life, and finally death, followed by a new generation and a new cycle.

The long-term success of the community depended on good harvests and the fertility of their herds of domesticated animals. In addition to nature's autumnal bounty in the form of fruit, nuts and berries, the first farmers had to store and conserve the food that they produced so that they could last through the cold winters and into the early part of spring. Excess animals had to be killed in late autumn, to help conserve winter feed for young animals, breeding females and a few stud males. The colder nights helped keep the meat fresh and it would have been a good time to make bacon, sausages and ham from the pigs they raised and then dried, smoked or salted the meat. Foods such as these have been a staple of our winter diet for thousands of years.

The people of Stanton Drew would have been very familiar with the natural cycle of the seasons. They could not have failed to notice that as the sun rises further to the southeast each day the amount of heat and light become weaker and weaker. The sun rises further south and lower in the sky until at the winter solstice its position at sunrise seems to stay in the same place for several days. Then the cycle changes and the sun is reborn and returns northward, growing stronger with each passing day. In spring, Nature itself is reborn with an explosion of plant and animal life, which we still welcome today. The cold winter is over and life renews itself.

Gradually spring turns to summer, the days become warmer, then hot and the harvest ripens, animals that were born in spring grow fast and reach adolescence. But all too soon the sun's power lessens and the summer heat is over and autumn comes again. The nights draw in and the days become colder. Then winter arrives. However the weather is not constant from year to year. The farmers may have got an early spring and a long summer or alternatively a long winter and a short summer. So the farmers would have needed a basic calendar to keep track of the farming year, particularly when it came time for sowing, since a temporary warm period towards the end of winter could easily be mistaken for the first days of spring, with disastrous results for the new shoots if the seeds were planted too early. The grain could sprout and then freeze solid, then thaw and rot in the ground, with the likelihood of a disastrously poor harvest later in the year. The maintenance of a calendar would also have been a priority for the priesthood, so that religious festivals could be held at the right times, to coincide with important moments of the solar and lunar cycles.

THE SOUTHWESTERN TEMPLE

The southwest temple (south southwest) is situated much farther away from the Great Circle than the northeast temple is. The circle is on higher ground, about 15 metres above the rest of the site, in a small field to the south. An important feature of this circle is its dominant position. In the past this would have given a 360-degree view although because it is on higher ground it is hidden from the other circles. And this suggests that it was the first temple to be built at the site. Various authors have given a surprising variety of measurements from the centre of the Great Circle to the centre of the southwest temple and yet the distance has not changed in thousands of years. The distance between the edges of the Great Circle and the southwestern circle is about 450 feet (137 metres). The same sort of variation in distances is true for the diameters of the different temples and I think what is needed is a definitive survey, based on the original positions of the stones before they fell over. The remains of the southwest temple are scattered around the edges of a low mound and none of the stones are standing upright. In summer they are often covered by long grass, so the temple is nowhere near as impressive as it would be if the stones were still standing. Some of them are geometrically shaped stones, which would have marked important seasonal and calendrical positions of the sun and moon. The tallest stone in the circle would probably have marked midwinter sunset in the southwest. However, the stones are no longer in their original positions, they have been dragged around, and some were used in a nearby wall and then returned to the circle.

There are twelve stones, (plus a small one in the middle, but this might have been added more recently) and I find that number significant since each stone could have represented a lunar month in the year, (although some years had twelve moons and other years had thirteen moons). For the people who lived near such an important site as Stanton Drew, it would have been vital to know the date for all sorts of reasons, to measure the passing years, for agricultural purposes and to predict the dates of festivals and ceremonies long in advance, so that people would know when to come. Women in particular always needed to know when it would be their next moon time, so they could plan accordingly and if their menstruation didn't start on time, they knew they were pregnant and could then work out when they would give birth.

Today there are twelve signs of the zodiac and although most astronomers and scientists are very sceptical about the influences of the stars and planets on humans, it does not alter the fact that over the millennia countless millions of people have believed very differently. Astrology has been with us for a very long time and has been used all over the world by different cultures at different times. (The earliest known Chinese characters are to do with divination.) I think that it is more likely that when they were making horoscopes, the ancients determined the time of conception, rather than using the time of birth for their predictions. Ceremonies involving ritual fertilisation can be easily arranged in advance, whereas the date and time of a birth is much more difficult to predict. One can imagine a cult worshipping Venus trying to make sure that more children were conceived under the beneficial light of its presence at the time of its greatest brilliancy. And one optimum time would have come every eight years, when Venus rises as a morning star just before the sun rises on the first day of the Neolithic New Year, the first morning after the winter solstice. So Venus, could also have been celebrated at Newgrange, and it may even have been symbolised by the eight crosses on the front edge of the window above the entrance.

Winter sunset in the southwest symbolises death and, given the size of the circle, with a diameter of 145 feet (44 m) it is very likely that the centre of the temple was used for celebrating the lives of the dead. Excavation is necessary to determine if, like several other stone circles, it was used for cremating the bodies, particularly since there is an absence of barrows or Neolithic graves around this part of the Chew Valley. The nearest chambered tomb is the Fairy Toot, nearly five miles away , near the village of Butcombe and this tomb did not belong to the Stanton Drew community. The position and alignment of the southwest temple reinforces the idea of cremation, after all, cremating bodies is smelly and so the additional height would help keep the smoke away from the rest of the site.

THE GREAT CIRCLE

There is an old local story that the stones of the enormous Great Circle at Stanton Drew are uncountable. This is probably due to the way that buried stones surface and then disappear again beneath the grass according to the season. Consequently the number of visible stones varies from year to year. Currently we know the positions of twenty-seven stones, although until there is a proper excavation we cannot know for sure how many others there were.

It was when I was walking round the Great Circle at Stanton Drew many years ago that I first noticed something special, something that seemed to have escaped everyone else's attention. I suddenly realised that, instead of being just lumps of natural rock, all the stones had been deliberately shaped. I saw that the outline of every stone was made up of parts or combinations of the three most basic geometrical shapes: circles, squares and triangles. There were nearly round stones, half circles, crescents, squares, oblongs, isosceles triangles and right-angled triangles.

One of the reasons that the stones have escaped such attention, until now, is perhaps because so many stones have fallen over. If all the stones of the Great Circle had still been standing upright, their shapes would have been much more obvious, as it is you need to examine each fallen stone individually, to work out how it would have looked when it was upright. Some of the stones are partly buried, others completely buried and some are missing. Some stones have fallen forward, others sideways and some have fallen backwards. And some of the stones have been moved and are no longer in the position where they once stood. In time I realised that, along with other stone circles, the symbol stones were originally positioned around a circle as a representation of places on the 360-degree horizon. They were arranged like a map, so that they could serve as a focus of attention and direction for rituals and ceremonies linked to the annual movements of the sun and the different cycles of the moon. But at Stanton Drew most of the horizon is not level, so many of the positions of the stones are due to local conditions and not the usual compass bearings associated with important rising or setting positions of the sun or the moon. So because the alignments were not always scientifically precise, I figured that what was more important was the correlation of a particular stone with a specific time of day and time of year and different stones related to sunrise at the spring equinox, sunrise at the midsummer solstice or the midwinter solstice sunset.

At Stanton Drew, certain symbol stones acted as a reminder of specific events such as the full moon, the two half-moons and the new moon, the lunar swing cycle, the points of the compass and possibly constellations of the brightest stars. Some of the artwork on the standing stones of Stanton Drew must also refer to religious and mythical associations of calendar events, in a similar fashion to the way that many religions celebrate special events in their own sacred calendars, by worshipping at special shrines or in front of particular religious images in their chapels, churches or temples.

The phase of the moon varies according to the time of the month. The moon changes from a left-facing crescent at new moon, waxes until completely round at full moon, then wanes to become a right-facing crescent at old moon and so, for the very first time, I realised that certain monthly lunar phases were reproduced on the ground in the same sequence, in stone. For example, the round

THE GREAT CIRCLE AT STANTON DREW

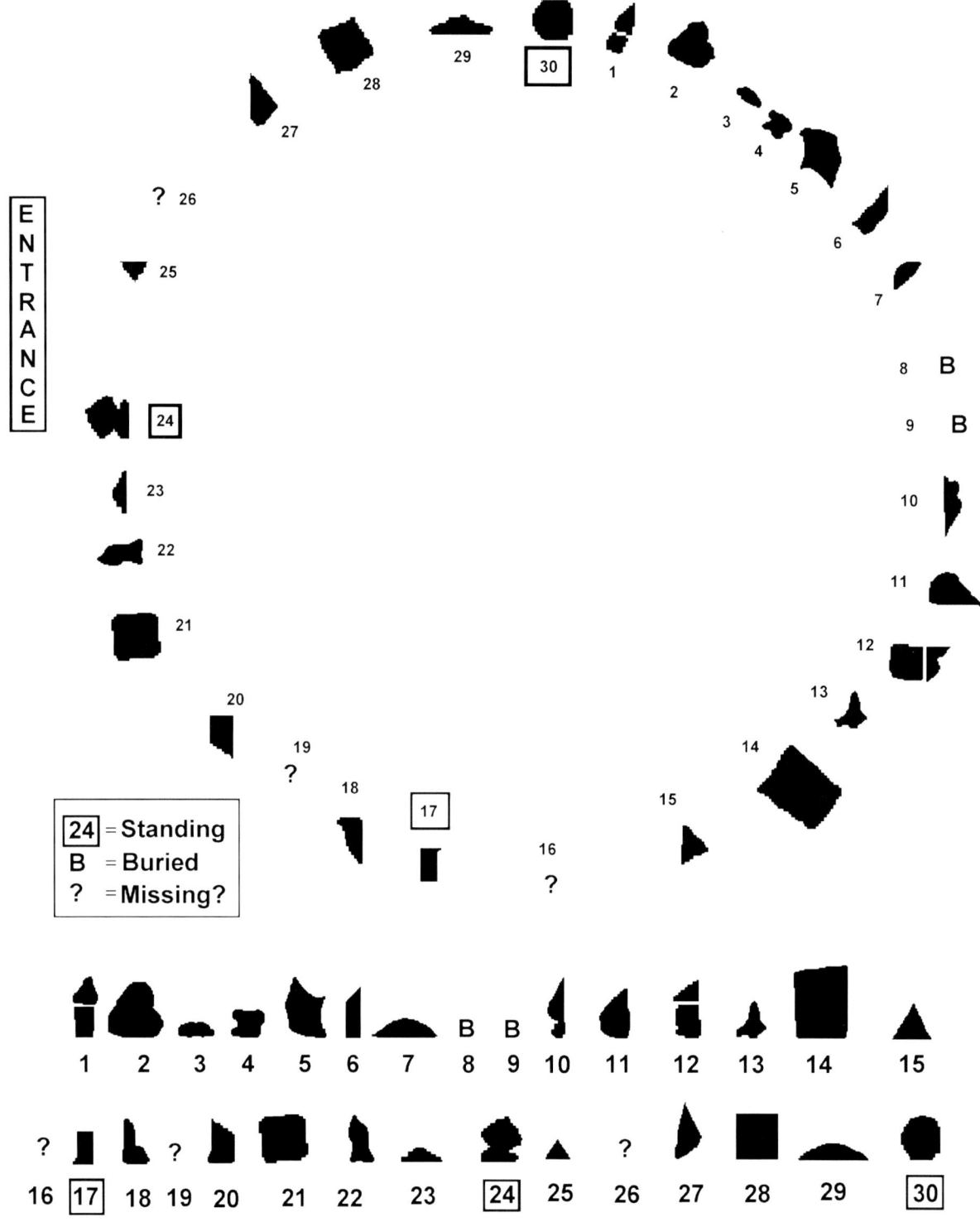

Many of the stones have fallen forwards, backwards or sideways and are lying in long grass. As a result, this plan is just intended as a guide. Only a professional survey, following excavation of the stones, will allow a much better interpretation of the shapes, position and astronomical meaning of the individual stones.

stone (30) in the northern sector probably represented the waning full moon and there are several different types of crescent (such as stone 7) around the circle to mark other lunar phases.

So I think that these stones were used as a reminder, and that by counting them in the correct sequence of stones you could tell how many days it would be before the next important ceremony. In other words, it was a Stone Age calendar... It was also a major step forward for me, I realised that instead of developing a written language, our ancestors had invented the next best thing, a language of permanent symbols.

There may even have been intentional gaps in the circle to denote the new moon, where no moon is visible for three nights. One of the gaps in the circle is due south and the side of the stone next to it (17) is divided into three by two diagonal lines. So if you were using the stones as a calendar, the missing part of the sequence, where stone 16 should stand, could mean 'no moon'. The entire lunar phase cycle is of twenty-nine and a half days and since stone 15 is a small triangle next to a much larger oblong stone (number 14), so stone 15 may refer to the half-day of the monthly cycle. (In a similar fashion to sarsen 11 at Stonehenge, which stands next to a full-size sarsen stone.)

In the same way as a sentence may not contain every single letter of the alphabet, the various codes at Stanton Drew are not complete sequences. The complete codes will need to be worked out by using symbol stones from other circles as well. The shape of the each of the stones may also have a second meaning and this refers to numbers. A circle has one side, the circumference; a semicircle has two sides, a round side and a flat side; a triangle has three sides and a square has four sides. Other numbers are obtained by adding the shapes together, for example, a triangle on top of a square, three sides plus four sides, gives seven. Some of the shapes bear a marked similarity to numbers and perhaps early numbers were written down in the form of these sorts of shapes.

For example, the number 8, is the combined shape of two circles (moons) and there are eight phases in two lunar cycles (eight weeks). As we saw with bluestone number 49, the symbol for midsummer sunrise is just like the number 1, an oblong with a slanted top and at Stanton Drew the chisel-shaped stone number 6 (which has rolled over) represented the summer solstice sunrise.

So I reasoned that it was the shape of the stone that served as a reminder of the event that it represented. Once you had been taught the meaning of all the shapes, the circle came to life in your mind, as a map of the cosmos and a representation of your religious beliefs.

Southwestern side of Great Circle stone 24

Stone 24 is a very strangely shaped stone, made up of a triangle behind an oblong. It is a very complex sculpture and represents the direction of sunset at the time of both spring and autumn equinox in the western sector. Each side of this stone shows a different group of eroded sculptures of people and animals. The view from the southwest shows several multiple images, including a complex group of strange creatures with a cat-like animal in the middle. This animal is standing upright with its paws raised high to hold a small creature lying on its back. The upper surface of the stone shows a sculpture of a face in left profile looking upwards to the heavens. In a previous era, the stone was upside down, and, since these carvings are very crude in comparison to the newer ones I have described, I think that this stone is very ancient indeed and in view of the erosion I think it was probably the first stone on the site. It reminds me of the Heel Stone at Stonehenge.

Northeastern side of Great Circle stone 24

One of the few stones still standing, stone number 17, marks the southern sector, with the remains of the Great Circle curving round to the east and west. Each side of stone 17 shows different sculptures. On the broad face towards the south are some large but very eroded carvings of people. The eastern side shows the left profile of the head and body of a flat-faced man, wearing a coat and hood. He has a rather stumpy arm at his left side.

Great Circle stone 17

(This picture reminds me of the small, thirty-two thousand year old, sculpture of *'the Lion Man'*, which was found in one of the Hohlenstein Stadel group of caves in the Swabian Alb, Germany.)

Directly opposite this stone, across the circle, is stone number 30, which marks the northern sector of the Great Circle. This stone is like a circle with the right hand side flattened, a bit like a letter D, but the other way round. Stone 30 was a very complex work of art, a real masterpiece, although it is faded and eroded today and the artwork is best seen when there is strong side lighting, near sunrise in summer or sunset in winter. There are several large images that were subsequently decorated in the multiple and composite style, with hundreds of tiny engravings and carvings of little people. However, this major alteration of the original surface has meant that the stone has suffered extensive erosion over time and these images are hard to see without image intensification. In the bottom left are several lions, large cats and a lynx with a dark muzzle and whose front and back left legs are delimited by cracks running half way up the stone. Above these cats, in the top left half of the stone, is the left profile of a large mythical animal with a broad face. This creature is perched on top of many other images of people. The area just below its eyes is a multiple image and it forms the head of a man wearing a fur hat who is looking to the right. To his right is a slightly shorter man in left profile, his left ear is quite visible. This is also a multiple image of another man with dark hair and a short black beard.

Great Circle stone 30

One of the most obvious images that remain is that of a large central figure, in right profile, of a man who is stooping over and surrounded by a crowd of other people. He is smiling and has a very pronounced jaw. Just below his chin are two smaller images of a young man and a woman. They are sitting next to each other and both looking to the left. The young man is wearing a white hat and the young woman has quite a dark face and is wearing a headscarf tied on with a braided band. To the left is another figure, this time of an older man with a beard and who is wearing a broad brimmed hat. Above and behind them is a priest who is wearing a headdress that looks a bit like a helmet. (This multiple image is within the right shoulder and body of the man with the big jaw.) I think this whole image is a wedding ceremony.

Opposite the young couple, on the right side of the stone, is quite a large picture of another standing figure in left profile. The left shoulder and body of this man forms a multiple image of a prancing horse, which is also the curly hair on the head of a young man in three-quarter right profile. The horse's foreleg forms the young man's forehead and nose. Running along the bottom of the stone is a long frieze of at least seven people who are sitting or squatting down. The most noticeable of these is a man with a pointed chin and a goatee beard. He is wearing a large fur hat. The stone itself is a massive sculpture and it reminds me of an animal's head, although of what creature I don't know. Stone 30 is on the north side of the Great Circle, and, in addition to being a representation of the waning full moon, the stone may represent the star Deneb, which was the northern polar star five thousand years ago.

New geophysics surveys by Bath and Camerton Archaeological Society (BCAS) in 2009 and 2010, revealed another entrance into the Great Circle from the southwest. (The original entrance/exit was along the second avenue, towards the local midsummer sunrise position in the east northeast.) The new surveys also revealed that there had been three rings of posts within the southwestern circle.

THE COVE

In the garden of the local pub, the Druid's Arms, is another megalithic structure that is known as the Cove. This was a wide, box-like arrangement of large stones originally comprising two uprights and a long, broad back stone. This is made of a different kind of stone to the rest of the site, dolomitic brecchia and when new would have shone brightly in the sun or by moonlight 4,500 years ago. By 1723, the back stone had already fallen over and since then it has split into two pieces. The larger of the two upright stones is very obviously artificially shaped and it was one of the first clues I had that our ancestors were skilled artists as well as stonemasons. The western face of this stone is in the form of a hafted axe and, although heavily weathered today, it was originally covered with many small images and faces arranged in a circular fashion around a central figure.

The gap between the two uprights is about two metres wide and this makes me think the Cove was originally used as a mortuary platform to store the bodies of the dead. If so, it is possible that dead bodies were placed on wooden scaffolding, ready to be carried in a funeral procession for cremation. The alternative is that the bodies were just left to decay naturally. Corpses rot away quite quickly under the effects of fly maggots and scavenging birds and animals. This process is known as excarnation or sometimes, sky burial.

These events occur at very specific times and I think it probable that the cremations were timed after sunset, when the funeral pyre would be most visible against the night sky and the rising smoke would take away the spirits of the dead, perhaps to journey to the moon or the stars. The Cove faces southeast, towards the winter sunrise and the summer moonrise, in other words at special times it is lit by the sun during the day and the full moon by night. I think the Cove predates the construction of the three temples because of its shape, rock-type and position. The southwest circle was probably the next to be constructed and then came the henge and roundhouse of the Great Circle. Then the northeastern temple was added, since there is an alignment from the centre of the northeast circle to the centre of the southwest temple. This alignment gives the most southerly moonset position. (The mass of broken and disturbed stones in the northeastern circle may also be the remains of a cove-like structure or perhaps some sort of shrine.) Only a few Coves are known, each is in a circle henge and there is one at Avebury, another at Arbor Low in Derbyshire and a third, far away at Cairnpapple in West Lothian, 15 miles to the west of Edinburgh. A recent geophysics survey (in 2009) suggested that the Cove was in fact the entrance to a chambered tomb, but until the site is properly excavated, the exact nature of the structure, and its meaning, are still unsure. It is also thought that it may predate the circle by many centuries, but again, until there is some firm dating of the henge ditch and this tomb it is unwise to speculate too much about it.

So why were there three different open-air temples at Stanton Drew? As I have said many times before, the northeast is associated with midsummer, the high point of the annual solar cycle and a celebration of life, whilst the southwest is associated with winter and death. The Great Circle would have been at the centre of everything. If there was indeed a huge roundhouse in the middle then it was their home, and it would have witnessed the birth of their babies, the everyday life of the community and the death of the old and the seriously ill. So I think that the annual cycle of birth, life and death was symbolically represented at Stanton Drew by the three circles and each of them represented one aspect of the three parts of the natural cycle of birth, life and death. This everlasting cycle would have been celebrated by ceremonies performed at the different temples. The carvings, sculptures and engravings on special stones would have been used to record religious themes as well as to picture different myth and legends and mark astronomical events and important calendar dates.

Like many other great ritual and ceremonial sites I think that Stanton Drew must have been an important centre of learning, so I think I had better explain my reasons for thinking this. Firstly its location. Stanton Drew is in a secluded area but close to an ancient river port, which was later to become the city of Bristol. Secondly, at several sites I have seen carved scenes of old men wearing long white beards, with children and young people sitting round them, listening. Thirdly, Stanton Drew is unusual and unique in that it had three circles and that the largest may well have contained a huge roundhouse. And lastly, there must have been some sort of organised diffusion of ideas, knowledge, artistic skills and religious beliefs because although each of the thousands of stone circles across the country was unique yet they were all based on common principles. At every site there are different systems of symbolic geometrical shapes, as though there was a selective use from a collection of accumulated knowledge and each designer used his or her own ideas for the construction of their local temple. As with so many other cultures, the religious and astronomical knowledge and techniques of construction and decoration of stone temples had to be diffused from centres where people could learn what to do and how to do it, in the same way as stone axes, flint tools and pottery were distributed from their centres of production. At a time when communication and travel was slow, students would have needed a place to stay for extended periods learning their trade and where better than a secluded place away from the main religious centres but in a location that was accessible and well provisioned, Stanton Drew.

The complex as a whole looks like an ideal place to teach the accumulated knowledge and wisdom of hundreds of years of cultural, religious and astronomical endeavour. There was plenty of room for living accommodation. The local farming and hunting community could easily support a lot of people through agriculture, rearing livestock, and from hunting, foraging and fishing. And although the stones are now badly weathered, initially the artwork was superb and so I think there must have been some sort of formalised training or apprenticeship for the artists and stonemasons that created the temples of Stanton Drew.

In societies that did not have written records, knowledge was learnt by heart, in the same way as an actor learns his lines. And indeed many epic poems were remembered in this way; the works of Homer such as *'The Iliad'* and *'The Odyssey'* were recited for many hundreds of years before they were finally written down. The thousands of lines of verse in the Viking Sagas were all learnt by heart, before finally being recorded in ink and in the Middle East, the local exploits of Alexandra the Great are still related by professional storytellers, nearly two thousand years after the events they describe.

In the Neolithic and Bronze Age the same oral techniques would have been used to learn and then pass on to the next generation the accumulated knowledge and history of their people, including their religious ideology and mythology, and their astronomical knowledge. Such knowledge, sometimes in the form of poetry and stories, was essential to the continuity of cultures and was an important part of maintaining the status quo, since those who were prepared to undergo years of intensive training kept all the real knowledge and the power that went with it.

I have seen several pictures of people wearing crowns, these are usually old men wearing long beards and surrounded by other people. The crowns are usually simple rings, probably of gold, and I think that they were a token of the priesthood, rather than of royalty. The golden crown may have been a symbol of the sun and the stone circle. My interpretation of this is that 'Your head was inside the circle and the circle was inside your head'. In other words, the wearer of the crown had achieved mastery of the circle, and all the astronomical, symbolic and mythological knowledge of their culture, and he was a sort of master of knowledge or High Priest. (If this sounds a bit fanciful on my part, then just think of how different headwear is used to denote special roles in modern society, everything from the mortarboard of a Professor, to the domed helmet of a policeman and the mitre of the Archbishop of Canterbury).

If we now look at the whole site again we see that it fulfils several roles, including religious, astronomical and practical ones. The three circles were probably linked to ceremonies involving birth, life and death; there were perhaps stone calendars for calculating and commemorating the cycles of the moon, the sun and Venus. With the temples we also have other levels of symbolism. When the midsummer sun rises in the northeast, the midsummer full moon sets in the southwest. When the midwinter sun sets in the southwest, the winter full moon rises in the northeast. So according to the time of year, the smaller northeastern and southwestern circles represented the extreme positions of the sun and the moon (summer), or, the moon and the sun (winter), although in each case the Great Circle always represents the Earth. In addition, the northeast temple perhaps represented Venus, the Great Circle the Earth and the southwest temple, the Moon. Three lots of Trinities.

With the small avenue leading into the circle we also have a womb in the northeast temple and the soul leaving as the corpse is cremated in the southwest temple, and the body was where people lived in the Great Circle roundhouse. Womb, body and soul, another Trinity. To a stranger, unaware of all the symbolism and the hidden meanings involved, the temples were just three circles of stones standing in some fields near a river.

At Stanton Drew, there is also an alignment from the centre of the southwestern temple through the centre of the Great Circle and from there across the River Chew, to an outlying stone called Hauteville's Quoit, a distance of about two-thirds of a mile (360 metres) away. This was originally a huge stone some thirteen feet high (4m) and it lies fallen and buried in the ground in the hedge next to the Pensford road, close to Quoit Farm.

It is now about seven feet long (2.2 m). The folklore quoted by John Aubrey, in 1664, claims that this was a stone thrown by a man called Hakewell (probably named after Sir John Hauteville 1216-72) from the top of Maes Knoll, about two kilometres to the north. There are several other country tales from our folklore about the throwing of large stones or quoits, usually by the Devil. The most famous of these is the Friars Heel, more commonly known as the Heel Stone at Stonehenge...There is also a row of three very tall standing stones that are known as the Devil's Quoits, near Boroughbridge, North Yorkshire.

Hakewell's Quoit is at the end of a long alignment from the centre of the SW temple and through the Great Circle, although from the main site it is now hidden behind a large barn at Quoit Farm. It has been claimed that this stone was used to mark the position of the midsummer sunrise. This is impossible since at the summer solstice the sun cannot be seen until it rises above the flat hill much further round to the east. Instead, I think the Quoit marked the boundary of the sacred area around the Temple and that the footpath which lead around it, has now become the main road from Chew Magna to the A37, the main route south from Bristol to Pensford and on towards Shepton Mallet.

On the map drawn by Seyer in 1821, he shows the position of two other stones in a field called Lower Tyning, about 760 yards to the west of the circles. These two stones could have marked the outskirts and entrance to the sacred site for people going towards the Cove or onwards to the south. In 1723, Stukeley said there was another outlying stone to the west, also near the road to Chew Magna but this has now disappeared. Perhaps it was broken up and used to repair the road, just as the Quoit was. The River Chew also provides a natural boundary to the site and, because of the bend, encloses the site on two sides. About a mile to the north of Stanton Drew, near Maes Knoll, is the end of a cross-country track that runs all the way to Bath and on to Avebury and beyond. It was the main trackway linking Avebury to Stanton Drew and then onwards towards the southwest and into Devon and Cornwall. This track was later changed and widened and many centuries later became known as the Wansdyke.

Maes Knoll, high above the nearby village of Norton Malreward, is an interesting place to visit.

Although originally of Neolithic origin, it was turned into a fortified hilltop during the Iron Age, but a few centuries ago the wall of stones that were part of the defences were cast down and pushed down the wooded hillside at the back. The footpath approaching the knoll opens out into a wide plateau that has a natural curved bank with tiers on the right, a bit like a natural amphitheatre and one can imagine that it was used for meetings, games, shows and ceremonies.

Detail of stone 30, showing a few large composite images, which are made up of hundreds of small carved images of little people.

At its peak, Stanton Drew must have been an extraordinary site, with its stones freshly carved and painted and crowds of people bustling about at the time of major festivals. The site was used for many hundreds of years and during its lifetime had an admiring audience who would have travelled from far and wide to assist at the religious ceremonies, to gain knowledge as students, to admire the artwork or to come simply as tourists or traders.

I would suggest that such an important site as Stanton Drew has many, many more secrets to show us, and if we are ever going to truly understand the complex systems that our ancestors created at Stanton Drew, the site must be surveyed and excavated fully and the symbol stones must be re-erected to show the works of art in all their former glory, not lying face down in the dirt as they are now. We have a duty to our long-lost ancestors to renovate Stanton Drew, to excavate the site and to reveal the symbols, artwork, history and knowledge of a deceptively simple civilisation.

Our next destination is forty miles to the east of Stanton Drew, to the sacred landscape around the village of Avebury, in Wiltshire.

12 AVEBURY

Seven thousand years ago, long before the beginning of the Neolithic period, most of mainland Britain was covered in dense primeval forest. The earliest inhabitants lived mainly along the coastal margins of the sea or alongside rivers, lakes and streams, but deeper inland there were few people, just hunters and their families who lived in small, natural clearings within the ancient forest. They lived in a world that had yet to be tamed but their inherited bushcraft skills would have allowed them to live well from the wealth of resources that the natural world had to offer, for generation after generation. But things started to change dramatically when the first farmers arrived from the Continent, some six and half thousand years ago.

The newcomers cut down trees and cleared land to produce pastures for their livestock. In the beginning they raised cattle and pigs, sheep and goats and created small fields for their crops of emmer and einkorn wheat and barley. Later on they added oats, beans and peas to their diet. In the beginning the rate of change was slow and most of the indigenous population of foragers, hunters and trappers continued to live along the coasts or hunt in the forests for the elusive red and roe deer. They also fished for salmon, trout and eels in the rivers and shot wildfowl such as ducks, geese and swans with their bows and arrows. But for those who made the slow transition to farming, their way of life would be changed forever because they would be ruled by a new order, the never-ending cycle of the farming year. And as we saw in earlier chapters, this change in lifestyle created changes in the way people thought about their lives and about their place in the world.
In time these produced changes in their religious beliefs, which led to the development of circular temples of earth and wood, and later on, stone. Incidentally, the benefits of a food supply derived from agriculture have often been exaggerated, after all, foraging and hunting had worked consistently well for over a hundred thousand years. The change to agriculture was slow at first, since in comparison to the excitement of hunting and the relatively easy rewards gained from gathering Nature's bounty, the growing of crops lacked appeal. The change would mean settling down in one place and everyone could see that clearing the forest to grow crops and then processing the grain would be incredibly hard work. The benefits really needed to outweigh all the disadvantages before people would make the decision to radically change their traditional way of life. That is one reason why it took nearly two thousand years for the majority of the population to become farmers.

To the west, across the Irish Sea, some of the first farmers settled around Carrowmore, near Sligo, in northwestern Ireland, and later on new people farmed along the banks of the River Boyne in the east, where their descendants would eventually build the great passage tombs of Newgrange, Knowth and Dowth. The climate was warmer than at present and even before 3000 BC farming people had already settled in some of the islands far to the north. The places that were particularly attractive to the newcomers were the Western Isles and the Orkneys, where there were fewer trees but plenty of good grass for their cattle and sheep. Only when the population had increased a great deal did they build the great ceremonial centres around Calanais and Brodgar. Most of Ireland and mainland Britain was covered in an ocean of trees and only in a few places had people made any sort of real impact on the dense, deciduous forest. This was mainly a mixture of elm and ash, oak, hazel, and broad-leaf lime, with a few alder and willow along the riverbanks. Although people had lived on the south coast for generations, the heart of the ancient wildwood was almost impenetrable and it seems that few places were inhabited for very long. Travel was difficult and so that they did not get lost in the dense deciduous forest, travellers in those early times used the ancient trackways that kept to the higher ground. Over time these developed into a network of paths that crisscrossed the land and are still known as the Ridgeways. And around 3700 BC some of the earliest settlers in a part of the country that is now Wiltshire journeyed up the Ridgeway and set up a seasonal encampment on Windmill Hill, a mile or so to the northwest of Avebury. During the centuries that followed, people built a massive causewayed enclosure that had three circular banks and ditches enclosing an area of twenty one acres, eight and a half hectares.

Gradually the area became more settled and the community grew as more and more children were born and new people moved to the area. From then onwards the surrounding area developed further and further, to become a thriving community and eventually it became what some have called 'the sacred heartland of Neolithic Britain'. As the decades passed more and more trees were felled to create pastureland for the ever increasing flocks of sheep and goats and herds of cattle. Timber was also needed for housing, tools and fencing and a great deal of firewood would have been needed for cooking, lighting and heating.

As the years rolled by, the human impact on the landscape intensified and with the rise in population, they had the time and energy, and the desire and the need to construct several very large communal graves. The most famous of these is the West Kennet longbarrow, which is situated near the A4 road to Marlborough, a few miles to the south of Avebury. The barrow dates from about five thousand seven hundred years ago. At that time the surrounding countryside was still wooded and so communal graves such as these were often built just below the brow of a hill, so that they could be seen from below, yet had a panoramic view from the top. The main idea seems to have been that by storing the bones of the dead in a specially built sacred place, the ancestral spirits would watch over their descendants, and these beneficial spirits would always look after them and protect them from harm. This heritage also gave the people a sense of purpose and place in the world and they knew that, even after they were dead, they would be revered and still be an integral part of community life. In short, the land belonged to them and they belonged to the land.

Over the ensuing centuries the landscape of rolling chalk hills seems to have helped to inspire them to design and build a very diverse collection of sacred monuments. Some of these were arranged into some sort of preordained pattern, in which each temple or tomb could be seen from its neighbours and each was part of the overall scheme. Around five thousand itself. They dug an enormous, roughly circular ditch that was more than 8,000 feet (1.3 km) in circumference and was originally an incredible fifty-five feet deep (17 m.). At the top, the ditch was about seventy feet (21m) twenty-one metres wide, although this narrowed down to a width of about 16 feet (5 metres) at the bottom. The spoil that was removed was used to create a massive earthwork, a ring of chalk that was set back slightly from around the outside edge and as much create the ditch and the bank they removed in the order of one hundred and sixty-five thousand tons of chalk... The modern ditch is silted up with chalk from this bank so that is now less than a half of its original depth. Estimates for the original height of the bank vary from about 20 to 55 feet (6.5 - 17 metres). To make it even a more of an impressive feat, all of this backbreaking work was done without the help of any complex machinery. The digging and construction was just done with simple hand tools made from wood, bone or antler.

Over the next few centuries they started to erect a huge circle of about a hundred very large stones around the inside perimeter of the massive ditch. (Estimates about the number of stones vary, many think there were 98 stones and this is based on quite good evidence, however it is not a number that makes much sense in terms of design, it would make more sense if there had been a hundred stones, the same number of fingers on the hands of ten people.) They were massive sarsen stones, some weighing as much as sixty tons, from the nearby Downs, and this is exactly the same type of very hard sandstone that was used a few centuries later to build the sarsen ring and the massive trilithons at Stonehenge, a day's walk to the south. Inside Avebury's Great Circle they added two small circles of sarsens and two long processional avenues of even more standing stones. One, the Beckhampton Avenue, led into the henge from the west and the other, the West Kennet Avenue, joined the henge at the southeast and went up a valley to another sacred site on Overton Hill, now on the busy A4 and known as the Sanctuary.

The Sanctuary.

This now bears little resemblance to the site seen by Aubrey in 1685 or recorded by Stukeley after his visit in 1719. He wrote that the sanctuary was a charming place, of two concentric circles of standing stones and much admired by the local people. Five years later a local farmer by the name of Green removed the standing stones and ploughed up the land. Since the time of the first excavation, by Maud Cunnington in the early 1930's, the Sanctuary has been seen as a sequence of large wooden roundhouses, which were constructed over several centuries on the same site next to the Ridgeway and the orthodox view is that the Sanctuary served as a shrine and mortuary house for many centuries.

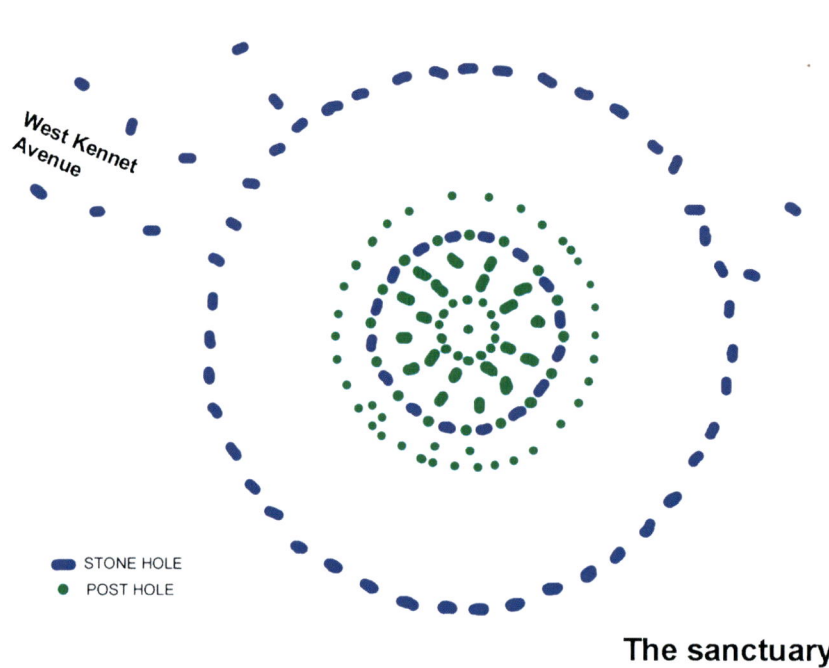

The sanctuary

The position of the two rings of standing stones that Stukeley saw is nowadays marked by sets of concrete oblongs, and inside these rings are small concrete posts, which mark the position of six rings of post-holes that have traditionally been seen as supports for the wooden buildings. The Kennet Avenue joined the Sanctuary at the northwest side of the outer ring of stones. This is quite an unusual direction for an avenue to join a stone circle. At Stanton Drew one avenue joins the Great Circle from the east, whilst another avenue joins the northeast temple from the southeast. At Stonehenge the Avenue joins the temple from the northeast, whilst at Calanais the avenue joins the circle from the north-northeast. This suggest to me that during ceremonial procession, people were entering the circle from the northwest, travelling towards the southeast, the direction of the midwinter sunrise and the start of a New Year and a New Life.

Stukeley's drawing of the Sanctuary, dated 8th of July 1723, shows that most of the stones had already fallen down, with just a handful remaining upright. In contrast to the monster stones of the main site, these were only waist-high stones, suggesting that at the time of construction only a small workforce had been available to move them from the Downs and this also suggests that the Sanctuary predates the main site by many centuries, simply because there were fewer people living in the area.

Once the ditch and bank of the henge had been constructed, they joined it to the Sanctuary by building a ceremonial corridor, the West Kennet Avenue. In May 1724 Stukeley wrote that during the previous winter the Sanctuary stones had been carted away and the land ploughed up by farmer Green, but I have since discovered that not all the stones disappeared, for in the lay-by across the A4 road are a dozen or so stones that are hidden in the long grass. And since some of them have been carved and shaped, I think that they may well be the remains of the original stone circles, so perhaps they could be moved back across the road to their former position, in place of some of the ugly concrete markers.

An excavation in 1999 by archaeologist Mike Pitts led him to make a re-evaluation of the Sanctuary and he has suggested that there never had been any wooden roundhouses there at all and that the Sanctuary was really just a series of five concentric circles of tall posts with two rings of standing stones. According to Pitts, the outer ring of posts acted as the supports for a fence that enclosed the concentric circles of stones and rings of freestanding posts. (However what has escaped most people's attention is the way that the third and fourth circles of posts form lines emanating from the centre - like the rays of the sun.)

For Mike Pitts, the Sanctuary was more likely to have been a temple or shrine, rather than a charnel house for bodies. The original excavation by Maud Cunnington in 1930 found only fragments of animal and human bones and one shallow, secondary burial of a young 'man' who had many broken bones and a skull that was crushed flat, but there are reports by both Aubrey and Stukeley that although the Sanctuary itself was clear, the ground nearby was the final destination for a mass of human bones from dozens of skeletons. Several other excavations in the area have also found human remains, including lower jawbones, as well as many Neolithic pottery sherds and numerous flint arrowheads. The shallow burial next to Stone C12 in the Sanctuary was the skeleton of an adolescent of about fourteen. This person was buried with their feet to the north, head to the south and they faced eastwards, towards the rising sun. It was often the case that Beaker women were buried with their head to the south, whilst men were usually buried the opposite way round. So it is likely that this was the skeleton of a young woman. Her meagre grave goods included a beaker and some animal bones and teeth. However, it would be unwise to think that these were the total sum of her possessions, for burial customs and funeral rites have always depended on a person's culture and religious beliefs, not just on their personal wealth.

Longbarrows were used for many, many centuries yet excavations have shown they rarely contained much in the way of grave goods. Apart from the bones of our ancestors and funeral urns, the tombs often contained just a few mundane items such as meat bones, flint knives and bits of broken pottery, the rubbish of funeral feasts and anniversary get-togethers. (But let's not forget that even in modern times we take little with us when we are buried or cremated. A lifetime of personal possessions are disposed of by bequeathing them to our family and friends or just thrown away.)

Only in a few cases were the grave goods of Neolithic people more than just a symbolic gesture, and only a few of the people who were buried in longbarrows took with them more than a favourite tool, choice weapon or a piece of jewellery. It is as though they would have no need for anything in the next life, either because they weren't going anywhere, or else because they thought that journey to the next world was only for the spirit or the soul, not for a person's body or any physical object. In some megalithic graves, both in Britain and in Denmark, the chambers contained groups of skulls and groups of long bones, with separate heaps for the vertebrae and other small bones all jumbled up together. It is as though the priests had kept the skulls separate because they had been using them for some sort of magical ceremony, perhaps at a time of great need, when the priests and the ancestors needed to get their heads together...

Much later on, during the Bronze Age, burials were no longer communal and important people were usually buried in individual round barrows. But even then only a small part of their possessions were buried with them, their real wealth was in their land, their crops, their livestock and their social standing. The most notable of the few burials with rich grave goods is that of the Bush Barrow chieftain, who was buried near Stonehenge with some rare gold ornaments, several bronze daggers and axes, and a small but very attractive stone mace. The excavation also showed that the man had worn a bronze helmet, for the remains of it lay next to his head. Another burial, sixteen miles to the south, was that of the Amesbury Archer, an immigrant from France who was buried with many of his belongings that included a great number of Beaker pots, bronze tools and weapons. Of course, people were rarely buried naked and it would probably have been customary for people to be dressed for their funeral in their finest clothes. Although their furs and woven fabrics have not survived in Britain, we know from several well-preserved ancient burials, in tree-trunk coffins in Denmark, that people were dressed to look their best for their last public appearance, just as they are today.

Over the centuries, there have been several small excavations at the main site at Avebury and many different theories as to its function and reasons for its construction. Harold St George Gray undertook the first major excavations over several digging seasons, between 1908 and 1922. Then, from 1934 until the outbreak of war in 1939, a wealthy businessman named Alexander Keiller excavated at Avebury, he cleared the henge, emptied the ditch of a huge amount of rubbish, cut down trees that had grown up in the wrong places and removed untidy sheds and buildings and demolished houses. He did his best to recreate the site, although hundreds of the megaliths had already been destroyed, particularly during the 18th Century. Keiller's excavations also gave us a better understanding of some of the details about the site that had not been recorded by Aubrey or Stukeley. He discovered buried and forgotten stones and re-erected as many as he could, particularly those of the South Circle and along the Kennet Avenue.

Some of the damage to the site may even go back to Roman times, when there was a purge of the Iron Age Druids in both France and Britain. In AD 54 Emperor Claudius ordered the desecration or destruction of many sacred sites of the old religions across Northern Europe. This was quite an unusual step since, rather than suppressing them, the Romans generally adopted and adapted local religions to their own culture as they enlarged their Empire. Later on a more systematic attack on the Avebury stones started in the 1300's when religious zealots destroyed many sculptures that they probably saw as some of the worst examples of pagan idols representing 'Devil Worship'. The damage continued slowly over the years, but from around 1700 onwards the process of destruction speeded up again when many stones were smashed up or buried by local land speculators, publicans and farmers. When Stukeley first visited Avebury, in 1723, much more of the site was intact than it is today and he was able to witness the remains of what had been achieved all those centuries before. He described the circle and two avenues of stones and recorded their sad decline as more and more of them were broken up. He saw how the stones were toppled over into specially dug fire pits containing wood and straw that heated up the stones until they were very hot. Next, water was poured in a line onto the stone and the surface struck with a heavy hammer. The sarsen stone would then break along the stress fracture caused by the sudden drop in temperature.

Over the next few years Stukeley developed the unusual idea that the Avebury complex had symbolised a snake, with the body of the serpent running along the Beckhampton Avenue, coiling up inside the henge and then running along the Kennet Avenue, with the head ending up at the Sanctuary. Unfortunately, to give credence to this strange theory he even went so far as to alter some of his old plans of the site and to rewrite his descriptions and findings. He also became obsessed with Druidism and founded a new belief system, *'the Ancient Order of Druids'*.

However, in spite of all this, we do owe him an enormous debt of gratitude, simply because he was one of the few eyewitnesses to record for posterity many of the things that have since disappeared. Since Stukeley's time, the site has changed considerably, and today's first-time visitor can find it hard to make sense of the ruins of this prehistoric wonder. The biggest problem of understanding Avebury is due to the presence of the modern village in the heart of the henge. It would be far easier for visitors to understand the temple as a whole without the presence of the buildings and the busy main road, the A4361 from Swindon to Devizes, which winds its way through the heart of the henge. It makes it hard to really appreciate the sheer size of the ditch and bank and the fact that is roughly circular. At the height of summer, the increased volume of traffic is particularly dangerous to the thousands of pedestrians that cross from one sector to another.

THE AVEBURY HENGE

Showing the full numbering & estimated positions of missing stones.
Also the estimated position of the original bank & ditch at the entrances.

This is an assembly of plans made by various artists at different times. Although every effort has been made to maintain accuracy it should only be regarded as an approximation.

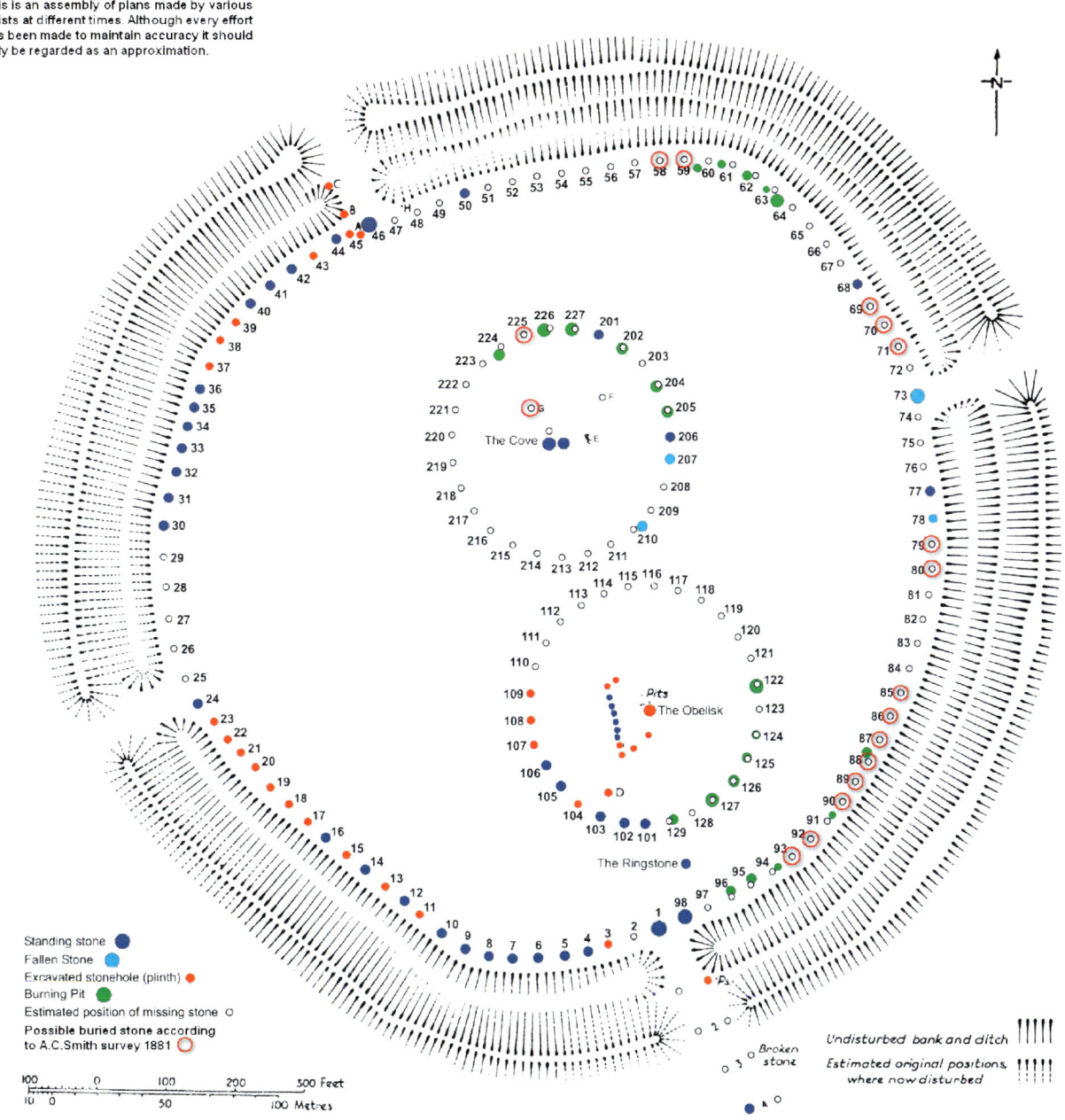

Plan courtesy of Peter Roberts 2011

Avebury is a World Heritage Site and a by-pass would solve some of these problems, and, without the incessant traffic passing through its heart, could even restore the henge to some of its former tranquillity.

In order to get a better understanding of Avebury one must first appreciate that the farming people who built the Avebury complex were very devout and very hard working. Their faith must have impacted greatly on their daily lives, because they were willing to expend a vast amount of energy on major construction projects in order to build their sacred places. The henge that they constructed was enormous. It was over a 1000 feet (>300m) in diameter and had four entrances, each of which was flanked later on by two massive guardian stones that acted as an impressive entrance portal. The ditch alone was a monumental task; especially since it was originally nearly twice the depth that it is today, and it has been estimated that they dug out an incredible 165,000 tons of chalk and earth, and piled it up on the outside of the ring, to form a high bank that was over a thousand paces in circumference. This is an astounding feat in its own right, especially when you consider the fact that it was all done by hand, just using simple tools, without any sophisticated earth-moving machinery. Even if they managed to remove a massive ten tons of spoil a day, every day, then it could still have taken them over forty years to complete the monumental task. Day after day, week after week, month after month, and year after year. And for many people this would have been the labour of their lifetime.

Some of the tools they used for digging into the hard chalk were made from the antlers of red deer. At a time before metals were around, the antler picks that they used were surprisingly efficient for the work that was done. They were made by cutting off most of the side branches, leaving just one thick tine at the bottom of the antler. They look a bit like the letter 'L' and were used as a sort of combination pick, lever and rake, and they probably used wooden spades and shovels as well. Other members of the teams would have used wicker baskets and rucksacks to carry away the spoil, and they would have used ropes, made from leather or the strong fibres of nettle plants or lime tree bark, to haul the chalk upwards and pile it onto the bank. When it was eventually finished, the bank would have shown up as a gigantic white ring, for at that time it was covered with the hard white tabular chalk from the bottom of the ditch. But nowadays the bank is green, because over the centuries a thin layer of wind-blown soil has built up and let the grass grow, although the underlying chalk does sometimes show through where the feet of thousands of visitors have passed, particularly along the top of the bank in the southeastern sector. (Incidentally, the idea of creating a huge white ring was also copied and adapted far to the north, in Yorkshire. The three henges at Thornborough, near Ripon, were built in a line running from northeast to southwest and each of the circular banks of soil was originally covered with a coating of sparkling white gypsum crystals.)

Archaeologists have found so many discarded antler picks at the bottom of large henge ditches that some of them think that the builders must have farmed red deer, because simply wandering around the woods and forests searching for the thousands of antlers that were shed in late spring, could have been a difficult and unrewarding task. (Although we now know them as living on moorland, red deer used to be mainly forest-dwelling animals). The farmers already had flocks of sheep and goats, herds of cattle and they raised pigs, so keeping semi-tame red deer in stockades would have had several benefits. It would have provided a guaranteed supply of venison to help feed the army of workers, the hides could have made into buckskin clothes and then there would have been a ready supply of tools from the cast antlers that the bucks shed each year in late spring. A good candidate for such a deer park would have been one of the large palisaded enclosures that were built down near the river, at West Kennet. Another of the curious things about these antler tools is that although many were just discarded and dumped in the bottom of the ditches, they were sometimes carefully buried in the soil, as though they were being planted, just like seeds. The tradition of burying the corpses of men with a full set of deer antlers was even older, since it dates back to the time of the hunters of the Mesolithic period and even beyond.

Archaeologists have often paid a great deal of attention to the weird and wonderful activities that were performed by some of our Neolithic ancestors. These included the digging of special pits and then using them to carefully bury odd things such as deer antlers, the skulls of cattle and deer, human and animal teeth and bones and sometimes charms and talismans such as small balls of chalk, special stones and pieces of worked flint. In some societies, these sorts of activities were often performed by witch doctors and medicine men and they give us a glimpse into an unfamiliar and alien world, one where the deliberate burial of goods and offerings seem to have been part of a magical act. The reason behind such an act could even have had a malicious intent, the forerunner of black magic and the casting of spells. Other reasons for the special treatment were perhaps as an act of appeasement to an evil spirit, or as thanks to the gods, or even as a prayer for good fortune. However, I think it can sometimes be a mistake to concentrate too much on such strange, mystical and magical rites, since they have sometimes overshadowed the more mainstream activities that would have taken place in the temples.

Although excavation has exposed the building techniques used, few excavations have revealed how stone circles were actually used, simply because the sacred area was often kept clean and clear of rubbish and all that has been found at many of the smaller sites is the odd bit of flint, a piece of charcoal or just a fragment of bone. But as I have tried to show in the preceding pages, the meaning and purpose of scared places was recorded in the form of special sacred symbolism and in the shapes and positions of special stones and in the works of art that were carved and sculpted on them. Digging holes in the ground has revealed little of this.

We should also remember that the activities on major sites, such as Avebury, Stanton Drew and Stonehenge, involved ceremonies and festivals that would have linked thousands of people to the high points of the cycles of the sun and the moon, and to the eternal cycle of Birth, Life and Death. Such special events marked the seasonal changes in the natural world, they celebrated important milestones in people's lives; and perhaps the stones were sometimes involved in special rites asking the gods for protection and for maintaining and increasing the fertility of the land and the fruitfulness of their herds, crops and families. Like festivals across the world, all these festivals and ceremonies would have been accompanied by the music of pipes and drums, and by chanting, singing and dancing. Then would have come the feasting and drinking. And sex.

The stone settings around the Avebury central enclosure date from after 2600 BC, long before their neighbours to the south began building Sunhenge. Although the exact start date for building the stone circles at Avebury is unknown at present, clearly such a gargantuan task would have taken many decades to complete, especially since some of the stones weighed more than fifty tons (the combined weight of eight adult elephants). Around the inner edge of the ditch they erected a circle of about a hundred standing stones. This arrangement is known as the Great Circle and inside this ring of stones were two much smaller open-air temples, the North and South Circles.

Although few remain today, the North Circle originally had twenty-seven standing stones. Inside this ring was a Cove, made from two tall uprights, one on each side of a wide back stone. The upright on the right side is missing. The South Circle was originally a circle of twenty-nine stones. To this was added an arrangement of small stones in the form of the letter D (a half-moon shape, known by scholars as the 'Z' feature) and in the middle there used to be an enormous rounded stone, known as the Obelisk, which was about twenty-one feet high (7m) and weighed over thirty tons.
In 1719, Stukelcy noted that there had originally been two long avenues of standing stones leading into and out of the henge. Each of these avenues was composed of about a hundred pairs of large stones and they are known as the West Kennet Avenue and the Beckhampton Avenue. Until quite recently the existence of the Beckhampton Avenue was disputed by many modern prehistorians, since even in Stukeley's day only a few traces of it could be seen and in modern times hardly any traces of it could be seen at all. But although he became a bit weird later on in his life, the Reverend Stukeley was usually a fairly reliable eyewitness and an excellent draughtsman, and he was eventually vindicated in 1999 by the discovery and excavation of some of the places where Avenue stones had stood. According to Stukeley, a Cove was also situated at the midpoint along each of the two Avenues.

When I first looked at a plan of Avebury I noticed that the arrangement of the two inner circles is quite peculiar, the axis across the centres of the two inner circles takes a different line to the one that you would expect. Instead of the axis going towards the midsummer sunrise position in the northeast, or towards the midwinter sunrise in the southeast, the axis seems to be based on the more unusual extreme lunar positions of the major moonrise in the south-southeast and the corresponding major moonset in the north-northwest. This immediately suggests that the two inner rings had a predominantly lunar function.

On his 1721 plan of the site, Stukeley called the northern circle, the lunar temple and the southern circle, the solar temple. And although this has often been criticised, it does seem logical to me.

However, as usual, things are much more complicated than they appear at first sight, for although it is quite easy to divide up a circle into four, eight, sixteen or thirty-two equal parts, it is far more difficult to set up circles of twenty-seven or twenty-nine megaliths of different sizes. So it must mean that the design was deliberate and that the choice of using such specific numbers for each of the inner rings must have been important.

Support for the idea that the northern circle was lunar is as follows: At the centre of the circle was a Cove and this was aligned roughly with the major northern moonrise. The northern ring had twenty-seven stones, and this is an important number, it could refer to the Draconic month of 27.212 days, the number of days that the moon takes to circle the earth and return to either the ascending or descending node. Or it could refer to the anomalistic month of 27.55455 days, the time between successive perigees, when the moon is closest to the earth. (This could be relevant at Calanais.)
In addition, several ancient cultures, including Babylonian, Egyptian, Hindu and Arabic, divided the sky into 27 or 28 mansions, usually centred around a prominent star, so that each stone in the Northern Circle at Avebury could have represented that mansion or star.

We have already seen multiple symbolism at many other prehistoric sites and have seen how the ancient artists illustrated more than one idea at a time with their multiple imagery, so perhaps the northern circle was a temple to the moon and a *'Temple of Death'*. And bodies were left in the cove for twenty-seven days, before the remains were removed for burial elsewhere, perhaps in the nearby longbarrows of East or West Kennet, or at Millbarrow, Manton, Old Chapel, Longstone, South Street, Horslip or many of the others, now lost and forgotten. (The U-shape of the cove also suggests a womb, a place where the dead could be reborn.)

The south circle had twenty-nine stones and I think that this must have been a reference to the phases of the synodic lunar month; this would also correspond to the monthly menstrual cycle of women, so in theory this would make it another lunar temple. But one of Stukeley's sketches shows that the destroyed Obelisk at the centre was quite a phallic stone and he also said that it was circular at the base. These sorts of stones have often had an important role in local folklore, they were said to promote fertility, love and health and it doesn't take much to imagine a circle of women and girls dancing around such a stone on the night of a full moon, in a bid to find a husband or to be blessed with a much-wanted child. At Kerveltré, near St Jean Trolimon in Brittany, France there is a tall, but now sadly shortened and damaged, very phallic-looking stone that was recarved in the Iron Age. An old postcard, dating from around 1900, shows a circle of a dozen women, wearing traditional Breton bonnets and dresses, holding hands and standing in a circle around the original stone, and looking rather embarrassed about the whole thing...

With the Obelisk in the centre of the ring, the overall design of the South Temple at Avebury would have looked like a cylinder within a circle. And in effect, this was quite a blatant way of representing the sexual act, since it was indicative of the way that it needed a male organ to impregnate the womb of a female in order to create new life. So I think that they planned the southern circle to symbolise the sun and the moon, male and female and it was a *'Temple of Life'* but the northern circle with its cove was just lunar, feminine and a *'Temple of Death'*. And yet again we see the same themes of duality present in many Neolithic religious centres: Sun and Moon, Male and Female, Life and Death.

So why did they go to all the trouble of building such an enormous earthwork surrounding the great circle and the two inner temples? It is hard to be sure, but it certainly makes sense to me that they would have tried to create a monument that incorporated as many aspects of divine symbolism as possible. And that it would probably be like so many other sites and have several layers of meaning, in other words, multiple symbolisms. When complete the site comprised a giant ring encompassing a huge circle of stones with two smaller circles inside. So, in addition to the other meanings outlined above, was it also the designers' intention to enclose within the high bank a representation of the world, with the sun and the moon moving across the heavens, like a mirror image of the sky acted out on the ground?

In an earlier chapter, we saw how the colossal burial mound at Newgrange in Ireland was a representation of the moon being lit up by the rays of the midwinter sunrise. And at Stonehenge we saw how the ring of sarsen uprights has been revealed as a representation of the sun (Sunhenge). So in its simplest form the circular temple at Avebury was a representation of the sun, with rays of sunshine being represented by the hundred sarsen stones around the rim and the huge circular bank representing the aurora around the sun. In this way the sacred enclosure, outlined by the ditch, symbolised the heart of the Sun, a place where Life was regenerated after Death and where light was created, so that it could maintain their existence and give new Life to plants and animals on Earth each spring. But there was also a very clear reference to the moon, since when it was freshly constructed the high, chalk bank of the henge would have shown up as a gigantic white ring. And so I think that this enormous, circular white embankment was also intended to be a gigantic representation of the rim around the moon, but perhaps the moon at a very rare and very special moment in time. I think that the major symbolism inherent in the bank and the inner edge of the ditch is therefore a combination of the moon and the sun, in other words, one of Nature's most awesome spectacles, *a solar eclipse.*

A solar eclipse can only occur when the moon passes directly in front of the sun, and a total eclipse can only happen when the dark moon (new moon) is exactly aligned with the sun and covers it completely. As the moment of totality approaches the temperature drops and the sky becomes darker and darker until the sun is hidden by the moon and night falls, although only for a few minutes. But sometimes, when the moon is a bit further from the earth, an annular eclipse occurs and a ring of bright light from the sun's corona can be seen all around the edge of the moon, and this ring must have been a truly awe-inspiring sight. A very powerful image that embodied the 'Circle of Life'. Therefore I think that Avebury was built as the physical representation of the coming together of the two most powerful entities in the heavens above, the sun and the moon. This meeting was acted out in the heavens above and then embodied on the ground below, by the construction of the gigantic white bank around a circular area of earth delimited by the ditch of the henge. This temple was built to re-enact and celebrate the joining together of the sun and moon and 'the Creation of New Life'. And perhaps the ancients saw this mystical and magical act of an eclipse as an auspicious, yet frightening, cosmic event, one that announced the dawn of a new era.

There is another level of symbolism. The site is so huge that the overall appearance of the design would not have been very clear from ground level, it would have been far more visible from overhead, and so it seems to me that one of the purposes of the construction was to send a message to the heavens above. When I looked at a plan I also thought that the whole arrangement of the henge with the two inner circles reminded me of a face, but one with no nose or mouth, just two round eyes. So perhaps another idea behind the design of this face was to communicate with the gods, or perhaps it was a way of sending a message to the spirits of their ancestors who had departed this life and were residing elsewhere, perhaps on the moon above. A message that tried to say something like: *"Here we are, look down on us and help us, for we are still watching the skies and thinking of you".*

(This is not a totally fanciful idea on my part. At some megalithic sites, such as at Stanton Drew and here at Avebury there are standing stones with sculptures of people on the top, with their faces looking directly upwards.)

The Art of Avebury

So far I have suggested various explanations for the meaning behind the design of the circles and the ditch and bank, but what about the stones themselves? Until now, conventional archaeology has not really understood the nature of the standing stones of Avebury. The really big question was not *'How did they construct the stone circles of Avebury'*, but *'Why did they do it?'*

Why did they go to all the trouble of quarrying, transporting and erecting hundreds of huge and very, very heavy stones? What did the stones mean to them?

Few archaeologists have attempted to answer these difficult questions. The nearest that some have come to the correct answer is to say that the stones were chosen for their shape. The conventional and traditional theory is that the megaliths are just rough, unworked, naturally shaped rocks and that any resemblance to a more artificial image is purely an accident, caused by geological forces when the sedimentary rocks were formed millions of years ago. Scholars think that the people of Avebury just chose stones for their interesting shapes, like some sort of grown-up version of a child playing with coloured stones and pretty seashells on the beach, and then collecting them and taking them home. And yet this theory of selecting interesting shapes has never really rung true, for it has never really made much sense that people would go to all the trouble of collecting, transporting and erecting such enormous stones and then not altering them in any way.

In the 1930's, Keiller noticed that some of the West Kennet Avenue stones were pillars whilst other stones were lozenge or rounded shapes, usually face to face across the path. He realised that this arrangement was deliberate and thought that the oblongs and pillars referred to male whilst the rounded shapes were female. And that is how matters have stood for seven decades, until I came along and realised that there are far more types than just two shapes and that the stones can relate to not just masculine and feminine but also to the sun, the moon and many other things as well.

In 1997, shortly after I started to take a real interest in our prehistoric past, I visited Avebury for the first time. But even then I was puzzled by all the mystery surrounding our distant past and it seemed very strange to me that even after so much time and effort, we still knew so little about who our ancestors were and why they built their amazing circles of standing stones. And the more I thought about it, the more I started to think that something was drastically wrong with traditional theories, attitudes and opinions.

And so I started to explore the distant past in my own way, rather than just accepting everything that the experts said was true. After another visit, and after taking more photographs, I began to realise that some of the stones were in fact prehistoric works of art. (Although for them, it was Modern Art.) This revolutionary way of looking at the standing stones was to think of them as natural sculptures, which had then been altered and improved on. For in fact many of them are no longer rough, natural stones at all, some are actually giant stone symbol stones, whilst others are complex prehistoric sculptures, and some are both at the same time.

Although hundreds of them are missing, the stones that remain were indeed originally chosen for their size and shape. But instead of laboriously removing large areas of unwanted rock, as a modern sculptor or even a Greek or Roman artist would have done, the prehistoric sculptors often used what nature had already provided, and they modified the existing bumps and hollows of the natural surfaces and incorporated them into their designs. This artistic technique of giving nature 'a helping hand' has its origins deep in the Upper Palaeolithic period, when some artists used natural rock formations inside caves to give three-dimensional relief to their painted images of Ice Age animals, particularly images of horses, bison and deer. The most obvious and perhaps the most remarkable of these is the carved head of a spotted horse that was painted inside the Pech Merle cave in south-western France. This work of art is about 25,000 years old. Another famous example of using what nature had generously provided is at another famous cave site at Altamira in Spain where some 15,000 years ago Palaeolithic artists used rounded parts of a cave ceiling to paint some bison that are lying down and curled-up. In other words, the technique of modifying and then decorating naturally shaped rocks had been invented a very, very long time before Avebury was conceived.

The basic mistake of misunderstanding the true nature of the standing stones at Avebury, and elsewhere, was probably caused by the religious beliefs and restricted education of the first investigators, Georgian antiquarians such as William Camden, John Aubrey, and William Stukeley. Many of them were deeply affected by Christian doctrine, which stated that the Bible was a true and accurate account of the history of Mankind. It would be a century and more before people started to question the belief that God had created the world in 4004 BC. (We now know that it is more than four thousand **million** years old!)

The major problem was that until the beginning of the 19th Century very few people realised just how old Britain's prehistoric ruins really were, some gentlemen scholars even thought that Stonehenge dated from the Dark Ages, not long after the Romans left Britain in about 400 AD. Many scholars were also deeply affected by the widespread racist attitude towards non-Europeans and their patronising sense of superiority toward other races included their own distant ancestors. The education and training of Georgian gentlemen included the Classical studies of Ancient Greece and the Roman Empire. Most academics believed what Julius Caesar had written about the Ancient Britons, how they were just barbarians and savages that rarely wore any clothes, just tattoos and blue body paint (there are even several illustrations that date from the 16th Century showing how this sort of thinking was already deeply engrained in our psyche).

But as we now know, recorded history of this period was very biased and one-sided, since only the victor's version of what actually happened was written down. And as a result our academics fell victim to Roman propaganda that has managed to endure for nearly two thousand years. (Anyone who was not Greek or Roman was automatically a barbarian.) And so many scholars believed the idea that our distant ancestors were just sub-human, pagan, sun-worshipping savages, with no concept of civilised behaviour, (despite the fact that thousands of years before the Romans arrived our ancestors had built such marvels as Calanais, Newgrange, Brodgar, Stonehenge and of course, Avebury). But if you are not wearing any armour and are going naked into battle it can also suggest that you believe you are invincible, or that even if you do die, you will go straight to paradise anyway. So being painted with woad was quite a good psychological battle tactic, since many of the soldiers in the Roman Legions were very superstitious and the idea of fighting naked blue aliens who were screaming at them in foreign tongues must have done their heads in!

This racism towards our distant ancestors continued until quite recently. In the 1960's, Atkinson wrote this about the culture of the first settlers on Windmill Hill: *"... it was the practise of agriculture and stock-raising, that is, the deliberate production as opposed to the mere gathering of food, that allowed the population of Britain for the first time to gain mastery of its environment, and to rise from brute savagery to the higher levels of barbarism."* And he wrote this about the previous native peoples: *"...the life of these Mesolithic inhabitants of Britain must have resembled in many respects the nomadic and precarious existence of the present-day aborigines of Australia."*

Another influential voice, V. Gordon Childe, was also instrumental in affecting both professional and public opinion. In his 1940's book, *'What happened in History'*, he named some of his chapters with titles such as *"Palaeolithic Savagery", "Neolithic Barbarism", "Higher Barbarism of the Copper Age", etc.* And one phrase in particular gives an insight into the way he saw Neolithic people: *"Societies of savages continued and continue to exist side by side with food producers."* He also wrote: *"The distinctive achievements of civilisations that differentiate them from barbarism are the invention of writing and the elaboration of exact sciences"*.

Until quite recently, such conceited, arrogant and frankly, racist, attitudes like these have drastically affected the way that people have perceived our Neolithic and Bronze Age ancestors. But as we have seen many times already in this book, generations of archaeologists have been blind to the achievements of our distant cousins, simply because instead of inventing writing, the ancient civilisations of Britain created other methods of recording knowledge and information. And they developed complex symbolism and created some amazing religious architecture, as well as many thousands of extraordinary works of art.

By the time the Romans arrived, over fifteen centuries had passed since the decline and fall of the megalithic cultures and their early forms of civilisation. When Caesar arrived with his legions, the local Iron Age tribesmen were part of an aggressive warrior society that was often in conflict with its neighbours. Consequently we have been consistently encouraged to think badly of our prehistoric forefathers and be ashamed of our distant roots. Although in the past many academics have had a grudging respect for the arduous work involved in building the Avebury henge and moving the stones from the surrounding area, our archaeologists, scientists and scholars have consistently failed to understand what the builders were actually doing at Avebury and to see the stones as they really are.

Looking up the West Kennet Avenue, towards Avebury

Even the 1990 guidebook to the site, published by English Heritage, states: *"None of the stones have been worked, unlike Stonehenge where they had been shaped by stone mauls (hammers)."* And in his book *'Circles and Standing Stones'*, Evan Haddington wrote: *"Although the stones were not artificially shaped in any way, they seem to have been chosen with some care."*

Yet, even a casual stroll along the West Kennet Avenue would show that scattered amongst the more natural-looking stones are stones that are obviously artificial, simply because they have straight sides that join at specific angles. Many of the stones are geometrical shapes with four, five, six or more sides, or in other words, they are rectangles, pentagons and hexagons

Although many of the giant stones are missing, either buried or destroyed, some of those that remain have symbolic shapes that are to do with the sun and the moon, male and female, whilst others refer to Neolithic mythology, astronomy and astrology. There are also stones that refer to the seasons, and other stones are representations of animals, people or supernatural beings.

West Kennet Avenue stones

I also think that many of the stones were originally painted but there are few, easily visible traces of this artwork left, simply because of the erosion caused by thousands of years of wind and rain, frost and snow. Even the edges of many of the sculptures and carvings have become softened with time, with the artwork slowly disappearing as the centuries have rolled by.

In addition to the more obvious sculptures and carvings on the stones, there is also a more subtle form of decoration. As at many other sites, a great deal of secondary carving was done over the centuries that followed their erection. This artwork showed scenes from their history and pictures from their myths and legends. There are also a great many, very small, engravings of people, but these have become blurred with time and the details have become very indistinct, although strong side lighting can sometimes help throw these into relief. But on some stones the outlines of the carvings are still visible due to the presence of lichen, as though the stones were decorated with black paint. Then in other areas the surface has eroded to such an extent that the carvings and engravings are only faintly visible, although as usual, the enhancement of photographic images using computer software packages, (such as Adobe Photoshop), can help reveal more of the detail. Although not every stone that remains is a work of art, many of the largest stones were altered to become superb sculptures and some of these were extremely complex. Different sculptures become visible on each stone as you move from left to right and then right to left, as the emphasis changes from one multiple image to another. The stones reveal different images at different times of the day. Some of the decorations remain hidden until a specific time when the light is just right. Strong side lighting, particularly at sunrise or sunset, or in winter when the sun is low on the horizon, can also have a part to play as to which of the images has the dominant role. The same stone can show many different images according to the viewpoint of the onlooker and the effects of sunlight and shadow that change according to the time of day and the weather. The moving images are quite magical in the way that they only appear for a few minutes and then disappear. However, because of erosion over the centuries, and the masking effects of moss and lichen, sometimes the images are best seen when the sky is overcast, rather than in bright sunshine. A good time to see some of them is after a rain shower, when the stones are still wet and the sky is dull.

Many of the sculpted stones are masterpieces of design, technique and subtlety, created by extremely gifted and talented artists. However it is not my intention to give a complete account of every single stone and every single image on that stone, just the stones that are particularly interesting or important and I will try and describe a few sample images on some of the sides of those stones. I hope this will encourage you to visit the site and discover the art for yourself.

The best art at Avebury is probably in the southwest part of the site. This includes the stones of the South Circle, part of the Great Circle and the West Kennet Avenue. Originally there were more than a hundred stones on each side of this avenue. The West Kennet Avenue was by no means a straight path as it wound its way downhill from the henge, then upwards to Overton Hill and on to the Sanctuary, and nowadays it even has the B4003 road running right through it in two places. The path between the stones is about seventy feet (21 m) wide, suggesting that it was specially designed to allow processions of large crowds of people to walk along it with ease. Some of the Kennet Avenue was excavated and recreated by Keiller, although the southern half still lies unexcavated and there are probably buried stones under the crops in the surrounding fields. Perhaps one day the rest of the avenue will be reconstructed and it will be possible to walk between the stones all the way up to the Sanctuary on Overton Hill.

Starting from what is currently the far end of the West Kennet Avenue, looking north and heading back towards the henge, the first stone on the right side is a stylised sculpture of the head of an animal with a sloping forehead. I think that it is more likely to represent the head of a lion rather than a horse because the neck is short and thick, and the muzzle is much wider than that of a typical horse's head. The eyes are slits and are set close together, with forward vision, unlike a herbivore that generally has its eyes more to the side. This is because carnivores focus on their prey, whilst herbivores have lateral vision and try and sense attack that can come from the side.

The lion is in left profile, has its mouth open and its head turned to the left. This stone was subsequently redecorated with hundreds of coloured images of little people, although, like so much prehistoric art, these are now faded and eroded. It is also a stone that has been turned upside and reused, the earlier image of a rugged face is now at the bottom of the stone, and it too was decorated with images of little people, particularly around the right eye and the mouth. Incidentally, when we think of lions we tend to think of the African species, but in the distant past other species of lion roamed across Europe. Of these only the Asiatic lion still survives, but during the last Ice Age there lived a massive variety, a huge cave lion that hunted animals as large as bison and aurochs.

Opposite the lion sculpture, on the west side of the avenue, is another very interesting sculpture, the head and neck of a stylised, rather rough-looking horse, similar in stance to the knight in a game of chess. This is deceptive. The stone is actually a very complex series of multiple images, with an amazing carving at the top. The image on the top of the stone is the head of a man who is bent backwards over the stone and facing upwards. His face is at the top but his eyes are closed and he is wearing a floppy hat. This is a multiple image, since the hat also forms the muzzle of the horse and the man's nose forms one of the horse's ears. And the large eye socket of the horse becomes a hole in the man's forehead. Two images, face to face, form part of the neck of the horse.

On the right is the head and torso of a man in left profile, opposite him, on the lower left side of the stone, is a curious, mole-like animal. This creature has strange protruding eyes, which make it

look as though it is wearing sunglasses! It is poking a hand at the nose and mouth of the man on the right. It is also part of another image, that of a rather distorted face of a man with big round eyes and who is wearing a goatee beard. And as usual, there are many other smaller works of art carved into this marvellous stone.

The second stone on the eastern side of the avenue, next to the lion, is a very complex sculpture with multiple carvings. The main sculpture is the head of a man wearing a domed hat, which slopes down from left to right. He has a bulbous nose and his chin is at ground level. A secondary image shows the left profile of a humanoid with a small beak-like nose, a very prominent chin. He has a long beard and long hair down his back. There are also images of a dog or wolf with its nose in the air. At the top, along the right side, is a small animal, like a bear cub, clinging on to another animal. Above the centre of the stone is the image of a bearded man wearing a hat with a white band. And just below the centre, on the left side, is another cat-like creature with pointed ears. All these main images were subsequently redecorated with smaller carvings and this megalith is also a symbol stone.

The third stone from the end, on the side nearest the road, is a tall, complex sculpture of a strange monster with a long oval head that is standing upright and hunched over. There are other strange animals around it, and there is also a large, multiple image of a human head, one image is looking down to the left, and looks like a child, and the other is in three-quarter right profile.
On the southern side of this extraordinary stone is a big triangle with a curved edge along the longest side and it has additional carvings forming a slitted eye, a nose and a small mouth producing an image that we all know as *'The Man in the Moon'*.

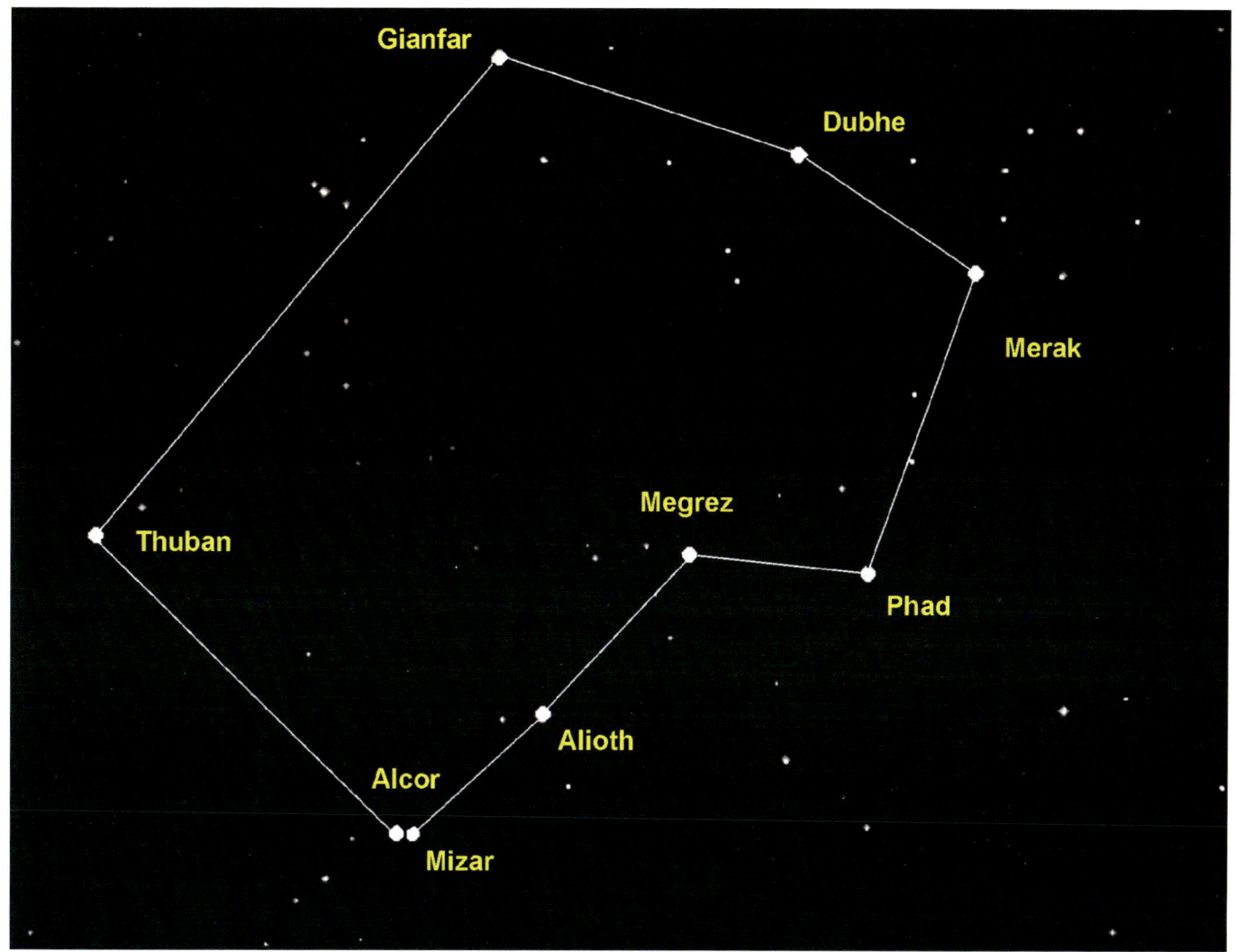

people saw five thousand years ago. It's why many people struggle with seeing the named pictures in many of the older constellations, especially the signs in the Zodiac.

Some of the remaining stones of the West Kennet Avenue show images that are very different from those at other sites. They show some quite disturbing images of demons, monsters and evil spirits. An example of this is on the side of another tall stone on the eastern side, which shows the brooding figure of a man facing into the Avenue. He is wearing a long cloak with a peaked hood over his head. (There is a similar sculpture on the side of the tall stone on the northern side of the West Kennet longbarrow.) At the time of nocturnal ceremonies, processions of worshippers would have moved along the avenue to and from the henge. Lighting their way by torchlight, the stones would loom up out of the darkness, and by the flickering light, images and faces would seem to come alive, producing a very scary experience for children and the more superstitious individuals. This impression may have been heightened by people taking 'magic mushrooms' (Psilocybe), or, much more dangerously, a drink prepared from dried Fly Agaric toadstools. They could also have had a stimulating drink prepared from wormwood (Absinthe), or much worse, from hallucinogenic plants such as henbane or even an extract of the fungus ergot. This is an infection of grasses and certain crops. Its hallucinogenic properties are caused by a natural form of LSD and they can be very powerful and even deadly. It was quite common for people in the Middle Ages to be poisoned by eating rye bread made from flour that had been contaminated with ergot.

The significance of the sculptures and carvings of grotesque faces and monstrous entities is going to result in a certain amount of controversy because I think that there are at least two opposing explanations. One possibility is that the images of such strange creatures were meant to alarm people, to make them more emotional and more susceptible to rituals performed at night, when their superstitious fears of evil spirits and demons were brought closer to the surface. The other possibility, the one that I prefer, is that the monstrous creatures were guardian spirits, protective agents who safeguarded the processional way between the lines of stones, acting as bodyguards on both a mystical and physical plane, allowing safe passage along a clearly defined sacred path. And if the records of other ancient religions are anything to go by, people would have believed that only the power of the temples and the priests could protect them from evil and malicious spirits. This idea was quite commonplace in ancient history, the entranceway into temple precincts was often guarded by strange and powerful supernatural beings or by sculptures of monsters that were part human and part animal.

Shortly before arriving back at the henge, the visitor walking up the West Kennet Avenue will pass a tall, oblong-shaped stone on their right, the eastern side. This is an interesting sculpture and it is also a geometrical symbol stone, an oblong with a sloping corner angled down the top right side. The artwork includes several amazing multiple and composite images.

One of the main pictures is in the top right quarter and this is the head of a dog-like animal in left profile. It is a multiple image and within this is the left profile of the head of a wild cat and another image that shows a rather humorous looking man. He has a very curved and beaky nose and has a bushy beard below his chin. He is wearing a sort of woolly hat and he looks a bit like the popular image that we have of a dwarf. Along the bottom left side is a seated figure of a bearded man wearing a long tubular hat, a bit like a fez. He has his back to the other images.

The Keiller excavation of the West Kennet Avenue revealed four different burials, two with beakers, at the foot of several stones and these burials supports the view that there was hallowed ground between the lines of stones and I suspect that the people buried there had a close connection to those stones, perhaps they were some of the artists. Another burial of a Beaker person was discovered next to Adam, one of the two Longstones that are all that is currently visible of the Beckhampton Avenue, to the west of the henge. Adam and its partner, Eve, are in a field close to the nearby village of Avebury Trusloe. They are incorrectly named since Eve is quite a phallic-shaped stone that has been badly damaged. Her partner, Adam, is a broad stone weighing well over thirty tons and it is quite an extraordinary work of art. Looking from right to left at the broad outer surface of the stone, the southern side can sometimes be seen as being one very large sculpture of a head in left profile, although this is a moving image that occurs mainly with lateral lighting.

Adam has a triangular nose, flattened forehead and a thin-lipped mouth, but this is perhaps not the face of a real human. From further round to the right, and looking at it from left to right, the face changes and the stone also appears to be some sort of huge animal with a bulbous nose and round tusks and it has a mass of people riding on its neck and back. Although these carvings are now

eroded and rather indistinct, I think that this picture is an artistic impression of a mammoth, perhaps based on a distant story or memory in their folklore.

Adam, part of the Beckhampton Avenue, Avebury Truslowe

THE GREAT CIRCLE

Before arriving at the henge, the end of the West Kennet Avenue originally turned to the left and then took a curve to the right. Some see this poor fit as an indication that the avenue of stones was constructed long before the henge was dug. But I think that this was deliberate and partly done to allow time for the congregation, particularly the very young and the very old to meet up and enter the henge together. The main road and a fence now block this route, so one needs to use the gate further up the road or scramble up the bank under some trees. The main road now passes between stones 1 and 4 of the Great Circle, but in ancient times, the avenue entered into the henge further to the right, across a causeway above the ditch, between stones 1 and 98. Portal stone number 1 is known as the Devil's Chair, and many people have had their photo taken as they sit on what appears to be a natural seat in the middle of the outer surface. Yet in earlier times it probably referred to a part of the stone a little to the left of this ledge, which is actually the sculpture of a seated figure, hence the name. This figure is most obvious with very strong lateral lighting and at that time it shows a complex sculpture of a young man with a white face, sitting in a high-backed chair.

the Devil's Chair, stone 1 of the Great Circle

This is a multiple style image but, because of erosion, it is quite difficult to make out all the different images of people and animals that surround the man. These include some children sitting on his lap whilst others are kneeling at his feet. The very bushy hat that he is wearing is also a multiple carving of a monkey, probably a Barbary ape, similar to the ones on the Rock of Gibraltar that originally came across the Mediterranean from North Africa.

To the left of the seated man is a much larger figure, that of a man wearing a parka with the hood up. And on the right side of the stone is a strange sculpture of an enormous ogre with a thin, very pointed nose and a goatee beard. There are several other quite large sculptures and many additional, secondary carvings. As usual, different images and scenes appear according to the season, the time of day and the weather. With different lighting you can sometimes see an interesting picture to the right of the chair. It is an old woman wearing a long coat and a red bonnet. She is holding out her hands to a bear cub, as though they are dancing. These moving images of sculptures and carvings seem to come to life as the sun moves round from late morning to early afternoon, the shadows forming, revealing and then hiding the different images.

On the right side of the Devil's Chair is the profile of another colossal head, with its chin at ground level. It has an overhanging forehead and a massive jaw but a snub nose and a small mouth. The outer surface of this megalith really was an extraordinary work of art, a true masterpiece of late Neolithic skill and creativity.

Southwest sector of the Great Circle

This was added to over the following centuries by successive artists. The bottom part of the inner surface of stone 1 shows a curious sculpture of a dog with its head raised in the air, its mouth is at top right. And on the left edge is a woman in left profile with her hair piled up on her head.

The other south portal stone, number 98, (pictured overleaf) stands on the right side of the entrance into the interior of the Great Circle was one of the most heavily and brilliantly decorated stones on the site. It was even decorated before it was turned upside down and reused. The most prominent sculpture on the outer surface, as it is today, is on the right side and it shows a man's face in right profile.

The sculpture of the man on stone 98 (*on the left*) has a short moustache and his mouth is at ground level, but as with so many images they have become eroded over the centuries and their visibility now depends a great deal on the time of day and the way the light brings the carvings to life. Before it was turned over, the stone showed the left profile of the head and torso of a young man on the right side. He was face-to-face with a much larger figure, a massive being, probably a god of some sort. This deity is holding his right arm out in order to support the young man. The left half of the stone showed the left profile of the head of another person and the surface was covered with dozens of full-length images of people. Extreme image intensification shows that these carvings and engravings were originally brightly painted in many different colours. On the inner left edge of the stone, along the top left part of the stone that faces the Devil's Chair, is a large triangular, kite-shaped face of a man wearing a hat.

The inner surfaces of portal stones 98 and 1, which flank the southern entrance into the Great Circle.

The inner surface of this huge portal stone was also heavily carved to show quite complex scenes. The main image seems to be some sort of large sledge, the driver is on the left side of the surface and he is bundled up against the cold. He has a beaky nose and is wearing a hooded coat of which the left arm is clearly outlined. His left hand is wearing a mitten. Behind him, towards the back of the stone are two reclining figures in left profile who are sitting next to each other. Behind these children is a much larger figure, the same size as the driver. She is wearing a hooded garment, a parka, against the cold and is looking to the left, towards the driver's back. Her back runs all the way down the edge of stone and the hood she is wearing forms the top right corner of the sculpture. Behind the driver, on the left side and looking towards them, is the head and upper body of a larger and rather grotesque figure with a bulbous nose and heavy features. He has a large white bushy beard. Behind him is a larger man who is wearing a sort of hat or helmet.

In the top left corner of the stone there is another face, looking to the right, he has a hood that ends in a peak. All along the bottom of the stone is another frieze of much smaller people, some are sitting down, others are standing up.

On either side of the causeway that is between portal stones 1 and 98 is the vast ditch that runs around most of the site and to the west there is the longest run of surviving standing stones that make up this part of the Great Circle. Most modern visitors to the site start their visit by entering from the High Street at the western end of this run of stones, because it is near the car park.

The megaliths are numbered 4 to 24 and unfortunately the very first stone that a visitor sees is stone 24, which has been severely damaged and has lumps of rock bolted back on. This stone epitomises the sorry state of one of the marvels of our prehistoric past. Nevertheless, Avebury is a very special place and well worth visiting and revisiting at different times of the year. It is particularly popular to pagans and druids as an alternative to Stonehenge at the time of the midsummer solstice. Stone 24 is now isolated, since stones 23 to 17 are all missing, as are stones 15, 13, 11, 3 and 2. (The missing stones were replaced with small concrete pillars.) Stone 12 is a geometric shape that has been balanced in the air, this has been achieved by having just one angle buried in the ground and as a result, it is a good example of 'modern' Late Neolithic art.

Great Circle, southwestern sector, inner surface of stone number 12

Stone number 11 is missing and is marked by a concrete post. Stone number 10 (*on the right*) however is a good example of the sort of complex sculptures that can show the masterful techniques of Neolithic and Bronze Age sculptors. It was the carvings on the top left of this stone that gave me the initial insights into the style of art I have since called **'multiple images'**. There are two strange faces that share the same eye socket, the left eye of the face on the left and the right eye of the face on the right. These are not human faces, nor is the other face further down the stone, they all look like spirits to me.

Outer surface of stone 10 in the southwestern sector.

The twin stars Castor and Pollux are the two brightest stars in the constellation of Gemini, which is also one of the twelve constellations of the Zodiac. These constellations follow the ecliptic, the apparent path of the sun in its annual journey across the heavens. In Classical mythology Castor and Pollux were the twin sons of Leda, but twins also feature in celestial mythologies across the world, including the ancient stories of the San Bushmen of the Kalahari. If you join up some of the main stars in Gemini (Pollux, Castor, Tejat, Ahena, Mekbuda and Wazat) you get a sort of oblong that resembles the inner surface of stone 10.

Inner surface of stone 10 in the southwestern sector, and on the left, the edge of the stone

The inner surface of stone 10 shows the heads and torsos of two rather strange bear-like creatures, standing close together, side by side. These are very prominent in early morning in high summer. In addition, the artificial diagonal line on the sculpture that separates the head on the left from the one on the right mimics a short imaginary line that connects Pollux down to Propus, another bright star within the 'oblong' of the constellation of Gemini.

The left side of the southern edge of this stone shows yet another sculpture. This is a hunched-over figure in left profile who is wearing a thick fur coat. He has a white face and a rather gloomy expression, and is wearing a tall hat, which comes down on one side to his left eye. However, the body of this individual doesn't look quite right to me and so I don't think that it is the representation of a human being since his head is low down on his chest. There are also several other strange sculptures and carvings of humanoid creatures as multiple images above the hunched figure's head.

Seen from the west side, the side nearest the bank, the outer surface of the next stone, number 9, is the stylised head of a woman in right profile. She must have been an important feature of Neolithic mythology because this image reminds me of the rather bird-like creature on sarsen 2 at Stonehenge (but she also reminds me of the Borg Queen from Star Trek!)

She has her chin at ground level and her hair piled up on top of her head. The area below her mouth is quite rough, as though it has been flaked off. Looking at the same surface from right to left, the image becomes a rather beaky head of a bird-like creature in left profile with its eye high up on the left.

On the left, outer surface of stone 9

This is a famous stone and it is known as the *'Barber-Surgeon Stone'* because of the 14th Century skeleton of a man that was found underneath it. The body had next to it a purse containing a pair of scissors, an iron lance or probe and some coins dating from between 1310 and 1320. Two of these were from the reign of Edward III and the other silver coin was French. The scissors suggest that he earned a living from working as a travelling barber and the other instrument was part of his equipment for 'doctoring' those of his customers with minor ailments such as boils, blocked ears and decayed teeth.

The traditional explanation for his unusual burial place is that the megalith fell on him while he was helping digging a hole, so that the stone could be burned and broken up, but it fell and crushed him to death. However, if this is true then it is very strange that no one bothered to dig out his body and bury him in the nearby churchyard! A recent re-examination of the skeleton, previously thought to have been destroyed during the Blitz, was inconclusive because the damage to his pelvis, neck and skull was not obviously caused by massive crushing at the time of death.
The damage may even have occurred afterwards, as the stone settled. However, the re-examination of the skull revealed that, even before his untimely end, he must have led an eventful and interesting life because there was a deep cut mark across his skull. This had enough time to heal over and since cuts such as these were often the result of a sword blow, it is unlikely that he was an entirely law-abiding citizen.

So, I think that it may well be that something else happened to him. I think it far more likely he had been murdered and his corpse was concealed by toppling the stone over on top of his body. By looking from slightly to the right of square on, the inner surface of the Barber-Surgeon Stone looks to me like the head of a dog (or a wolf) with its nose buried in the ground. In other lighting conditions new images appear including a strange sheep-like animal head in left profile. There are also secondary images of faces on the stone, including an image in the top right corner of a hooded man with a long beard. He is in right profile with his head turned to look to his right and he is carrying someone or something on his back.

The inner surface of the Barber-Surgeon Stone, stone 9. *Inner surface of stone 5.*

One side of another interesting stone, number 6, shows the headless torso of a man wearing a long coat. And the outline of stone 5 shows a very classic lunar image, the reversed D of the second half-moon (3rd quarter).

This symbol stone portrays several large multiple images of faces, both animal and human. One of the most interesting of these is the left profile of a man's face near the middle left edge of the stone, this another *'Man in the Moon'* image. He is facing outwards, towards the southwest. This a multiple image, there is another face looking to the right, and is wearing a domed hat. There is another carving, at top right, which shows the left profile of a strange creature with its mouth wide open as though it will swallow the man with the domed hat. At the top left of the stone is the flat face of a grumpy-looking person. He has a snub nose and his mouth is turned down in a frown.

The South Circle

Of the original twenty-nine stones of the south circle, there are only five very large stones still in position today. But these include several extraordinary sculptures of animals that were important to the early farmers. The stones have been numbered from 101 to 106, with stone 101 being nearest to the southern entrance and 106 nearest to the village. Seen from inside the southern circle the basic shape of stone 101 suggests that it is a symbol stone for south, although the top slopes upward from left to right, then curves round and down. Although much wider and taller, it reminds me of the small sarsen circle stone number 11 at Stonehenge, the southstone.

According to variations in the lighting, the inner surface of 101 has many multiple carvings of people and animals, including a hooded man with a long white beard and a seated man on the right side of the stone. When the stone is looked at from the left and when the winter sunlight is low down and from the south, the outer surface of the stone becomes the head of a dog in left profile. This hound has small ears and a wavy line shows it has a large mouth. It is sitting down and its nose points high up into the air, to the left. The stone is also the head of someone in left profile wearing a hat, his nose is on the edge of the stone and his chin is at ground level. There are also many secondary images carved into the stone and, like so many other works of art at Avebury, these moving images change according to the viewpoint, the time of day, the time of year and the lighting conditions.

Outer surface of stone 102

Stone 102 is one of the most interesting of the entire site. Its outer surface is a sculpture of the head of a horse on top of a sheep (which is also a white wolf in three-quarter profile). The stone was originally upside down and at that time it was a sculpture of the head of an ewe with a lamb nestled under her chin. The horse was one of the very first ancient sculptures that I saw and I have since found out that other people have seen the same thing, although when they sought expert advice, they were told it was just a coincidence and that it just resembled an animal. They were told that the people of Avebury had simply selected a stone that was an interesting shape, created entirely by natural processes. In some lights the lower part of the right half of the stone can show the head of a cat-like creature in right profile, particularly if the viewpoint is square on and you are looking from right to left. The whole stone then looks like this creature is wearing a hat.

Looking from the right, the **inner** surface of stone 102 is sometimes shaped like an arrowhead. But when you look at it from more to the left it becomes more of an inverted Z-shape and it can then show the stylised profile of the head of a seated lioness that is looking outwards and to the right. On the left side of the stone is the left profile of the head of a deer, with the end of its nose curved slightly downwards. In addition, when looking just at the narrow right edge of the stone, the lower part forms the image of a man's head and upper body. He is wearing a hooded coat and below his bearded chin his left arm clutches the folds of his coat together. Seen from square on, and looking from left to right, the head of the lioness becomes much more apparent. Looking from right to left, the left side of the stone becomes the head of someone who is wearing a close-fitting hat with a flat top and with the sides just covering his ears.

Inner surface of South Circle stone 102

Next is stone 103. On its outer surface is a sculpture of the head and compact body of a ram that is sitting down. It is facing to the right, with the tip of its nose almost at ground level. When the light is from the right side the curve of its right horn is quite clear. This sculpture of a ram has suffered badly at the hands of later artists, who carved and then recarved a host of other images into the rock surface. In the centre is a multiple image of a bearded face with a squashed nose, its left eye is also the right eye of the ram. Looking from right to left, the stone becomes two very large heads in left profile, they are standing next to each other but they don't look human, the one on the left looks particularly strange.

At an earlier time the stone was the other way up and it showed quite a large variety of different medium-sized images of people and animals. Near the centre of the stone is the head and body of a white horse with a rider, both in left profile. It is following another horse and they seem to be galloping since the hind quarters of the front horse are bunched up. Above them is seated woman who is wearing a long dress.

South Circle stone 103, outer surface, and below, the inner surface of stone 103

Seen from the centre of the circle, the inner surface of stone 103 looks to me like the head of a small mammal such as a mouse or perhaps a pine marten or a weasel, although at first I thought it was the very characteristic head of a Great Crested Grebe. Sometimes you can see a beaver that is standing up at the back and on the right. Sometimes there is a very curious image inside the dip in the middle of the stone that shows people sitting down, they are wearing furs and fur hats and it looks as though they are riding in some sort of huge sledge with a sort of wooden or leather windshield. As usual, the images that the casual visitor may see will vary according to the time of day and the lighting conditions, and other images will become apparent at different times of the year.

Stone 104 has disappeared and its place is marked by a concrete pillar, but the rounded stone 105 is particularly interesting since it has an alignment with the sun around the time of the summer solstice and because of its colour and its images, I think it was meant to represent the moon as well as the sun.

The inner surface of stone 105 *(right)* is less rounded and looks bashed about, however the right half forms a rough half-moon shape. The left half shows the head of a bearded man in left profile with his nose right on the edge of the stone. This is a composite image and there are two smaller images of rather strange-looking people in right profile. On the left is someone with a very white, flat, rounded face, probably female and she is wearing her bunched up hair in a cap. Next to her, on her left, and slightly overlapping, is a more rugged image of a man with a beard. These two people are also parts of several other multiple images on the sculpted stone.

On the outer surface of Stone 105 *(below)* are many

other carvings, and some of them show a group of people riding on the back of a very large, but rather strange animal with short tusks. Its head is to the far left. Superimposed on top of this picture is a white horse, with its bridled head at top left, next to this horse are several people including the head and body of a bearded man in left profile. He is wearing a fur hat and coat.

Next to this sculpture is number 106, which is one of the most intriguing standing stones on the site. An experiment conducted by Dr Terence Meaden, and first shown on television at the end of 1998, re-enacted the effect of a Mayday sunrise, with the shadow of the recreated Obelisk passing across stone 106. Meaden called this *'the Goddess Stone'*. In Meaden's scenario, the penis-shaped shadow of the obelisk symbolised the Sky God fertilising the Earth Goddess, during a *'Marriage of the Gods'*.

According to his theory, the Avebury people had built the whole complex to worship the Earth Goddess, but this idea ignores the fact that representations of such a deity, which were common in Turkey and central Europe, during the Palaeolithic period, are absent from Neolithic and Bronze Age Britain. But as I have shown time and time again, the ancient people of these islands revered the sun and the moon, not just a goddess and so they created circular images and circular monuments to celebrate the sun and moon. However the scenario recreated by Meaden is similar in some respects to the lighting effect at Newgrange and the fertilisation and recreation of Life by the rays of the midwinter sunrise. The people of Avebury did not create any obvious images of a Goddess that I have seen - *well, apart from the enormous breast that is the nearby Silbury Hill...*

The inner surface of stone 106 *(above)* is actually the sculpture of the head of a bird in left profile. With its long bill folded down along its neck I believe it represents a stork. This image can be seen by looking from left to right, but in early afternoon the shadows across stone 106 produce another image as well. Standing in front of the stone, and looking from right to left, you may be able to see the profile of a humanoid with heavy features and a thick, protruding chin. He is looking to the right and is wearing a long, floppy headdress that is hanging down his back, a bit like a Victorian nightcap. And at the bottom of the stone are the head of a stylised wolf in right profile and another face, this time of an ogre with very thick features, a bulbous nose and whose head is just protruding from the ground. There are several other carvings of people on the stone as well.

As to the meaning of stone 106, May Day is about half-way between the spring equinox and the summer solstice, so the stork sculpture probably symbolises the beginning of summer.
Until the 1800's, white storks were once a very common sight in Britain, but today only a dozen or so migrants are recorded each year, although they are still widespread in southern Europe. So I wonder if the Christian persecution of pagan traditions included an extermination of one of the old pagan symbols, after all, it would not be the first time that Man has reduced an animal to near extinction for religious reasons.

If the idea that the early farmers used the symbol of a bird to represent a change in season seems a bit odd, then it may help to remember that birds were commonplace in many other mythologies, both historical and prehistorical. Perhaps this was because of the way that certain types of birds appeared and disappeared according to the time of year. Some species, such as sand martins, swifts and swallows spend the summer here, whilst other species of birds, including several types of swans, ducks and geese spend part of the winter here. And perhaps there were so many special stories about birds because they could do something special that ancient man could only dream of doing. Fly.

In the mythology of Ancient Egypt, the god Horus was the son of Osiris and grandson of the sky goddess Nut and earth god Geb. Horus was often represented as a man with the head of a falcon, with the sun as his right eye and the moon his left eye.
There was also the ba, a sort of non-corporeal double of the deceased that was represented as a bird with a human body. Another common image was Thoth, the ibis-headed god of the scribes. In addition, depictions of the bennu, a heron-like bird, that was sometimes used in heiroglyphs to represent the planet Venus. This bird was also known by the story of the phoenix, a golden bird that was said to rise from the ashes of its own funeral pyre. In this manner the phoenix is an obvious candidate to represent the everlasting cycle of life, death and rebirth.

(Please note that I am definitely not suggesting that our prehistoric ancestors had links with Ancient Egypt, no Egyptian artefacts have been found, I have simply used some of the many Egyptian deities to show how their mythology used similar astronomical phenomena and represented their gods with birds and other animals.)

For a long time we had our own symbolic way of representing birth, children were often told that babies were brought by a stork, until the days of a more modern approach to sex education. But this myth has persisted into modern culture by the use of greeting cards to announce the arrival of a new addition to the family, by using images of a baby, wrapped in a blanket and carried by a flying stork. And we still have plenty of old sayings about birds in our folklore, such as *"the sound of the first cuckoo of spring"* and *"one swallow does not make a summer"*, and even, *"like water off a duck's back"*.

So if the inner side of stone 106 marks the date and direction of Mayday sunrise, then the image of the stork represented the start of summer. The first of May and later on, in the Iron Age Celtic calendar, this became the time for the fire festival known as Beltane.

There was also an alignment in the opposite direction, between the setting sun, stone 106 and the Obelisk, which took place at the start of winter, midway between the autumn equinox and the shortest day of the year, the winter solstice. (This was on the 1st of November, the date of the fire festival of Samhain in the Iron Age ritual calendar.) At sunset the shadow of the Obelisk went further across the circle towards a stone that used to be opposite stone 106. It is possible that this missing stone was the sculpture of a bull or another ram, especially since Samhain was the traditional time of year when farmers culled their excess animals. This was done for two main reasons. Firstly to produce a large quantity of dried, smoked and salted stores for winter and secondly, so that there would be enough hay for the rest of the herd to last them through the winter. Traditionally, the animals that were slaughtered were usually old females who could no longer have calves (or lambs) and most of the young males, since one stud bull, or prize ram, is usually enough to cover many females.

The inner surface of stone 106 faced towards the rising sun on Mayday, the start of summer and the outer surface corresponded to the setting sun at Halloween, the start of winter. The **outer** surface of stone 106 is covered in eroded, multiple and composite images of animals and people, but according to the lighting, the main picture is that of a bear that is standing upright or else it is a representation of something countless generations of children have made every winter, and a fitting symbol of the coming cold, *a snowman.*

Outer surface of South Circle stone 106, summer and winter

So in effect, special stones were used to mark the high and the low points of the seasonal cycles of nature for all to see and to be celebrated with feasts, rituals and ceremonies. The shadow of the Obelisk marked the moment by acting as the gnomon (pointer) of a sort of colossal sundial. I think that some of the missing stones in the south circle corresponded to a particular event or celebration relating to the moon and to the rising and setting points of the sun at other times of the year, particularly at the equinoxes and the solstices. Other images represented the quarter days and would have corresponded to festivals, such as Imbolc in early February, this was when ewes came into milk and lambs were born and Lugnasadh, in early August, was the traditional time when the successful gathering of the crops was celebrated with a Harvest Festival. Secondary carvings on the main sculpture are young animals, including two bear cubs, a puppy and some human faces.

The group of small stones inside the South Circle (usually known as the Z feature) are in a half-moon shape. The Obelisk stood at the apex of the curve and at a 90-degree angle to the centre of the row of stones making up the base line. This D-shaped arrangement strongly indicates a lunar function, especially since there were about twelve stones along the base line, reminiscent of the number of moons in a year. (There are also twelve constellations in the Zodiac.)

What is still unclear at the moment is just how many other stones there were along the curved sides of the D-feature, because if there were an additional seven stones then the total number of nineteen stones would be indicative of the lunar swing cycle and the Metonic cycle of nineteen years.

Five of the stones in the half-moon shape within the South Circle

Some of the small stones that make up the D-feature are quite interesting sculptures. One stone, near the middle, is the sculpture of the head of a hound with its nose buried in the earth, however its neck has been shortened drastically so that it can then becomes a multiple image of another dog looking upwards to the right. The left side of this stone is also the head of a man with a very big nose, which in the multiple style is also the large, floppy ear of the second dog sculpture.
This complex of sculptures probably represents the constellations of Canis Major and Canis Minor, the two companion dogs of Orion the Hunter. (Canis Major includes Sirius, the Dog Star and the brightest star in the night sky.) The constellation of Orion is a well-known group of stars because it straddles the celestial equator and it contains five very bright stars, including Bellatrix, Betelgeuse and Rigel. The constellation is easy to find in the night sky because it includes a line of three stars that are grouped close together near the middle of the figure and these are known as Orion's Belt. Incidentally, some people think that a row of three small pyramids were built at Giza to recreate the alignment of the three Belt stars of Orion. These pyramids were for the ancient kings named Cheops, Chephren and Mycerinus.

The Northern Sector

Very few stones remain of the northeastern quadrant of the Great Circle, however there is a run of standing stones (numbers 30-46) in the northwest sector, near the Great Barn. And judging from the style and poor quality of the artwork here, I think that the sculptures and carvings on the stones of the northwest row are some of the oldest decorations on the site. Some are obvious sculptures of animals and people. One in particular, number 35, is even known as the Headstone. This is probably because of the rather rough sculpture of a woman's head on the southern side. Stone 30, the first in the row, on the right of the photograph, has a carving of a strange-looking man with a pointed beard on the south side and his bent left arm is quite noticeable. He is holding a smaller person in his arms. The right side of the outer surface of stone number 32 has picture of a woman with her long hair pulled back. The whole stone is a peculiar sculpture of an ape-like creature with a domed head and deep-set round eyes. Its chin is at ground level. Another nearby stone shows the head of a cat on the side nearest the ditch, and this stone has been recarved to show many other images of animals as well.

The large photograph of part of the northwestern sector, on the next two pages, gives an indication of how much the ditch has filled in over the centuries, the bottom of the ditch was originally more than twice as deep, with quite sheer sides. The lane and the garden to the right, show how the land surface has been altered since antiquity, because the bank and ditch have disappeared.
The last stone in this sector, just next to the main road, and conveniently situated near to the pub, is a huge diamond-shape that is usually known as the Swindon Stone (46) and this enormous polygon has many different carvings of monstrous images on it. The Swindon Stone (*below*) has been turned clockwise through ninety degrees, but in its current orientation the most obvious carving on the northern side is the eroded image at top right of a strange looking creature with a wide open mouth. This creature is looking outwards and downwards, towards the right. A bit lower down on the left side is the head, and the left side of the upper body, of a dog-like creature in left profile.

This creature has a broad head but a short, narrow muzzle. In one of the stone's earlier orientations, (when it was turned anti-sunwise through ninety degrees), the most noticeable carving was the head and torso of a very large figure along the right edge (now the top). He is in left profile, but his face is not quite human, his broad face has a big, bulbous nose and a sloping forehead and his massive left arm hangs down to his waist, ending in a paw. I think he is probably some sort of god. His left shoulder now forms a rotated multiple image with the open-mouthed creature. Facing him is a much smaller figure of a woman wearing her hair bunched up in a net hanging down her back. She is wearing a dress with a collar.

Inner surface of Swindon Stone

On the other side of this stone, the inner surface, there are some very curious images. Just to the right of the centre is a scene that looks like some sort of creature that is holding out a lamb to a bearded man. The right front leg of the lamb is quite prominent but it looks as though there is no muscle control, as though the lamb is dead. Behind him to the right are several other people, but it is hard to make out what is going on. There are several very large faces, in right profile, in the bottom left quarter of the stone. There is another strange looking face, with angular features and a hooked nose in the top left quarter of the stone. The whole stone is a sculpture of a giant head wearing a flat-topped hat and has its mouth and chin buried into the ground at the bottom left corner.

The Swindon Stone marked the northern entrance to the site, its partner, the other portal stone (47) of the northern entrance, had already fallen over and was destroyed in Stukeley's time, in 1722. This megalith was one of the largest on the site. It was roughly similar in shape to the Obelisk and at 22 feet long (6.7 metres) a sketch by Stukeley shows that it could have weighed more than the enormous Swindon Stone and one can only guess at the amount of time and effort needed to transport these monster stones from their place of origin on the Downs. Around the ditch to the east of the northern entrance are two standing stones and one fallen stone, 50, 68 and 73, these are all that remain of a run of at least twenty-four megaliths in the northeastern sector.

One of these upright stones is stone number 68 and although a relatively small stone, it is nonetheless another very interesting work of art. It is a broad stone with a distinctive hump on its back, similar to that of a bull, an aurochs or a pig. The main sculpture on the inner side is of a rather strange, pig-like creature with a broad head. The animal's head is to the left and its rump is to the right. Its wide-open mouth is at ground level, as though it is eating or biting something.

Great Circle, northeastern sector, inner surface of stone 68

Its left front leg is very easy to spot, since it is bent, as though the animal was moving forward quickly. There are also several other animals that are arranged parallel to this beast so that they overlap one another and all of them seem to be moving in the same direction at the same time. The first one is another strange creature, with an obvious rounded eye and a broad, rounded head and distinctive nose.

Behind this, near the top of the stone, is the head a large dog, his skull forms part of the bump along the back of the main image and his floppy left ear is quite clearly visible as it overhangs the surface of the stone. Just to the left of the centre of the stone is the head of yet another image in the group. This is the face of another dog in left profile. It has an overhanging forehead and quite a triangular chin. Its forehead is part of a multiple image that also forms the ear of the other dog. In addition to all these images, there are many other eroded decorations, including several large and medium-sized faces of people and a host of small scenes of various people. This stone is yet another masterpiece of Neolithic art, and it serves to highlight the tragedy of just how much ancient art was destroyed and vandalised by a handful of people during the Georgian era.

Incidentally, several fallen stones in this part of the site could be re-erected, and there may be as many as fifteen others that are still buried in the ground. Only if these sculpted stones are restored to their former upright positions can the amazing work of the ancient artists, our direct ancestors, be admired once again. To the west of stone 68, not far from the northern entrance, is another survivor of the Great Circle, stone 50.

Great Circle, inner surface of stone 50

The inner surface of this very complex stone has an unusual sculpture that shows the head of a cat in left profile, on the right half of the stone whilst the left half of the stone is the head of a horse that is looking downwards to the left, its snout (muzzle) is at ground level and very clear. Both images share the same pair of ears, and as usual, there are a host of secondary images covering the surfaces of the two main sculptures These multiple images include the head of a woman in left profile, which is on top of the cat image, which is also part of another multiple image. This is a rat-like animal in left profile that is standing up on its back legs, and it is on top of another animal that it is biting in the neck. This whole area is also the head of another horse in left profile, the outline of its chest and left foreleg are quite visible as the wavy line running down part of the stone to the right.

The Northern Circle

It is such a great shame that nearly all of the original 27 stones in the inner northern circle are missing, I think they would have been some quite amazing sculptures, judging from the few remaining stones. One of these is stone 201. The southern side of this megalith is the sculpture of a very strange head in right profile, but I don't think that it is a human face, it doesn't look quite right. Although the back of the head looks rounded and overlaps slightly, (like someone with a long hairstyle), the right side of the stone slopes down from a very high forehead towards the nose, which then curves round and down. The eye is just a slit and the jaw doesn't look quite right either. In addition, the stone also has a line of a darker colour running all the way along its circumference, as though it had been buried

North Circle, stone 201

a yard (a metre) of so lower down at some moment in time. The surface is covered with small engravings of little people, which are highlighted by the black and green lichen that covers the surface.

Another large upright stone of the northern circle, 206, (*on the left*) is a very complex sculpture. This stone presents lots of small sculptures on each side of the stone, some of them are quite scary images and it would have been quite frightening to see them lit up at night by the light of flickering torches. One image in particular stands out as a sort of *'Man in the Moon'* image. The left side of his face is tucked inside, under the main overhanging surface of the stone. He has a very pronounced chin. The sculpture looks as though he is wearing a very bulky fur coat and has a big floppy hat that falls down onto his fur-covered shoulders.

One of the most bizarre images that I have seen is on the edge of stone 206, it doesn't look quite human. It shows a rather grumpy-looking humanoid with a beaky nose and a pronounced chin. This is a multiple image. The bottom of the creature's nose is also the left side of the head and upper torso of a man with long, shoulder length hair. He is wearing a hat and is facing towards the stone, held in that position by the very long left arm of another strange ogre-like creature.

N.B. The main carving of this creature was independently identified by Terence Meaden and featured on the cover of his book *'The Secrets of the Avebury Stones,'* in which he correctly identified the presence of a few carved faces on some of the stones.

detail of North Circle stone 206

THE COVE

The Cove stood at the centre of the Northern Circle of twenty-seven stones, but since so many of them are missing it is hard to get a sense of what this would have looked like. The Cove was originally composed of three stones arranged in a sort of open box shape and according to a plan of the site, drawn in 1724 by Stukeley, the right hand stone was already missing. It had been destroyed eleven years earlier. The two remaining stones of the Cove are set quite far apart, with the five-sided backstone being the wider and larger of the two. The inner surface of this backstone, and hence the Cove itself, is orientated approximately towards the major northern moonrise, not towards the rising sun at midsummer. On the inner surface, near the base, are some very deeply carved lines and in the past these have been wrongly interpreted as being the outline of an ox.

One reason for this is due to a lack of understanding that the stone was used several times in different ways and different orientations. Previously the stone was upside down so the top third is now buried. In each orientation, the stone was recarved and the carvings now form a chaotic series of images. The engravings are mainly in straight lines and as such they are quite unlike any carvings, engravings or other outlines of Neolithic or Bronze Age art that I have seen. They do however represent a host of animals including an owl, horse's heads, birds and men's faces and a running animal, looking vaguely like a wolf, with its left front leg outstretched. The most obvious engraving is in the middle and this is a very basic image of a bird, with two lines coming out of its back for wings.

Detail of the inner surface of the back stone.

These engravings were done on top of much earlier pictures and I think that these very crude engravings date from a much more recent period, probably from the late Iron Age, or even later, during the Dark Ages, in the centuries after the Romans left Britain in 410 AD.
In complete contrast, the outer surface of the back stone is quite an amazing work of art, as you would expect from such an important structure. The outer surface of this five-sided stone (the side facing towards the north-northwest) looks like the head of an animal in left profile, and I think this is another wildcat.

The two remaining stones of the Cove

It has a very, very complex assortment of dozens of eroded multiple and composite images across its surface. One of the largest, running across most of the stone, is the head of a young man in right profile. We are looking at his back and right shoulder and arm (this is the wavy line running down the centre of the stone) and the top of his head is in the top right corner. Apart from a small moustache, he is clean-shaven. He has curly hair and is looking downwards, towards the bottom right corner. Behind his head and draped across his left shoulder is the body of an animal, perhaps a fox, with its head hanging at a 45 degree angle to the left.

This animal is part of a multiple image, the head of the animal that can also be seen as that of another creature with a white face, it is standing upright and looking down to the left. Its eye sockets are particularly visible and it has a white streak between them that gets wider as it goes upwards. This suggests to me that it may be a badger. On the far right, about half way up the stone is another animal that is standing upright, its back is right on the edge of the stone. It has a very narrow muzzle and it is looking to the left. I think this is a fox. Just above this is the head of a bearded man in left profile. His back extends all the way down to the ground and it looks like he is wearing a cloak, or else it is a sheepskin coat with a white seam where the inner fur is turned over. (This coat can also be seen as the body of the standing fox or wolf.) The man is wearing a strange, triangular white hat with a very distinctive curved brim. In different lighting conditions a whole host of other art becomes visible, including two major, full length figures of a woman and a man facing each other. The woman on the left is in right profile has her head at the top left corner, the other figure is in left profile and occupies the top right corner. She looks very pregnant, as she has a large, rounded belly. This is outlined by the curve running down the middle of the stone.

To the right of the backstone is the remaining upright, a very white stone that in the photo is standing side on. About half way up this stone is the side view of the eroded face of a man with a bulbous nose. He is wearing a very tall hat, (like a chef's hat, but without the pleats), this goes all the way up to the top edge, producing a hat that slopes down to the right. This makes me think that this edge of the stone represents a winter sunset symbol stone. Winter, the time when Nature dies.

The art on the inner side of this stone is very hard to make out because the surface is so eroded and partly covered with lichen. However, I think that the main image is that of a burly, bearded man, in three-quarter right profile. He has a bulbous nose, is wearing a fur coat and a fur hat with a white brim and seems to be riding a horse. There are other images but these are hard to make out due to the erosion and the lichen. However there is the head of a horse in right profile above the centre of the stone and there is some sort of strange burial scene going on about half way up the right side. These images may become more apparent under different lighting conditions. This is certainly the case for the outer surface of this stone. In sunny conditions many more images are apparent than when the sky is grey and overcast. The main decoration on the outer surface is yet another extraordinary set of images. One of these shows a full-length figure of a man in right profile. His head is in the top right corner and his body extends all the way down to the ground. His face is covered with green lichen, so it makes it hard to see if he is wearing a hooded parka, or else a coat, or whether it is just that he has a mass of very long hair.

Three-quarters of the way up the outer surface of this stone, on the right, is a picture of a man and a woman. They are standing face to face. He has a beaky nose, a short beard and his face is in left profile. He is looking slightly downwards towards the woman who is standing close to him. She is wearing a headscarf and a coat, and she is carrying a child. Both their bodies are covered by many images of children in the composite style.

The outer surface of the stone on the southern side

These images blend into a group of a dozen or so people, some of whom are standing up and others are sitting on the ground. Below the child the woman is carrying, and to the left of the centre of the outer surface of the stone, is a large and curious circular depression, divided by a slit down the middle. It is probably part of a fossilised tree that was caught in the sandstone and became petrified millions of years ago. However, I do not think that the image is an entirely artificial one, there have been some small carvings added to it, particularly at the top.

Since this shape was not removed, to provide a clean surface for the artists to work on, it must have been something that was important to them. Perhaps it had a multiple role. This sort of image is generally considered a representation of womanhood, a vulva. And this portrayal of the very essence of femininity reinforces my opinion that the northern temple of 27 standing stones, containing the Cove in the centre, was lunar and female, and perhaps even dedicated to a lunar goddess. The mark may also represent a navel. This is a physical representation of the link of a new-born baby to its mother, and as such it is a very potent symbol of pregnancy and birth. The creation of a new life. At the bottom of the stone is a big, burly man with a bushy beard. He is in right profile and is sitting down, face to face with another person who is also seated.

This area of the stone is covered with a multitude of images of children and adults, both in the composite and multiple style. Erosion, caused by sheep rubbing themselves against the surface, has made the images hard to separate from each other. There were also several other stones in different arrangements within the Great Circle, but their settings are still unclear, especially since so much of the central area was covered over with houses, sheds, workshops, gardens and roads. Several stones from the southern side of the north circle once stood in what is now the High Street, and other stones were arranged within the ring and some accounts suggest that they formed an inner circle of twelve stones, with the Cove in the middle.

It is a great shame that the standing stone on the northern side of the Cove no longer exists, Stukeley wrote that it was similar in shape to the thin left stone and its carvings may have provided a greater insight into the different uses that the building had over the centuries. However, as I noted earlier, I think that the main use of the Cove was as a temporary repository, where bodies were left to decompose, perhaps for twenty-seven days. (Just to remind you, this the time the moon takes to orbit the earth and the number of stones in the northern ring.) Archaeologists have discovered that in Neolithic times, bodies were left on wooden platforms, in the open, to decay naturally, a rather smelly process known as excarnation. This process was aided by fly maggots and by scavenging birds and animals such as crows, rooks, dogs and rats. Radiocarbon dating of skeletons has shown that in some places, the practice of excarnation was used over very long periods, so it may well have been common practice around Avebury.

The animal sculptures and the sundial calendar at Avebury probably indicate a seasonal round of festivals and ceremonies based around the annual cycles connected with growing crops and raising livestock. In many early societies, people were very concerned with the way their herds, flocks and fields would produce a maximum return for the work spent on them. If animals became diseased and died before they could reproduce, their numbers diminished. So fertility was all-important issue for a successful farmstead. With a high mortality rate amongst children, it would have been essential to try and have a large family, to help with tending the animals, weeding and guarding the crops from birds, deer and even wild boar. They would also be expected to help with bringing in the harvest and grinding grain for bread. A bad harvest could result in a difficult winter, with famine and starvation just round the corner. The high infant mortality was probably caused by a lower resistance to disease because of a poor diet, from food poisoning from poor hygiene or from diseases such as diphtheria and tuberculosis caught from domesticated cattle. Many late Neolithic and Bronze Age teeth and skeletons show evidence of long periods of malnutrition and also the effects of hard manual labour, as well as the results of accidents, disease and dental problems This is exactly the same as in many parts of the world today, some four and a half thousand years later.

Because of the new obsessions and worries about health and fertility, actions were sometimes taken by the early farmers to try and get help from benevolent spirits and from the gods. These would have been the sources of different religious rites and customs from one group to another, sometimes these were benign, just offerings to appease the gods in the form of a small part of the last harvest to ensure success in the next. This was the forerunner of the Harvest Festival. Agricultural fertility rites continued until fairly recently in many rural areas of Britain but these have changed dramatically over the centuries, the ancient rituals were diluted and disguised to become more acceptable in a changing social background. Dances around the Maypole were still quite common in many English villages in the first half of the 20th century. For those unfamiliar with this rite, a mixed group of children danced around in a circle, each holding a long coloured ribbon attached to the top of a post and as they danced and moved in patterns, weaving in and out, and round and around, with the ribbons becoming shorter and shorter. The ribbons ended up plaiting themselves round the pole, until finally, the lengths of ribbon were so short that the dancers could no longer move and so they let the ends fall. This is probably a relatively recent version of Mayday ceremonies. A much older version of the rite used a pole of hawthorn or birch that was decorated with garlands of flowers and leaves plaited into circular wreaths that were suspended from the top.

Perhaps the basic idea of decorating a pole dates back even further in time, to the early Neolithic, when causewayed enclosures were decorated with posts from which they probably suspended charms and talismans made from antlers, horns, feathers, furry animal tails, and both animal and human bones and skulls. These could have acted as wards that kept away evil spirits from the newly dead who had been left to decay naturally in the open. This idea of spiritual protection was retained when more permanent guardians, in the form of sculpted and carved stones, replaced the wooden posts around the edge of the henge ditch.

A Celtic fertility rite, dating from the Iron Age, and more in keeping with the agricultural cycle, was that of John Barleycorn, the mythical spirit of barley. Each spring seeds from the previous harvest were sown, they grew, were harvested and then turned into beer and songs were sung in John Barleycorn's honour. But not all the barley was turned into ale, some of the seeds were always kept back, to be sown the following spring. Another Celtic tradition used the last sheaves of harvested crops to be turned into corn dollies, which are small, woven figures of straw that represented the different aspects of the vegetation goddess, as she changed from child to virgin and from mother to old hag. And a corn dolly was 'planted' in the fields the following spring, completing the cycle. But I think that both of these Celtic traditions were simply updated versions of a much more ancient Birth, Life, Death and Rebirth saga.

Other rituals were far more dramatic and in some societies they even included human sacrifice to appease angry or jealous gods. Roman propaganda by Julius Caesar accused the Druids, the Celtic priests of the Ancient Gauls, of setting fire to huge figures of the Wicker Man, which contained people who were then sacrificed to the Gods.

The countryside around Avebury was a religious site for thousands of years and during that time many different structures were constructed as part of the religious landscape. Far too many of these ancient monuments no longer exist, but they included several small stone circles, numerous longbarrows and a multitude of round barrows. These were nearly all removed or ploughed out by farmers. At the height of its importance as a ceremonial site, Avebury would have looked truly astonishing. With its elaborate sculptures, carved and painted stones and its extraordinary earthworks, it was home to a thriving religious and secular community. During the main construction phase, it would also have attracted some of the most talented artists in the Ancient World. As time passed, Avebury would have become the centre of attraction for visitors from all over the country. This shows up in the archaeological record by the presence of many different types of trade goods and pottery, some from as far away as the Orkneys. People coming from remote areas would travel along the prehistoric routes known as the ridgeways. As its name suggests, the Ridgeway near Avebury was an ancient route that ran along the high ground for over 150 miles, starting near St Albans, to the north-west of London, until it arrived in the Avebury area at the Sanctuary, on the top of Overton Hill. Much of the trade in heavy consumer goods along the ancient ridgeways would have been by oxen and packhorses, after all, there is a limit to how many stone axes, raw flint, grain, meat or pottery one person can carry.

The first builders of Avebury used a particular type of earthenware pottery known as Mortlake. The bowls were thick and robust and they had a round bottom and a thick collar around the rim, suggesting that they could be placed in the ashes of a fire or securely and then suspended over the campfire to cook potage, soups and stews. Pots and beakers of that time were made by hand, without the benefits of the potter's wheel and after decoration and drying they were baked in a hot campfire, rather than in a kiln. The decoration was often quite simply achieved, by scratching and impressing marks in the wet clay to form the designs. Although the pots were quite skilfully made, it is curious that the pottery and ceramics of Neolithic Britain were not up to the same standard as the marvellous artwork that the artists produced when they worked with stone. Furthermore, on the Continent, particularly in Southern Europe, Greek and Balkan artisans had already been producing beautifully shaped, highly decorated and brightly coloured ceramics for several centuries. As the time of major ceremonies approached, people from far and wide would travel down the ridgeways to arrive near the Sanctuary and from there walk down the valley, past Silbury Hill and on towards the henge complex at Avebury. Even with so many of the West Kennet

Avenue stones missing, it is still possible to get an idea of the sort of experience the Neolithic visitor would have had as they walked in a ritual procession towards the Great Circle. And let's not forget that lunar ceremonies would often be held at night, when the light from countless torches in the darkness made everything seem far more dramatic and much more exciting, if not scary. With a little imagination, you can still get a sense of what it would have been like to walk down the avenue in the darkness to witness a moonlit ceremony.

Throughout the year there would have been festivals and ceremonies, with special rites to honour the gods, to celebrate the Circle of Life, the turning of the seasons, to give thanks for a good harvest and pay tribute to the ancestors. In particular, people would celebrate the rising sun at midsummer and the start of a new year at midwinter. Holy relics in the form of bones and skulls were periodically moved to and from burial chambers such as the West Kennet longbarrow. These activities have been the subject of a great deal of speculation to do with ancestor worship by archaeologists and a distant echo of these sorts of ceremonies still remains with us, in the religious processions of statues and relics of Christian saints and martyrs.

The building sequence of the tombs, henge, avenues and stone circles of Avebury is something of a puzzle. The radiocarbon dates for the main site are few in number and not very conclusive. However my view of the sequence of construction is as follows: Windmill Hill was the first site, followed by the Sanctuary, and then around 3700 BC they built some of the longbarrows in the Kennet area. Then some five hundred years later a large construction team started to build the ditch and bank. Over the next few centuries groups of the strongest people moved about six hundred stones from their source on the nearby hills to form the circles and avenues. Whilst this was going on, the artists were hard at work transforming the stones that had arrived into extraordinary works of art and symbolical images. Some time around 2400 BC they started on the construction of Silbury Hill. Then around 2300 BC there was a dramatic change in society when Beaker people came to power. They closed off the West Kennet longbarrow and altered some of the images and the arrangement of the standing stones in the circles and avenues.

Whether or not this sequence is exactly as it happened is hard to say for sure, but there is no getting away from the fact that it would have taken the combined efforts of many generations of people to accomplish. They dug an enormous circular trench, created a huge hill and moved tens of thousands of tons of earth, chalk and stones, without any machinery, just using physically demanding labour and simple tools, but with a great deal of skill and ingenuity. The result was a fitting tribute to the amazing determination of people devoted to their religious beliefs and their way of life.

The facade of the West Kennet longbarrow

The West Kennet longbarrow

I have already mentioned this burial site several times and this is now a good time to look at in more detail. Built about 5,700 years ago, this Neolithic monument to the dead is deservedly world famous. It is situated on the top of a hill a mile or more south of Avebury and it can be reached by means of a long footpath from the busy A4 road to Marlborough. It has a panoramic view of the whole of the surrounding countryside, including great views of nearby Silbury Hill, the East Kennet Longbarrow (on private land), the Sanctuary and Windmill Hill.

The original shape of the longbarrow was a long, narrow mound flanked by a ditch on either side. The earth for the mound came from the ditches and in Stukeley's time the sides of the mound were smooth and angled to form a ridge along the top. An illustration that he drew shows that the top of the barrow was originally decorated with small megaliths. The barrow was over 100 metres long when finished and its construction started out as a line of sarsen stones and boulders that were piled up in a line to form a spine. Later on large sarsens were used to build a communal tomb in the eastern end and this was then covered over with earth and chalk.

The finished tomb had five burial chambers inside, comprised of two small chambers on either side of a long passage that opened out into a larger end chamber and at present these are open to the public. The burial chambers were used by more than fifty generations (far longer than Westminster Abbey) but it is thought that the privilege of being deposited there was retained for a select few, possibly the families of the leaders or perhaps those of the priests who were in charge of Avebury. However, the skeletal deposits were probably only temporary since the bones of only about fifty people were recovered from excavations. There was a mixture of men, women and children, and their bones were separated into groups in some of the chambers. Nearly all of the adults had suffered from arthritis of the spine. Some had diseased hip joints and others had medical problems with their arms, wrists, hands and feet. Several skeletons showed evidence of spina bifida, possibly a genetically related ailment that suggests that some of them were related to each other. In one chamber the longest arm and leg bones were piled up and some of the skulls were missing. This has led to the idea that the bones of the ancestors were sometimes used in rituals, ceremonies and processions. Archaeologists have established that the long bones and skulls from many burials were moved in and out of the chambers for ceremonies involving *'ancestor worship'*. One is also tempted to think that some of the sacred rites and rituals performed by the priests may have involved the summoning of the spirits of the ancestors and the casting of bones to foretell the future.

Storing their skeletons was also a way of having continuity with the ancestors. The people who were buried in the chambers must have once been important individuals in the community since such small numbers can only represent a fraction of the tens of thousands of people who had lived in the surrounding area during the many centuries that the tombs were in use. But the missing skulls also remind me of the report by Julius Caesar of an Iron Age custom, which involved setting the heads of vanquished enemies on spikes outside the home of victorious warriors. This also ties in with the excavated remains of skulls and jawbones that have been found in the ditches of causewayed enclosures. Life in the Neolithic was not always peaceful and some tribes may well have been more aggressive than others, so it is not hard to picture a row of posts decorated with the heads of enemies all along the top of the bank around some enclosures.

The last person to be buried in the West Kennet longbarrow, shortly before it was closed up, around 2,500 BC, was an elderly man who seems to have been shot in the throat with a flint-tipped arrow. Did this killing mark a profound change in society with the end of power for one group and the beginning for another? It certainly looks that way, although some Beaker people had already been in Avebury long before these dramatic events unfolded.

Along the front of the chambered tomb is a row of large sarsen stones. These were originally arranged in a crescent shape, with the passageway leading into the mound at the centre. At the end of its use the entrance to the tomb was sealed with two very large sarsens, which were placed in line with the other stones across the forecourt. These were originally carved and sculpted but they are in such an exposed position at the top of the rise that they have become very eroded by wind-blown grit. The largest, a rounded, roughly D-shaped stone is now heavily eroded and covered in lichen but it is still recognisable as the head of some sort of animal in right profile. (It reminds me of the round stone, number 30, at Stanton Drew, but the other way round.) On the top left surface, starting from the top of the stone is the forehead, eyes, nose and mouth of a face looking out of the stone. Although hard to see, the whole surface of this stone still bears the remains of an extraordinary scene from Neolithic mythology. The picture shows a large group of people and several large spirits or gods. (This may well be the origin of a local legend that relates how a white priest appears at sunrise on the summer solstice.)

Below the large face on the top left is the seated figure of a man who is in three quarter left profile. In front of his knees is a composite image of a baby that is being held up. Above and also to the left are two rather sinister figures. In the centre of the stone are two people, face to face in profile. The one on the left occupies about two thirds of the height of the stone. He is wearing a tall, domed hat and has his mouth open. Opposite him is a woman wearing a tall headdress and between them is a smaller figure in left profile, this person is younger and I think it is an adolescent male. He has a white face, long dark hair and is wearing a black cloak. He is looking upwards towards the woman with the headdress. To her right is another strange-looking creature with pointed ears and a very furry coat, a sort of mixture between a bear and a lynx. The entrance to the passageway inside the longbarrow is just behind the large stone to the left of this D-shaped stone. The passageway leads into a stone tomb. There are two small chambers on each side of the passage, ending in a much larger chamber.

The stone next to it on the left is roughly oblong and it shows the very eroded remains of quite a complex form of decoration that was a sculpture of many animals.

The most noticeable is the weird animal at the top that still protrudes out to the left and over the top of another cat-like animal. Further down the stone are the eroded remains of several humanoid figures in the composite style at are sitting down on the ground. They are facing down to the left, towards a group of much smaller human figures. On the extreme bottom left is a strange face with white skin and very thick lips.

The lintel over the passageway is yet another intriguing sculpture, this is the head of a red deer with an unusually small, rounded ear, which sticks out at the back of its stretched-out face. I am not sure of the religious or symbolic significance of this picture. I think it only makes sense if the animal is a buck that has shed its antlers, and is ready to grow another set for the autumn rut. Another annual cycle.

When the barrow was finally sealed, the inner chambers were filled up with chalk, rubble and earth and further access into the tomb was prevented, by the addition of the two large forecourt stones. In Stukeley's time, a local doctor named Toope dug into the earth of the longbarrow on several occasions and plundered many bones to grind up to make a 'medicine' for his patients. Later on, in 1859, a Dr Thurnam excavated the passage and the end-chamber, removing the skeletons he found there. In the 1950's, the longbarrow was re-excavated and Professors Piggott and Atkinson discovered the side chambers. Amongst the earth, bones and pottery they removed they found a number of small ox bones. Each of these had each been drilled with a small hole. Some archaeologists think these were whistles, but I think it equally likely that they were strung together to form a baby's rattle or perhaps even a bracelet or necklace. I have often wondered about the lack of traces of children in our distant past, although they have been found as the occasional skeleton, and they can be seen in groups in various pictures, but even so, they must have outnumbered the adults by a factor of three or four. Perhaps they weren't considered to be worth picturing unless there was special role for them in the story that was being recorded.

The excavations also revealed the broken remains of over 250 pots in a large variety of styles and fashions spanning nearly a thousand years and the work of many generations of potters. Also present in the chambers were many flint tools, particularly scrapers and arrowheads and some of these look like tiny versions of the huge sarsen symbol stones at the main site. This suggests to me that the symbols were a sort of alphabet, whereby their shape had as much, if not more, meaning as the individual words you are reading...

Archaeologists have also been puzzled by the alignments of longbarrows, especially since not all of them follow the same pattern of facing towards a point somewhere within the seasonal arcs of the sun. Many longbarrows were built so that the broader end was facing towards the eastern horizon, but this was not universal, others range between north-northeast to south-southeast. This is the complete arc of the major moonrise during the nineteen-year swing cycle. So I think that each site had its own orientation depending on when the barrow was constructed and the particular beliefs of the people who built it. However, according to the astroarchaeologist John North, longbarrows were built in alignments with specific stars. According to him, the astronomer/priests would stand in the ditches and use the line formed by the ridge of the mound to observe the rising and setting positions of special stars. Visually it was as though the stars entered, then left the mound, as though they were paying a visit to the bones of the ancestors. But I am not convinced by this theory, particularly since very few individual stars are bright enough to show up until they have risen well above the horizon. It is far more likely that it was the whole constellation, such as Orion, Ursa Major, the Great Bear or Taurus, the Bull that were being observed on a nightly basis.

The photograph on the left is another fantastic work of art. It is placed above the entrance to the longbarrow. The main sculpture is a cat-like creature at the back of the stone and it has quite a human face. At the front are several complex scenes, including at least four seated figures on the

left. They are facing to the right and in front of them are some children and animals. Just below the adults at the back is another set of smaller images and right in the middle is the head of a horse, so I think that this sculpture is another sleigh scene. But in view of the position of the stone, I think that the cat-like creature represents a guardian spirit, placed there to give protection over the dead.

The entrance of the West Kennet longbarrow faces east, towards the rising sun at the spring and autumn equinoxes, so originally the sunlight would have streamed all the way down the passageway right to the end chamber, until the blocking stones were replaced. East is the direction of sunrise twice a year, at the spring and autumn equinoxes, whilst west is the direction of the setting sun. And since spring is the time of rebirth and renewal in the vegetation and animal cycles, and autumn a time of senescence and old age, leading to death and decay, so it is that I think that for some communities, spring sunrise and autumn sunset were the key times of the symbolic year. I see this orientation as a symbolism for the midpoint between winter and summer, and then between summer and winter, and as a sort of halfway stage between death and rebirth. Such deliberate alignments of stone and earth monuments with the sun or moon gives a clear indication of how knowledgeable, skilful and sophisticated Neolithic designs could be, even if they did have some very strange beliefs and performed bizarre rituals. Yet one important feature of longbarrows remains to be explained:

Why were the barrows made so long when the actual burial chambers were just a small part of the total length? And in some earlier versions, why was there was no burial chamber at all?

I think that the symbolism of the longbarrow is complex and involves many different ideas and themes; its shape may be symbolic of a penis, with the passageway and end chamber representing the vagina and the womb, and possibly the Earth Mother. But the most obvious likeness of all (and yet again, one that has remained totally unappreciated by the experts) is that the standard shape of an early longbarrow was the same shape as a Neolithic flint axe. The polished stone axes of the Neolithic period followed a standard shape, they were long and narrow with sides that gradually grew further apart to reach a wide, rounded end. Stone burial chambers were invariably placed near the widest end of the longbarrow, what would be the business end of a stone or flint axe, whilst the other end, the thinnest part, fitted through a socket in the wooden handle. And as I have demonstrated in earlier chapters, landscape symbols such as circles and rings were invariably based on very simple ideas, so that they could be seen and easily recognized by everyone.

The symbol of an axe to represent death was one that would have been widely understood. Flint axes were used to cut down trees, slaughter and butcher animals and occasionally kill people, so what could be a more explicit way of symbolising death than by building a special place for the dead in the shape of a giant version of a flint axe? More than a thousand years later, the carvings of bronze axes on some of the sarsens at Stonehenge fulfilled the same role, to symbolise Death.

An additional feature lies at the heart of some longbarrows. A line of wooden hurdles or a long line of stones was placed along the middle of the mound with radial lines branching out and then it was covered over by earth, like the backbone and ribs inside an animal. So, was this simply a construction technique to hold everything together or was it intended to represent the body of Mother Earth?
The details of the design and length of longbarrows varies considerably over time and place. In many instances longbarrows started out as a wooden hut or house, later on, perhaps after the owner's death, this was covered over with earth, sometimes with the dead occupants inside. Other longbarrows were simply communal graves that had been used for decades, before having a stone chamber added and then the whole thing covered with earth. There are several theories about the length of the earthen part of the barrows, some think that the longbarrow was an expression of the power and prestige of a local ruler, others think that they were symbols of the different communities involved, in a sort of one-upmanship with the neighbours.

Consequently the empty barrows are sometimes thought to have been an expression of owning the land, and even to give the impression that people had been there for generations, when in fact they were newcomers. This last bit seems rather contrived to me. What is widely ignored in archaeological textbooks is the fact that several longbarrows near Avebury had an oval of standing stones erected around the perimeter. John Aubrey illustrated this in the 17th Century with his sketches of the West Kennet longbarrow and the now vanished tombs of Manton and Millbarrow.

As I mentioned earlier, the East Kennet longbarrow is on private land and is in a bad way. There is a local tale that the barrow was destroyed by a falling bomb during the Second World War, but such an isolated target for a bombing mission is very unlikely. And I think that it is far more likely that the barrow was the victim of someone who was testing the destructive power of military explosives, since Salisbury Plain has been a military test site for many years.

Until a few centuries ago, there was a retaining drystone wall around the earth of the mound at West Kennet but local villagers and farmers took the handy stones of this kerb away for their own uses. The drystone walling inside the chamber, and between the forecourt stones, comes from further to the west, from the Bath/Wellow area, up to 35 km away. (Wellow is a town near the site of the Stoney Littleton longbarrow, which still has drystone walling all around its perimeter.) There are several tons of stones and they may have come by oxen or packhorses to Avebury or else they just came in rucksacks on people's backs. There are several possible explanations for transporting the stones from so far away; perhaps it was the custom for people moving to a new area to bring part of their old territory with them, to act as a reminder and as a form of solidarity with their ancestral background. Or then again, perhaps it was just a fashion.

Incidentally, this confirms that the local farmers were already expert masons and that drystone walls already surrounded some of their fields. The walls that they built helped to clear the land and kept wild (and domestic) animals out of their crops, just as they do today. Although they generally fall apart after only a few centuries, several ancient drystone walls have been discovered in the Western Isles and Ireland that are almost intact, despite having being buried under peat bogs for more than three thousand years. There were regional variations in drystone walling techniques across the British Isles. There are several styles of decoration, such as the herringbone pattern on Mortlake pottery, that look similar to the patterns of diagonal stones on the top layers of some ancient drystone walls, such as those at the Tinkinswood burial chamber in South Glamorgan. So I wonder if the decorations on some types of ancient pottery were also the same as they used to identify the boundary walls of their fields?

SILBURY HILL

The countryside around Avebury was a religious site for thousands of years and during that time many different structures were constructed as part of the religious landscape. Far too many of these ancient monuments no longer exist, but they included several small stone circles, numerous longbarrows and a multitude of round barrows. These were nearly all removed or ploughed out by farmers. However, one outstanding monument that does remain is the enormous mound we know as Silbury Hill, the largest man-made mound in Europe, which contains an estimated 250,000 cubic metres of chalk and clay and stands some forty metes high (131 ft.).

If the radiocarbon dates are correct, then Silbury Hill was finished after the henge at Avebury was completed, probably sometime around 2400 BC so it would have been visible from many of the monuments that had already been constructed in the landscape, as though it was always going to be at the centre of attention. One of the strangest things about it is that the mound was not built on top of a hill, which would have made it even higher. Instead, it was built in a valley, with the top of the man-made hill at a similar height to the surrounding high ground. However, as I mentioned earlier, from the top of this hill the priests would have been level with the local horizon. During the year they, and their students, would have seen how the sun and moon rose and set at different places along the horizon, giving valuable insights into the passage of time throughout the changing seasons. They could also have watched the night skies and kept track of the seasonal changes of the stars, planets and constellations, and over time they would have become aware of the regular reappearance of comets and meteor showers. Folklore has said that the hill was the burial mound of King Sil or Zel.

Silbury Hill, next to the busy A4 road to Marlborough

But although several tunnels have been dug into the mound over the centuries, none of the excavations, old or new, have revealed why the hill was built. It was certainly not an enormous burial mound because no trace of any burials have been found. So, for the moment, the exact purpose of Silbury Hill remains an intriguing mystery.

What must now be very clear to the reader, is that Avebury was much, more than the scared heartland of Neolithic and Bronze Age Britain. It was not only a massive religious site, it was also an enormous, open-air art gallery and museum, where an admiring public could come to look at the works of art and be entertained by the way that the moving images came to life as the light changed. The sculptures and carved stones showed images and scenes that were an important part of their history and culture. They gave a sense of belonging to generations of children who were taught about the stories, myths and legends of their forefathers and they would have learned about the religious beliefs of their world and about the sun, the moon and the skies above.

13 CONCLUSIONS

I am sure that people will say that the preceding pages are full of controversial ideas, that a great deal is unproved or at the very least, pure speculation. I am also sure that many years will pass before my ideas are widely accepted by the scientific establishment, but that is the nature of all revolutionary discoveries. Even Darwin was vilified in the Press, denounced in society and generally ridiculed for his theory of evolution, because it vigorously opposed religious doctrine and was such a departure from the traditional scientific wisdom of the time. It is still going on.

Although some of the minor details I have outlined in the previous pages may prove to be wrong, in my defence I would ask:

Why is it that thousands of years of our ancient culture have remained such a mystery for such a long time long?

Why has so much remained misunderstood or overlooked by the people we trusted (and paid) to investigate the past for us?

How did the 'experts' miss the significance of the different shapes of standing stones, understand the astronomy and the symbolism of prehistoric structures and above all, fail to see the multitude of art forms that our ancestors created?

In the last thirty years, a great deal of physical evidence relating to tools, crops, climate, industry, vegetation and soils has provided very valuable insights into the lives our pre-Roman forefathers. However, all this new evidence has done little to reveal how our ancestors lived their lives, what they thought about their world and what motivated them to do the things they did. The material that has been found through excavation has given a very lop-sided view of who our ancestors were and what they were like. What has been missing, until now, are the records or images that could have revealed what they looked like, how they dressed and some of the true nature of the customs and culture of these ancient societies, and in particular, their religious beliefs, history and mythology.

Until now, the religious and cultural life of hundreds of thousands of our forefathers has remained almost a complete mystery, simply because mistakes made during the last three centuries have never been corrected and each subsequent generation of scholars, academics and scientists has followed blindly in the footsteps of those who came before. Until now, the study of British prehistory has been handicapped by a persistent belief that many of the old theories were correct, but a lack of insight, and some very basic observational skills, has meant that vital evidence has been persistently overlooked or ignored, even though with hindsight much of it is remarkably obvious.
In addition, a purely scientifically basis for looking at the few things that have survived from the distant past has been singularly ineffective in understanding the motives for the actions of the people who were our ancestors. As a direct result of all these mistakes, generations of us have been prevented from knowing, and enjoying, the artistic legacy that our prehistoric forefathers created and left behind for us to admire and enjoy.

We owe our forefathers a huge apology.

At the beginning of this book I mentioned how the nature of prehistoric societies has been poorly understood because the invention of written languages has created an artificial barrier in time, between history and prehistory, and how far too much emphasis has been placed on written records and outdated theories. The study of prehistory evolved from the work of Georgian and Victorian antiquaries who, through social and intellectual racism, religious bigotry and prejudice, had very little empathy with their own distant forefathers. They saw our ancestors as sub-human savages, as sacrilegious sun worshippers, uncivilised barbarians, or just simple farmers and herdsmen, with bleak, empty lives of unceasing toil, barely able to scratch a living. Such erroneous conclusions have dramatically hindered a better understanding of the true nature of those early societies that did not invent writing, and some of these old attitudes have persisted, generation after generation after generation, right up to the present day. Even now, a few highly influential prehistorians, archaeologists and palaeontologists are still depressingly negative towards the intelligence, skills and abilities of our predecessors. Despite having been proved wrong many times, they continue to act as dead weight, hindering progress towards a better understanding of who we are and where we came from. And although it is right to be cautious and critical, yet it is something completely different to be totally negative towards new ideas without examining the new theories and new evidence in an open-minded manner. That is how real progress is made.

My amazing discoveries and revolutionary insights are just the first steps on the long road to a more accurate understanding of our origins. These discoveries will effectively open a window on the distant past because the images will show, rather than tell us, how our distant forefathers saw themselves.

We can be proud of them. Even though our Neolithic ancestors did not have a written language, it does not automatically mean they were stupid, far from it. Instead of recording their thoughts, ideas, history, knowledge, mythology and sacred beliefs in small characters inscribed on baked clay or on wax tablets or marked in ink on paper, papyrus or parchment, they had other methods of storing and passing on information for future generations. Although they undoubtedly had an extensive oral tradition of passing on their knowledge of the world around them, they also encapsulated their sacred beliefs in symbolic structures of earth, wood, and stone and recorded aspects of their culture as paintings, sculptures, carvings and engravings. Their thoughts and deeds were not stored as letters or words or numbers but were recorded as images, shapes and symbols. After all, this was the Stone Age and so their knowledge was written in stone.

The words of the ancient storytellers, priests, poets and historians may have gone forever, but a proportion of the images that the artists created so long ago still remain. Once the works of art have been better documented, preserved and understood, we should be able to link them with radiocarbon dates, pottery types and genetic information, so that we can get a better understanding of who did what, when and why. In other words, to further unravel the unwritten history of Ancient Britain, and ultimately, ourselves.

You may have noticed that throughout this book I have tried to refrain from using the word *'primitive'*. This has been very deliberate action on my part because of all the connotations the word has had. It has engendered an elitist way of looking and thinking about ancient people, one that has prevented the truth from emerging from the mists of time. The complexity of their marvellous art and the wonderful architecture, engineering and landscaping prowess of Newgrange, Calanais, Stonehenge, Silbury Hill, Avebury, Stanton Drew and dozens of other sites, eloquently show what could be achieved by *'primitive'* people. It also shows that it was not the sort of technology that they invented and used that counted, but rather just how much could be achieved through intelligence, skill, dedication and sheer hard work.

Yet despite all that we have seen in the preceding pages, the Neolithic and Bronze Age investigations into astronomical phenomena may not have fully developed into what we would term a scientific discipline (despite the efforts of modern scientists and mathematicians to prove the contrary). They don't seem to have developed a complex form of mathematics. So it seems to me that their astronomical knowledge was developed primarily as a means of predicting the correct times for their festivals and sacred ceremonies, rather than for any purely abstract scientific reasons. They studied the sky so that special ceremonies could be accurately linked to the seasonal changes of the natural world; the seasonal extremes of the solar cycle; and the phases of the moon, especially the Metonic cycle and the extremes of the lunar swing cycle. It is likely that if purely scientific pursuits had been their intention, then the ancients would have developed the system of symbolically shaped sunstones and moonstones into a more complex and exhaustive form, but in a smaller version and used it to develop written records. In time they would have done as other civilisations did and invented better technology and industrial processes that would have left traces behind. They were on the brink of these major breakthroughs, but rather than developing their sciences they concentrated their attention more on tradition, religious belief and creating their wonderful works of art.

The population of was predominantly young and the work was very hard. The bones and joints of the early farmers and temple builders show the signs of the wear and tear of heavy manual labour and often reveal traces of malnutrition when the harvest was bad. Many skeletons from Bronze Age round barrows show evidence of a brutal end to their lives. There is a depressing list of wounds and injuries, including cleft and battered skulls, arrow heads and spear heads lodged in the spine or vital organs, heads, hands and feet cut off. etc. etc. (But it should also be remembered that murder and extreme violence are still with us today, it is only the weapons and the technology that have changed!) The people who received special treatment by being buried in barrows were only a small percentage of the local population. The vast majority of people have disappeared without trace.

Over time, many ancient constructions were built with passages or incorporated alignments towards the direction of the setting or the rising of the winter sun. A special relationship was perceived between death and the coming of night, and between birth and the dawn of a new day. So in this way the end of a person's life was symbolised by the end of the day and marked by the setting sun, whilst rebirth was heralded by the dawn of a new day and marked by the rising sun. The direction of the setting sun was the direction for the spirits or souls of the dead to travel towards the next life. So clearly, the intent behind the construction of many prehistoric tombs and ceremonial monuments was an overwhelming desire for a better life in the hereafter.

For the ancient farmers and herdsmen the true source of wonder and reverence was the regenerative power of the sun and its control over the natural world. Just as it is now, the sun was the driving force behind the eternal cycle of the seasons. During the winter much of the natural world was either dead or asleep, but in spring, nature came alive again, seeds germinated and lambs and calves were born. Then in summer the crops ripened and the animals grew up and in autumn there was a multitude of seeds, fruit and nuts to harvest. But winter was a time of hardship for animals and people alike and many didn't last through the cold months to see another spring. In short, the sun had the power of life and death over the natural world. At a time when many people did not live long enough to see their fortieth birthday, thoughts of their own mortality must have weighed heavily on their minds. Death was an unwelcome but frequent visitor to many households, particularly during the long, cold, wet winter months. For generations, people did the same things as their families had done before and they attained stability in an unpredictable world, a world filled with unknown and unseen dangers, where death could occur without warning. They were brought even closer to their ancestors by keeping the old traditions alive, providing a link between past and present in a world where the future was uncertain. (And this provided them with the security and stability that we in the modern urban world sometimes lack.) But it didn't last. Society changed profoundly with the coming of metals, firstly with copper, then bronze and finally iron, although by 1500 BC there was already evidence of a decline in soil fertility, followed by a worsening of the climate. There were major changes in society and religious belief with the coming of iron tools and weapons. People suffered and warfare became rife. It has never left us.

We tend to look back at prehistory as a time of linear evolution and progression through the inventions and technology that was developed. This is most obvious in tools that were initially made from stone, then copper, then bronze, then iron. But in many ways the people of the Neolithic and Bronze Ages were superior and more civilised than those of the Iron Age that followed. Although the Iron Age is characterised by better metal working technology, it was also a time of great social unrest, when many communities lived in fortified villages or had to seek refuge in purpose-built hillforts. And by the time our written history starts, with the arrival of Julius Caesar in 55 BC, much of central and southern

Britain had already degenerated into a period of chaos and confusion because tribes were constantly feuding with each other. To the Romans they were truly barbarians and if Celtic Britons united, it was only on a temporary and partial basis and it came about because of the threat posed by the invading forces from across the sea.

Incidentally, Caesar was a very good publicist, since even now he and his culture are renowned as having had a wonderfully civilising influence on the hordes of 'pagan barbarians'. What is less well known is that in his conquest of Gaul (France) he and his legions are reputed to have killed and enslaved well over two million people. Various modern terms spring to mind to replace the word 'civilisation', they include extermination, mass murder, ethnic cleansing, genocide, crimes against humanity, etc., etc. Civilisation really means that people lived in cities, not that they were caring and morally responsible. The price that many paid was very high, just so that a few people could live a life of luxurious ease. Sounds familiar?

In terms of social organisation, cooperation, monument construction and artistic culture, the populations of the earlier millennia were far more peaceful and better organised for the benefit of the local and surrounding communities. This cohesion in the first half of the Neolithic period is evident from the construction of vast ritual centres, such as those along the Boyne Valley in Ireland, at Calanais in the Western Isles, on mainland Orkney and far to the south, at Stanton Drew, Avebury and Stonehenge.

With over a thousand stone circles, spread across most of western and northern England, Wales, Scotland and Ireland, the feeling I get is one of great cultural and religious unity (and diversity) spread out across the country over several millennia. Yet although there was social harmony in some areas for very long periods, this does not mean that things were always peaceful, far from it. There is evidence of murder and mayhem, starvation and disease, just as there has been throughout the long centuries that have followed. Nevertheless, I think that you will agree with me that our ancestors deserve our respect and admiration for all that they achieved. They weren't barbarian savages after all, far from it.

So were they really sun worshippers? Were the sun and the moon their gods?

The answer must be yes, but the actual celestial orbs themselves were only part of the story. Our ancestors have often been maligned as primitive sun worshippers when in reality it was the physical embodiment of the regenerative powers of the sun that they revered the most. They honoured the immense power necessary to melt the snow and ice of winter, to warm the land in spring so that it could revive the natural world and to give rise to new Life.

Their monuments clearly show that they understood how the annual cycle of the sun mirrored all the other life cycles of the natural world, and the endless turning of the seasons reflected the everlasting circle of birth, life, death followed by rebirth and the start of a new cycle. And this cycle of events, together with those of the lunar cycles, culminated in the building of the most famous prehistoric building in the world, Stonehenge. Many of their buildings, at places such as Newgrange, Calanais, the Ring of Brodgar and Stonehenge, were intended to witness and to commemorate the links between the solar and lunar cycles, and to match the human life cycle with that of celestial bodies, symbolised by **'the Circle of Life'**. Although they may well have studied the stars and planets as well, scientific knowledge was secondary to the religious aspects of celestial mechanics, the measurement of sacred time, and the protection of the living from evil forces by enlisting the aid of the ancestral spirits. Their shamans or priests may well have used astrology for predicting the future and used astronomy to give warning of impending events such as another lunar eclipse (by the Metonic cycle), the conjunction of planets or the return of a comet or meteor shower. Over time the basic philosophies changed with the evolution of a multitude of different cults with different beliefs. After all, nothing stays the same forever, not even stone.

I have tried to show in the preceding pages how each prehistoric site had works of art that were true masterpieces, sometimes they developed a particular style of art that reflected the religious and cultural beliefs of the local inhabitants. Yet even at the same site these varied considerably because the sites were used over vast periods of time by successive cultures. With their henges, barrows and burial mounds and their circles and rows of standing stones the Neolithic and Bronze Age people produced enormous landscape symbols and some of the most marvellous works of art ever created. I have also demonstrated how astronomy was linked to mythology and religion and how this affected the way monuments were built and used. They recorded at their ancient ceremonial centres, a part of their historical, mythical and religious culture, not in books, but in stone, so that it would last forever. And we should also admire how they recorded their understanding of astronomy by developing systems of geometrically shaped stones and celebrated their scientific discoveries at special sites by mapping out important aspects of the solar and lunar cycles and then they incorporated the sacred numbers that they found into their religious architecture. I have also revealed how they used symbols and images to mark the passage of time, the high points of the solar year and the changing seasons.

At Stonehenge they celebrated the discovery of the twenty-nine and half days of the monthly lunar cycle by incorporating it into the sarsen circle. They marked the lunar swing cycle with the Heel Stone and the four Station Stones and they chronicled both nineteen-year lunar cycles with the Bluestone horseshoe. I have also shown that the reason the Bluestones were brought all the way from southwest Wales was because they were part of a system of symbolic geometrical shapes. Other stones show sculptured images of people and animals linked to Neolithic mythology, agricultural cycles and the changing seasons. As time went by, society changed and the Beaker People and their descendants transformed many sites. At Stonehenge for example, many of the older stones were used and re-decorated time and time again, sometimes in different orientations.

The stones of the South Circle at Avebury were linked to the seasons and the agricultural cycle and these, together with the portal stones, were possibly the finest works of art at the site. Yet the images of the West Kennet Avenue and the remaining Great Circle stones were not always pleasant. It seems to me that at Avebury it was astrology that took precedence over astronomy, and perhaps it was fear of the spirit world, conjured up by their priests and shamans, that eventually led to its desertion, sometime around 1600 BC.

The archaeological evidence also points to the arrival of a different kind of people in the Avebury area, very few pieces of Grooved Ware pottery have been found at Avebury, whereas this type of pottery was prevalent in the area around Stonehenge. At the settlement sites of Durrington Walls, Woodhenge and at Marden, the henge halfway between Avebury and Stonehenge, thousands of Grooved Ware pottery sherds have been excavated. Grooved Ware originated far to the north, in the Orkneys, so clearly the astronomical knowledge of the Orcadians spread south, along with their pottery, although how the knowledge was used varied from site to site. A Grooved Ware jar that was found at Durrington Walls is particularly interesting. Although the bottom is missing, the decoration on the side shows a series of long angled marks between vertical lines. These verticals look like posts to me, and the overall pattern is very reminiscent of a decorative wattle and daub wall. Above the wall is a series of angled, parallel lines, very reminiscent of reed thatching, and above this roof is a large quantity of thin, oval, impressions in the clay that look like rain drops! So the big question is, what other pictures did they put on their pottery?

So much has been destroyed, yet the overall picture I get from the Avebury images is one of fertility rites and ancestor worship mixed with superstitious beliefs, a reverence for the moon and a fear of the dark side of human nature. It was different at Stanton Drew. The people celebrated life and living, rather death and the supernatural. The best works of art are probably the stones that are still standing. In the Great Circle, the near circular stone number 30 was a triumph, a work of genius with its infinite variety of multiple and composite imagery, which shows just how complex prehistoric art could be. In addition to the geometrically shaped symbol stones our ancestors created, they developed many works of art using the new styles of art that they had created: including natural art, composite images, multiple images, moving images, overlapping art, inverted images, symbolic images and landscape art.

But by the end of the Bronze Age the great tradition of building with giant stones faded away and the skills of the artists were no longer practised on new circular monuments, leaving just a very vague memory in our folklore of the artistic greatness that had been achieved centuries before. This memory was retained in our folk stories of the stones having been people that had been turned to stone. Like other ancient civilisations, our forefathers were well aware of the eternal battle between good and evil and many of the images they produced show that they feared death and that they associated death with the night, populating it with evil spirits and demons.

One of the most fascinating aspects of the ancient art I have discovered is that it shows pictures of strange mythical creatures and of spirits, monsters, *'Little People'*, giants, imaginary animals and even the carving of priests with a pointed hats at Stonehenge and those at other sites, particularly in the Western Isles and Orkney. Such images have resisted the passage of time and have remained firmly fixed in our racial memory and folklore, in the form of nursery rhymes, fantasy and fairy tales. The monstrous images of nightmarish creatures seem to show that we have changed very little from such remote times; we still like to be scared silly! Their universal appeal is as vivid today as it was five thousand years ago. Modern versions of the truly ancient concepts of day and night, and of good versus evil, have been recaptured in works of fiction such as Dracula, the novels of James Herbert and by the film industry in blockbuster movies such as Harry Potter, The Lord of the Rings and Star Wars.

So what did they look like, these Neolithic and Bronze Age people?

By now you will probably have realised from the countless images and portraits in this book that they looked like us! Or rather, like some of the faces of people you see in a large crowd, but perhaps with stronger and more pronounced features than us. You can see it in the shapes of their faces and heads and in their hair, their noses, eyes and chins. This is not all that surprising since we carry the genes of these special people within us, even though their genes have become mixed and diluted over the intervening centuries.

The more I discover and learn about our distant forefathers the more I am amazed by them. Instead of being the primitive people we were told they were, they produced a series of early civilisations, rich in artistic and cultural heritage and living a very different way of life, a way of life linked directly to the natural world. This way of life led to a true partnership with Nature, in which even their tombs and temples seem to be part of the natural landscape, but as time went by intensive livestock rearing and agriculture had dramatic consequences on many parts of the country. From the Bronze Age onwards the demand for more and more pastureland and larger fields for crops meant that the trees that covered much of the countryside were cut down. Soil erosion followed on the heels of deforestation, just as it does today in many parts of the world, with the same catastrophic consequences. In England it created Dartmoor, Exmoor, the North Yorkshire Moors and many other barren areas. At times it seems as though we have learned nothing from the mistakes of our ancestors and that it is only from the 1960's onwards that we are finally wakening up to our responsibilities as guardians of the planet so that our descendants, five thousand years from now, will have somewhere to live.

But will the records of our history, of our societies and cultures survive the test of time? Will our very distant grandsons and granddaughters be able to understand us? And more to the point, what will they think of us?

I hope this book will motivate you to explore the prehistoric world for yourself and that you will make your own set of extraordinary discoveries. And I hope that my insights and theories have helped you to appreciate the achievements of our forefathers and to dispel the idea that they were just members of a simple, primitive, farming culture. It is to our shame that so much of our prehistoric heritage has been neglected or destroyed. Many tombs, standing stones and stone circles have been ruined, the sculptures and symbol stones lie in the grass face down, buried in the ground, or worse still, broken up for building material or road repair. It is an absolute tragedy that so much has been needlessly destroyed.

We owe an enormous debt to our ancestors and a duty to our descendants. We must put the stone temples back together again. We must restore the fallen stones and care for our artistic heritage, only in this way can future generations appreciate and enjoy the skills, intelligence and artistry of their distant families. We can then be proud of our inheritance, of who we are and where we came from and we must do our utmost to restore and preserve the work of the exceptionally talented artists, so that their accomplishments are not forgotten, *again.*

                Martin Ringer. Bristol. 15th May 2012.

Bryn Celli Dhu passage grave, Anglesey, north Wales

A view from Carn Meini, Preseli Mountains, southwest Wales, source of some of the Stonehenge bluestones

Sculpture of the head of a wolf with its nose in the ground. Duloe Stone Circle, Cornwall

A multiple image, showing the head of a dog with its nose in the air, and the head and body of a bird, with its bill pressed against its chest. Machrie Moor, Arran, Northwest Scotland.